Shakespeare Beyond English

Tackling vital issues of politics, identity and experience in performance, this book asks what Shakespeare's plays mean when extended beyond the English language. From April to June 2012 the Globe to Globe Festival offered the unprecedented opportunity to see all of Shakespeare's plays performed in many different world languages. Thirty-eight productions from around the globe were presented in six weeks as part of the World Shakespeare Festival, which formed a cornerstone of the Cultural Olympiad. This book provides the only complete critical record of that event, drawing together an internationally renowned group of scholars of Shakespeare and world theatre with a selection of the UK's most celebrated Shakespearean actors. Featuring a foreword by Artistic Director Dominic Dromgoole and an interview with the Festival Director, Tom Bird, this volume highlights the energy and dedication that were necessary to mount this extraordinary cultural experiment.

SUSAN BENNETT is University Professor in the Department of English at the University of Calgary, Canada. Her interest in contemporary performances of Shakespeare's plays dates back to her 1996 monograph, *Performing Nostalgia: Shifting Shakespeare and the Contemporary Past*. Her latest book, *Theatre and Museums*, was published in 2013. A current research project is concerned with the circulation of performance in global markets where Shakespeare, not surprisingly, is a premium brand. She hopes to see some of the Globe to Globe Festival performances again at different international venues and with other audiences.

CHRISTIE CARSON is Reader in Shakespeare and Performance in the Department of English at Royal Holloway University of London. She is co-editor of *The Cambridge King Lear CD-ROM: Text and Performance Archive* (2000) and the Principal Investigator of the AHRB-funded research project *Designing Shakespeare: An Audio-Visual Archive, 1960–2000*. She has published widely on the subject of contemporary performance and co-edited *Shakespeare's Globe: A Theatrical Experiment* (2008) with Farah Karim-Cooper and *Shakespeare in Stages: New Theatre Histories* (2010) with Christine Dymkowski. She hopes to continue to document international gatherings of this kind from a vantage point that takes in both the onstage action and the audience response.

SHAKESPEARE BEYOND ENGLISH
A GLOBAL EXPERIMENT

Edited by

SUSAN BENNETT

and

CHRISTIE CARSON

CAMBRIDGE
UNIVERSITY PRESS

CAMBRIDGE
UNIVERSITY PRESS

University Printing House, Cambridge CB2 8BS, United Kingdom

Published in the United States of America by Cambridge University Press, New York

Cambridge University Press is part of the University of Cambridge.

It furthers the University's mission by disseminating knowledge in the pursuit of education, learning and research at the highest international levels of excellence.

www.cambridge.org
Information on this title: www.cambridge.org/9781107674691

© Cambridge University Press 2013

First published 2013

Printed in the United Kingdom by T. J. International Ltd, Padstow

A catalog record for this publication is available from the British Library

Library of Congress Cataloging in Publication data
Shakespeare beyond English : a global experiment / edited by Susan Bennett and Christie Carson.
    pages   cm
Includes bibliographical references and index.
ISBN 978-1-107-04055-7 (hardback) – ISBN 978-1-107-67469-1 (pbk.)
1. Shakespeare, William, 1564–1616 – Dramatic production.   2. Shakespeare, William, 1564–1616 – Translations.   3. World Shakespeare Festival.   I. Bennett, Susan, 1955– editor of compilation.   II. Carson, Christie, editor of compilation.
PR3092.S53   2013
792.9′5 – dc23   2013005740

ISBN 978-1-107-04055-7 Hardback
ISBN 978-1-107-67469-1 Paperback

CONTENTS

ILLUSTRATIONS

COLOUR PLATES

The colour plates are to be found in two inserts, pp. 70–1 and pp. 198–9.

1   *Troilus and Cressida*, Ngākau Toa. Photograph by Donald Cooper ©Donald Cooper/photostage.co.uk

2   *The Merry Wives of Windsor*, Bitter Pill and the Theatre Company, Kenya. Photograph by Marc Brenner, reproduced by permission of Shakespeare's Globe.

3   *Twelfth Night*, Company Theatre. Photograph by Simon Annand, reproduced by permission of Shakespeare's Globe.

4   *A Midsummer Night's Dream*, Yohangza Theatre Company. Photograph by Donald Cooper ©Donald Cooper/photostage.co.uk.

5   *Cymbeline*, the South Sudan Theatre Company. Photograph by Ellie Kurttz, reproduced by permission of Shakespeare's Globe.

6   *Richard II*, Ashtar Theatre. Photograph by Donald Cooper ©Donald Cooper/photostage.co.uk.

7   *The Tempest*, Dhaka Theatre. Photograph by Donald Cooper ©Donald Cooper/photostage.co.uk.

8   *Macbeth*, Teatr im. Kochanowskiego. Photograph by John Haynes, reproduced by permission of Shakespeare's Globe.

9   *2 Henry IV*, Elkafka Espacio Teatral. Photograph by Ellie Kurttz, reproduced by permission of Shakespeare's Globe.

10 *King Lear*, The Belarus Free Theatre. Photograph by Simon Kane, reproduced by permission of Shakespeare's Globe.

11 *As You Like It*, Marjarnishvili Theatre. Photograph by John Haynes, reproduced by permission of Shakespeare's Globe.

12 *Coriolanus*, Chiten. Photograph by Simon Annand, reproduced by permission of Shakespeare's Globe.

13 *Antony and Cleopatra*, Oyun Atölyesi. Photograph by John Haynes, reproduced by permission of Shakespeare's Globe.

14 *The Merchant of Venice*, Habima National Theatre. Photograph by Simon Kane, reproduced by permission of Shakespeare's Globe.

15 *Henry VIII*, Rakatá. Photograph by Simon Annand, reproduced by permission of Shakespeare's Globe.

16 *Timon of Athens*, Bremer Shakespeare Company. Photograph by Simon Annand, reproduced by permission of Shakespeare's Globe.

BECKY BECKER heads the BA program in Theatre at Columbus State University in Columbus, GA, and currently she holds the position of International Studies Certificate Coordinator for the university's Center for International Education. Her interest in international studies extends to many parts of the globe, including England, Nigeria and Japan, where she led a study-abroad programme in May 2013. Becky's directing credits include *A Midsummer Night's Dream*, *The Laramie Project*, *Cloud Nine*, *Eurydice* and *Caroline, or Change*. Her published work may be found in *Theatre Journal*, *Feminist Teacher* and *Theatre Symposium*.

SUSAN BENNETT is University Professor in the Department of English at the University of Calgary, Canada. Her interest in contemporary performances of Shakespeare's plays dates back to her 1996 monograph, *Performing Nostalgia: Shifting Shakespeare and the Contemporary Past*. Her latest book, *Theatre and Museums*, was published in 2013. A current research project is concerned with the circulation of performance in global markets where Shakespeare, not surprisingly, is a premium brand. She hopes to see some of the Globe to Globe Festival performances again at different international venues and with other audiences.

JACQUELYN BESSELL is Programme Leader, MA Acting, Guildford School of Acting, and has directed and taught at several conservatoires and regional theatres across the USA, as well as in New York City and London. Her research interests came into focus during her time as Head of Research at Shakespeare's Globe, and include the complex of relationships between performer, audience and space in early modern drama. She convenes the Performance Research Group, a practitioners' collective which explores early modern and postmodern approaches to performance, and her recent publications examine the application of post-Stanislavski actor-training techniques to Shakespeare's plays.

TOM BIRD was Director of the Globe to Globe Festival and is now Executive Producer at Shakespeare's Globe. In producing the Festival, he travelled around the world from Armenia to Zanzibar in search of performance groups working with Shakespeare. Tom successfully applied for a major Arts Council England grant, as part of The Space project, to ensure that all the performances at the Festival were filmed in high definition.

DAVID CALDER received his BA in French from Trinity College in Hartford, CT, and is currently a doctoral candidate in the Interdisciplinary PhD in Theatre and Drama at Northwestern University. His dissertation examines how contemporary French street theatre companies and former industrial workers jointly negotiate urban redevelopment in converted factory spaces. More broadly, his research addresses the material conditions of production and reception in contemporary European theatre. In Chicago, he has served as a dramaturge on works by Corneille, Ionesco and Sartre.

CHRISTIE CARSON is Reader in Shakespeare and Performance in the Department of English at Royal Holloway University of London. She is the co-editor of *The Cambridge King Lear CD-ROM: Text and Performance Archive* (2000) and the Principal Investigator of the AHRB-funded research project *Designing Shakespeare: An Audio-Visual Archive, 1960–2000*. She has published widely on the subject of contemporary performance and co-edited *Shakespeare's Globe: A Theatrical Experiment* (2008) with Farah Karim-Cooper and *Shakespeare in Stages: New Theatre Histories* (2010) with Christine Dymkowski. She hopes to continue to document international gatherings of this kind from a vantage point that takes in both the onstage action and the audience response.

JUAN F. CERDÁ is Lecturer at the University of Murcia and has worked on the Shakespeare in Spain research project since 2006. He has written mostly about Shakespeare's role in Spanish culture, including Shakespeare's presence in the work of actors, directors and the Spanish avant-garde in the first decades of the twentieth century, on Shakespeare's relationship with García Lorca and on the infrequent adaptation of Shakespearean drama for Spanish film. At present, he is collaborating on an annotated bilingual bibliography of Spanish criticism on Shakespeare from 1764 to 2000.

MALCOLM COCKS was born in Zimbabwe, where he lived until 1999. His current research projects focus on aspects of nineteenth-century intellectual history, literature and culture. Malcolm is interested in the idea of Shakespeare as a global commodity, and particularly in the complex political, imperial and moral roles that Shakespeare studies have come to assume in secondary-school curricula around the world. These interests stem from his work as a teacher: he has taught Shakespeare and performance in various educational contexts in southern Africa, Europe and the United Kingdom.

EMMA COX is Lecturer in Drama and Theatre at Royal Holloway University of London. Her research engages with contemporary performances of Shakespeare and Jonson in postcolonial and intercultural contexts. Recent publications include a chapter with Elizabeth Schafer on The Alchemist in Ben Jonson: A Critical Reader (2013) and Theatre and Migration (2013). This essay attempts to locate the different Shakespeares that were thrown up by this Kenyan Merry Wives: Shakespeare the global commodity, Shakespeare the tool of imperial pedagogy and Shakespeare the raucous comic ally.

MICHAEL DOBSON is Director of the Shakespeare Institute in Stratford-upon-Avon. Between 1999 and 2008 he reviewed every major production of a Shakespeare play in England for the journal Shakespeare Survey. His publications include Shakespeare and Amateur Performance (2011) and Performing Shakespeare's Tragedies Today (2006), as well as programme notes for Shakespeare's Globe, the Royal Shakespeare Company (RSC), Peter Stein, Mokwha, TR Warszawa and others.

DOMINIC DROMGOOLE was appointed Artistic Director of Shakespeare's Globe in 2006; prior to this he was Artistic Director at the Oxford Stage Company and Bush Theatre in London. Under Dominic's leadership the Globe Theatre has become a champion of new writing, significantly increased its audience size, won several major awards, created regular national and international touring circuits, and filmed many of its productions for distribution in the cinema, on DVD and on TV, and online. Dominic has written two books: The Full Room (2001) and Will and Me (2006).

ALEKSANDAR SAŠA DUNDJEROVIĆ completed his PhD at Royal Holloway University of London and is currently Senior Lecturer and Head of the Drama Department at University College Cork. He was born in Belgrade, Serbia, where he studied theatre directing at the Faculty of Dramatic Arts. He is also a professional theatre director who has worked in Serbia, Romania, Brazil, Canada and the UK. Aleksandar's expertise is in international theatre and multimedia performance practice, devising and theatre directing. He has published a number of books and articles on the creative opus of Robert Lepage. His most recent book is on performance practices in Brazilian contemporary theatre.

CHRISTINE DYMKOWSKI, at the time of writing her chapter, was Professor of Drama and Theatre History at Royal Holloway University of London; she has since retired. Her work on the performance history of The Tempest is extensive: she wrote the volume on The Tempest for CUP's Shakespeare in Production series (2000; reprinted with minor revisions 2005) and is also Theatre History editor of the forthcoming New Variorum *Tempest* being prepared under Andrew Gurr's editorship. Other work on Shakespeare includes *Shakespeare in Stages*, co-edited with Christie Carson (Cambridge, 2010). With David Wiles she co-edited *The Cambridge Companion to Theatre History* (2012).

BRIDGET ESCOLME is Senior Lecturer in Drama at Queen Mary University of London, where she researches and teaches early modern drama in performance, the performance of mental health, and theatre costume, in theory and through practice. She has worked as a teacher, a performer, a director and a dramaturge. Her published work has explored the ways in which staging convention and the relationship between performer and audience generate meaning in the theatre, so she has been particularly interested in the conventions and traditions that the Globe to Globe Festival have brought to the performance of Shakespeare.

JEANNIE FARR lectures in Performing Arts in London. She achieved her MA in Shakespeare and Theatre at the Shakespeare Institute in December 2011. Her research interests are focused on experimental approaches to classical performance, including cross-gender, single-sex and politically informed interpretations.

SUZANNE GOSSETT is Professor Emeritus at Loyola University Chicago and is the Past President of the Shakespeare Association of America. She is a General Editor of Arden Early Modern Drama and a General Textual Editor of the Norton Shakespeare Third Edition. Her most recent editions are of *Pericles* (2004), *Philaster* (2008) and *Eastward Ho!* (Cambridge University Press, 2012).

TAMARA HADDAD is a doctoral student at the University of Kent, where her research focuses on site-specific performance and audience reception of late medieval and early modern drama. She is also interested in the adaptation of early English drama into a Middle Eastern context, especially in relation to regional Arabic dialects.

PETER KIRWAN is Lecturer in Shakespeare and Early Modern Drama at the University of Nottingham. His primary research and teaching interests are in authorship and collaboration in the Renaissance, early modern book history, digital media and contemporary Shakespearean performance. He reviews theatre for several academic journals and on his blog, The Bardathon (http://blogs.nottingham.ac.uk/bardathon). His work on previous Shakespeare festivals has dealt with questions of intercultural performance, the subjectivity of the reviewer and the UK reception of foreign-language productions. He is a trustee of the British Shakespeare Association.

ADELE LEE is Lecturer in English Literature at the University of Greenwich, London. She is the author of numerous articles on Shakespearean appropriation and

Renaissance travel writing, and has published works in such journals as *Shakespeare Bulletin*, *Early Modern Literary Studies* and *Quidditas*, among others. She is currently completing a book for Fairleigh Dickinson University Press entitled *The English Renaissance and the Far East: Cross-Cultural Encounters* and contributed to a new critical introduction to Shakespeare's *Richard III*.

LEE CHEE KENG is Assistant Professor in the Visual and Performing Arts Academic Group, National Institute of Education (Singapore), Nanyang Technological University. He is the Chinese translation co-editor of the Asian Shakespeare Intercultural Archive (A|S|I|A), and has written, translated and directed plays in Chinese and English. His research interests include visual metaphor in performance, Shakespeare performance in Asia and cultural policy.

RANDALL MARTIN is the editor of the Oxford World's Classics edition of *Henry VI Part Three* (2001) and has written extensively about the *Henry VI* trilogy. He has also co-edited a stage-oriented edition of *The Merchant of Venice* (2001) with Peter Lichtenfels and a collection of essays, *Shakespeare/Adaptation/Modern Drama: Essays in Honour of Jill L. Levenson* (2011), with Katherine Scheil.

SONIA MASSAI is Reader in Shakespeare Studies at King's College London. She has published widely on the global and intercultural dimensions of contemporary Shakespearean performance. Her publications on this topic include *World-Wide Shakespeares: Local Appropriations in Film and Performance* (2005), scholarly essays in journals and collections, and feature-length articles and reviews in newspapers, blogs and literary magazines, including the *Guardian* and *Salon Magazine*. In 2009 she organized a large international conference on 'Local/Global Shakespeares' with Globe Education, and she is currently completing her new book, *Shakespeare and Global Modernity*.

KATIE NORMINGTON is Vice Principal and Professor of Drama at Royal Holloway University of London. She researches medieval drama, including contemporary productions of medieval texts. She has also published on contemporary theatre and practice, and has previously studied Russian theatre director Meyerhold's techniques and investigated the application of these to theatre rehearsal processes.

ROBERT ORMSBY is Assistant Professor at Memorial University of Newfoundland and his primary area of research is the performance of early modern drama. He is currently completing a monograph on *Coriolanus*. He is also working on a project about Shakespeare, Canada and globalization that is concerned with how Shakespeare is used to produce both local and international identities. His work has appeared in *Cahiers Élisabéthains*, *Canadian Theatre Review*, *Modern Drama*, *Shakespeare Bulletin* and *Shakespeare Survey*.

STEPHEN PURCELL is Assistant Professor of English at the University of Warwick. His research focuses on Shakespeare in contemporary performance and popular culture. He is the author of *Popular Shakespeare* (2009), as well as numerous articles on Shakespeare on stage, television and film. His writing on the World Shakespeare Festival also appears in *A Year of Shakespeare: Re-Living the World Shakespeare Festival* (2013) and *Shakespeare Survey 66* (2013). He directs for the theatre company The Pantaloons.

KEVIN A. QUARMBY is Assistant Professor of English at Oxford College Emory University. His previous career was as a professional UK actor, appearing in Shakespeare productions throughout the country. A theatre reviewer in the UK and US, he offers detailed theatrical records, both informed and critical. He is co-director of the World Shakespeare Project, a model for interactive pedagogy in a new media world. His book, *The Disguised Ruler in Shakespeare and His Contemporaries* (2012), considers *Measure for Measure* as one of several interrelated plays. Focusing on Shakespeare, performance and editorial decision-making, his research questions the intersection between contemporary performance practice and canonical mediation of the text.

DEANA RANKIN is Senior Lecturer in English and Programme Director for English and Drama at Royal Holloway University of London. After graduating, she lived in Japan, where she saw as much contemporary and traditional Japanese theatre as she could; she was then Belfast co-ordinator for the Japan–UK Festival 1991. She is the author of *Between Spenser and Swift: English Writing in Seventeenth-Century Ireland* (Cambridge University Press, 2005) and is currently writing a book about assassination on the early modern English stage. She maintains a strong interest in Japanese performance and Japanese film versions of Shakespeare.

KIMBERLY RICHARDS is a doctoral student in the Department of Theater, Dance and Performance Studies, University of California, Berkeley. She received the Award for International Research at the Canadian Association of Theatre Research conference in May 2012. Her research focuses on performances from places of war, trauma studies and globalization.

ABIGAIL ROKISON began her career as a professional actor. She completed her PhD at Cambridge University in 2006, after which she was a Lecturer in Drama and English there. In January 2013 she became a Lecturer at the Shakespeare Institute, University of Birmingham. Abigail has written a number of journal articles and chapters on Shakespeare and children's literature. Her monograph, *Shakespearean Verse Speaking* (Cambridge, 2010), won the inaugural Shakespeare's Globe first book award (2012). She has recently completed her second book, *Shakespeare for Young People: Productions, Versions and Adaptations.*

DAVID RUITER has taught at the University of Texas at El Paso for the past fourteen years, where 80 per cent of the student population is of Mexican descent. David and his students live and work in a dynamic, bilingual and binational environment, and in his time teaching there he believes his views of Shakespeare have altered and expanded – indeed, have been translated – by this experience. David and his colleague Ruben Espinosa have recently completed an edited collection entitled *Shakespeare and Immigration*.

KATE RUMBOLD is Lecturer in English Literature at the University of Birmingham. Her research focuses on the reception and quotation of Shakespeare from his own lifetime to the present day (and in particular in the eighteenth century), and she has recently completed a co-authored book with Kate McLuskie on the cultural value of Shakespeare in the twenty-first century.

JULIE SANDERS is Professor of English Literature and Drama at the University of Nottingham and currently Vice Provost for Teaching and Learning at Nottingham's Ningbo, China campus. As well as researching early modern drama in its historical and geographical contexts, she has particular interests in adaptation theory, not least in relation to intercultural performance and global contexts for performing and interpreting Shakespeare. She is the author of *Novel Shakespeares* (2002), *Adaptation and Appropriation* (2006) and *Shakespeare and Music* (2007).

ELIZABETH SCHAFER is Professor of Drama and Theatre Studies at Royal Holloway University of London. Her publications include *Ms-Directing Shakespeare: Women Direct Shakespeare* (2000) and Cambridge University Press's Shakespeare in Production volumes on *The Taming of the Shrew* (2002) and *Twelfth Night* (2009). She is also co-author of *Ben Jonson and Theatre* (1999). Her *Lilian Baylis: A Biography* (2006), was shortlisted for the Theatre Book Prize 2006. She edited *The City Wit* for the Richard Brome online project and is currently completing a performance history of *The Merry Wives of Windsor*.

BENEDICT SCHOFIELD is Lecturer in German and Senior Tutor of the School of Arts and Humanities at King's College London. He has worked on the development of German theatrical theory, realism and the 'Bestseller', as well as the notion of a German Shakespeare. He has also worked extensively on the wider representation of Germany within the Cultural Olympiad 2012, and the ways in which the 'world stage' provided by the Olympiad provides new avenues for assessing German culture in transnational contexts, and the manner in which this further problematizes the German appropriation of Shakespeare.

CATHERINE SILVERSTONE is Senior Lecturer in Drama, Theatre and Performance Studies at Queen Mary University of London. Her research is concerned with the cultural politics of contemporary performance and includes work on Shakespeare in relation to trauma, sexuality, national identity and theatrical reconstruction. She has published articles on the performance of Shakespeare in Aotearoa New Zealand, including in *te reo* Māori (Māori language), and Shakespeare's Globe Theatre. She is the author of *Shakespeare, Trauma and Contemporary Performance* (2011) and is co-editor with Sarah Annes Brown of *Tragedy in Transition* (2007).

P.A. SKANTZE is a director and writer for theatre and performance, and works internationally with her performance company, Four Second Decay. Author of *Stillness in Motion in the Seventeenth-Century Theatre* (2003), Skantze employs practice as research as a methodology suitable not only for contemporary investigations but also for explorations of early modern performance and for Shakespeare. Writing on sound and the sonic arts practised by makers and receivers of seventeenth-century theatre, she explores the practice of spectating across nations, across centuries and across media. Currently she is Reader in Performance Practices at Roehampton University.

KIM SOLGA is Senior Lecturer in Drama at Queen Mary University of London, and Associate Professor of English at Western University, Canada. Her first book, *Violence Against Women in Early Modern Performance: Invisible Acts*, was published in 2009 and appeared in paperback in 2013. She is part of Western University's Africa Institute and travelled for Western to Rwanda in 2010.

JANET SUZMAN was born in Johannesburg, graduated from the University of Witwatersrand, trained at LAMDA and was at the RSC for a decade playing many of the heroines, culminating in a memorable Cleopatra. She has since pursued a rich and varied career. Her production of *Hamlet* opened the RSC's Complete Works Festival in 2006, and her *Antony and Cleopatra* began life at the Liverpool Playhouse in 2010. She was appointed DBE for services to drama in 2011. She edited *Antony and Cleopatra* in 2012.

ANN THOMPSON is Professor of English and Director of the London Shakespeare Centre at King's College London. She is a General Editor of the Arden Shakespeare series and has (with Neil Taylor) edited all three texts of *Hamlet* for Arden (2006); an updated edition of *Hamlet* will appear in 2016. In addition to numerous publications on *Hamlet*, she has also published on a number of other Shakespeare topics, mainly in the areas of editing, source studies, language studies and feminist criticism.

HARRIET WALTER has worked extensively in theatre, television, film and radio since training at LAMDA. Of her many roles with the RSC, where she is an Associate Artist, the most recent have been Cleopatra in *Antony and Cleopatra* alongside Patrick

Stewart, Beatrice in *Much Ado About Nothing* and Lady Macbeth opposite Anthony Sher, all directed by Gregory Doran. Her film credits include *Atonement*, *Babel* and *Sense and Sensibility*. She has also published three books: *Other People's Shoes*, an actors' edition of *Macbeth* and a photography book, *Facing It: Reflections on Images of Older Women* (2011).

SAMUEL WEST is an actor and director. He has played Hamlet and Richard II for the RSC, and Jeffrey Skilling in *Enron* in the West End, and is the voice of Pongo in Disney's *101 Dalmatians II*. He has also played Hal, Benedick and Octavius Caesar on stage, and Henry V, Richard II, Coriolanus, Bertram, Bassanio and Lysander on radio. Sam has toured Palestine twice with the Choir of London and directed *The Magic Flute* for the Palestine Mozart Festival, the first fully staged opera to visit the West Bank.

YONG LI LAN is Associate Professor in the Department of English Language and Literature, National University of Singapore. She is Director of the Asian Shakespeare Intercultural Archive (A|S|I|A), an online multilingual archive that presents Shakespeare performance videos from East and Southeast Asia alongside scripts and data in English, Chinese, Japanese and Korean (http://a-s-i-a-web.org). She has published essays on Shakespeare and intercultural performativity in the theatre, cinema and internet, and is co-editor with Dennis Kennedy of *Shakespeare in Asia: Contemporary Performance* (Cambridge, 2010).

KEREN ZAIONTZ is a post-doctoral fellow in the Drama Department at Queen Mary University of London. She researches experimental performance practices such as site-specific theatre and relational aesthetics, and is particularly interested in how artists engage audiences as co-creative participants. Her research into the Belarus Free Theatre links her interest in theatre to her own family history. In the early 1930s her grandfather, Mischa Zaiontz, was convicted of being a counter-revolutionary because he refused to purchase state bonds. He was sentenced to a gulag in north Russia, returning to Kiev on the cusp of World War II.

FOREWORD

Dominic Dromgoole

It was only four days in to the Globe to Globe Festival. We had already seen the sublime Isango come and go with their sung and danced *Venus and Adonis*, that afternoon we had premièred the Vahktangov's cerebral and monochromatic *Measure for Measure*, and tonight was the second and last performance of the Māori *Troilus and Cressida*. They had erupted onto the stage the day before with their visceral tribal version, their bodies almost naked, their buttocks painted with swirling green Pacific patterning, eyes popping and feet stamping, as if they were trying to pound their way through the earth back to New Zealand. The acting was exhilarating and supple, turbo-charged and witty. The show finished, and the curtain call exploded into a *haka*, that articulate yell which thrills the blood. No sooner had they finished than the audience erupted in turn. But not with conventional applause. About sixty Māori, who had discreetly placed themselves around the back of the yard, shrieked back at the stage, doffed their coats onto the floor and hunkered down, pounding out a combative rhythm straight at the stage. The audience was thrilled and terrified, caught in the no man's land between two groups of mammoth Māori rehearsing an old tribal war rite. When it finished there was more mad applause. I was up in the Upper Gallery in one corner, and watched the thrilled and babbling audience filter out of the vomitoria. They left one group in the middle. It was the Deafinitely Theatre troupe, later in the Festival to play *Love's Labour's Lost*, all of them hearing-impaired, vigorously signing their responses and ideas to each other. 'Hello,' I thought, 'we may be on to something here.'

That night was, of course, a long way down the road from the moment when the idea for the Festival first popped up. A big, simple, stupid idea, which like all stupid ideas took very little translating or explaining: to do all the plays of Shakespeare, each in a different language, each by a premier company from a different country, all in the same space in just six weeks. Our great good luck is that through the vision of Sam Wanamaker, who made the Globe happen, and through the brilliant early leadership of Mark Rylance, who enshrined boldness and experiment at its heart, the theatre has become an iconic space within a very short time. Companies from all around the world wanted to come and play with us, and wanted to play raw, human and dirty as the simplicity of the Globe demands. No concepts, no mediation, no filter, just the plays, those remarkable and eternal human documents, told straight from the lit eyes of the actors to the lit eyes of the audience.

Our greater good luck is our audience, a remarkable congregation of collaboration and goodwill, who lift every experience here to a greater height than we could ever imagine. Our own audience turned out in strength, about 200 of them seeing each and every show, with many others seeing 5, 10, and more. And they welcomed the huge influx of new audiences who really made the Festival all that it could be. Whether it was five generations of a Bengali community sitting together in a bay, the deaf audience all waving their hands in the air in celebration, the Palestinians waving their flag, a group of Albanian children holding an impromptu birthday party in the yard, or the South Sudanese invading the stage and refusing to leave – whoever they were, it was essentially their Festival. And to them goes our greatest gratitude for making it work.

I hope these essays give some idea of the range, the variety and the wit of the work. The bar was set high early and was constantly raised. Since the Festival happened, we at the Globe have spoken surprisingly little of it. It is almost as if it defies language. Hopefully, this book will start the process of trying to make some sense of it.

ACKNOWLEDGEMENTS

Without the co-operation and encouragement of people at Shakespeare's Globe this book would not exist. Tom Bird, the Festival Director, and Farah Karim-Cooper, Head of Research and Courses, provided remarkable support from day one, for which we are both tremendously grateful. Our thanks go equally energetically to Sarah Stanton at Cambridge University Press whose initial enthusiasm for a collection of scholarly essays about the Globe to Globe Festival sent us looking for contributors. She has, rather remarkably, continued to show confidence in this book as it grew substantially from initial thoughts of a dozen or so chapters to this collection of more than forty contributions. Her willingness to give us the flexibility to shape the project as the Festival unfolded has been much appreciated, and we hope that this volume rewards her commitment. We would also like to thank Fleur Jones and Jodie Hodgson at the Press who shepherded the book through the publication process.

Along with Tom and Farah, many others at the Globe have helped during the complex process of assembling this text. A big thank you goes to Dominic Dromgoole, as well as staff members Claire Godden, Amy Kenny and Penelope Woods. Jordan Landis, the Globe's librarian, and Ruth Frendo, their archivist, were ever helpful in providing information. Sian-Estelle Petty, the Globe's Digital Officer, enabled access to the website for contributors' blog responses. David Bellwood was extraordinarily efficient in managing our requests for photographs. All of them welcomed our very many questions and answered them promptly and fully. It has been a real pleasure to work with this terrific group of people.

Christie Carson would like to acknowledge the funding of the Research Strategy Fund and the Faculty Research Initiative at Royal Holloway University of London that allowed for marking release during the Festival and part-supported the publication of the images in the volume. Additionally she would like to thank colleagues in the English Department for their support and forbearance during the editing of this book, but in particular her Shakespeare colleagues Kiernan Ryan, Deana Rankin and Eric Langley, who took up the marking load in her absence. She would like to thank Neil and Edwina Carson, and Lynne, Mark, Anna and Cameron Rickards for their continuing support and enthusiasm, and Uli Kress, Jo Robertson, Jeannie Farr and Liz Fisher for their good humour and sustaining conversations. Finally, and perhaps most crucially, she would like to thank Susan Bennett for the ongoing collaborative working relationship they have shared which has enabled this project to happen at short notice and across great distance.

Susan Bennett would like to thank the Social Sciences and Humanities Research Council of Canada for their financial support for travel, tickets and research assistance, as well as the University of Calgary Faculty of Arts for the award of University Professor research funds in part-support of publication of the images in this volume, as well as for a perfectly timed Research and Scholarship Leave. She would also like to thank her family for putting up with more absence than presence during the summer of 2012. And, of course, she is delighted that Christie Carson agreed to take on this project with her and would like to record here that only Christie saw every production in this six-week Festival, more often than not stalwartly enduring adverse weather conditions in order to do so – a sign, no doubt, of a 'real' Canadian identity.

We would both like to acknowledge the timely support of the Centre for International Theatre and Performance Research at Royal Holloway, financing two working meetings for contributors at crucial junctures in the project's development. We also have an enormous debt of gratitude to our research assistant, Kimberly Richards, who was level-headed and calm when we were less so. Her ability to keep track of everyone and everything has been indispensible. Finally, we would like to thank all our contributors who came to Shakespeare's Globe at short notice, travelling by plane, train and automobile with nothing more promised than a ticket to a show. Since that time, they have worked to punishingly tight deadlines and have done so with good cheer and real purpose. It is our great pleasure and good fortune to collect their thoughtful and engaging work on the Globe to Globe Festival here.

Editors' Note: All references to the plays use the New Cambridge Shakespeare Editions for character names and line numbers. All of the names of performers and scholars visiting from Asia use the Eastern ordering, which places the surname first (Yong Li Lan rather than Li Lan Yong). For performers and scholars living, working and publishing in the West, the surname follows (Adele Lee rather than Lee Adele). Translations are by the chapter authors unless otherwise stated. A website exists to accompany this volume which will contain any developments that occur after the book has gone to press. To keep up with the ongoing impact of the Festival and this collaborative research project, please see: www.rhul.ac.uk/english/showcase/staffprojectsinitiatives/showcaseitems/shakespearebeyondenglishaglobalexperiment.aspx

INTRODUCTION

Shakespeare Beyond English

Susan Bennett and Christie Carson

On 6 July 2005 the International Olympic Committee announced that London would be the host city for the 2012 Olympics Games.[1] Some two years later (4 June 2007) the 'London 2012' brand was launched with the motto to 'inspire a generation' – an objective that would be met not just by the main event but also through the staging of a Cultural Olympiad, 'the largest cultural celebration in the history of the modern Olympic and Paralympic Movements'.[2] And at the heart of this giant undertaking (more than 2,500 cultural projects bore the London 2012 imprimatur)[3] was Shakespeare. As the British Museum–British Petroleum 'Shakespeare Staging the World' exhibition (mounted as a centrepiece of this Cultural Olympiad) proclaimed, he is 'Britain's greatest cultural contribution to the world'.[4] Similarly the nationwide World Shakespeare Festival was announced as 'a celebration of Shakespeare as the world's playwright'.[5] Representing the most widely distributed and banner component of the Cultural Olympiad celebrations, this Festival was '[p]roduced by the Royal Shakespeare Company, in an unprecedented collaboration with leading UK and international arts organisations, and with Globe to Globe, a major international programme produced by Shakespeare's Globe'; according to the World Shakespeare Festival's website, 'it's the biggest celebration of Shakespeare ever staged'.[6]

Shakespeare Beyond English is about the Globe to Globe Festival, staged 21 April–9 June 2012 at Shakespeare's Globe, comprising performances of all thirty-seven plays and *Venus and Adonis* delivered in more than forty different languages (when including the pre-Festival 'Sonnet Sunday') and bringing a diversity of international content to audiences as well as to the umbrella organizations of the World Shakespeare Festival, the Cultural Olympiad and London 2012. Contributors to *Shakespeare Beyond English* review and reflect on these productions to examine questions of cultural authority and global markets, along with ideas about language, nationhood, power, pleasure and more. Why, this book asks, should Shakespeare be at centre stage in London's remarkable year, and why, when the world was coming to London for such a large-scale sporting event, should Shakespeare be such a dominant and compelling part of London 2012's brand identity? What was at stake in these global performances at Shakespeare's Globe, and who were their audiences? The essays address, too, a variety of challenges that these Festival performances, individually and collectively, present to ongoing scholarly debates about the contemporary relevance of Shakespeare's plays.

The genesis for this project was, however, simpler and certainly less ambitious. It was partly wonder – could the Globe really be planning to bring in thirty-eight different theatre companies, none of which would be English-speaking, to perform in a six-week period? – and partly cynicism – would this be yet another assertion of Shakespeare's universality by way of the exotic 'other' on an English stage? Christie Carson and Farah Karim-Cooper had worked together on *Shakespeare's Globe: A Theatrical Experiment,*[7] so when the editors of this volume were curious to discover more about this mammoth event, it was to Karim-Cooper, Head of Research and Courses at the Globe, that we naturally turned. Giving us a snapshot of the Globe's plans, she asked if we would be interested in spearheading a scholarly response to the Festival, but without specifying what shape that might take. And so we thought, rather predictably, that there was scope for a collection of scholarly essays that might bring new evidence and different points of view to debates about 'foreign Shakespeare' that have interested the field at least since Dennis Kennedy's landmark book of the same name.[8] But Karim-Cooper urged us to consider all of the performances in the Festival rather than a select few and to engage with the full breadth of the 'world' that would be showing London audiences their Shakespeare.

In a few short months *Shakespeare Beyond English* evolved as a remarkable collaborative enterprise among an international group of scholars and theatre professionals – some Shakespearean specialists, others theatre and performance practitioners and/or researchers; some experts in or native to particular language communities, others without any knowledge of the language of the production they saw – whose ideas, arguments and criticisms have developed from the night of the performance and a subsequent blog review on the Globe's website through to the diverse and thoughtful essays collected here. As readers will notice, the initial plan remains the backbone of this volume: longer essays that explore in-depth a key issue in thinking about Shakespeare 'beyond' his homeland and natural tongue. Shorter essays allow for a full record, as well as a much wider variety of perspectives about the Festival: some look to specific national traditions 'with' Shakespeare, others assess interpretive or performance practices, and yet others dwell on an audience's engagement with a show. In some instances, we commissioned more than one contributor, so as to pry out particular complexities (political, aesthetic and cultural among them) in a production or group of productions. As a whole this book must serve as a scholarly archive of the Globe to Globe Festival, but it is our hope that it is a great deal more. The more than forty contributors collectively challenge the business of Shakespeare, whether that business takes place in the classroom, in the scholarly journal or monograph, on the stage, or in the audience. If there is a common thread among the very different analyses gathered here, it is that the Festival was unlike anything any of us had seen before, and that fact inevitably challenged familiar and sometimes fiercely held assumptions time and again – whatever those assumptions were and however they had been formed.

A press release sent out by the Globe on 7 June 2012 heralding the end of their Festival summed up in rightfully glowing terms the six weeks of theatre that had just passed: 'Since the celebratory opening weekend on 21 and 22 April, Shakespeare's Globe has welcomed artists from all over the world to perform in the hugely ambitious multilingual Globe to Globe Festival as part of the London 2012 Festival. For the first time ever, 37 international companies performed all 37 of Shakespeare's plays in 37 different languages'.[9] Their statement recorded the more than 85,000 tickets sold and revelled in the knowledge that 80 per cent of bookings were made by first-time visitors to the theatre. As Ruth Mackenzie, Director of the London 2012 Festival, commented, 'The Globe has exceeded expectations by gaining . . . new audiences, many of whom were from the communities represented on stage'; its success, she suggested, was a model for the Cultural Olympiad at large.[10] If our contributors were experienced – indeed, generally, expert – audiences for Shakespearean performance, what they saw and with whom they saw it strayed far from usual theatre-going conditions. As readers will discover, the experience of watching a Shakespeare play with audiences drawn predominantly from non-English-language communities in London changed the conditions of reception in ways that few of us well rehearsed in Shakespeare spectatorship could ever have imagined. What, then, is 'Shakespeare beyond English'?

Certainly, the idea of an international Shakespeare festival is not new (nor, of course, is the idea of a 'Complete Works' festival – the RSC had one in 2006); what was new, different and special about this Festival was the stated aim to speak to local communities through the gateway of the Globe stage. In this way, the Globe to Globe Festival had at its heart ideas dearly held by its founder, Sam Wanamaker, about giving back to the local population at the same time as reaching out to an international audience. Furthermore, the idea of the theatre welcoming a different community each night, and specifically a different London community, recalls the 'physical, soulful and spiritual experience' that the Globe's first artistic director, Mark Rylance, had sought for his audiences.[11] But the process that brought thousands of first-time Globe attendees to the theatre was, without doubt, a novel one. The foreword to this book by the current artistic director, Dominic Dromgoole, and the question-and-answer introduction to the Festival by its director, Tom Bird, suggest how keen companies were to participate; as Dromgoole puts it, 'Companies from all around the world wanted to come and play with us, and wanted to play raw, human and dirty, as the simplicity of the Globe demands.'[12] In the same vein, Bird describes in the Festival programme the eighteen-month journey that he and Dromgoole undertook 'to meet theatre people in every corner of the world', marvelling that '[e]verywhere, Shakespeare, or perhaps the name of the Globe Theatre, seems to have a currency that affords one a special welcome, a mutual recognition – or, in the case of the Republic of Armenia, complete immunity from border controls'.[13]

Selection of the companies to perform at the Globe to Globe Festival started with productions that Dromgoole or Bird knew or had heard about and subsequently saw: this accounted for nine plays.[14] Their stroke of genius, it seems to us, was to move ahead with commissions for the other twenty-nine groups driven by the potential to connect with the many diasporic populations that make up contemporary London. Not all the new productions were by companies that met this criterion, but very many did. The capital city could easily generate 'natural' audiences for performances in languages such as Arabic, Bangla, Hindi, Polish, Spanish, Turkish and Urdu, but the question must have always been, 'Will they come?' As the attendance statistic perhaps implies, they certainly did. Almost all of the performances benefited from the pleasure of audiences predominantly populated by speakers of the language on the stage – often, of course, these spectators were long-time residents of London and their families. And, inevitably, some of these spectators had never been to the country where the theatre was from, but had spoken the language at home, growing up in this large metropolitan city. From this shared experience of language came so many expressions of delight, pride and, occasionally, national fervour.

Many of the essays in this book address the complexities of these language relationships and the dangers that an enthusiastic and celebratory mode masks continuing inequities both locally and abroad, but, for now, it is worth remarking how successfully the Globe to Globe Festival met current goals articulated by the Arts Council. In their ten-year vision, 'Achieving great art for everyone', the Council argues for 'excellence, founded on diversity and innovation, and a new collaborative spirit to develop the arts over the long term, so they truly belong to everyone'.[15] In a year when the Council took an almost 30 per cent cut in its government revenue, it could justifiably seem that any kind of art for everyone has been made an impossible goal, but the Festival successfully modelled one way at least that new audiences can be brought into premium arts venues. Of course, the cultural weight of Shakespeare and his plays has much to do with this appeal for performers and spectators alike. Kyu Choi from the Yohangza Theatre Company of South Korea (a fan favourite for their charming version of *A Midsummer Night's Dream* populated with the sprites of Korean folklore) commented, 'As an artist, if you're really into Shakespeare's work, performing in Shakespeare's home at the Globe, that's a great honour for us.'[16] It was the joy of being in 'Shakespeare's home' as well as 'at home' in one's language that produced the festive, high-spirited atmosphere that characterized Festival performances, irrespective of the weather or the subject matter. For English-speaking audience members, this almost always proved infectious.

In the context of language, Bird suggests in his introduction that three different notions were in fact at work when developing the programme for the Festival. The first was this commitment to London's languages, but the second he calls a 'Shakespeare language',[17] by which he sees the plays engaged with local debates about identity and often, also, the nature of art – something that also produces the Globe's now iconic presence on London's South Bank. The third is what Bird calls 'big languages', languages spoken by a great many people in the world. If the English that presides as a global lingua franca is set aside, what other languages hold sway politically, socially and culturally in our world? Are those the same languages as or different ones from the languages of London's diasporic communities or from the Shakespeare language that he suggests unites people and art? The organizers seemingly recognized the limits of their language selections, something they suggested through the Sonnet Sunday event that took place on 22 April, the day before the official Festival opening. This was a six-hour marathon staging of Shakespeare's 154 sonnets, performed in a variety of languages not included in the Festival proper – among them Latin, Finnish, Czech and Cornish.[18] Above all else, then, the Globe to Globe Festival brought to the fore questions of language and its effects, on stage and off.

But can language be separate from nation? That it can was a presumption of the Festival organizers, and they tried very hard to avoid flag-waving, national anthems and political protests. All of these things took place on different occasions during the Festival, moments that only enforced the sense of how hard it is to acknowledge that a language can be spoken by many people outside a nation without that acknowledgement standing as a nationalist statement. The elision of language and nation produced some of the Festival's more controversial or at least thought-provoking occasions. As Bird notes in the programme:

The festival has found itself at the mercy of international politics (Cymbeline from the world's newest country, South Sudan, The Comedy of Errors from Afghanistan, Richard II from Palestine); ash clouds, the Eurozone crisis (the National Theatre of Greece join us with Pericles); delicate sensitivities (the Polish Macbeth is one of the most badly behaved performances you will ever see); censoring dictatorships (the Belarus Free Theatre's King Lear will be harder-earned than most) and many other hurdles besides.[19]

He does not mention in this list the arguments that were played out around the invitation to the Habima Theatre of Israel to contribute *The Merchant of Venice* to the Festival. In advance of its performance dates (28 and 29 May), a letter was published in the *Guardian* (29 March) that opened 'We notice with dismay and regret that Shakespeare's Globe Theatre in London has invited Israel's National Theatre, Habima, to perform.'[20] The thirty-seven signatories – among them arts luminaries such as Caryl Churchill, Mike Leigh, Jonathan Miller, Mark Rylance, Emma Thompson and Harriet Walter – expressed support for the inclusion of a performance in Hebrew but asked 'the Globe to withdraw the invitation so that the festival is not complicit with human rights violations and the illegal colonisation of occupied land'.[21] Among other responses, one from Howard Brenton (3 April) suggested to the protestors 'Denounce, don't censor; argue, don't ban.'[22] Interestingly, he ponders whether the invitation to the National Theatre of China (*Richard III*) might be considered support 'for the occupation of Tibet',[23] throwing a political spotlight onto yet another of the Festival's productions. Wherever one stands on the political appropriateness or otherwise of the Habima, and perhaps other, invitations, what the Festival inspired was critical debate – before, during and after what took place on the stage.

The location of the Globe to Globe Festival within the larger Cultural Olympiad, branded for London 2012, and in relationship to the Summer Olympic Games, also raises questions about national (rather than linguistic) competition. But this Festival might well have served to challenge the logic of the Olympics: after all, the most cursory look at the parade of athletes in the Games' opening ceremonies demonstrates that this is not an even playing field among countries. Moreover, national identity for some athletes is not one of birth but of other circumstances, including a choice that serves both competitor and country in maximizing the chances of reaching the podium. But at the Globe to Globe Festival all the visiting companies had the same on-site considerations, 'a break-neck three-day schedule of rehearsal, technical rehearsal, and two performances on consecutive days, an equally warm send off, then home',[24] and tickets for the Festival were definitely easier to obtain than for the Olympics' more popular events. Like the Summer Olympic Games, the performances themselves and the audiences they reached inspired an almost visceral experience of identity formation. It is not coincidental that so many of our contributors (and both editors) have experience of expatriate life and hybridized culture. If we have come to an historical moment when more nations are significantly multicultural than monocultural, this asks us, too, to better measure the plurality of cultural expression in Shakespeare's London as much as in our own time. Thus, many of the contributions explore what it is about language that makes people feel included socially and culturally. Many of the plays discuss in detail migration – indeed, banishment – from home, cutting across propositions of national identity with issues about conflict at familial and more local governmental levels – topics that seemed to have a special resonance with Festival audiences.

The opacity and obscurity of Shakespeare's language is the common battle cry of reluctant high school and university students, and many Festival companies sought a linguistic equivalent by deploying old or poetic forms of their mother tongues. The Globe's useful provision of brief plot synopses ahead of scenes through surtitles – a remarkably Brechtian strategy – was, it seemed, often as much appreciated by the native speakers in the audience as by the English-only spectators. Some of the most impressive productions used more than one register of language, slipping back and forth between these with seeming effortlessness. In the early days of the Festival, many of the companies opted for selected words in English to ensure moments of interaction with the entire audience. Often this provided a linguistic punchline that the actors could be sure everybody would understand. But, part-way through the Festival, the organizers asked companies to stop using English words – an injunction that imposed an extremely artificial restriction on the way that many of the actors normally express themselves. Use of English words and phrases, particularly in reference to technology or popular culture, is one of the defining characteristics of our global economy. To restrict this practice and to ignore the commonplace hybridization of language as much as culture produced a particular artifice that insisted on the performances as 'other'. Furthermore, in some productions where older forms of the language chosen were unfamiliar to the actors themselves, this required learning new words and phrases in their own languages that might be incomprehensible to compatriots in the audience. Other companies took the opportunity provided by the Festival to raise awareness of languages in need of protection or promotion (as in Ngākau Toa's Māori *Troilus and Cressida* or even Deafinitely Theatre's British Sign Language *Love's Labour's Lost*). If we are to propose a common purpose in the expression of language at the Festival, it would be the desire to be understood, to have stories witnessed, identities and languages recognized, and for all of this to happen in a place that passes as hallowed ground. In short, the Globe in these six weeks was a deeply affective space.

At the same time, it is important not to overestimate the shock value that English-speaking spectators might be presumed to experience in hearing 'their' Shakespeare in so many different tongues. Certainly there were resistant spectators and critics. It was not unusual to hear a few voices grumbling in the intermission about the injustices being done to Shakespeare – non-naturalistic theatrical practices and often irreverent approaches to the texts were sometimes too much for audience members raised in the English performance tradition of the plays that depends on naturalism and textual fidelity. For the more adventurous theatre-goer, however, there was the cumulative effect of Festival performances: over a six-week period, repeat customers simply got better at working with different languages and different performance styles. More generally, it is surely the case that over the last two decades there have been more and more opportunities to experience Shakespeare outside those two encoded places of 'authenticity', the RSC's Stratford theatres and the Globe itself in London. International festivals market diversity of experience fostered by a roster of participants drawn from across the world, and audiences have come to expect, and become familiar with, non-English-language performance of all kinds. Equally, the Globe itself has long had an audience base believed by many not to understand Shakespeare anyway – or at least not to properly understand him, as W.B. Worthen noted in reviewers' 'general condescension to (and ritual skewering of) the Globe's foreign, tourist audience'.[25] Tourist audiences have sought out Shakespeare not just at the Globe in London but at very many different venues around the world, not all of whom deliver the plays in English. Indeed, there is, by now, an established history of the 'foreign Shakespeare' which Kennedy introduced in his 1993 monograph, reminding readers there that Shakespeare was not just 'by far the most popular playwright in England and North America' but 'actually the most performed playwright in the world at large. He regularly crosses national and linguistic boundaries with apparent ease.'[26]

More recently, Kennedy revisited his ideas, this time in an essay for the Festival's souvenir programme, where he suggests that Shakespeare's global popularity is not so much the result of 'the *universality* of his texts'; rather, we should understand it 'as the result of their *flexibility*'.[27] Kennedy reminds us that Shakespeare has been seen in a variety of Asian cinemas, as well as in Manga comic books, along with many styles of stage performance. In an examination of both film and performance interpretations of Shakespeare's work 'world-wide', Sonia Massai has argued for a complex and interactive relationship between 'local' Shakespeares designed for local audiences and those intended for national or international reception that both evidences and challenges the idea that Shakespeare 'has become one of the powerful global icons through which local cultural markets are progressively Westernized'.[28] In other words, audiences have been explicitly and implicitly prepared by the Shakespeare marketplace for the Globe to Globe Festival; what was new, in the end, was not the 'foreignness' of the experience. The excitement derived more thoroughly from the 'specialness' of each performance to its constituency spectatorship and, as much, to other theatre-goers who got a double show – watching the action both on and off stage. The Olympians, as they were called, who saw every show in the yard (for the bargain inclusive price of £100), were in many ways keener to talk about the ways audiences interacted with the action and with each other than to discuss what was or wasn't Shakespearean about the performances.

This volume takes the form of a chronological record of the productions not just to document the events in the order in which they appeared on the stage but also to trace the debates that developed over the Festival's six weeks. For example, the first week was characterized by the novelty of each production, and responses rarely moved beyond the celebratory. Each new show was received as a discovery and a joyful theatrical gift. But as the weeks and productions accumulated the stories from around the world became more complicated and more apparently political. Parts of the audience began to develop a collective understanding of how to shift from one culture to the next as a new audience appeared and took over the dominant language (spoken, of course, but as much physical, cultural, social, religious and theatrical) of the hour. Everyone else in the theatre had learned to adapt very quickly. The pattern of constant arrival, technical rehearsal, matinee performance, evening performance and departure for each company meant that there were five companies at some stage in this process every day. Tickets for the groundling Olympians required them to attend the matinee performances, and, given the afternoon shows were the first of the company's usual two performances, this often created the feel of a dress rehearsal, where the audience was leading and teaching the actors in their use of the Globe space rather than the other way around. The back and forth between the audience and onstage action was often wonderful to watch.

What exactly performers and spectators learned from the Globe to Globe Festival remains hard to quantify, and Kennedy's suggestion of flexibility is a useful one. For an audience comfortable in their knowledge of the plays and of the space, the challenge of each new day and each new play was significant. For an audience unfamiliar with Shakespeare's plays the challenge was certainly different, and, time and again, it was simply important to be there. The essays that follow examine the ways we have come to think about Shakespeare in the present and recent past – as national and international, as colonial and postcolonial, as a cultural icon and intercultural paradigm, as conservative and radical. The Globe to Globe Festival was the host to thirty-eight performances, each with its own story to tell, and this book tries to achieve something of the same: each essay here addresses some element(s) of Shakespeare beyond English, and together they suggest, like the performances themselves, the limits of contemporary assumptions about and expectations for these plays. Readers may well dip in and out of the volume as audiences did with the Festival, preferring to pursue their particular interests (whether geographical, thematic, generic or other), but however these essays are engaged, we hope they bring new ideas about how and where Shakespeare makes a home.

ENDNOTES

1 'London beats Paris to 2012 Games', 6 July 2005, news.bbc.co.uk/sport2/hi/front_page/4655555.stm, 27 October 2012.
2 Official London 2012 website, 'Cultural Olympiad', www.london2012.com/about-us/cultural-olympiad/, 27 October 2012.
3 Ibid.

4 Display at 'Shakespeare Staging the World', British Museum, 19 July–25 November 2012.

5 World Shakespeare Festival 2012, 'About the Festival', www.worldshakespearefestival.org. uk/about/, 27 October 2012. This site records seventy productions under its sponsorship that took place across the UK.

6 Ibid.

7 Published by Cambridge University Press in 2008.

8 Dennis Kennedy, ed., *Foreign Shakespeare: Contemporary Performance*, first published in 1993 by Cambridge University Press. In an afterword to this, the first collection to address performances by non-English-speaking companies, Kennedy provided a field-changing critique of the Anglo-centrism of Shakespeare studies.

9 Globe press release, 'Shakespeare's Globe announces success of the Globe to Globe Festival as it completes its six-week marathon', 7 June 2012, www.shakespearesglobe.com/ about-us/press/releases/globe-theatre, 27 October 2012. There are inconsistencies in how the number of plays/performances are counted. Thirty-seven represents the number of Shakespeare's plays; the staging of *Venus and Adonis* raises that count by one. The number of 'languages' is also the subject of some debate in the essays and elsewhere, particularly in reference to Deafinitely Theatre's *Love's Labour's Lost* and the Q Brothers' hip-hop version of *Othello*.

10 Ibid.

11 Mark Rylance, 'Discoveries from the Globe Stage', in Christie Carson and Farah Karim-Cooper, eds., *Shakespeare's Globe: A Theatrical Experiment* (Cambridge University Press, 2008), p. 103.

12 See p. xxiv.

13 Shakespeare's Globe Theatre, *Globe to Globe, 37 Plays 37 Languages*, Souvenir programme (London: Shakespeare's Globe, 2012). p. 10.

14 See pp. 13–14 in this volume.

15 Arts Council England, 'Achieving great art for everyone: A strategic framework for the arts', 4 November 2010, www.artscouncil.org.uk/publication_archive/strategic-framework-arts/, 27 October 2012.

16 Globe press release, 7 June 2012.

17 See p. 14 in this volume.

18 For further discussion of the event, see Rob Hand, 'Year of Shakespeare: Review of "Sonnet Sunday"', http://bloggingshakespeare.com/year-of-shakespeare-sonnet-Sunday, 7 November 2012.

19 Shakespeare's Globe Theatre, *Globe to Globe*, p. 11.

20 'Dismay at Globe invitation to Israeli theatre', *Guardian*, 29 March 2012, www.guardian.co. uk/world/2012/mar/29/dismay-globe-invitation-israeli-theatre, 27 October 2012.

21 Ibid.

22 Howard Brenton, 'Denounce, don't censor: Globe's invitation to Habima should stand', *Guardian*, 3 April 2012, www.guardian.co.uk/stage/2012/apr/03/denounce-dont-censor-habima-globe?intcmp=239, 27 October 2012.

23 Ibid.

24 Globe press release, 7 June 2012. In fact, several companies had three, and not two, performances, scheduled over weekends (*Venus and Adonis, Richard III, Othello, Romeo and Juliet, Antony and Cleopatra* and *Hamlet*, along with the Globe's own *Henry V*).

25 W.B. Worthen, *Shakespeare and the Force of Modern Performance* (Cambridge University Press, 2003), p. 102.
26 Kennedy, *Foreign Shakespeare*, p. 2.
27 Dennis Kennedy, 'Flexible Shakespeare', in Shakespeare's Globe Theatre, *Globe to Globe*, p. 3.
28 Sonia Massai, ed., *World-Wide Shakespeares: Local Appropriations in Film and Performance* (London: Routledge, 2005), p. 4.

THE GLOBE TO GLOBE FESTIVAL: AN INTRODUCTION

Tom Bird

An extraordinary number of people have asked me questions about the Globe to Globe Festival, from the moment in late 2010 that we announced the event would be going ahead. I was asked questions in scores of different languages and in the street, in theatres, on BBC Breakfast News, in bars and restaurants, wherever I went. A breathtaking wave of curiosity seems to have been generated by Dominic Dromgoole's idea of putting on all the Shakespeare plays in thirty-seven different languages. Some questions were easier to answer than others ('Why have you offended the people of *x* by not including a company from *x* in the festival?'), but on the whole there emerged a series of queries that everyone seemed to want answered, and I have attempted to answer these questions below, by way of giving some background to the critical reactions that followed.

HOW DID THE GLOBE FIND THESE COMPANIES?

In the first instance, we talked and talked and talked. To theatre people, to academics, to journalists, to cultural attachés and ambassadors: who do you know who is doing Shakespeare in a way that might work for a festival like this? We wanted wonderful storytellers, of course – the best actors and directors and musicians we could find – but we also wanted companies that could play anywhere at a moment's notice, light-of-foot groups who would be able to make the Globe space their own without five days of technical rehearsal. After talking at home, we began to travel and talk more, and then to watch as much work as we possibly could in the ten or so months we had in order to programme the Festival.

Happily, productions of Shakespeare's plays are happening in more than thirty-seven countries. For a finite festival like Globe to Globe (thirty-seven different plays plus *Venus and Adonis*, all in different languages) we would need some kind of vague selection criteria as to which languages were crucial to have around. The first and most important of these was London language. It was vital to us that a large proportion of the productions we chose should be in languages that are widely spoken in London, and in turn that we attracted speakers of those languages to the Globe for the Festival. The most straightforward example is probably what we did with *The Tempest*. Tens of thousands of people in the London Borough of Tower Hamlets, about a mile from the Globe, speak or understand Bangla. So we decided that we would have a show in Bangla, talked to many theatre-makers who had worked in Bangladesh and south Asia, and the same name kept appearing: Nasiruddin Yousuff's Dhaka Theatre. We looked at their work, felt it would suit us and invited them.

Another way we selected groups was by what I called 'Shakespeare language', by which I mean languages in which there is a long history of Shakespeare's plays being performed. Even if those languages aren't necessarily major London tongues (Armenian, Japanese, Georgian), we felt this was perhaps a way of ensuring that the most exciting work from the most vibrant Shakespeare (or theatre) scenes would be with us. So, in the case of the Caucasus, Dominic travelled to Georgia and I travelled to Armenia to watch the work of various companies, and we ended up with two spectacularly memorable shows: the Marjanishvili State Theatre's *As You Like It* and the Sundukyan National Theatre's *King John*.

Beyond those criteria, there were curveballs. We never wanted to shut any doors, so despite the fact that not many Londoners speak Juba Arabic, the language of the capital city of South Sudan, the proposal from that company's fledgling national theatre group was too heartfelt, genuine and mouth-watering to turn down. Other times, the work was simply so fine that we wanted it at the party no matter what criteria it did or didn't fill. As ever at the Globe, we broke our own rules and had great fun in the process. The end product was a mind-expandingly massive programme of work, from every inhabited continent, from Buenos Aires to Kyoto to Cape Town to Lahore to Moscow to Istanbul, and many more places in between.

WHICH PLAYS?

The idea was always to do all of Shakespeare's plays, but of course this depends on whom you believe. In the end, we made the somewhat arbitrary decision to lose *The Two Noble Kinsmen*, to keep *Henry VIII*, and to throw in an adaptation of *Venus and Adonis* for good measure. None of this reflects Globe 'policy', for want of a better word, on which plays are by Shakespeare and which are not. It's just that this was the way it worked out. If, say, a ground-breaking production of *The Two Noble Kinsmen* appeared in Inuit or Thai or Punjabi, then we would have been glad to look at it, but that didn't happen.

HOW MANY SHOWS EXISTED ALREADY?

A few of the shows that ended up at the Festival predated Globe to Globe. They were: Grupo Galpão's *Romeo and Juliet*, Bremer Shakespeare Company's *Timon of Athens*, Tang Shu-wing Theatre Studio's *Titus Andronicus*, Two Gents' *Two Gentlemen of Verona* (though in a different language), Meno Fortas' *Hamlet*, Teatr im. Kochanowskiego Theatre's *Macbeth*, the Vakhtangov Theatre's *Measure for Measure*, Yohangza Theatre Company's *A Midsummer Night's Dream* and Compagnie Hypermobile's *Much Ado About Nothing*. Everything else in the programme was developed with the Festival in mind.

WHICH PLAY GOES WHERE?

Once the shows above were programmed, and we had begun to decide which groups we wanted to work with, we had to begin the rather odd process of matching a company to a play. Of course, this starts easy and ends up difficult once there aren't many plays left available. In the vast majority of cases, the process was a collaborative one. We would ask a director or a group if there was a particular Shakespeare play that interested them, they would reply with a couple of titles, one would already have been taken but another wouldn't have been. As we reached the end of the programming period, it was, predictably, a case of 'we'd love to have you here, and if you want to come you have to do play *x* or play *y*'. In the end, even the plays that were 'given' to groups unexpectedly inspired and thrilled those who might rather have taken *Hamlet* or *Romeo and Juliet* at the outset. It was a real pleasure to talk to artists absolutely enthralled and enraptured by Shakespeare's less popular work.

WHAT INFORMATION DID THE GLOBE PROVIDE FOR EACH COMPANY? WERE THERE ANY RULES?

The companies were sent documents from the Globe's Associate Movement Director (Glynn MacDonald), Voice Associate (Martin McKellan), and Head of Research and Courses (Farah Karim-Cooper) – just guides through the many idiosyncrasies of working on that particular stage. We asked artists to use language, costume, music and movement as their storytelling tools, and not to bring large sets. As a special dispensation for the Festival, we allowed companies to play electronic music if they wished to – a departure for the Globe, but one that some groups exploited beautifully. Finally, we asked that each group keep their performance to less than two hours and fifteen minutes including an interval – mainly because of the very tight scheduling of a festival taking place in only one space over a relatively short period of time. This rule was broken by nearly everyone. Otherwise, we didn't interfere. We wanted companies to bring their own work, as though they were playing the show outdoors to an audience back home.

WHAT ABOUT SURTITLING?

We had three choices: line-by-line surtitling, no surtitles, or a compromise of scene-by-scene synopses. Line-by-line would be disastrous in the Globe, in my opinion – 1,500 heads in common light with the actors turning every few seconds would be spectacularly distracting. No surtitles seemed elitist – why should people be expected to know the plot of *Pericles* if they didn't speak Greek? In the end, after some growing pains, the synopses solution worked extremely well, as it avoided both the unattractive scenarios listed above. I hope other theatres or opera houses might be influenced by what we did with surtitles during the Festival.

WHAT WAS THE AUDIENCE REACTION TO THE FESTIVAL?

We had absolutely no idea what to expect with regard to audiences, but what we got was utterly exhilarating. Well over 80 per cent of those who attended had never been to the Globe before, and a huge number of native speakers of each language who told us they were not regular theatre-goers joined us for 'their' show. So for *Measure for Measure* we were a little Moscow, for *All's Well That Ends Well* a little Gujarat, and so on. Any regular London theatre-goer knows that audiences in London remain far too white and middle-class for our art to be considered as something that appeals to a wide spectrum of modern British society, so it was a great joy to see that if you programme work that appeals to non-traditional audience groups and you make them aware of it, they will come, and laugh and cry and whoop. This extraordinary audience reaction made me incredibly proud to have been part of the Globe to Globe Festival.

WHAT MIGHT BE THE FESTIVAL'S LEGACY?

The Festival received a huge amount of press, and the critical response was more positive than we could have dreamed of, so I hope those factors encourage other programmers to bring more international work to the UK. Furthermore, I hope this leads to greater engagement with new audiences, and even a consultation with those potential audiences before programming takes place at all. For the Globe itself, the Festival represented perhaps the ultimate manifestation of Sam Wanamaker's internationalism, and I hope marks the beginning of a myriad relationships with lovers of Shakespeare in performance, no matter what language they speak or which country they live in.

The Globe to Globe Festival was, in a way, far too colossal to sum up in any amount of words, but I hope that these answers help those interested to understand how we put it together, and that this book conveys just how joyous, extraordinary, wild and beautiful a party it was, and continues to be.

PERFORMANCE CALENDAR

Date	Play	Language(s)	Company	Director	Translation	Number of actors	Supporters	Performance history
21–2 April	Venus and Adonis	IsiZulu, IsiXhose, SeSotho, Setswana, Afrikaans, English	Isango Ensemble from Cape Town, South Africa	Mark Dornford-May	Isango Ensemble Company	Twenty-three actors		– Debut in Cape Town in 2012 – The Globe April–May 2013 – La Bohème, The Ragged-Trousered Philanthropists and Aesop's Fables at the Hackney Empire, London, from 11 May to 1 June 2012 – Yiimimangaliso – The Mysteries at Wilton's Music Hall, London in 2001 and at Garrick's Theatre in 2009 – The Magic Flute at the Duke of York Theatre and the Young Vic in 2007–8
23–4 April	Troilus and Cressida	Māori	Ngākau Toa from Auckland, New Zealand	Rachel House	Te Haumiata Mason	Twenty-two actors	Rawiri Paratene	– Debut at the New Zealand International Art Festival in March 2012
24–5 April	Measure for Measure	Russian	Vakhtangov Theatre from Moscow, Russia	Yuri Butusov	Osi Soroka	Seventeen actors	Alina Frolenko; Kiril Krok; Rimas Tuminas	– Debut in Moscow in 2010 – regular season in Moscow in September 2012 – Uncle Vanya at the Noel Coward Theatre, London in November 2012
25–6 April	The Merry Wives of Windsor	Swahili	Bitter Pill and The Theatre Company, from Nairobi, Kenya	Daniel Goldman and Sarah Norman	Joshua Ogutu	Eight actors	Kuona Trust; the Italian Institute of Culture; Stichting DOEN; HIVOS	– Workshop at the Harare International Festival of Arts in association with Theory X in May 2009 – the Oval House Theatre, London in June 2009 – tour throughout East Africa May–July 2012 – 'It's Shakespeare' Festival, Bangalore, India in November 2012

(cont.)

(cont.)

Date	Play	Language(s)	Company	Director	Translation	Number of actors	Supporters	Performance history
26–7 April	Pericles	Greek	National Theatre of Greece from Athens, Greece	Giyannis Houvardas	Dionisis Kapsalis	Twelve actors	Victoria Solomonidis at the Embassy of Greece; Aegean Airlines; London Greek Radio	– Debut in Athens in November 2011 – tour throughout Greece following the Festival – continues in repertoire in Athens
27–8 April	Twelfth Night	Hindi	Company Theatre from Mumbai, India	Atul Kumar	Amotish Nagpal	Nine actors, two musicians	Tulika Pandey; the Bhavan Centre; Rajat Kapoor; Namit Das; Shruti Vyas; Sumit Vyas; Yamini Das; Poorva Naresh; Shubrjyoti Baarat	– Tour throughout India in June 2012 – film screening during the South Asian Literature Festival at the Bush Theatre, London, on 4 November 2012 – Hamlet: The Clown Prince at the Hackney Empire, London in March 2011 – 'It's Shakespeare' Festival, Bangalore, India in November 2012
28–9 April	Richard III	Mandarin	National Theatre of China from Beijing, China	Wang Xiao Ying	Lv Rui	Twelve actors	Xinjiang Tech-Art Science Co. Ltd.	– The Capital Theatre, Beijing in July 2012 – the National Centre for the Performing Arts, Beijing in August 2012 – Shanghai International Arts Festival in October 2012 – Bitola Shakespeare Festival, July 2013
30 April–1 May	A Midsummer Night's Dream	Korean	Yohangza Theatre Company from Seoul, South Korea	Yang Jung-Ung	Yang Jung-Ung based on Lee Kangsun's translation	Eight actors	AsiaNow Productions; the Art Council Korea	– Debut in 2002 – performances in Tokyo, Japan; Quito, Equador; Manizales and Bogotá, Colombia; Psnan, Poland; Edinburgh, Scotland; Habana, Cuba; San Salvador, El Salvador; Bristol, UK; Neuss, Germany; Gdansk, Poland; Sydney, Perth and Adelaide, Australia; Chennai, India; and Brussels, Belgium – London debut at the Barbican Centre in June 2006

Date	Play	Language	Company	Director	Translator/Adaptor	Cast	Partners and supporters	Notes
1–2 May	*Julius Caesar*	Italian	369 Gradi/Lungta Film in collaboration with Teatro di Roma from Rome, Italy	Andrea Baracco	Vincenzo Manna and Andrea Baracco	Six actors	Teatro di Roma	– Production of Acts 1 and 2 at the Teatro della Cometa in Testaccio, Rome in January 2011 – debut in late spring 2012 in Gualtieri – Teatro di Roma in Rome, Italy in March 2012 – continued tour of Italy 2012–13
2–3 May	*Cymbeline*	Juba Arabic	South Sudan Theatre Company from Juba, South Sudan	Joseph Abuk and Derik Uya Alfred	Joseph Abuk and Derik Uya Alfred	Thirteen actors	The British Council; Gregory Thompson; Raz Shaw; Friends of Ibba Girls' School; Refugee Action	– Debut in Juba, South Sudan on 14 April 2012 – 'It's Shakespeare' Festival, Bangalore, India in November 2012
3–4 May	*Titus Andronicus*	Cantonese	Tang Shu-wing Theatre Studio from Hong Kong	Tang Shu-wing	Rupert Chan	Twelve actors, one musician	Hong Kong Arts Development Council; Perfect Stage Professional Make-up Company	– Debut at the 2008 Hong Kong Arts Festival – revival in 2009 – performances in Bytom, Norway; Wroclaw, Poland; and at the Nanluoguxiang Theatre Festival in Beijing, China, following the Festival
4–5 May	*Richard II*	Palestinian Arabic	Ashtar Theatre from Ramallah, Palestine	Conall Morrison	Bryan Shbib and Iman Aoun, based on a translation by Mohammad Anani; text editor, Gassan Zaqtan	Thirteen actors	The National Palestinian Authority; the National Security Forces; the Embassy of Palestine in the United Kingdom; Mr Mohammad Masharqa; Mojisola Adebayo; Razanne Carmey; Creation Theatre, Oxford; Oxfam, Oxford; Rebecca Watts; Lucia Conejero Rodilla; Jon Revell; Sakura Fujibayashi; Patrick Baldwin; Nabiha Naji; the Palestine TV; the Palestinian Ministry of Culture; the Ministry of Tourism and Antiques; Jericho Governorate; Al-Nasher; Ramallah Municipality; the British Council; Padico Holding	– Oxfam House, Oxford on 7 May 2012 – Multiple performances at Hisham Palace, Jericho; Al-Qasabeh Theatre, Ramallah, Palestine, 2012 – Performed in Dubai, 2012 – performances of *The Gaza Monologues* in several locations across the UK

(cont.)

(cont.)

Date	Play	Language(s)	Company	Director	Translation	Number of actors	Supporters	Performance history
5–6 May	Othello	Hip hop	Q Brothers/ Chicago Shakespeare Theater/ Richard Jordan Productions from Chicago, USA	JQ and GQ; developed with Rick Boynton	JQ and GQ	Four actors, one musician	The John D. and Catherine T. MacArthur Foundation; the Davee Foundation; the Julius Frankel Foundation; American Airlines; Arc Worldwide; the Best Portion Foundation; The Boeing Company; ComEd; Eric's Tazmanian Angel Fund; Hyatt; Lew and Susan Manilow; Raymond and Judy McCaskey; the Robert R. McCormick Foundation; the Donna Van Eekeren Foundation; City of Chicago Mayor Rahm Emanuel; the United States Embassy in London	– The Shakespeare-Festival im Globe Neuss in Neuss, Germany, 6–7 July 2012 – the Edinburgh Festival Fringe, 1–27 August 2012 – Chicago Shakespeare, from 12 March to 15 June 2013
7–8 May	The Tempest	Bangla	Dhaka Theatre from Dhaka, Bangladesh	Nasiruddin Yousuff	Rubayet Ahmed	Thirteen actors	UCB Bank Bangladesh; THEWHATWORKS; Bengali International	– Debut at the Shilpakala Academy in Dhaka, Bangladesh, on 27 April 2012 – the Selim Al Deen Festival, Dhaka, on 25 August 2012 – 'It's Shakespeare' Festival, Bangalore, India in November 2012 – Cox's Bazaar, Bangladesh in December 2012
8–10 May	Macbeth	Polish	Teatr im. Kochanowskiego from Opole, Poland	Maja Kleczewska	Antoni Libera	Sixteen actors	Londoneynek.net; the Polish Cultural Institute	– Debut at the Jan Kochanowski Theatre in Opole, Poland in December 2004
9–10 May	The Two Gentlemen of Verona	Shona	Two Gents Productions from London/ Harare, Zimbabwe	Arne Pohlmeier	Noel Marerwa	Two actors	Annika Brown and the Oval House Theatre; the Watermill, Rich Mix; Tara Arts	– North Wiltshire, Nottingham, Aldershot and Tara Arts, London in May 2012 following the Festival – Australian tour February–March 2013 – previously performed in English at the Oval House, Theatre London, as well as in Germany, Zimbabwe, Hungry, Poland and Bath, UK

(cont.)

Date	Play	Language	Company	Director	Translator	Cast	Sponsors	Notes
11 and 13 May	1 Henry VI	Serbian	National Theatre Belgrade in association with the Laza Kostic Fund from Belgrade, Serbia	Nikita Milivojević	Zoran Paunović	Twelve actors, three musicians	Laza Kostic Fund; Jat Airways; Mona	– Debut in Belgrade on 15 June 2012 – the Belgrade International Theatre Festival (BITEF) 2012 at the National Theatre Belgrade, on 15 September 2012 – Henry VI trilogy with the National Theatre of Albania and the National Theatre of Bitola, Bitola Shakespeare Festival, July 2013
12–13 May	2 Henry VI	Albanian	National Theatre of Albania from Tirana, Albania	Adonis Filipi	Shpresa Qatipi, Piro Tanku	Twenty-two actors	The Embassy of Albania in London	– Henry VI trilogy with the National Theatre Belgrade and the National Theatre of Bitola, Bitola Shakespeare Festival, July 2013
12–13 May	3 Henry VI	Macedonian	National Theatre of Bitola from Bitola, Macedonia	John Blondell	Dragi Mihajlovski	Thirteen actors, two musicians	The Ministry of Culture of the Republic of Macedonia; the Municipality of Bitola; Lit Moon Theatre Company, Santa Barbara, USA; Jim and Colleen Sterne	– Workshop in Santa Barbara, USA in February 2012 with the Lit Moon Theatre Company – Ohrid Summer festival in Ohrid, Macedonia in July 2012 – Henry VI trilogy with the National Theatre Belgrade and the National Theatre of Albania, Bitola Shakespeare Festival, July 2013
14–15 May	1 Henry IV	Mexican Spanish	Compañia Nacional de Teatro from Mexico City, Mexico	Hugo Arrevillaga Serrano	Alfredo Michel Modenessi	Eight actors, four musicians	Susan Chapman at the Anglo-Mexican Foundation and the Mexican Embassy in London; Mexico City's Ministry of Culture; Mexico City Theatre System; Scaffolding Dalmine; the Anglo-Mexican Foundation: MAC Cosmetics; Paulette Jonguitud; Dr Guillermina Solé; Manuel Monroy; Federico Ramírez Bustamante; Ariel Cavalieri; Claudia Cervantes; Francisco Gastelum; Architect Juan Morano Gasca; Elena Cepeda; Paco Arquero; Nina Serratos; Ricardo Rojas; Luigi Renato	– Debut at the National Theatre, Mexico City in April 2012

(cont.)

Date	Play	Language(s)	Company	Director	Translation	Number of actors	Supporters	Performance history
15–16 May	2 Henry IV	Argentine Spanish	Elkafka Espacio Teatral from Buenos Aires, Argentina	Rubén Szuchmacher	Lautoro Vilo	Fifteen actors	The Argentine Embassy in London; Dirección General de Asuntos Culturales del Ministerio de Relaciones Exteriores de la República Argentina; Complejo Teatral de la Ciudad de Buenos Aires; Instituto Nacional de Teatro (Argentina); PROTEATRO (Gobierno de la Ciudad de Buenos Aires)	– The Complejo Teatral de Buenos Aires in Buenos Aires, Argentina, July–September 2012
16–17 May	King John	Armenian	Gabriel Sundukyan National Academic Theatre from Yerevan, Armenia	Tigran Gasparyan		Ten actors, three musicians	The Embassy of the Republic of Armenia; the Saint Sarkis Charity Trust	– The National Theatre in Yerevan in June 2012
17–8 May	King Lear	Belarusian	Belarus Free Theatre from Minsk, Belarus now exiled in London	Vladimir Shcherban	Nicolei Khalezin	Thirteen actors	The Kevin Spacey Foundation; Hamish Jenkinson; the British Foreign and Commonwealth Organization; the Arts Council England; Julie Farrington and Mike Harris from Index on Censorship; Albina Kovaleva; the British Embassy in Minsk; Rosemary Thomas, HM Ambassador to Belarus	– The Globe in September 2013 – Being Harold Pinter at the Soho Theatre in February 2008 – Discover Love and Numbers at the Young Vic Theatre in December 2010 – Minsk, 2011: A Reply to Kathy Acker at the Young Vic in June 2012 during the London International Festival of Theatre (LIFT) 2012
18–19 May	As You Like It	Georgian	Marjanishvili Theatre from Tbilisi, Georgia	Levan Tsuladze	Lasha Bugadze	Fourteen actors	Tbilisi City Hall and the Ministry of Culture and Monument Protection of Georgia; the British–Georgian Chamber of Commerce; the British Georgian Society	– Tbilisi, Georgia in September 2012 – 'It's Shakespeare' Festival, Bangalore, India in November 2012 – The Globe in May 2013
19–20 May	Romeo and Juliet	Brazilian Portuguese	Grupo Galpão from Belo Horizonte, Brazil	Gabriel Villela	Onestaldo de Pennaforte	Ten actors	Petrobras; Paul Heritage and the team at People's Palace Projects; the Brazilian Embassy in London; the Williams Charitable Trust	– Debut in Ouro Preto, Brazil in 1992 – performances in more than sixty Brazilian cities, as well as in Spain, England, Holland, Germany, the USA, Uruguay, Venezuela and Colombia – The Globe in 2000

Date	Play	Language	Company	Director	Translator	Cast	Supporters	Additional performances
21–2 May	Coriolanus	Japanese	Chiten from Kyoto, Japan	Motoi Miura	Tsuneari Fukuda (福田恆存)	Five actors; two musicians	The Japan Centre; the Daiwa Anglo-Japanese Foundation; the Japan Foundation, London; the Great Britain Sasakawa Foundation; the Agency for Cultural Affairs, Government of Japan; EU–Japan Fest Japan Committee; Kyoto Art Centre	– Moscow and St Petersburg, Russia in May 2012 following the Festival
22–3 May	Love's Labour's Lost	British Sign Language	Deafinitely Theatre from London, UK	Paula Garfield	Translation team including Andrew Muir and Kate Furby	Ten actors, two musicians	The Arts Council England	– Ipswich, Wolverhampton, Derby and Brighton, UK, following the Festival – 'Spring and Winter' poem at Potter's Fields, London Bridge and the Boundless Festival, Peckham Square on 2 September 2012 and the Liberty Festival 2012 in Trafalgar Square
23–4 May	All's Well That Ends Well	Gujarati	Arpana from Mumbai, India	Sunil Shanbag	Mihir Bhuta	Nine actors, three musicians	Tulika Pandey and the Bhaven Centre	– Debut in Mumbai, India in May 2012 – tour throughout India in July and August 2012 – 'It's Shakespeare' Festival, Bangalore, India in November 2012 – Lagos, late 2013
24–5 May	The Winter's Tale	Yoruba	Renegade Theatre from Lagos, Nigeria	Olúwolé Ogúntókun	Ayantadel Padeola	Thirteen actors, three musicians	Professor Wole Soyinka; Bayo Oduneye; Ronke Fetuga; Femi Sunmonu; Jide Odusolu; Goke Coker	
25–6 May	The Taming of the Shrew	Urdu	Theatre Wallay from Islamabad, Pakistan	Haissam Hussain	Aamna Kaul, Mariam Pasha and Zaibun Pasha	Fifteen actors, five musicians	Shakespeare's Globe; Theatre Walley; Kashf; the Northwall; Oxford and Open Minds; Rotherham; the Ministry of Foreign Affairs; the Government of Punjab; Lahore Arts Council; Pakistan International Airlines; the Nauman Taseer Foundation; the Rangoonwala Foundation; British Council; Arts Council England; the North Wall Arts Centre	– Rotherham and Bradford, UK, in May following the Festival – film screening during the South Asian Literature Festival at the Bush Theatre in London, on 3 November 2012

(cont.)

(cont.)

Date	Play	Language(s)	Company	Director	Translation	Number of actors	Supporters	Performance history
26–7 May	Antony and Cleopatra	Turkish	Oyun Atölyesi from Istanbul, Turkey	Kemal Aydoğan	Bülent Bozkurt	Twelve actors	Avrupa Gazette; T.C. Kültür ve Turizm Bakanlığı Telif Hakları Genel Müdürlüğü	– Istanbul Theatre Festival in June 2012 – continues in repertoire
28–9 May	The Merchant of Venice	Hebrew	Habima National Theatre from Tel Aviv, Israel	Ilan Ronen	Dori Parnes	Twelve actors, five musicians	The Friends of Habima; Mr Igal Ahouvi	– Habima National Theatre in Tel Aviv, Israel in September 2012
29–30 May	Henry VIII	Castilian Spanish	Rakatá from Madrid, Spain	Ernesto Arias	Jose Padilla	Twelve actors, five musicians	The Spanish Embassy in London; Instituto Cervantes in London	– The Teatros del Canal in Madrid, Spain in September 2012
30–1 May	The Comedy of Errors	Dari Persian	Roy-e-Sabs from Kabul, Afghanistan	Corinne Jaber	Nahal Tajadod	Nine actors, three musicians	Dr Paul Smith; Cathy Gomez and Daud Rasool of the British Council; Dr Sarah Fane; Paula Swanborough; Anne Eberhard; Bruce Myers; Giannis Koskinas; Qais Akbar Omar; Shiv and Urvashi Khemka; Tommy Wide; Christopher Morris; Leena Tukhi; Professor John Baily and Goldsmiths College London; Viscount Cranborne; Mirwaiss Sidiqi; Rory Stewart; Sir Sherard Cowper-Coles; Sir William Patey; Lord Dalmeny; Christian Destremau; Diane Adriaenssen; Simon and Mary Robey; Alexander and Libby Russell; Christopher and Brigitte Granville; Julian and Louisiana Granville; Dame Vivien Duffield; Dr Mai Yamani; Lord Marks; Malú Ansaldo	– Debut in Bangalore, India, on 12–13 May 2012 – the Sheldonian Theatre in Oxford, UK, on 6 June 2012 – the Shakespeare-Festival im Globe Neuss in Neuss, Germany, on 11 June 2012

Date	Play	Language	Company	Director		Cast	Supporters	Notes
31 May–1 June	Timon of Athens	German	Bremer Shakespeare Company from Bremen, Germany	Sebastian Kautz	Sebastian Kautz	Five actors	The Higher Education Academy; the Goethe Institut	– Debut in Bremen on 14 October 2010 – Concordia in Bremen, Germany in March and November 2012 – *The Merry Wives of Windsor* on the building site for the Globe Theatre in 1993
1–2 June	Much Ado About Nothing	French	Compagnie Hypermobile from Paris, France	Clément Poirée	Jude Lucas	Ten actors	Ville de Paris; Les Productions Somnambules; Jeune Théâtre National; Institut Français Royaume-Uni	– Debut at Théâtre de la Tempête in Paris in November 2011 – Le festival d'Anjou in Anjou, France in June 2012 – le Centre des Bords de Marne in Paris, France in April 2013
2–3 June	Hamlet	Lithuanian	Meno Fortas from Vilnius, Lithuania	Eimuntas Nekrošius	Aleksas Churginas	Eleven actors, one musician	The Ministry of Culture of the Republic of Lithuania; the Lithuanian Embassy in London	– Debut at Meno Fortas in May 1997 – performances at numerous European festivals in 1998 and 1999, as well as in Montreal (1998) and Toronto (2002) – fall 2012 season opener in Vilnius, Lithuania
7 June–26 August	Henry V	English	Shakespeare's Globe from London, UK	Dominic Dromgoole	N/A	Seventeen actors, four musicians		– National tour April and May 2012 – performances during the Globe regular season June–August 2012

WEEK ONE

CHAPTER ONE

U VENAS NO ADONISI

Grassroots theatre or market branding in the Rainbow Nation?

Malcolm Cocks

The Isango Ensemble from Cape Town, South Africa, kicked off the Globe to Globe Festival with a glorious interpretation of Shakespeare's epic poem that left the audience grinning from sheer exhilaration. The compelling story of desire, power, attempted seduction and loss unfolds through a seamless medley of song, dance and music, drawing on elements from Western operatic traditions, South African *a cappella* and contemporary pop music. This was Shakespeare with marimbas, drums, beatboxing, hand-clapping, whistles and improvised instruments I can't even name. An all-black cast on the Globe stage in a multilingual production incorporating six of the nine major South African languages, including IsiZulu, IsiXhose, SeSotho, Setswana, English and a sprinkling of Afrikaans: this was Shakespeare like never before.

As I stood in the yard, waiting for the performance to start and watching the all-black cast kitted out in their quasi-Elizabethan but also somehow unmistakably South African costumes, I did find myself wondering about the project. Shakespeare performed in thirty-eight languages? A pernicious example of the continuing success of Western cultural colonization? Or an eloquent testimony to the ways that shared human values successfully cross the cultural divide? A lot rides on the idea of a global Shakespeare festival.

My curiosity and scepticism were thoroughly piqued by the selection. Who puts on *Venus and Adonis* anyway? Shakespeare in translation performed by a group of South Africans, however talented, in the place where it all began is a daunting enough undertaking without choosing a poem that no one has successfully adapted for the stage into the bargain. It's a wonderful poem, to be sure, but it sits oddly in the canon, and there are good reasons why the poem has rarely been staged, even at the Globe. One challenge is that the poem is effectively a series of beautiful but static verbal tableaux, a monologue rehearsing the entire verbal artillery of female seduction.

None of my initial reservations about the stageability of the poem withstood the performance. The performance was a consummate feat of artifice from start to finish. But nothing felt contrived. All the elements were integral to the telling of the story. They brought the poem to life in a way that felt spontaneous and homegrown, while remaining completely consonant with its unique emotional appeal and with the elements of the story that we still find most compelling today. At no point did the motley audience of Globe *aficionados*, Shakespeare-lovers and tourists lose the narrative thread. To judge from their riveted expressions during the performance, the audience might have been firmly convinced that it spoke IsiXhose. The resounding applause it bestowed on a slightly startled cast at the end seemed to suggest that no one remembered or cared that the poem had been written in English. The messages of the poem were made universal by wonderfully simple but innovative casting and staging decisions which produced an astonishing range of emotional effects, from poignant sympathy for a woman spurned, to amused incredulity at the powers of a peevish youth to resist so many eloquent arguments, to amorous sport, to the much rarer but very real empathy for male innocence menaced by overbearing female lust.

Led by a bewitching Pauline Malefane, seven women of distinct parts and persuasive lyrical talents play the insatiable Venus. The lusty, highly sympathetic female ensemble are complemented perfectly by a slight but sprightly Mhlekazi Whawha Mosiea, who plays the testy Adonis. The decision to multiply Venus so as to create an overwhelming chorus of formidable femalehood in all its stages of desire, loss and mourning is an example of the simple genius that made this production so successful. Mark Dornford-May's innovative production also exploited choric elements of the Greek tragic drama and overcame the issue of staticness by relying on a stunning array of visual and dramatic effects. These included an improbable but, in the event, rather successful incarnation of Adonis' horse in the form of a massive horse-head puppet fashioned from recycled tin. Katlego Mmusi's stark embodiment of death as a bald, painted, scythe-wielding skeleton with a lolling, slithering tongue of blood-red who gyrated with macabre elegance across the stage was among the most memorable of the imaginative dramatic elements employed to bring the poem to life on the stage.

But this intelligent production also contributed to our experience and understanding of the poem's central issue: the frank exploration of transgressive human sexuality and the radical questioning of gender conventions. Venus dominates the poem in all senses. The passive Adonis barely speaks. At one point, straddled, pinned and wriggling beneath the weight of Venus' bosom, a distraught Adonis cries out, 'You crush me, let me go!' The shock of much of the violence is diffused, but not dismissed, by the frequent resort to physical comedy. In another scene, Adonis finds himself compelled to skip to escape becoming ensnared in a twist

Fig. 1 Adonis (Mhlekazi Whawha Mosiea) with five Venuses, *Venus and Adonis*, Isango Ensemble from Cape Town, South Africa; director Mark Dornford-May.

of sheets wielded by a chorus of singing Venuses. Some of the resonance of the scene derives from its association with the rituals of southern African marriage ceremonies and the amusing (but also potentially distressing) public compulsion for the groom to consummate the marriage while the wedding guests literally sing the couple to bed. The Isango Ensemble were able to adapt this little-known poem for the stage so successfully because they understood the poem's own freeness with genre and convention and because, as a successful international repertoire company, they are aware of the (now global) contexts for performance which continue to make Shakespeare available and meaningful for contemporary audiences.

In a production that brought so much joy to the audience, it seems almost churlish to dwell on any criticisms. But it was precisely what the production had to say about what 'global Shakespeares' might mean which persisted as a niggling residue after the wonder and exhilaration of the performance itself had subsided. I wondered about the kind of audience, if any, U *Venas* might expect to enjoy in South Africa, and, indeed, about its appeal for a Cape township audience. In his interview with Globe Education, assistant director Lungelo Ngamlana admitted frankly that 'most of the people who attend a theatre in South Africa are still predominantly white'.[1]

Part of the company's challenge, and therefore part of the meaning of their performances, would always include breaking down certain cultural expectations about who should perform theatre from the Western canon and where. This is a good thing. But it also reminded me that meaning in theatre is transactional and culturally determined. It always depends on a contract between the performers and audience to create the meaning together. A version of U *Venas no Adonisi* might go down as well with a township audience in the Cape as it did with the motley collection of largely Western spectators who flocked to the Globe. But if it did, some of the reasons for their enjoyment would be different and the meanings created would also be different. In fact, it would be a different production altogether. The question of audience should prompt us to reflect on what happens when a Western audience in London enjoys a multilingual performance of a poem from the Western canon by Africans from the townships in Cape Town who sing and dance and smile. We might want to think about the meanings that are so effectively suppressed or, indeed, enabled by all that Shakespearean wonder and exhilaration.

This issue is perhaps even more fraught in the case of the Isango Ensemble because, for astute economic reasons of its own, post-independence South Africa has become a remarkably efficient machine for marketing a certain global image of the not-so-new but still shiny Rainbow Nation. The need for this image and the effectiveness of the campaign is such that we in the West continue to consume it with astonishingly complacent insouciance. But it elides or suppresses certain realities about some of the stark social and economic inequalities which divide South Africa and which inevitably impinge, I think, as a negative or largely invisible condition determining the meaning of such global performances, even when we say to ourselves, 'Isn't it amazing? They come from the townships in Cape Town.'

These observations are not intended as a criticism of the Isango Ensemble's almost flawless production. Nor do I wish to censor their efforts as a global repertoire theatre company, or to suggest that the production could somehow have been different. But I do think their participation in the Globe to Globe Festival affords us the opportunity to acknowledge the peculiar conditions which make the idea of a global Shakespeare possible, and for whom.

ENDNOTE

1 *Culture Works*, 'Lungelo Ngamlana interview excerpt', http://vimeo.com/40974737, 29 July 2012.

CHAPTER TWO

FESTIVAL SHOWCASING AND CULTURAL REGENERATION

Aotearoa New Zealand, Shakespeare's Globe and Ngākau Toa's A Toroihi rāua ko Kāhira (Troilus and Cressida) in te reo Māori

Catherine Silverstone

English-language productions dominate performance traditions for Shakespeare in Aotearoa New Zealand and can be traced to visiting English troupes in the nineteenth and early twentieth centuries, a legacy that survives today in visits by the RSC and the National Theatre, among others.[1] Performances of Shakespeare have also developed locally, especially since the expansion of amateur and professional productions from the mid twentieth century on.[2] Significantly, there is also a small but growing body of work in te reo Māori (Māori language), inaugurated by Pei Te Hurinui Jones' translations, *Owhiro: Te Mua o Weneti* (Othello, 1944), *Te Tangata Whai-Rawa O Weniti* (The Merchant of Venice, 1946) and *Huria Hiha* (Julius Caesar, 1959).[3] Of these translations, to date only *Te Tangata Whai-Rawa O Weniti* has been performed, directed most notably by Don C. Selwyn as the landmark film *The Maori Merchant of Venice* (2002).[4] There have also been some smaller-scale Shakespeare projects in te reo Māori, including Merimeri Penfold's translation of nine of Shakespeare's sonnets, *Nga Waiata Aroha a Hekepia* (2000), Toby Mills' short film *Te Po Uriuri* (The Enveloping Night, 2001), based on a translation of Sonnet 147, and Te Haumihiata Mason's 'Oriori 18' (2009), a translation of Sonnet 18.[5] Mason subsequently translated *Troilus and Cressida* for Ngākau Toa's production *A Toroihi rāua ko Kāhira* (Troilus and Cressida), performed at the Globe to Globe Festival.[6] Rawiri Paratene (Ngākau Toa's founder and *A Toroihi rāua ko Kāhira*'s executive producer) recalled his dream after first performing at the Globe to 'one day... bring a company of Māori back here and... blow this place apart'.[7] The realization of this dream – *A Toroihi rāua ko Kāhira* – opened the main Festival on 23 April 2012, and Paratene situated the production as a continuation of Selwyn's 'legacy of taking Te Reo Maori to the

I am grateful to Susan Bennett, Christie Carson, Julia Cort and Mark Houlahan for comments on earlier drafts of this chapter.

World'.[8] This production is the most significant performance of Shakespeare in *te reo* Māori since Selwyn's film.

Directed by Rachel House and co-directed by Jamus Webster, Ngākau Toa's production transported the action of Shakespeare's play from Ancient Greece to Te Ao Māori, the world of the Māori prior to the arrival of European explorers, traders and settlers. In this respect it relates to work produced primarily since the 1990s that draws attention to Aotearoa New Zealand as a site of production, especially in the context of historical and contemporary race relations between Māori and *Pākehā* (white New Zealanders of predominantly British and Irish origin) following the signing of the Treaty of Waitangi/Te Tiriti o Waitangi between Māori and the British Crown in 1840.[9] Unlike Annie Ruth and Rangimoana Taylor's production (2003) for Toi Whaakari (New Zealand Drama School), where the action was set in the context of New Zealand's mid nineteenth-century land wars, with the Trojans identified as Māori and the Greeks as British, the war was here refigured between fictional Māori tribes, the Kariki and Toroi.[10] The names of Shakespeare's characters were given Māori equivalents (e.g. Toroihi for Troilus and Kāhira for Cressida), and the spiritual and social world of the play was recast in terms of Māori culture and traditions. Thus, Kātiti (Calchas) was performed as a *tohunga* or priest who is able to mediate between the *atua* (ancestors) and the *iwi* (tribe), and the text was saturated with references to Māori gods. Opening with a powerful *whakaeke*, or entrance onto the stage, used to deliver the prologue with a *haka* (dance) and *karanga* (ceremonial call), the production employed Māori *taonga* (cultural treasures) throughout (see Colour Plate 1). These included *kapa hapa*, or Māori performing arts, comprised of *haka*, *waiata* (song), *poi* (swinging balls) and *mau rākau* (Māori weaponry); *nga taonga puoro* (traditional Māori instruments); and *te reo* Māori. Costumes designed by Shona Tawhiao incorporated traditional Māori designs (including tattoos) and weaving techniques, as well as acknowledging the play's Western origins in the bodices and full satin skirts worn by some of the women.

For Paratene, who also performed the role of Panātara (Pandarus), the production provided the opportunity 'to showcase some of our great Maori actors, to show off our beautiful reo rangatira [esteemed, revered language] but also to showcase a selection of Maori performing arts'.[11] This designation of the production as a 'showcase' is reiterated on the company's website and by other members of the project, including Jamus Webster.[12] Further, Chris Finlayson, the New Zealand Minister of Arts, Culture and Heritage, asserted that '[i]t is a great opportunity to demonstrate the strength of Maori Theatre performance and to showcase Te Reo Maori', which, in the context of his ministerial role, positions the production as a type of cultural export.[13] Cultural 'showcasing' is symptomatic of how international festivals, as Ric Knowles suggests, tend to model '"exchange" . . . on international diplomacy, intercultural tourism, and transnational trade'.[14] The support offered variously by the British Council, cultural institutes, foundations and embassies, though not New Zealand's, to sixteen of the thirty-seven productions included in the Festival highlights this phenomenon.[15] Showcasing can certainly serve these 'international' ends, but it can also be situated in relation to specific local histories and interests, even as these can be put under pressure by international contexts of production. The remainder of this chapter accounts for Ngākau Toa's Festival 'showcase' by considering some of the factors that enabled it, the implications of the performance, especially with respect to the regeneration of *te reo* in relation to the Globe and Shakespeare, and the effects of performing as part of an international festival dislocated from the culture of production.

I have previously written about Shakespeare's Globe Theatre and Shakespeare in Aotearoa New Zealand, including Shakespeare in *te reo* Māori, and here extend my discussion of the effects of colonization in aspects of this earlier work through a consideration of festival performance.[16] This chapter is also inflected by my experiences as a New Zealander. I have lived in the United Kingdom since 1999, but my primary, secondary and tertiary education in Aotearoa New Zealand in the 1980s and 1990s coincided with developments by Māori communities and the New Zealand government, initiated in the 1970s, to redress the effects of the British colonization of Aotearoa, measured in lower educational achievements, poorer health records and lower life expectancy for Māori than their Pākehā counterparts.[17]

Regeneration initiatives include the recovery of traditional cultural practices such as carving, weaving and tattooing; the creation of *te reo* Māori immersion schooling, encompassing *kōhanga reo* (language nests) in 1982, *kura kaupapa* (primary schools) in 1985 and *wharekura* (secondary schools) in 1989; the designation of Māori as an official language alongside the creation of the Te Taura Whiri I te Reo Māori (the Māori Language Commission) in 1987; and the establishment of grant-awarding bodies to support Māori arts and artists on stage, film, radio and television.[18] In addition to these wider developments, members of Ngākau Toa have been instrumental in improving access to and regenerating *te reo* and other aspects of Māori culture: the production's website records Paratene's involvement in a delegation to Parliament on 14 September 1972 that presented a petition requesting that Māori language courses be taught in schools, which also marked the inaugural Māori Language Day; Mason is the Language Standards Manager at Te Taura Whiri I te Reo Māori; *nga taonga puoro* expert Richard Nunns has done significant work in researching traditional Māori instruments and sounds; Kimo Houltham (Toroihi (Troilus)) is a presenter on IAMTV, a youth-focused television programme with an emphasis on Māori culture; Waihoroi Shortland (Netāhio (Nestor)) has worked in Māori broadcasting as a cultural adviser and as an actor in *te reo* Māori, which includes his performance in *The Maori Merchant* alongside Scotty Morrison (Akamēmana (Agamemnon)); Morrison is also a presenter on *Te Karere*, a *te reo* Māori news television programme, and is co-presenter of *Marae Investigates*, a bilingual current affairs programme, as well as Adjunct Professor and Director of Māori Student and Community Engagement at Auckland's Unitec Institute of Technology.[19] *A Toroihi rāua ko Kāhira* thus emerged in relation both to historical and ongoing regeneration efforts, as did Selwyn's *The Maori Merchant* produced a decade earlier.[20]

The effects of these efforts can be seen in Ngākau Toa's onstage performance of *te reo*, *kapa haka* and *nga taonga puoro* (performed on stage by Richard Nunns and James Webster, who also played Menerau (Menelaus)). They can be seen in the biographies of some cast members, too, such as Kimo Houltham, who benefited from Māori immersion education programmes and is fluent in *te reo*. In addition to being enabled by these broad cultural shifts, the production was supported by public bodies set up to develop Māori language and culture. Specifically, Mason's translation was funded by Te Taura Whiri I te Reo Māori, and development of the production was also supported by Te Puni Kōkiri (the Ministry of Māori Development) and Te Waka Toi (the Māori Arts Board of Creative New Zealand). In turn, involvement in the production also enabled participants to develop their skills and knowledge. For instance, although Mason is a skilled translator, she reports that her 'confidence has grown in [her] ability to translate' through her work on the script.[21] In some cases, expertise was also developed where there was little pre-existing experience: Jamus Webster notes that '[m]ost of the people in this production didn't grow up in kapa haka but were hungry to learn', and House notes that 'it was great having Tweedie Waititi helping the less fluent cast members with their understanding and pronunciation'.[22] Ngākau Toa also promoted *te reo* and Māori performing arts through print, television and media interviews, and by maximizing attendance for their performances at Te Marae in Te Papa Tongarewa (the Museum of New Zealand) in Wellington for the New Zealand International Arts Festival (2012) and at the Auckland Town Hall Concert Chamber (2012). This was achieved by performing for *koha* (donation) rather than selling tickets, with the exception of one fundraising performance in Auckland in April to support the trip to the Globe.

In the context of the many opportunities that the production offers for cultural development, language regeneration has been repeatedly cited as one of its key contributions. Indeed, Paratene and Morrison commented respectively that *A Toroihi rāua ko Kāhira* is 'an important part of the journey [of the] . . . recovery of our language' and that it is 'helping to rejuvenate the Maori language'.[23] In light of such claims, I will now focus on the work that the Globe and 'Shakespeare' (as text and cultural icon) do in relation to this project. As the language performed at the main Festival that is perhaps most in need of protection and nurturing, *te reo* nonetheless shared a position with some of the languages spoken at Sonnet Sunday on 22 April 2012. This was a free event that offered 'a marathon of all 154 sonnets in over 20 different languages NOT represented in the Festival'.[24] Some of these languages including Scots, Gaelic, Cornish, Noongar (an Australian Aboriginal language) are, like *te reo* Māori, spoken within English-majority language contexts and are, variously, similarly endangered and subject to language and cultural recovery projects. The Globe thus provided a pre-Festival platform for some endangered languages, but in the case of *te reo* Māori it also influenced how the language was presented: Mason recalls that 'Shakespeare's Globe Theatre didn't want the new Maori language of today. Instead, they wanted the classical language used by our ancestors', which suggests a desire for cultural authenticity and linguistic 'purity' outside the grip of English.[25] While the vision of an authentic precolonial language is perhaps impossible to achieve, given the powerful effects of colonization and interlinguistic borrowing on classical as well as contemporary Māori language, the Globe's brief did help to stimulate a translation that enhances understandings of classical Māori. Mason used a form of the language known as *kupu tawhito* (ancient language) or sometimes as *te reo kōhutu* – also used by Jones in his translations in the 1940s and 1950s – that is devoid of transliterations characteristic of modern Māori (e.g. *motokā*/car). She thus employed classical phrases, words and what Houltham describes as 'old Māori *kīwaha*' or colloquialisms to produce a version of *te reo* that Paratene says is 'pretty difficult', even for fluent speakers.[26] Shakespeare's language was employed, then, as it was in Jones' and Selwyn's work with *The Māori Merchant*, as a means through which to revitalize historical aspects of *te reo*.[27] The translation is, though, similarly shadowed by the irony of using English to help rejuvenate a language that it has historically subordinated and in many ways does still.

Given this drive towards a precolonial linguistic authenticity, it is striking how those involved identified a synergy between Shakespeare's language and classical *te reo* Māori. Paratene commented that 'the classical Maori language is very poetic, very bawdy, very prosaic – it's got all the different forms of the language that Shakespeare uses', while Morrison noted that 'Shakespeare is incredibly metaphorical and poetic, which is actually very much the way Maori used to be spoken as well', also suggesting that 'our language actually fits perfectly with the rhythm and emotion of Shakespeare'.[28] House also asserted that 'the whole story fits with Maori culture like a glove'.[29] Paratene further noted similarities between the theatre and the *marae*, or the open area in front of a *wharenui* (meeting house) where formal discussions and greetings occur; he claimed 'the Māori performer . . . will feel right at home', that the stage is 'like the contact that you can only have on a *marae*' in its directness, intimacy and grandeur.[30] Such claims show how cultural differences can be incorporated under the signs of Shakespeare and the Globe as if they were self-same. They also, however, advantageously position *te reo* and Māori cultural practices as having equivalent status (and attendant cultural capital) to that of 'Shakespeare'. Further, in some accounts, *te reo* is elevated above Shakespeare's language, with Paratene reporting that non-speakers claimed that the play is 'more accessible in *te reo* Māori'.[31] Here he stakes a claim less for *te reo* rejuvenating Shakespeare's text, as Morrison does elsewhere, and more for the primacy of the translation over Shakespeare's text, which situates it in a relation of dominance to its powerful textual origin.[32]

The company's commitment to *te reo* Māori and performing arts and its work in promoting these practices inside and outside Aotearoa New Zealand does, however, take place in the context of significant work still to be done in supporting the once profoundly endangered language. The fact that Paratene, House and other members of the company are not fluent speakers of *te reo* emphasized, in the midst of extremely well-attended and positively received productions in Wellington, Auckland and London, wider issues regarding the health of the language that were occluded by reviewers in the UK, although highlighted by some commentators in Aotearoa New Zealand.[33] The last census (in 2006) records, for instance, that 157,110 people, or 3.9 per cent of the total population, and '131,613 [people] (23.7 per cent) of Māori could hold a conversation about everyday things in te reo Māori'.[34] Further, a 2011 report by the Waitangi Tribunal – a commission of enquiry created in 1975 to investigate breaches of the Tiriti/Treaty – asserts that in 2010 'the health of te reo remains fragmentary at best' and notes that 'if trends continue, over the next 15 to 20 years the te reo speaking proportion of the Māori population will decline further, even as the absolute number of speakers continues to slowly climb'.[35] It remains to be seen whether Mason's hope that the translation will 'promote the Maori language being spoken wherever the stage may be' and Te Puni Kōkiri's projection of 2028 as the year when 'the Māori language will be widely spoken by Māori' will be realized.[36] While the production invests the future state of *te reo* with promise, I want now to consider some more immediate implications of the 'showcase' for audiences, both in Aotearoa New Zealand and London.

Critical work on international festivals has examined the effects of dislocating productions from their cultures of origin, especially for audiences.[37] Knowles suggests that '[c]ultural differences . . . tend either to be packaged for consumption as exotic or charming . . . or, as in high modernist formalism, to be treated as interesting and energizing but fundamentally incidental local variants on a (therefore more important, or essential) universalist or transcendent humanism'.[38] This dynamic certainly operates with respect to *Toroihi rāua ko Kāhira*, as some reviewers in the UK commented on the actors' tattoos, exposed buttocks and performance of *haka*, almost as if they were objects of outmoded forms of anthropological enquiry.[39] Further, the double-page photographic spreads of the opening *whakaeke* in the *Independent* and the *Guardian* offered spectacular images of cultural otherness on the Globe's stage, contrasting with the theatre's usual publicity shots, which tend, though not exclusively, to feature white actors in period costumes.[40] Simultaneously, the production was situated as a variant of one of Shakespeare's texts, and reviews in Aotearoa New Zealand and the UK made appeals to Shakespeare's universal and transcendent qualities.[41]

Knowles argues that although it is tempting 'to consider the constraints and containments of the international marketplace to be virtually all-confining', there are 'fissures'.[42] As such, it is important not to replay the exotic/universal dynamic as a totalizing assessment of festival performances. Thus, while the production was subject to 'othering', it also participated in the creation of reductive representations by recycling a set of predictable gay stereotypes evident in Rangi Rangitukunoa's camp performance of Patokihi (Patroclus) and the reiteration of a masculine/feminine dynamic in the relationship between Patokihi and Matu Ngaropo's Aikiri (Achilles). These performances did little to draw attention to the cultural specificity of *takatāpui*, which historically refers to a close or devoted friend of the same gender and which in contemporary contexts is used as a term of identification by some Māori in preference to (or alongside) lesbian, gay, bisexual, transgender or queer.[43] Rather, the production presented Patokihi and his relationship with Aikiri as objects of fun, bordering, at times, on ridicule, evidenced by the laughter elicited from some members of the audience in New Zealand and at the Globe, which also occurred in relation to Paratene's camp portrayal of Panātara, even as others were critical of these representations.[44] Further, the production worked to invest the relationship between Patokihi and Aikiri with sincerity only after Patokihi's death, negating much of the potential both the play and the production's historical and cultural setting offer to acknowledge and affirm queer affiliations and desires.[45]

As these examples suggest, companies are not (usually) completely devoid of agency in their choice of representations and are capable of affecting their audiences in different ways, even as they cannot control the reception. Accordingly, House's comment that 'we are keen to show the sexiness of our culture, through our unique costumes and Maori movement' and her 'susp[icion that] people will freak out about the tattooed bums at first but I'm sure they will get used to it' show a deliberateness in the representations and an awareness of their potential effects in an international context.[46] House also positioned the production's specially composed *haka* as expanding an international audience's understanding beyond 'the ["Ka Mate"] haka before the [All Blacks'] rugby' matches.[47] In addition, James Webster saw part of the project as 'show[ing] this play to Maori people there [London] who yearn for their Maori identity and their language'.[48] Here the production is cited as offering cultural sustenance to Māori, diversifying its range of meanings beyond those produced through a cultural showcase for an international audience.[49]

Displaced 'local' audiences are also capable of expanding the range of meanings that a geographically dislocated production might generate in international festival contexts. One of the most arresting elements was the sight of a group of spectators in the yard who honoured the performance at its end with a *haka*. This employed the traditional Māori protocol of 'call and response' familiar from the *marae*, staged here between the spectators and the performers. The *haka* positioned the spectators in a relation of kinship to the performers, circumventing discourses of touristic cultural consumption as novelty that are often used to characterize festival-going experiences.[50] The Globe subsequently described the repetition of the *haka* in the yard as an example of 'true Globe style', seamlessly appropriating the occasion into the mythology of their theatre.[51] This reception exemplifies what Knowles, in a different context, describes as '[t]he dangers of displacement and loss of cultural specificity' that festivals can effect.[52] In contrast, paying attention to the cultural specificity of the final *haka*, performed outside the 'official' showcase of the Festival, enables it to stand, alternatively, as it did for me, as a profound reminder and acknowledgement of the importance of community and *whanau* (familial) networks. These networks not only helped to enable the production but also continue to support and develop *te reo*, *kapa haka* and other *taonga* beyond the event of a high-profile performance such as this.

Support was also mobilized in Aotearoa New Zealand through appealing to feelings of pride. These appeals derived, at least in part, from the production's status as a *representative* at the Globe variously of *te reo*, Māori and New Zealand in the context of a high-profile international festival that it opened, a position that Paratene frequently drew attention to as a 'great honour'.[53] For example, he addressed his fundraising appeal to support the trip to the Globe to 'proud New Zealanders', elsewhere describing the production as 'a proud thing for New Zealand in general but especially for our language'.[54] Morrison spoke of being 'very proud to be representing our people', and Pita Sharples, co-leader of the Māori Party, claimed that '[w]e as New Zealanders can all be so proud'.[55] Discourses of pride appeal to a collective sense of self-esteem and solidarity. They can function effectively to counter histories of violence and dispossession; honour developments in cultural and linguistic regeneration; increase awareness, understanding and participation in language acquisition and cultural practices; and enhance the cultural capital of these practices. It is, though, worth remembering that the machinery of a high-profile festival, especially the external validation it offers of an individual production, can also work to eclipse multiple local instances of language learning and cultural development, as well as work still to be done in redressing inequalities. Further, Paratene noted that 'it's very easy for New Zealanders to think that we are a peaceful nation but we're a nation that's founded on war', and House suggested that the production's narrative of historical intertribal conflicts resonate today.[56] Pride can thus occlude violent histories, cultural differences and inequalities under the signs of an undifferentiated Māori and, on occasion, New Zealand identity.

Toroihi rāua ko Kāhira emerges, then, from a commitment to *te reo* Māori and cultural practices. Enabled by a range of community-led and government initiatives, it, in turn, promotes *te reo* and Māori culture both locally and internationally through the form of the performance 'showcase'. The showcase does, nonetheless, risk being consumed as exotic, universal or an object of cultural tourism and is capable, variously, of both marginalizing and homogenizing difference. *Toroihi rāua ko Kāhira* privileges and affirms Shakespeare and the Globe (and in the context of a festival such as this, it would be difficult not to), but it also deploys these institutions and attendant cultural capital for its own ends of cultural and linguistic regeneration, so as to create and affirm networks and generate feelings of pride. Alongside developments in Māori cultural practices, *te reo*, film, radio, theatre, television and education more broadly, this production offered a vibrant and high-profile performance that looked, as Selwyn's film did a decade earlier, to a future in which *te reo* and other cultural *taonga* are yet more secure. The overall health of the Māori language and the comparative rarity of local and international performances in *te reo*, however, provide a sobering reminder of the work still to be done.

ENDNOTES

1 Aotearoa is the Māori name for New Zealand; the compound 'Aotearoa New Zealand' attempts to acknowledge the nation's dual heritage.
2 For an account of the history of Shakespeare in Aotearoa New Zealand from the presence of a copy of the *Collected Works* in the luggage of Sydney Parkinson, the ship's artist on James Cook's 1769 voyage, through the settler period to the late twentieth century, see Mark Houlahan, 'Shakespeare in New Zealand', in Roger Robinson and Nelson Wattie, eds., *The Oxford Companion to New Zealand Literature* (Oxford University Press, 1998), pp. 489–91.
3 Jones also translated *waiata* (songs) into English and contributed to a translation of the Bible (1949).
4 Selwyn first directed *Te Tangata Whai-Rawa O Weniti* in 1990 as part of Auckland's Te Koanga Spring Festival of Māori Arts. *The Maori Merchant of Venice*, released early in 2002, has the distinction of being the first feature-length film in *te reo*.
5 Mason's sonnet was performed at Shakespeare's Globe by Rawiri Paratene and presented by Belinda Brown, New Zealand's Deputy High Commissioner in London, in August 2009 as a gift on behalf of the Shakespeare Globe Centre New Zealand (established 1991) to mark the 400th anniversary of the publication of the *Sonnets*. This gift is one of the latest markers of the relationship between the Globe and its New Zealand counterpart, which has seen students, teachers and actors, including Paratene, spend time performing, studying and interning at the Globe (see Shakespeare Globe Centre New Zealand, 'About Us', www.shakespeare.org.nz/about-us, 9 July 2012).
6 Following guidance offered by Te Puni Kōkiri (Ministry of Māori Development), I have used macrons to 'indicate long vowel sounds in the Māori language', except where they are absent from the texts I cite (Te Puni Kōkiri (Ministry of Māori Development), 'Macrons', http://www.tkm.govt.nz/about/, 9 July 2012).
7 Paratene, interview with Paul Diamond, 'Rawiri Paratene – *The Maori Troilus and Cressida*', *Sunday Morning*, National, Radio New Zealand, 11 December 2011, www.radionz.co.nz/national/programmes/sunday/20111211, 9 July 2012. Paratene had previously spent time at

the Globe on an International Actors Fellowship (2007); he subsequently performed Friar Lawrence in Dominic Dromgoole's *Romeo and Juliet* (2009) and Theoclymenes in Deborah Bruce's *Helen* (2009).

8 Paratene, quoted in *Toroihi rāua ko Kāhira*, sponsorship document, p. 9, accessible via *The Maori Troilus and Cressida*, http://themaoritroilusandcressida.com/support/, 9 July 2012.

9 Examples of performances that engage with contemporary contexts include a plotline from the local soap opera *Shortland Street* (1997); Oscar Kightley and Erolia Ifopo's *Romeo and Tusi* (1997–2000) for Pacific Underground; and Lemi Ponifasio's *Tempest: Without a Body* (2007), devised with his company Mau. For discussions of *Shortland Street*'s *Othello* storyline and *Romeo and Tusi*, see respectively Catherine Silverstone, 'Othello's Travels in New Zealand: Shakespeare, Race and National Identity', in Pascale Aebischer, Edward J. Esche and Nigel Wheale, eds., *Remaking Shakespeare: Performance across Media, Genres and Cultures* (Basingstoke: Palgrave, 2003), pp. 78–84; Mark Houlahan, 'Romeo and Tusi: An Eclectically Musical Samoan/Māori Romeo and Juliet from Aotearoa/New Zealand', *Contemporary Theatre Review*, 19.3 (2009): 279–88.

10 For a discussion of Ruth and Taylor's production and its historical setting, see Julie McDougall, 'The Mutability of History: Troilus and Cressida', *Contemporary Theatre Review*, 19.3 (2009), 331–41. Other productions that have situated Shakespeare's plays in the context of the nineteenth-century land wars include Theatre at Large's appropriation of *Othello* in *Manawa Taua/Savage Hearts* (1994), Cathy Downes' *Othello* (2001) and Jonathon Hendry's *Othello* (2007). For a discussion of *Manawa Taua*, see Silverstone, 'Othello's Travels', pp. 84–9.

11 Paratene, quoted in 'Paratene to take Reo Shakespeare to London', Waatea 603 am, 3 October 2011, www.waatea603am.co.nz/news/2011/october/paratene-to-take-reo-shakespeare-to-london, 9 July 2012.

12 'Our Journey', in *The Maori Troilus and Cressida*, http://themaoritroilusandcressida.com/about/, 9 July 2012; Jamus Webster, interview with Kawariki Morgan, 'Troilus and Cressida', *Waka Huia*, series 2012, episode 8, directed by Morgan, subtitled English translations by Mariana Whareaitu, One, TVNZ, 6 May 2012, http://tvnz.co.nz/waka-huia/s2012-ep8-video-4867851, 9 July 2012.

13 Finlayson, quoted in 'Maori on an International Stage', in *The Maori Troilus and Cressida*, www.themaoritroilusandcressida.com/the-cast/, 9 July 2012.

14 Ric Knowles, *Reading the Material Theatre* (Cambridge University Press, 2004), p. 187.

15 Shakespeare's Globe Theatre, *Globe to Globe, 37 Plays, 37 Languages*, souvenir programme (London: Shakespeare's Globe, 2012), p. 33.

16 See Catherine Silverstone, 'Shakespeare Live: Reproducing Shakespeare at the "New" Globe Theatre', *Textual Practice*, 19.1 (2005): 31–50; 'Othello's Travels'; *Shakespeare, Trauma and Contemporary Performance* (New York: Routledge, 2011), pp. 55–79, which expands 'Speaking Māori Shakespeare: The Māori Merchant of Venice and the Legacy of Colonisation', in Mark Thornton Burnett and Ramona Wray, eds., *Screening Shakespeare in the Twenty-First Century* (Edinburgh University Press, 2006), pp. 127–45.

17 See Statistics New Zealand, www.stats.govt.nz/browse_for_stats.aspx, 9 July 2012.

18 For a book-length account of efforts to regenerate *te reo* Māori between 1972 and 2008, including interviews with many key advocates, see Chris Winitana, *My Language,*

My Inspiration: The Struggle Continues, Tōku Reo, Tōku Ohooho – Ka Whawhai Tonu Mātou (Wellington: Huia Publishers and Te Taura I te Reo Māori, 2011).

19   See 'Key Personnel' in *The Maori Troilus and Cressida*, www.themaoritroilusand cressida.com/the-cast/, 9 July 2012.

20   See Silverstone, *Shakespeare*, pp. 57–8, 68–70.

21   Mason, interview with Morgan, 'Troilus and Cressida'.

22   Jamus Webster, interview with Morgan, 'Troilus and Cressida'; House, quoted in Sharu Delilkan, 'Preview: Troilus and Cressida (Auckland Town Hall to the Globe Theatre)', *Theatre Scenes*, 6 April 2012, www.theatrescenes.co.nz/preview-troilus-and-cressida-auckland-town-hall-to-the-globe-theatre/, 9 July 2012.

23   Paratene, interview with Diamond, 'Rawiri Paretene'; Scotty Morrison, quoted in Kerry McBride, 'Te Reo Fits Shakespeare "Perfectly"', *Dominion Post*, 8 March 2012, www.stuff. co.nz/dominion-post/culture/arts-festival-2012/6541903/Te-reo-fits-Shakespeare-perfectly, 9 July 2012.

24   Shakespeare's Globe Theatre, 'Sonnet Sunday', www.shakespearesglobe.com/theatre/special-events, 9 July 2012, emphasis in original.

25   Mason, interview with Morgan, 'Troilus and Cressida'.

26   Houltham and Paratene, interview with Matai Smith, 'Kimo and Rawiri', *Good Morning*, One, TVNZ, 20 March 2012, tvnz.co.nz/good-morning/extra-210312-kimo-video-4789438, 9 July 2012.

27   See Silverstone, *Shakespeare*, pp. 63–7.

28   Paratene, quoted in 'Maori Troupe Kicks off Shakespeare Fest', *New Zealand Herald*, 24 April 2012, www.nzherald.co.nz/entertainment/news/article.cfm?c_id=1501119&objectid=10801104, 9 July 2012; Morrison, quoted in McBride, 'Te Reo Fits'.

29   House, quoted in Delilkan, 'Preview'.

30   Paratene, interview with Diamond, 'Rawiri Paretene'.

31   Paratene, interview with Smith, 'Kimo and Rawiri'.

32   Morrison, quoted in McBride, 'Te Reo Fits'.

33   See for example Dionne Christian, 'The Language is the Thing', *Stuff.co.nz*, 23 April 2012, www.stuff.co.nz/entertainment/arts/6786794/The-language-is-the-thing, 9 July 2012; Paul Diamond, 'An Awe-Inspiring Marvel', Review of *Troilus and Cressida*, Te Marae, Te Papa, Wellington, *Theatre Review*, 20 March 2012, www.theatreview.org.nz/reviews/review. php?id=4641, 9 July 2012.

34   'Language Spoken', Statistics New Zealand, www.stats.govt.nz/Census/2006CensusHome Page/classification-counts-tables/about-people/language-spoken.aspx, 9 July 2012; 'Language/Ko te Reo', Statistics New Zealand, www.stats.govt.nz/Census/2006Census HomePage/QuickStats/quickstats-about-a-subject/maori/language-ko-te-reo.aspx, 9 July 2012. The census scheduled for 2011 was delayed until 5 March 2013 due to the 2011 Christchurch earthquake. At the time of writing the census had not taken place.

35   Waitangi Tribunal, 'Chapter 5: Te Reo Māori', *Ko Aotearoa Tēnei: A Report into Claims Concerning New Zealand Law and Policy Affecting Māori Culture and Identity*, vol. II, WAI 262 Waitangi Tribunal Report (Wellington: Legislation Direct, 2011), pp. 387–487 (pp. 441, 440), www. waitangi-tribunal.govt.nz/scripts/reports/reports/262/52823D9E-6BD4-465E-86EE-8A917BAE12D1.pdf, 9 July 2012.

36 Mason, interview with Morgan, 'Troilus and Cressida'; Te Puni Kōkiri, *Te Rautaki Reo Māori: The Māori Language Strategy*, (Wellington: Ministry of Māori Development, 2003), http://www.tpk.govt.nz/en/in-print/our-publications/publications/the-maori-language-strategy/download/tpk-maorilangstrat-2003.pdf, p. 5.

37 See Knowles, *Reading*, especially pp. 88–91 and 180–200; Karen Fricker, 'Tourism, the Festival Marketplace and Robert Lepage's *The Seven Streams of the River Ota*', *Contemporary Theatre Review*, 13.4 (2003): 79–93.

38 Knowles, *Reading*, p. 187.

39 Indicative examples from the UK: Andrew Dickson, review of *Troilus and Cressida*, Shakespeare's Globe Theatre, *Guardian*, 24 April 2012, www.guardian.co.uk/stage/2012/apr/24/troilus-cressida-review, 9 July 2012; Dominic Cavendish, review of *Troilus and Cressida*, Shakespeare's Globe Theatre, *Telegraph*, 24 April 2012, www.telegraph.co.uk/culture/theatre/theatre-reviews/9224440/Maori-Troilus-and-Cressida-Shakespeares-Globe-review.html, 9 July 2012. Some reviewers in Aotearoa New Zealand commented on similar characteristics, but they tended to be framed as shared cultural reference points rather than exotic curiosities; examples include John Smythe, 'Poetic, Vibrant, Physical, Visceral', review of *Troilus and Cressida*, Te Marae, Te Papa, Wellington, *Theatre Review*, 10 March 2012, www.theatreview.org.nz/reviews/review.php?id=4594, 9 July 2012; Diamond, 'An Awe-Inspiring Marvel'.

40 Contrast images by Tony Nandi ('Is This a Haka I See Before Me?', photograph, pictures of the Day, *Independent*, 24 April 2012) and Facundo Arrizabalaga ('Shakespeare's Globe Theatre, London', photograph, Eyewitness, *Guardian*, 23 April 2012), with, for example, the Globe's promotional photograph of Jamie Parker as Henry V (2012).

41 Indicative example from New Zealand: Paul Simei-Barton, review of *Troilus and Cressida*, Auckland Town Hall, *New Zealand Herald*, 23 March 2012, www.nzherald.co.nz/theatre/news/article.cfm?c_id=343/objectid=10794079, 9 July 2012; indicative example from the UK: Cavendish review of *Troilus and Cressida*.

42 Knowles, *Reading*, p. 188.

43 See Jessica Hutchings and Clive Aspin, 'Introduction', in Hutchings and Aspin, eds., *Sexuality and the Stories of Indigenous People* (Wellington: Huia Publishers, 2007), pp. 15–24.

44 See, for example, Diamond, 'An Awe-Inspiring Marvel'; Hannah August, 'Globe to Globe Week 1: Part One', *Stet: An Online Postgraduate Research Journal*, 2 May 2012, www.stetjournal.org/blogs/author/haugust/, 12 October 2012.

45 I am grateful to Mark Houlahan for drawing my attention to this shift in representation.

46 House, quoted in Delilkan, 'Preview'.

47 House, quoted in Tim Masters, 'Globe to Globe: *Maori Troilus and Cressida* Puts *Haka* into Shakespeare', *BBC News*, 22 April 2012, www.bbc.co.uk/news/entertainment-arts-17769799, 9 July 2012.

48 James Webster, interview with Morgan, 'Troilus and Cressida'.

49 A small sample of post-show audience interviews suggests that the production attracted Māori keen to see aspects of their culture represented in London (and on stage); see Penelope Woods, interview with audience members, 'Year of Shakespeare G2G Troilus and Cressida 1', Shakespeare Institute, 20 June 2012, http://soundcloud.com/shakespeare-institute/year-of-shakespeare-g2g-16, 9 July 2012; Woods, interview with audience members, 'Year of Shakespeare G2G Troilus and Cressida 2', Shakespeare Institute,

20 June 2012, http://soundcloud.com/shakespeare-institute/year-of-shakespeare-g2g-17, 9 July 2012.

50 See, for example, Dennis Kennedy, 'Shakespeare and Cultural Tourism', *Theatre Journal*, 50 (1998): 175–88; Fricker, 'Tourism', 79–83.

51 Shakespeare's Globe Theatre, 'Globe to Globe Opens to Rave Reviews', *Globe News*, Spring 2012, mass-publicity e-mail to the author, 27 April 2012.

52 Knowles, *Reading*, p. 89.

53 See for example Paratene, 'Help Us in Our Journey to the Globe', in *The Maori Troilus and Cressida*, www.themaoritroilusandcressida.com/, 9 July 2012.

54 Paratene, interview with Lynne Freeman, 'The Maori Troilus and Cressida', *The Arts on Sunday*, National, Radio New Zealand, 18 March 2012, www.radionz.co.nz/national/programmes/artsonsunday/20120318, 9 July 2012; Paratene, interview with Freeman, 'Rawiri Paratene', *The Arts on Sunday*, National, Radio New Zealand, 15 May 2011, www.radionz.co.nz/national/programmes/artsonsunday/20110515, 9 July 2012.

55 Morrison, quoted in 'Maori Production of Troilis [*sic*] and Cresida [*sic*] Prepares to Open the World's Largest Shakespearean Festival', *Marae Investigates*, One, TVNZ, 22 April 2012, www.youtube.com/watch?v=vc6b8Dkyteo&list=UUd_uV1LZOdOeTUuehv10-ZA&index=60&feature=plpp_video, 9 July 2012; Pita Sharples, 'Māori-Language Play to Open Globe to Globe Festival in London', press release, *Māori Party*, 27 April 2012, www.maoriparty.org/index.php?pag=nw&id=1860&p=m257orilanguage-play-to-open-globe-to-globe-shakespeare-festival-in-london.html, 9 July 2012.

56 Paratene, interview with Garth Bray, 'Maori Production of Shakespeare Play at the Globe', *One News*, One, TVNZ, 23 April 2012, tvnz.co.nz/entertainment-news/maori-production-shakespeare-play-globe-video-4847299, 9 July 2012; House, quoted in Delilkan, 'Preview'.

CHAPTER THREE

'WHAT'S MINE IS YOURS, AND WHAT IS YOURS IS MINE'

Measure for Measure, Vakhtangov Theatre, Moscow

Kevin Quarmby

The Vakhtangov Theatre, established in 1922, is named after Stanislavski's protégé, Evgeny Vakhtangov.[1] The theatre perpetuates the distinctive dramatic technique of its founder, embodied in Vakhtangov's Imaginative or Fantastic Realism (*fantasticheskii realism*), which contrasts fundamentally with Stanislavski's own naturalistic dramaturgy.[2] With its ironic style of acting and emphasis on elements of the grotesque, Vakhtangov's experimental physicality and psychological intensity continue to inform the company's artistry.[3]

For this Russian *Measure for Measure*, Vakhtangov's 'grotesque' and 'ironic' formulations served to highlight the visual and aural intensity of the drama. Since the play is not particularly well known in Russia, its director, Yuri Butusov, felt free to adapt it to suit the company's stylistic needs.[4] Butusov's most radical alteration was to double Duke Vicentio (*sic*) with Angelo. The impressively tall Sergy Epishev, who towered menacingly over his fellow actors, played both duke and deputy. As the duke, Epishev presented a self-controlled aristocrat whose effeteness accounted for Vienna's moral decline. As Angelo, Epishev became a gangling bureaucrat, uncomfortable in his ill-fitting suit and straitjacketed in his moral outwardness. It was, however, in disguise as Friar Lodowick that Epishev's physicality offered the most striking visual analogue. In black-hooded habit, Epishev appeared more Mephistophelean opportunist than ducal manipulator.

Epishev's menacing portrayal complemented Butusov's equally radical narrative alterations. Since the duke and Angelo would no longer meet in the Act 5 scene of retributive justice, the 'duke of dark corners' (4.3.148) could freely mirror the moral corruption of his wayward deputy. The comic agony of this disguised duke, as he fought his desire to fondle the derrière of Anna Antonova's seductive Mistress Overdone, was juxtaposed, however, with his despicable assault against a helpless Isabella in the closing moments of the play. As the duke lunged at the distraught young woman, the true depths of his depravity, and of the society he so obviously failed to control, came into sharp and violent focus.

The foregrounding of Vicentio's failings, and the character's obvious identification with his deputy since the same actor played both roles, served to highlight the production's overarching theme: the domination and oppression of powerless young women by powerful men. Fundamental to this theme was the representation of women as objects of innocent, though corruptible, purity or of fetishized male fantasy; either might invite abusive treatment in this violent world, whose period setting seemed both timeless and frighteningly contemporary. First to appear was the diminutive Juliet, played with fecund innocence by Maria Berdinskikh. Like a heavily pregnant wren, Berdinskikh hobbled alongside her beloved Claudio (Vladimir Beldiyan) as he discussed his plight with the perpetually drunk and clownish Lucio (Oleg Lopukhov). Huddling close to the father of her unborn child, though no more than a child herself, Berdinskikh's Juliet gazed with adolescent adulation into her lover's eyes while proffering him a personally lit cigarette to ease his shackled pain. Even the dutiful cupping of her hand to create a human ashtray added to the utter devotion and subjugation of this tiny creature. Berdinskikh's representation of Juliet's helplessness served to emphasize the phallocentric power of the play's male protagonists; even in chains and led to prison, Claudio commanded dutiful obedience from his besotted devotee.

If Juliet was a wren, then Isabella was but a feather. Evgeniya Kregzhde portrayed the teenaged Isabella as a Lolitaesque innocent in a predatory Humbert world. When first asked to plead on her brother's behalf, Isabella depicted the nimbleness of youth by energetically tiptoeing into Angelo's office. The lightness of her footfall also facilitated a *coup de théâtre* of breathtaking beauty. Isabella was not goaded into pleading for her brother's life. Instead, she was literally blown into the arms of Angelo like a wisp of gossamer captured on the wind of Lucio and his male associate's breath. The soft sound of two actors blowing Isabella about the stage was accompanied by the novitiate's involuntary wafting backwards and forwards. The breeze-tossed balletic beauty of Isabella's movements was nevertheless tarnished by the sexual predation of its male intent.

Once in Angelo's arms, this vulnerable female fired his sexual passions. Angelo's offer of Claudio's life in exchange for Isabella's virginity was greeted, however, not with justifiable outrage, but with incredulity and disdainful rejection. All Isabella's lightness and feathery innocence seemed shattered and debased in that instant. From that moment on, Isabella's feet remained firmly planted on the ground as she painfully and visibly matured. Isabella's disdain was greeted, however, by Angelo's vicious slap across her face. Angered and frustrated, Angelo then overturned stage furniture as he grabbed the distraught Isabella and forced her onto a table-top. This

Fig. 2 Angelo (Sergey Epishev) and Isabella (Evgeniya Kregzhde), *Measure for Measure*, Vakhtangov Theatre from Moscow, Russia; director Yuri Butusov.

horrific act, so near to actual rape, left Angelo momentarily powerless and strangely emasculated. Skulking sullenly offstage, Angelo left the lone and abused Isabella sobbing with fear.

Isabella's distress was compounded by her brother's arrogant disregard for her plight. Although Isabella needed desperately to return to the childhood innocence of their 'catch-if-catch-can' sibling relationship – which ended in the tender moment of her kneeling to tie up her brother's shoelace and then patting his leg in sisterly approval – Claudio rejected her with an emotional violence no less painful than Angelo's attempted rape. Yet again, Isabella was forced to carry alone the weight of her femininity.

Rejected by her brother, Isabella found her isolation horrifically complete with the duke's later attack, which, as already alluded to, altered Shakespeare's ending in a fundamental way. Shockingly mirroring the encounter with Angelo, the duke's own lustful lunges at Isabella duplicated precisely his deputy's earlier movements in choreographic detail. Each overturning of the multiple tables, and swipes at the unfortunate female victim, was repeated by the frenzied duke. There was one significant difference, however. When the duke mirrored Angelo's vicious slap across Isabella's face, in response to her dismissal of his equally unwelcome proposal, the 'victim' was no more. Instead, if only for a moment, Isabella found her own strength. She returned the slap full force on the Duke's cheek. Isabella might be man-handled screaming onto the table. She might be left sobbing and laughing uncontrollably at her insane new plight. Nevertheless, this moment of female rebellion was to situate the Vakhtangov production in the realm of Ibsenite social discourse, the problematic construct that has haunted *Measure for Measure* since the late nineteenth century.

Isabella might be mentally unhinged by her ordeal, but, as this production's narrative alterations graphically allowed, her virginity seemed, for the moment at least, guaranteed. That would be until the next predatory male fantasized over the innocence of a youthful novitiate. The unpleasantness of these multiple representations of abusive male power confirmed Isabella's utter helplessness and hopelessness. Only Mistress Overdone knew truly how to manipulate male desire to her advantage; for innocents like Isabella, male desire would hound them until its ardour was sated, or until the bloom of youth had faded from their cheeks.

The Vakhtangov Theatre presented their spectacular and psychologically stimulating production as if they belonged in the open-air Globe space. Although the company feared the loss of their traditional sets, lighting and props, the physicality, wit and humour of the actors' performances complemented the darkness of the subject matter, as well as the open barrenness of the stage.[5] The Globe audience was noticeably divided between native Russian speakers and their English counterparts. This resulted in a disjunctive duality in appreciation of the play's wit and violence. One distinctive section of the audience would laugh at comic lines delivered in Russian, their amusement attracting as much interest as the onstage action, whereas everyone cherished the visual comedy in temporal unison.[6] The intriguing topicality of Shakespeare's narrative, and its alteration and relocation to Russia, ensured that this socially troubling play took on a Putinesque modernity whose comprehension by a mixed Globe audience seemed as surprising to the actors as it was to those lucky enough to see it. An alternative ending for *Measure for Measure* added an unusually focused nuance to the play's elusive and disquieting message. Insatiable lust from deputy and duke alike debased the individuals concerned while defining the society in which they lived. The victims remained, however, the women.

ENDNOTES

1 The Vakhtangov Theatre, 'Vakhtangov Theatre History', promotional website (2012), www.vakhtangov.ru/en/history, 1 July 2012. See also Andrei Malaev-Babel, ed., *The Vakhtangov Sourcebook* (Oxford: Routledge, 2010), pp. 127–8.

2 Stephen V. Bittner, *The Many Lives of Khrushchev's Thaw: Experience and Memory in Moscow's Arbat* (Ithaca, NY: Cornell University Press, 2008), pp. 76–8.

3 Ibid., p. 78.

4 Anton Prokhorov, '*Measure for Measure*: International Insights', audio interview (interviewer/translator unknown), Shakespeare's Globe London (2012), http://globetoglobe.shakespearesglobe.com/plays/measure-for-measure/interview, 24 June 2012.

5 Prokhorov, '*Measure for Measure*'.

6 See Matthew Evans, '*Measure for Measure* Reviewed by Young Directors' http://blog.shakespearesglobe.com/measure-for-measure-reviewed-by-the-young-directors, 1 July 2012.

CHAPTER FOUR

'THE GIRL DEFIES'

A Kenyan *Merry Wives of Windsor*

Emma Cox

At the end of the 1980s a renewed push to Africanize Kenya's secondary school literature curriculum prompted Kenyan President Daniel arap Moi to intervene and insist that Shakespeare, who he declared a universal genius, retain a permanent position in the nation's schools; today, Shakespeare continues to appear in a curriculum that otherwise centralizes African literature in English.[1] A chuckling admission by Kenyan actor Sharon Nanjosi when asked by a member of the Globe research team about her experience of Shakespeare offers another perspective on the cultural and political matrix that informed the Swahili *Merry Wives of Windsor* that she and her compatriots brought to the Globe to Globe Festival in 2012: 'I never grew up with Shakespeare. I only saw *Romeo + Juliet*, the movie... the one with Leonardo DiCaprio.'[2] It is no great insight to point out that the only Kenyan name that would come as trippingly off the tongue of the average Westerner as DiCaprio does off Nanjosi's is, as history would have it, Barack Obama. What is more telling is the fact that Nanjosi attributes her awareness of Shakespeare's work more to a product distributed globally by 20th Century Fox than to her Kenyan education.

The Africanization of the literature curriculum was hard won. Following Kenya's independence in 1963, debates concerned not only authors' backgrounds but also the language in which they wrote. Born some two generations before Nanjosi, the acclaimed Kenyan writer Ngũgĩ wa Thiong'o recalls that when a state of emergency was declared in Kenya in 1952 and all schools came under the authority of the British, 'English became more than a language: it was *the* language.'[3] Despite a landmark 1974 conference at the University of Nairobi (spearheaded by Ngũgĩ) on the teaching of African literature in secondary schools, the drive for an indigenous literature curriculum only gained pace in the 1980s.[4] Even in the context of Swahili advocacy, former president of Tanzania Julius Nyerere's Swahili translations of *Julius Caesar* (1963, revised as *Juliasi Kaizari* in 1969) and *The Merchant of Venice*

(*Mapebari wa Venisi*, 1972) implicitly bolstered the perception that Shakespeare had cultural validity for Africans.[5]

A Kenyan education system that has in part disentangled itself from British cultural inheritances and fostered in its young people an appreciation of previously debased indigenous writing; a production of *The Merry Wives of Windsor* by actors who claim no particular affiliation with Shakespeare, performed as part of a Cultural Olympiad initiative designed to show how cosmopolitan London (and Shakespeare) is in 2012: the hallmarks of 'soft' neo-imperialism are undeniable. But upon closer inspection a more complicated (and interesting) picture starts to coalesce of the Swahili *Merry Wives*, of how it might have served the interests of global Shakespeare, as well as how Shakespeare might have served the interests of the Kenyan practitioners. A collaboration between UK-based Bitter Pill and The Theatre Company, Kenya, the production was performed once in Nairobi before coming to the Festival; it toured to Hyderabad, Bangalore and Pune in November 2012 before returning to Nairobi the following month.[6] Like most who saw the production in London, I don't speak or understand Swahili (the dozen or so Kenyan audience members at each performance were identifiable when they quietly joined in the Kenyan national anthem at the start, enacting their allegiances among the otherwise silent crowd), so my observations of the performance come out of an experience of estrangement, but they are also informed by an enhanced appreciation of just how far good comic acting can transcend linguistic boundaries in the theatre.

The work was directed by Daniel Goldman (of UK company Tangram Theatre) and Sarah Norman (the Zimbabwean artistic director of Bitter Pill). Norman had directed a Zimbabwean production of *Merry Wives*, in English, which was work-shopped in Harare and performed at London's Oval House theatre in 2009, and she was also assistant director on Christopher Luscombe's celebrated 2008 Globe production and 2010 revival. One of my points of departure for discussing the Kenyan *Merry Wives* is a comment made by the wonderfully versatile Nanjosi (who played Sir Hugh Evans, Anne Page, Pistol and Robert) in the aforementioned interview, where she articulates something that, for her, seems to lie at the heart of this Swahili Shakespeare: 'The girl defies; but you can't defy in Kenya.'[7] (The fact that a girl couldn't defy in Shakespeare's England either is not immediately relevant here, but it is worth pausing over in light of the zeal with which Shakespeare can be shoehorned into narratives of empancipatory individualism.) With the provocation of *defiance* or, more precisely, the intrinsically political question of who is defying whom (or what) foremost in mind, I want to investigate the Swahili *Merry Wives* with reference to its theatrical form (particularly its metatheatricality) and to its engagement with issues of gender, sexuality and marriage.

While the men's performances tended to be marked (as I will discuss) by various degrees of camp flamboyance, the women, particularly the wives, comprised the formidable core of this production (see Colour Plate 2). Shakespeare offers some scope for such dynamics: for a play about the jealous guarding of marital property, *Merry Wives* represents women with some room to manoeuvre within the contract. As Mistress Ford and Mistress Page, Lydiah Gitachu and Chichi Seii were feisty, strikingly beautiful and in command of those around them. While Shakespeare establishes Falstaff's motivation primarily in terms of economic opportunism, it was the confident sexuality of the two wives that was prominent in this production. They knew exactly how to make Falstaff weak at the knees, how to orchestrate his and their husbands' desires; a hilarious stag-and-doe courtship ritual between Falstaff and Mistress Ford in Act 3 Scene 3 illustrated just how far the matriarchs were prepared to excite Falstaff's lust. The production also conferred greater agency on Anne Page than she has in the text: the start of Act 3 Scene 4 was performed as a touching duet between Anne and Fenton (Neville Sanganyi), and Anne was an active presence in Act 4 Scene 6, speaking for herself in a scene that in Shakespeare's text consists of Fenton enlisting the help of the Host of the Garter Inn (here, Hostess of the Windsor Hotel, played by Seii). Nanjosi portrayed the young woman as determined, somewhat impatient and passionately in love with Fenton. Norman notes that in her Zimbabwean *Merry Wives* she had been 'particularly inspired by the possibility of rural women succeeding',[8] and similarly, from Nanjosi's perspective, a narrative in which 'the girl defies' may pose an alternative to community cultural norms if a planned east Africa production tour goes ahead.[9]

That the production might have challenged or *defied* certain conventions seems against all odds: of the thirty-seven plays that were performed during the Globe to Globe Festival, *The Merry Wives of Windsor* is the one most saturated in 'Merrie England' nostalgia. Certainly, Luscombe's Globe production did little to shift an image of Elizabethan picturesque. On the (London) face of it, the Swahili *Merry Wives* stuck to fairly recognizable means of attracting laughs – physical comedy, innuendo, sly winks at the audience and participation with audience plants. If this sounds like a production made for the Globe, that is because it was. Norman was living in Kenya when the Globe to Globe project was announced, and it was she who suggested a Swahili production of the play.[10] Joshua Ogutu Muraya (who also performed in the work) translated Shakespeare's text, first into contemporary English, and then into contemporary Swahili.[11] Neither Goldman nor Norman speaks Swahili, so the project involved cross-linguistic and cross-cultural transactions right from its inception. Goldman's role was in large part to assist the actors in tailoring their performances to the Globe stage, offering insight into the space's volume and dimensions, its configuration, its 'weak' and 'strong' spots – and with the playful, interactive performance techniques that work so well in the space.[12]

The production employed modern costume and minimal set, placing the focus squarely on the shoulders of eight youthful actors who performed twenty roles.

In the opening scene, Shallow (James Gathitu), Slender (Sanganyi, who hilariously played all three of Anne Page's suitors) and Evans entered through the yard, comprising a motley trio: Shallow in a tweed jacket and bent over a walking stick; Evans, in long black frock coat with a large wooden cross around his neck, similarly bent with age; and Slender, in a bright orange suit jacket and purple shirt, flamboyantly flicking a white handkerchief in the air and holding his free hand aloft. His camp, flouncing manner attracted laughs throughout the performance. An effective piece of comic business in Act 1 Scene 1 established a mode of gentle interaction with the audience. Slender prissily called out for Simple (Eric Wanyama) three times, and when the dolt-like man arrived, Slender asserted his superiority by gesturing the servant to stand further and further aside until finally Simple was forced to get off the side of the stage and stand awkwardly at the edge of the group of groundlings while Slender spoke with Anne Page. Afterwards, Simple was unable to clamber back up onto the stage, and, after several attempts, was forced to make his way through the laughing audience until he reached the central steps. Seii's cool Hostess of the Windsor Hotel (Host of the Garter Inn) also interacted effectively with the crowd in the first act; spotting a couple of groundlings to distribute bottles of beer to, she toyed with them momentarily before removing the bottle caps with her teeth and handing out the drinks. As she chatted with the crowd, she casually held out her hand for payment of the beer, much to the crowd's – and her own – amusement. Moments of metatheatrical blurring between actors and their characters were also well received; in Act 3 Scene 1 an aggressive Caius roared at Evans, prompting the cowering Evans to run screaming through the groundlings, only to return, cautiously, when the other actors called out 'Nanjosi' by name.

The actors attracted appreciative responses to a few deft onstage character changes. In the transition to Act 1 Scene 3, Nanjosi as Evans stood upstage and pulled off her black gown and, grinning conspiratorially at the audience, revealed a dark grey hoodie and tight black trousers; as she pulled the hood onto her head and shifted her bent posture to a swagger, she was joined by several actors who entered, singing, as they set up the next scene. But it was Sanganyi whose quick-fire changes of character repeatedly drew applause. In Act 3 Scene 4 Fenton dashed from stage left to right to become Slender after Shallow called out 'Neville' by name (interrupting a kiss between Fenton and Anne), only to run back across the stage shortly afterwards, hurriedly retrieving his orange jacket as he went, after Page reminded him (using his name, Neville, once again) that Slender was called for at stage left. A couple more mad dashes were required before the end of the scene. These hilarious onstage changes became increasingly chaotic, as in Act 5 Scene 3, when Slender became Caius by wriggling out of his orange jacket just before the wives draped Caius' long white gown precariously over his front. Such moments where the world of the play was breached necessarily exceeded Shakespeare's text; in this case extra-textual comic work became crucial opportunities for forging complicity with an audience that for the most part was missing the words.

Not surprisingly, a lot of audience interaction derived from Falstaff. Played by Tanzanian actor and poet Mrisho Mpoto (the only non-Kenyan performer), he wore a garish purple (and later orange) shirt, lime-green cravat and outrageous fat-suit, and was met with a cheer upon his first entrance, grinning widely at the audience, arms open. A distinct departure from the grey-haired old rogue with which audiences are familiar, the dreadlocked, fat-suited Mpoto exuded libidinous energy combined with a good dose of childlike cuteness. His non-verbal shorthand for indicating the wives was to trace an hourglass shape with his hands, and in Act 1 Scene 3 this provided him with an opportunity to communicate with the audience: after Pistol and Nym (Ogutu Muraya) refused to pass Falstaff's letters on to Mistress Page and Mistress Ford, Falstaff handed the letters to two groundlings, miming an hourglass figure to explain his request. In Act 3 Scene 3, two audience plants were invited on stage and commandeered into helping pull off stage the large wicker basket containing Falstaff. In the matinee performance, but not the evening, the two men re-appeared after the interval to perform an Olympic-themed slow-motion race with Falstaff – out of which Falstaff emerged victorious – to the iconic theme music from the 1981 film *Chariots of Fire*. The charismatic Mpoto had the audience on side from the start, but particularly so after his unceremonious dunking in the river, after which he appeared, fluffy blue towel on his head, in angry childish tears. After he was pinched and tormented by 'fairies' at Herne's Oak – prompting inconsolable sobbing – and finally unmasked, his dejection elicited a sympathetic 'awww' from the crowd.

The actors' vocal techniques were more than adequate in the outdoor space – as one reviewer observed, '[r]esonant voices effortlessly project in a space which resident Globe actors sometimes struggle to fill'.[13] The cast also appeared entirely adept at the interactive, metatheatrical comic techniques I have outlined. But these were not familiar to the company. Nanjosi explains that whereas at the Globe, 'it is more about the audience – you are very generous with the audience . . . in Kenya, it is most about the actors on stage'; Ogutu Muraya agrees: 'we are used to having that fourth wall . . . the audience is not there'.[14] Nanjosi describes the challenge of mastering the exaggerated comedy that the production called for, noting that in rehearsal the actors had to remind one another to give '10 per cent more'.[15] What Nanjosi and Ogutu Muraya's comments imply is that their work with Shakespeare, created for Shakespeare's Globe, facilitated their departure from another European theatrical inheritance, one rooted in naturalism.[16] To the extent that *Merry Wives* was a departure from conventional practices at The Theatre Company, Kenya, this was lost in translation: the energetic cast's presentation of what was, in the end, a skilfully managed and often uproarious actor–audience rapport was entirely in accordance with what a Globe spectator would have expected from the only domestic farce in the canon.

The cultural capital that is tangled up with the idea of the Globe as a space where theatrical innovation may take place – specifically, in this case, where the Kenyan actors could extend their usual performance techniques – is illuminated by a comment made by Chichi Seii in a BBC Africa video report. Of the Globe, she enthuses: 'this is *old* and this is *special* and we are saying the words, although translated, that were written over 400 years ago; that's amazing. As you know, in Kenyan culture, we don't have anything written 400 years ago.'[17] In his book *Decolonising the Mind*, his 'farewell to English as a vehicle for any of [his] writings',[18] Ngũgĩ refers to the 'cultural bomb', which he describes as 'the biggest weapon wielded and actually daily unleashed by imperialism against . . . collective defiance'.[19] The cultural bomb 'makes [people] see their past as one wasteland of non-achievement . . . It makes them want to identify with that which is furthest removed from themselves; for instance, with other peoples' languages rather than their own.'[20] It is worth acknowledging that the last part of Ngũgĩ's description does not apply to the Swahili *Merry Wives*, but the fact that centuries-old Swahili literature written in localized Arabic script[21] can be so readily discounted puts into stark relief the theatrical liberation Shakespeare might be seen to offer, as well as the reflected international glow that bathes him in the process.

As a means of further contextualizing the Kenyan performers' adaptation to a Globe style of audience-centred comedy, Ngũgĩ's work offers a great deal of insight, particularly his mapping of the interconstitutive relationship between education, the status of English in Kenya and theatrical practice. Describing the suppression of performance traditions that originated in precolonial Kenya, Ngũgĩ writes, '[b]oth the missionaries and the colonial administration used the school system to destroy the concept of the "empty space" among the people by trying to capture or confine it in government-supervised urban community halls, schoolhalls, church-buildings, and in actual theatre buildings with the proscenium stage'.[22] Alongside such playwrights as Francis Imbuga and Mĩcere Mũgo, such directors as Seth Adagala and Waigwa Wachiira, and such companies as the Tamaduni Players, Ngũgĩ sought in the mid to late 1970s to redevelop grassroots, spontaneous and, most importantly, indigenous language performances, and to challenge the dominance and governance of the Kenya National Theatre, which had been established in the 1950s and was still 'run by a wholly expatriate governing council, with the British Council retaining a representative many years after Independence'.[23] The Kenya National Theatre and others like it, Ngũgĩ observes, 'specialised in West End comedies and sugary musicals with occasional Shakespeare and George Bernard Shaw'.[24] Infamously, Ngũgĩ's *Ngaahika Ndeenda* (*I Will Marry When I Want*), a nationalist production involving Kamĩrĩĩthũ villagers speaking and singing in the Gĩkũyũ language, was forcibly closed by the Kenyan authorities six weeks after opening in 1977, and Ngũgĩ, stripped of his position at the University of Nairobi, was arrested and imprisoned without trial for over a year. In Ngũgĩ's words, the government was 'attempting to stop the emergence of an authentic language of Kenyan theatre'.[25]

Thirty years later, on another continent and in another play about power and marriage choice, two Kenyan actors assert that Shakespeare's Globe – neither the empty space Ngũgĩ refers to (via Peter Brook) nor a proscenium stage – is what enabled (indeed, *required*) them to connect directly with the audience, in an African language. That this Swahili work came from The Theatre Company, which develops and produces work by local writers in English, Swahili and other Kenyan languages, indicates simultaneously how much things have changed since Ngũgĩ's imprisonment and how much they have stayed the same. This *Merry Wives* was a Swahili reterritorialization of an English playwright, but it existed only because of its involvement in a London cultural initiative. I mentioned a 'matrix' at the start of this chapter, and in this context it is important to draw out a point of confluence with regard to performance techniques and spaces of resistance. In the preface to *Decolonising the Mind*, Ngũgĩ recalls the deep impression made by a Māori welcome that he received when he gave a lecture in Auckland in 1984 and describes Māori culture as possessing 'the vitality, strength and beauty of resistance'.[26] In her interview at the Globe, Nanjosi explains that the necessity for '10 per cent more' was finally driven home when the *Merry Wives* cast witnessed the thundering Māori *Troilus and Cressida* the evening before their own performance. In such instances of cross-cultural illumination Shakespeare stands, just briefly, at the margins. It is perhaps these moments of unexpected encounter and recognition, between fellow artists or between artists and audiences, which surely must have criss-crossed the Globe to Globe season, that are at once the most intangible and the most valuable aspects of the project.

A couple of reviewers picked up on similarities between the Swahili *Merry Wives* and the Māori *Troilus and Cressida*, to do not with theatrical vitality, but with the performance of gender and sexuality. These responses bring into focus a curious aspect of this *Merry Wives*, and that is the extent to which it transformed male authority into camp petulance. One reviewer notes, 'I did have some concerns . . . about the cheaply camp portrayal of Slender; as in the Maori *Troilus*, this shortcut to characterisation seems misplaced.'[27] Why the reviewer felt Slender's campness was 'misplaced' is not entirely clear; certainly, it is not a stretch to argue that homosexual innuendo is a witty means of explaining Slender's lack of interest in Anne Page – this, indeed, was something Luscombe's *Merry Wives* tapped into with a similarly camp Slender, quite happy to find himself accidentally married off to a man at the end of the play. The more unexpected camp performance was Gathitu's effete Master Brook, whose costume (that is, Ford's disguise) consisted of a shirt knotted to suggestively reveal his midriff and a bright yellow neck-scarf tied in a bow. A critic observed, 'I could have done without another camp stereotype to follow the ones in the Maori *Troilus* when [Ford] impersonates "Brook."'[28] Interestingly, the same reviewer was not bothered by another exaggerated performance of gender, in this case the cross-dressing Ogutu Muraya as Mistress Quickly, even crediting his 'energetic drag' performance for giving a 'much needed kick' to the play's 'slow-kindling subplot'.[29] It is tempting to speculate that a man performing as a woman challenges gender norms less than a man performing effeminate masculinity, and that, specifically, the feminizing of Ford's alter-ego materialized anxieties about men's dominance in marriage that lie at the heart of this domestic comedy and linger in contemporary societies.

Whether dismissed as 'cheap' or praised as 'energetic', campness and cross-dressing are recognizable modes of characterization in British comedy, and in the Kenyan *Merry Wives* they served as a key means of attracting laughs from the audience. The preening and flouncing of Slender, Brook and Quickly were followed at the denouement with Wanyama's appearances as the accidental brides, first in a puffy white wedding gown and then a green satin dress, both of which tapped into a pantomime-drag tradition. But any reading of the production's campness has to be context-specific. While camp performance has now become all but synonymous with homosexuality in a Western context, it does not necessarily have to be read this way; certainly, if the planned tour of *Merry Wives* to regional Kenya and other east African nations where homosexuality is illegal goes ahead, the reception of the production's gender and sexual politics will be of particular interest.

In addition to its simultaneously amusing and baffling performances of gender, particularly the un-manliness of a husband driven to jealousy, the Swahili *Merry Wives of Windsor* raised a whole host of complex questions about the way Shakespeare, the Globe and the Swahili language functioned as symbols, theatrical facilitators and cross-cultural unifiers. These questions are necessarily weighted by a troubled relationship between Britain and Kenya, and between English and Swahili, whose histories stretch back long before London 2012. But this weight was not something that constrained the sharp ensemble cast. An equally relevant question has to be the one posed by an enthralled *Guardian* reviewer: '[H]as an English-language version of Falstaff's failure to seduce two married women ever raised so many laughs?'[30] This expertly performed production succeeded in pulling off that most elusive and vital theatrical feat of being great fun and genuinely funny.

ENDNOTES

1 See Alamin Mazrui, *Swahili Beyond the Boundaries: Literature, Language, and Identity* (Athens, OH: Ohio University Press, 2007), p. 128; Richard Dowden, 'Shakespeare and

Africa – Richard Dowden Reviews an Africanised Production of *Julius Caesar*, *African Arguments*, 4 July 2012, http://africanarguments.org/2012/07/04/shakespeare-and-africa-richard-dowden-reviews-an-africanised-production-of-julius-caesar/, 28 July 2012; KCSE Past Papers, *The Elimu Network*, www.elimu.net/Secondary/Kenya/Kenya_Sec.html, 1 August 2012. In his doctoral research on the Kenyan English curriculum, Peter F. Masibo Lumala reviewed teachers' preferences regarding the texts set by the Ministry of Education for the KCSE secondary literature programme and found that most teachers were not in favour of the prescribed Shakespearean text, *The Merchant of Venice*. He observes: 'Plays by African writers were regarded quite highly apart from Gogol's *The Government Inspector*. The latter received better ranking ostensibly due to of [sic] its social political relevance to the Kenyan context.' Peter F. Masibo Lumala, 'Towards the Reader–Text Interactive Approach to Teaching Imaginative Texts: The Case for the Integrated English Curriculum in Kenya', thesis submitted to the University of Nottingham for the degree of Doctor of Philosophy, February 2007, http://etheses.nottingham.ac.uk/1406/1/438383.pdf, pp. 153–4.

2 Amy Kenny, audio interview with Sharon Nanjosi and Joshua Ogutu Muraya, 25 April 2012, Shakespeare's Globe, London, 8 May 2012, http://globetoglobe.shakespearesglobe.com/plays/the-merry-wives-windsor/interview.

3 Ngũgĩ wa Thiong'o, *Decolonising the Mind: The Politics of Language in African Literature* (London: James Currey/Heinemann, 1986), p. 11.

4 Kevin M. Lillis, 'Africanizing the School Literature Curriculum in Kenya: A Case-Study in Curriculum Dependency', *Journal of Curriculum Studies*, 18.1 (1986): 69–78, and Ngũgĩ, *Decolonising the Mind*, p. xi.

5 Julius Nyerere's translations became a core feature of Kenyan secondary school curriculums. Mazrui, *Swahili*, p. 134.

6 There were some casting changes for the recent performances in India and Nairobi.

7 Kenny, audio interview.

8 Sarah Norman, e-mail correspondence with the author, 30 April and 8 May 2012.

9 Kenny, audio interview.

10 Norman, e-mail.

11 Angela Ngendo, 'Shakespeare Play Performed in Swahili at the Globe', BBC Africa, 4 May 2012, www.bbc.co.uk/news/world-africa-17960227, 16 June 2012.

12 Kenny, audio interview.

13 David Nice, 'Globe to Globe: *The Merry Wives of Windsor*, Shakespeare's Globe', *The Arts Desk*, 27 April 2012, www.theartsdesk.com/theatre/globe-globe-merry-wives-windsor-shakespeares-globe, 21 July 2012.

14 Kenny, audio interview.

15 Ibid.

16 However, before drawing the conclusion that Nanjosi and Ogutu Muraya are characterizing their practice as 'naturalistic' in a European sense, it is important to place their comments alongside the videos posted online of performances by The Theatre Company, Kenya, which reveal a good deal of engagement with the audience, via a diversity of contemporary and traditional dance and dramatic modes. See for example an excerpt from The Theatre Company's production of *My Moving Home* by Rogers Donatus Otieno, www.youtube.com/watch?v=30UP_EIYctk&feature=relmfu, a dance segment from Joshua

Muraya Ogutu Muraya's *Are We Free Yet?*, www.youtube.com/watch?v=YkMuRlPeNlY& feature=related, and a traditional dance and drama excerpt from the company-devised work, *Shungwaaya*, www.youtube.com/watch?v=9m7CaQiDMFE&feature=youtu.be.

17 Ngendo, 'Shakespeare Play'.

18 Ngũgĩ, *Decolonising the Mind*, p. xiv.

19 Ibid., p. 3.

20 Ibid.

21 Mazrui, *Swahili*, pp. 6, 16–17.

22 Ngũgĩ, *Decolonising the Mind*, pp. 37–8.

23 Ibid., p. 40.

24 Ibid., p. 38.

25 Ibid., p. 58.

26 Ibid., p. ix.

27 Megan Murray-Pepper, 'Globe to Globe Week 1: Part Two', *Stet: An Online Postgraduate Research Journal*, 2 May 2012, www.stetjournal.org/blogs/tag/merry-wives-of-windsor/, 21 July 2012.

28 Nice, 'Globe to Globe'.

29 Ibid.

30 Andrew Gilchrist, 'The Merry Wives of Windsor – Review', *Guardian*, 27 April 2012, www.guardian.co.uk/stage/2012/apr/27/merry-wives-of-windsor-review?INTCMP= ILCNETTXT3487, 16 June 2012.

CHAPTER FIVE

PERICLES AND THE GLOBE

Celebrating the body and 'embodied spectatorship'

Becky Becker

As an American theatre professor at a small regional institution in Columbus, Georgia, I have been fortunate to experience many Globe performances since it opened in 1997. While I do not consider myself a Shakespeare 'expert', my experiences as an academic and director interested in cross-cultural theatre provided a rich connection with the Globe to Globe Festival's interplay of cultures. More specifically, as a study-abroad instructor in London, I have, time and again, and with up to ten students in tow, waited in the queue outside the Globe an hour or more before show time to secure the most coveted 'front row' groundling spaces in the yard.[1] Given this experience, I approached the Globe to Globe production of *Pericles* by the National Theatre of Greece with the anticipation of a 'regular' Globe audience member. As such, I have come to expect the free interplay between actor and audience, stage and space that the Globe offers. It is largely the actor–audience relationship that provides each production its essential magic – something I have often pondered as we move further away, culturally, from live performance towards digital entertainments.[2] After experiencing the Greek *Pericles* (and Hindi *Twelfth Night* – the other production I saw live), I have come to view the Globe's capacity for engaging audiences as an extension of the space itself – and the ways in which that particular environment interacts with bodies.

In preparing to see *Pericles*, I wondered how this company would manage this art of connection, especially in the absence of a common language. From the outset, however, it was clear that this would be an engaging production, as the actors bounded on stage from the audience, with Dimitris Piatas inviting: 'Let's play!' And play we did, riding on a poetic tide of Greek till we were stopped short by select phrases in English.[3] One subtext-filled moment brought down the house: when a shipwrecked Pericles (Christos Loulis) failed to beg food from three ambivalent fishermen (Minas Chatzisavas, Kostas Vasardanis, Giorgos Glastras), he deadpanned to the audience: 'Please, I'm starving – I'm Greek!' Later, a gang of men waved £20 notes at Pericles' daughter Marina (Stefania Goulioti), who had been stolen away to a brothel. In a production so carefully conceived to connect, references to the current state of the Greek economy were both funny and poignant. Yet, of the two moments described, the one more carefully constructed to engage all audiences was not Pericles' momentary lapse into English; rather, director Giannis Houvardas' choice of British pounds sterling in the brothel seemed a more literal sign for the audience, given the fraught relationship of the Euro to the British pound and Greece's precarious place in the European Union. Perhaps more importantly, the physical nature of the symbol held more impact for the combined Greek-speaking and non-Greek-speaking audience.

But, for me, it was the use of the actors' bodies on stage and in relationship to the spectators' bodies in the space that ultimately spoke the language of the play. Weaving deliberately between tragedy and comedy, poetry and song, broad physical comedy and quiet realism, the ensemble moved through Pericles' life-journey with the audience *physically* in tow. Not that we weren't willing to go, but this is a difficult play in any language. The Greek-speakers led the way, while the rest of us held tightly to the eloquent body language of the ensemble. It was the overtly visceral quality of this *Pericles* that joined Greek-speakers with those who, like me, are not. In retrospect, I would argue that spatial relationships served to deepen the level of engagement in the production – both with the actors on stage and among the audience as a whole.

One way of understanding spatial relationships in the theatre is through the lens of cognitive science, an interdisciplinary study of the processes of the human mind as 'embodied' – that we acquire language through the body and conceptual metaphors.[4] According to Bruce McConachie, 'play is fundamentally an emotion, a neuronal and chemical system in the mind/brain'.[5] While we may perceive language to be a solely intellectual endeavour and play a primarily physical enterprise, both are similarly conceived extensions of the embodied mind. When we are at 'play', the body's spatial relationship with the world around it contributes to perception and understanding. In the case of the Globe, I would argue, spatial relationships support audience engagement even when the performers' language is not shared.[6] But what is so special about the Globe as a performing space? Why might it engage audiences differently, and thereby lend itself to a unique kind of audience engagement?

Admittedly, part of the pleasure of this *Pericles* was watching the Greek-speaking audience whose love for it was so apparent. While most of my own experience at the Globe has been as a groundling this time I sat in the second gallery. From stage right I had a wonderful vantage point not just to see the actors but also much of the audience, seated and standing. If I struggled to perceive without the common tool of language, I could still witness the joy of those who understood. Ultimately,

Fig. 3 Members of the company, *Pericles*, National Theatre of Greece from Athens, Greece; director Giannis Houvardas.

however, I experienced an understanding beyond language that was illuminating – a new perspective of heightened awareness that may best be described as 'embodied spectatorship'. The spatial orientation of the fourteen-sided Globe is based, in part, on the class system of Elizabethan England: groundlings paid a penny to see a play, while those in the galleries paid more. Current Globe ticket prices reflect a similar difference, but it is the relationship, spatially, among audience members that seems most significant today. Frequently I have enjoyed the visceral experience of standing in the yard, listening carefully to Shakespeare's language and following the physical cues of the actors as guide – all the while feeling the press of bodies pulsing around me. 'Embodied spectatorship', as I perceive it, provides a heightened understanding of shared physical experience within an audience. My experiences as a groundling certainly afforded me this kind of spectatorship, but my awareness as an audience member – and moreover *of* the audience – for *Pericles* was more strategically heightened as a dialogue with the bodies of the actors on stage and the bodies of the other audience members. From the gallery I found myself reading the physical cues of the audience almost as intently as I did the actors'. Feeling the chill of an unseasonably cold English spring, I wondered whether the groundlings felt this cold as intensely as the actors must have. Reading their approval of the action on stage, I was bolstered by their heartiness.[7] Pairing reactions of the Greek-speaking audience with my own body knowledge, I empathized with Pericles' journey. Remembering my own past standing in the yard, I imagined other seated spectators, whose own engagement might also be affected by the heightened awareness of shared experience. The Globe circled back on me – much like the plot of *Pericles* circles back on itself.

Perhaps the most enlightening moment occurred near the end of the play, when Pericles visits Diana's temple to recount his life's journey. Making his way around a semi-circle of characters from his past, Pericles seemed to meet his life anew, as if it were flashing before his eyes prior to death – an inspired turn by director Houvardas. Subsequently, Thaisa and Marina happily rejoined Pericles – seemingly in life, though quite possibly in death, as this interpretation seemed to suggest. A lively party song rounded out the evening, the circle of connection complete. While I do not speak Greek, I carry the metaphorical journey of language acquisition in my body. I also carry the literal journey of being in the world and experiencing successes and struggles through my body. Despite my inability to share the words, I could hear Pericles' body speaking even when his words did not readily translate. Perhaps, in the end, the Festival was not a celebration of Shakespeare's works so much as a celebration of our ability to make dialogue through bodies that share a remarkable connection via the acquisition of language and the metaphorical journey it entails – an embodied spectatorship like no other.

ENDNOTES

1 Beyond excursions with students, I have seen the potential of Shakespeare as a rehabilitative tool within American prisons after interviewing Agnes Wilcox, brilliant artistic director of Prison Performing Arts in St Louis, Missouri in 'Converting the Audience: A Conversation with Agnes Wilcox', *Feminist Teacher*, 16.3 (2006): 225–37. The ability of Shakespeare's words to convey universal ideas and emotions through specific characters and circumstances has never been so keenly communicated to me than when I witnessed productions of *Julius Caesar* and *Macbeth* in two different correctional facilities in Missouri.

2 I have written about cognitive science and its relationship to theatre more directly in the article 'Prosceniums and Screens: Audience Embodiment into the Digital Age', in John C. Countryman and Noreen Barnes-McLain, eds., *Theatre Symposium: A Publication of the Southeastern Theatre Conference* (Tuscaloosa: University of Alabama Press, 2012).

3 Not much later in the Festival, the Globe would ask companies not to insert English into their productions.

4 According to George Lakoff and Mark Johnson, we acquire language through the body and conceptual metaphors arising from bodily experience in the world (*Philosophy in the Flesh* (New York: Basic Books, 1999)). A primary example of conceptual metaphor describes it thus: 'Affection is Warmth because our earliest experiences with affection correspond to the physical experience of the warmth of being held closely' (Lakoff and Johnson, *Metaphors We Live By* (University of Chicago Press, 2003), p. 255).

5 Bruce McConachie, *Engaging Audiences: A Cognitive Approach to Spectating in the Theatre* (Basingstoke: Palgrave Macmillan, 2008), p. 51.

6 If human beings acquire language through bodily experience and conceptual metaphors, then our perception of a language we don't understand or speak must also be somehow embedded in a physical understanding of thought, emotion and lived experience. While language and the conceptual metaphors through which we acquire it are not necessarily 'universal', there are still connections to be made cross-culturally, according to Alice Deignan in 'Metaphorical Expressions and Culture: An Indirect Link', *Metaphor & Symbol*, 18.4 (2003): 255–71.

7 I found myself especially emboldened by the Company Theatre of India's Hindi production of *Twelfth Night*. The evening I saw it, it was particularly cold and it rained on and off throughout the entire production. Despite this, the company of actors maintained energy and humour throughout. While some audience members did not return following the intermission, I took note of the groundlings, in particular, who remained in impressive numbers.

CHAPTER SIX

TECHNICOLOUR TWELFTH NIGHT

Elizabeth Schafer

The Company Theatre of Mumbai's all-singing, all-dancing Hindi Twelfth Night turned Shakespeare's comedy into a technicolour romp. Whereas recent British Twelfth Nights have tended to be angsty, lugubrious, Shakespeare-as-Chekhov, with Malvolio needing to get in touch with Amnesty International, this production offered a cheekily filleted version of the play, cut radically to fit the two-hours running time stipulated by the Globe.[1] Physicality, energy and verve were the keynotes as Twelfth Night was given a bold Bollywood make-over (see Colour Plate 3).[2]

Director Atul Kumar's remixed Twelfth Night was bright and breezy but often worked in tension with the Globe's theatre-in-the-round element;[3] the presentational, Bollywood smile-at-the-camera playing style was essentially end-on, and the production pushed the action further down stage by using an upstage 'offstage' area, demarcated by a large, rectangular carpet. Here the musicians sat and here the actors gathered to watch any action they were not involved in, often applauding and calling out encouragement to each other. This onstage 'offstage' worked well with the production's enthusiastic show-and-tell approach that acknowledged and played to the audience, especially the groundling groupies with their elbows parked on the front of the stage. But anyone who was not end-on to the action risked missing much of the fun.

The production opened with the players bursting on stage, filling the Globe with whirling, swirling and energized dancing. The leading figure in this extravaganza was a jokey, rather portly man, wearing a tweedy pork-pie hat and glasses, who announced in English, 'My name is Orsino.' The clarification was a great help, as this vibrant comic figure was not easily identifiable as the traditionally debilitated, lovesick duke. But this recasting of Orsino was merely one of many refreshing and robust demolition jobs that the production carried out on current British pieties in relation to the staging of Twelfth Night.

Key to the production was Amitosh Nagpal's Sebastian, who was also responsible for translating *Twelfth Night* into Hindi. Nagpal first appeared as a storyteller figure at the opening of Act 1 Scene 2, when he simply announced that Viola had been shipwrecked. This eliminated any need to worry about staging a storm. Nagpal quickly established a jokey relation with the audience, and as some of his jokes used English, he was able to connect with both the Hindi-speaking and the non-Hindi-speaking groundlings.[4] Nagpal's narrator disarmingly admitted that he had decided to make some changes to Shakespeare's play, and, in particular, as Shakespeare had given his character of Sebastian so few lines, Nagpal had decided to expand Sebastian's role. Later, in character as Sebastian, Nagpal also explained that he had persuaded his friend Antonio not to accompany him into Orsino's dukedom because it was too dangerous. This audacious manoeuvre not only excised an entire plotline but also repositioned *Twelfth Night* in terms of sexual politics. Since 1968 and the removal of the Lord Chamberlain's powers of censorship in Britain, directors have often constructed Antonio as gay; the ending of the play then offers Antonio at best a muted, and at worst a tragic, conclusion as he cannot keep his beloved Sebastian. Jettisoning Antonio eliminated the possibility of undercutting the happiness of the play's ending in this way and un-queered the play.

Un-queering was also in evidence in the relationships between Olivia and Viola, and Cesario and Orsino. There was no investigation of a possible lesbian desire in Olivia, and Orsino was confused by his feelings for Cesario but nothing more. When Mansi Multani's Olivia gazed on Geetanjali Kulkami's Cesario and fell in love with 'him', the accompanying comic percussion signalled that Olivia's plight was not to be taken seriously. Multani's Olivia was a gorgeous prima donna, posing around in bright pink and turquoise, faking grief. For her first appearance she entered laughing, only shifting into a performance of mourning – posturing with her veil, repeatedly covering and uncovering her face – when she saw Malvolio. This Olivia was very affected but so delightfully ridiculous that the character was not unsympathetic. Meanwhile Kulkami's small, wiry, but very perky Viola/Cesario carried on crossing her arms over her breasts whenever Orsino got too close and resetting her voice to a male register when singing alongside her master.

Viola's transformation into Cesario took place on stage and was assisted by the entire cast. Viola's skirt was taken off, revealing trousers underneath, and her hair was spun up into a turban. Kulkami then pencilled on a moustache and practised being manly; she chewed gum, did knee-bends, and strode up and down. But immediately before the interval a more enigmatic piece of physical theatre added some nuance to this clowning. Having agreed to take Orsino's jewel to Olivia at the end of Act 2 Scene 4 Cesario was left alone on stage. 'He' unwound his turban, let Viola's long hair fall down her back and rubbed off her moustache; she paused sadly and then lay down to sleep at the front of the stage as Sebastian (or was it the narrator?) hovered over her protectively. Was Cesario turning back into Viola? Was Sebastian/the narrator guarding Viola as she slept? Was he a reassuring or a dominating figure? Was he a patriarchal overseer or a tender brother? Was he the narrator promising her a happy ending?

A particularly memorable example of how this production reconfigured *Twelfth Night* appeared in the production's rendition of the duel of Act 3 Scene 4. As Kulkami's street kid Cesario extricated herself so rapidly from the duel – she just ducked and ran – the entire 'duel' took place between Andrew and Sebastian. Each duellist positioned himself facing front with a crowd of enthusiastic supporters behind him; the duellists then took it in turn to sing jeering songs at each other, using a call-and-response structure. The duellists' supporters called out encouragement to them, as well as asking the audience to clap in time to the music. It wasn't what Shakespeare wrote, but it was theatrically engaging and exuberant.

The cakes-and-ale plotline had none of the nastiness that modern British directors often find. Toby was young, virile and a clown who had a close, warm and fun-loving relationship with Maria throughout. Andrew was tall, pale and thin, and beautifully dopey, completely oblivious to the fact that Toby was picking his pocket at every opportunity. Meanwhile Neha Saraf's Feste, an uncomplicated jester, had little to worry about except fighting for focus alongside Toby and Andrew. There was very little sense of a feud between her and Saurabh Nayyar's Malvolio, who was characterized as less Indian than the other characters and more connected to the remnants of the British empire. Amid the technicolour costumes of the other characters, Malvolio stood out in his sober costume of a black coat and white trousers. The confrontation between this Malvolio and the cakes-and-ale party was never dangerous, and so it seemed appropriate that Malvolio's subsequent punishment was so mild; according to the surtitles he was thrown out of Olivia's house, but there was no scene in the 'dark house'.[5] And when Malvolio reappeared at the end of the play to complain about his treatment, it seemed he was still 'sick of self-love' (1.5.73). For, after Cesario had metamorphosed back into a beautifully dressed Viola, and the soon-to-be-married couples had exchanged wedding garlands, Malvolio went up to a woman in the audience and offered a garland to her. The moment it looked as if the woman might accept the garland, Malvolio changed his mind and put his garland around his own neck.

For me, this Indian *Twelfth Night* particularly raised questions about a recent fashion in Anglophone productions of *Twelfth Night* for 'Indianizing' the play, often in a generalized, unnuanced way, which on occasions casually elides class and caste.[6] India is, of course, evoked in *Twelfth Night* when Maria speaks of 'the new map with the augmentation of the Indies' (3.2.62–3); in addition, connecting 'India' and 'Illyria' gestures towards word play. However, Poonam Trivedi has trenchantly critiqued the 'Indianization' of Shakespeare, particularly when Western gender

1 Haka by the company, *Troilus and Cressida*, Ngākau Toa from Auckland, New Zealand; director Rachel House.

2 *Mistress* Ford (Lydiah Gitachu), Mistress Page (Chichi Seii) and Anne (Sharon Nanjos), *The Merry Wives of Windsor*, Bitter Pill and the Theatre Company, Kenya from Nairobi, Kenya; directors Daniel Goldman and Sarah Norman.

3 Maria (Trupti Khamkar), *Viola* (Geetanjali Kulkarni) and Feste (Neha Saraf). *Twelfth Night*, The Company Theatre from Mumbai, India; director Atul Kumar.

4 Puck (Kim Sang-bo) and Jeon Jung-Yong (Duduri, Dot's little brother), *A Midsummer Night's Dream*, Yohangza Theatre Company from Seoul, South Korea; director Yang Jung-Ung.

5   Innogen (Margret Kowarto), lying down with Cloten's body, and members of the company, *Cymbeline*, the South Sudan Theatre Company from Juba, South Sudan; directors Joseph Abuk and Derik Uya Alfred.

6 *Richard II* (Sami Metwasi) and Northumberland (Edward Muallem), *Richard II*, Ashtar Theatre from Ramallah, Palestine; director Conall Morrison.

7 The wedding of Miranda (Esha Yousuf) and Ferdinand (Khairul Islam Pakhi), *The Tempest*, Dhaka Theatre from Dhaka, Bangladesh; director Nasiruddin Yousuff.

8 Duncan (Grzegorz Minkiewicz) at the microphone with members of the company, *Macbeth*, Teatr im. Kochanowskiego from Opole, Poland; director Maja Kleczewska.

norms are imposed on Indian actresses.[7] Trivedi asks us to think more carefully about who is empowered, who benefits from Indianization, and this is important in analysing the Company Theatre of Mumbai's *Twelfth Night*. An indubitably 'Indian' product, which, at the Globe, played to a mixed audience of Hindi-speakers and Anglophones, this production's Indianness resided more in the aesthetics – the emphasis on telling a story, on singing and dancing, on creating physical comedy – than in thematics. But the critique it offered of fashionably 'silver', uncomic *Twelfth Nights* was trenchant, unapologetic and in many ways salutary; Atul Kumar's festive *Twelfth Night* was certainly not a production for the Malvolios of the world. But any *Twelfth Night* that can generate laughter on a night when the freezing, drenched groundlings were being pummelled by the wind and the rain deserves respect.

ENDNOTES

1 For *Twelfth Night* and Shakespeare-as-Chekhov see Elizabeth Schafer, ed., *Twelfth Night*, Shakespeare in Production (Cambridge University Press, 2009), pp. 38–40.

2 Jen Harvie, discussing a moment, around the turn of the millennium, when a Bollywood-derived aesthetic became very marketable in British theatre, cautions against the over-enthusiastic use of the term 'Bollywood', which 'some see . . . as patronising, derivative, homogenising, and inaccurate', while others see it as 'affectionate and a fair reflection of popular Hindi cinema's unabashed populism and commercialism': *Staging the UK* (Manchester University Press, 2005), p. 186, n. 2. Although I was brought up in Handsworth, Birmingham, during the 1960s, when the South Asian community was growing rapidly and Bollywood films were playing every week, I managed to remain largely oblivious of the art form apart from its dazzling posters. So I use the term 'Bollywood' as a non-specialist in a generalized and populist sense.

3 Kumar has directed English and French classics previously, often with an emphasis on clowning. His *Hamlet, Clown Prince* played at the Hackney Empire in 2011, and his *Nothing Like Lear* toured India and internationally in 2012.

4 The slippage from English to Hindi and back again was a feature of the production.

5 5.1.321. The cutting of Act 4 Scene 2, when Malvolio is in what he describes as a 'dark house', is not unprecedented; for example, in the nineteenth century the scene was cut by Augustin Daly in his commercially successful production starring Ada Rehan.

6 For Indianized *Twelfth Nights* see Schafer, Shakespeare in Production, pp.33–5. One of the most influential Indianized *Twelfth Nights* was Ariane Mnouchkine's 1982 *La nuit des rois*, which quoted Kathakali performance in an attempt to create an intercultural Illyria Indianized for Parisian consumption.

7 Poonam Trivedi, 'Shakespeare and the Indian Image(nary): Embod(y)ment in Versions of *A Midsummer Night's Dream*', in Poonam Trivedi and Minami Ryuata, eds., *Re-playing Shakespeare in Asia* (London: Routledge, 2010), pp. 54–75.

WEEK TWO

CHAPTER SEVEN

PERFORMING CULTURAL EXCHANGE IN *RICHARD III*

Intercultural display and personal reflections

Lee Chee Keng

At the end of the National Theatre of China's (NTC) first performance of *Richard III* on the afternoon of 28 April 2012 at the Globe to Globe Festival, when the actors took the curtain call with a traditional Chinese bow – something they don't usually do when performing in China – the audience could feel in the actors a release of tension as well as an overwhelming sense of pride and fulfilment. The actors must have felt they were representing China in a 'Shakespeare Olympics', but the production's set and costumes had yet to arrive and they had had to perform in hastily put-together stand-ins. Nevertheless, the virtuosity of their craft held the audience rapt throughout the performance.

Theatre critics from the Chinese media had been invited to a special preview on 14 March 2012, before the set and costumes were shipped to London. Press publicity materials released for the occasion highlighted the fact that the production had been specially created for the Globe to Globe Festival to 'bring Chinese culture out to meet with the world's different races, different languages, and different cultural backgrounds, to interact and communicate with one another under the banner of Shakespeare'.[1] In an interview with Phoenix TV in China, Wang Xiao Ying, director of the production, recalled looking through posters of other participating productions and noticing that most would be dressing their characters in ethnic costumes. So Wang decided on classical Chinese costume for his production, especially to add elements of classical Chinese culture.[2] From the initial stage of conceptualization, Wang invested the production with Chinese cultural symbols that he felt would most effectively achieve the goal of cultural exchange.[3] This was important to him in the context of the Festival's association with the London Olympics, and the fact that his *Richard III* would be performed on Shakespeare's 'home ground' together with productions in thirty-six other languages. Key props in the production (a throne, masks and staff) had designs that drew upon totems found in the San Xing Dui (literally 'three stars mount') archaeological site – an enigmatic dynasty dating back to 1600 BC – to imbue them with an aura of distant and oriental mysticism. The site is believed to be the home of the earliest civilization in the Yangtze Valley, an ancient culture that had remarkably advanced bronze-casting technology. The costumes were based on the traditional long-sleeved *han* robe. The masks that the actors wore fused elements of Greek masks and *xi qu* (Chinese opera) painted faces. The inclusion of elements of Greek mask was strategic, as both the Olympics and theatre can trace their sources back to Greece.

Xi qu was another important element in the production. Three *jing ju* (Peking Opera) performers were invited to join the team of actors from the NTC. Zhang Xin played both Lady Anne and young Prince Edward. Her portrayal of Lady Anne drew heavily from the codified portrayal of *qing yi* (maiden in distress role type) in *jing ju*, in terms both of her spoken lines and her movements. Her young Prince Edward, on the other hand, was that of a *wu sheng* (young warrior role type) – wearing pheasant-plumes headgear and warrior boots, and carrying a horsewhip. In the murder-of-Clarence scene (Act 1 Scene 4), Xu Meng Ke and Cai Jin Chao, who played the two assassins, borrowed extensively from the famous *jing ju* fighting-in-the-dark scene in *San Cha Kou*.[4] In addition to these three *jing ju* actors, a musician from the China Opera Company was also invited to be part of the team; he would play more than ten kinds of percussion instruments – both Chinese and Western – to provide live musical accompaniment throughout the performance.

A huge white backdrop formed the centrepiece of the production design. Twelve words were printed on it: 'power', 'curse', 'benefit', 'lie', 'nightmare', 'war', 'destroy', 'conspiracy', 'having', 'pretense', 'kill' and 'appetite'. Each English word was custom-designed to resemble a Chinese character, with the word in roman script alongside – square-word calligraphy designed by internationally renowned Chinese artist Xu Bing.[5] At first glance, each word appeared to be a Chinese character but was in fact a rendering of an English word. Viewers who only understood Chinese and expected to be able to read it would find that they could not; viewers who understood only English, on the other hand, were likely to be surprised and delighted when they discovered that they could!

In the event, all these carefully wrought references were not to be. Wang and the team arrived in London on 26 April and learned that the container delivering their props and costumes had been delayed. Wang called an emergency meeting at the hotel lobby to reassure everyone that the performance would go on in spite of the circumstances. In a TV interview later Wang recalled saying to everyone, 'We have worked hard and spent more than half a year in preparation for this. The fact that we will perform on the Globe's stage is already our greatest achievement.'[6] The production department of Shakespeare's Globe helped to assemble an essential set, props and costumes. A yellow cushioned chair served as the throne, with two tables as bed and platform, and there were several functional chairs. All the actors were costumed in basic black, except for Edward IV and Richard III in yellow robes, Queen Elizabeth in a purple one, and Richard as duke of Gloucester in a green robe. Wang was full of praise for the Globe's production department. When he gathered his team on the stage to announce that they had helped put together all the stand-in props and costumes, Wang related how he was being shown a website and asked to identify the weapons required: 'They told me: in London, you can get any weapon, no matter which part of the world or which era it came from, because London is the number one theatre capital in the world.'[7] Right up to the last performance, Wang was still hopeful that the props and costumes would arrive so that the originally intended performance of *Richard III* could be performed on the Globe's stage. But they never did.

Instead of an East–West collage that infused Shakespeare's play with Chinese visual elements, the skills of the Chinese actors, trained in either contemporary spoken drama or traditional *xi qu*, were brought into sharp focus as a vivid re-creation of Shakespeare's characters. Two of the most memorable scenes were Richard's courting of Lady Anne, where the contrast between the naturalistic acting of Richard and the *xi qu* acting of Anne expressed the changing dynamics between them; and the killing of Clarence by murderers played as *xi qu* clown roles, who performed the task of murder under the cloak of darkness in the Globe's broad daylight, injecting the scene with a potent blend of comic poignancy. Because of the unlucky/lucky mishap of international shipping, their acting, in its bare bones and stripped of visual spectacle, shone with a perhaps accidental brilliance.

Zhang Dong-Yu (in his 30s) was a Richard with no deformity but driven by a desire to prove his abilities and hold absolute power. When Richard courted Lady Anne, Zhang, who was trained for and has always performed on the proscenium stage, could be seen working hard to adapt to the more intimate actor–audience relationship on a thrust stage, surrounded on three sides by a visible audience. Just as Zhang's Richard became more self-assured and unstoppable after successfully winning Lady Anne's hand, Zhang the actor found his metier through this scene.

In a private conversation with the writer after the first show, Zhang, still recovering from the intense performance, was in deep contemplation on the first experience of performing on the Globe's stage that afternoon. Trained as a *hua ju* (spoken drama) actor, playing to the audience meant playing his understanding as well as his interpretation of the character, and showing off his skills, Zhang said. He realized that the Globe was not simply another theatre space the moment he came, literally, face to face with the audience. In Act 1 Scene 2, in which Richard courts Lady Anne, there was a moment when Richard, to show how much he was pained by his love for Lady Anne, knelt down in anguish. When he lifted his head, Zhang came face to face with an audience smiling knowingly barely a metre away. He recalled being startled for a moment by the proximity and immediacy

Fig. 4 Richard III (Zhang Dong-Yu), *Richard III*, National Theatre of China from Beijing, China; director, Wang Xiaoying.

of the actor–audience interaction, and realized he had to adjust his usual acting method:

You could see the eagerness in their faces. I knew I cannot simply present Richard and his actions to the audience. They want to know what Richard will do next. They also want to see how, as an actor, I will do it. I have to simultaneously play with two realities. I have to unfold my actions step-by-step as if every moment I'm thinking, judging and deciding what to do next, and I have to take the audience along with me.

Conscious of the different reality the Globe architecture imposed on audience and actors, Zhang attempted to explore the different possibilities it offered. He had initially felt that the lack of lighting to focus audience response would be a major challenge. However, he soon realized that in the shared natural lighting, perhaps coupled with a certain excitement associated with watching a performance at the Globe, the audience was actively looking to become part of the action. Zhang compared the approach he then attempted to that of a storyteller-actor, sometimes acting inside the story, sometimes outside watching, commenting and interacting with the audience. The most fulfilling moments for Zhang were those when he felt engaged in a dialogue with the audience as if they were different parts of Richard's consciousness, sometimes cheering, sometimes objecting to, and sometimes even sneering at his actions. The audience response might not always be 'rationally expected' by a Chinese actor. When Lady Anne dropped the sword Richard had handed her, Zhang smiled confidently and made knowing eye-contact with the audience in the pit, many of whom cheered his success in wooing Lady Anne, before he said to Lady Anne, 'Take up the sword again, or take up me.' The relationship between actor and audience was, Zhang felt, alive and visceral: 'The space and the audience in the Globe have led me to play in a way I've never experienced before. They have helped me experience Shakespeare coming to life when I speak and move the audience in the present, moment to moment. As an actor, I've learnt so much from that theatre this afternoon.' In an interview with Phoenix TV after he returned to Beijing from the Festival, Zhang, once again, related the experience vividly:

I had prepared in great detail how to play the role. When I was on the stage in that theatre, the audience was very close, so close I could instantaneously feel their every reaction. As I was playing, there were many moments I was wondering to myself, why are they reacting here? There shouldn't be any reaction here. After the performance, I went back and studied the script to try to understand why they had reacted that way, and I discovered I had indeed overlooked the drama in that particular segment. There were many such segments. Those moments of discoveries were almost magical.[8]

After its performances at the Festival, the NTC's *Richard III* was premièred in China on 4 July 2012 at the Capital Theatre, Beijing, as part of the Beijing People's Art Theatre's sixtieth anniversary celebrations.[9] Besides the trial performance in March, this was the production's official première in China. In fact, it was the world première of the originally intended version of the NTC's *Richard III*. Neil Constable, chief executive of Shakespeare's Globe, was invited to attend the performance in Beijing, and he was reportedly very excited after watching its originally intended form and went on stage to congratulate the cast.[10] A news article on the Sina Entertainment website reported him giving a brief speech in which he praised the NTC's *Richard III* as one of the best productions at the Globe to Globe Festival, saying,

'People in the UK often think Shakespeare belongs to them, but I think Shakespeare belongs to the world. And today, Shakespeare belongs to China.'[11] Constable represented Shakespeare's Globe and the Globe to Globe Festival (including, arguably, its audiences), and the fact that he saw this première of *Richard III* and gave it his strong endorsement, in front of a Chinese audience in Beijing no less, would have soothed any disappointment over the mishap that resulted in the originally intended version not being staged in London.

The NTC organized a seminar on 23 July 2012 entitled 'Shakespeare and China, Classic and Modern, *hua ju* and *xi qu Richard III* seminar at which several established theatre directors, critics and academics were invited to critique and comment on the production for an audience that included the NTC's senior management. Wang Yu Sheng, a theatre critic, commended the production for its 'display of unique Chinese characteristics and bravura.'[12] Another theatre critic, Li Chun Xi, called it 'a work saturated with the artistic spirit of *xi qu*'.[13] Xu Xiao Zhong, a respected theatre director and educator, contemplated the visual expression of the English square-word calligraphy and the aural expression of the percussion instruments played throughout the performance, and observed that cultural elements from both the East and West were visually and aurally strategic to the production. While most reviews showered praises on the NTC's *Richard III*, a few critics questioned some of the key artistic choices the production had made. A London-based Chinese writer, Zhong Yi Ling, who saw the performance at the Globe, questioned the decision to portray Richard without any deformity, as well as the addition of three witches who provoked Richard into action just as the three witches did in *Macbeth*.[14] Another writer, Xu Cheng, who saw the performance at the Capital Theatre, took issue with opening the play with King Edward's enthronement and giving him Richard's famous speech, 'Now is the winter of our discontent'.[15] While Zhong praised the production for its use of *xi qu* elements, Xu questioned whether the NTC's *Richard III* can be hailed as a milestone of success by virtue of its extensive use of various Chinese elements.[16]

Dominant discourses positioned the NTC's *Richard III* as a successful cultural exchange for China through its modernizing and fusing of various traditional Chinese artistic and cultural elements. The performance had, undoubtedly, extended the range of possibilities for performing Shakespeare, both in London and in China. The actors might have most personally and deeply felt their range being expanded by the experience of performing at Shakespeare's Globe, and, among them, Zhang might have felt it the strongest when, at the curtain call, he prostrated himself and kissed the stage. The actors' performances there were a testament to the centrality of their craft to the production. Multiple layers of cultural exchange were happening simultaneously at a personal level as the NTC's *Richard III* was being performed. The audience saw Shakespeare's text brought to life through an 'other'

80

cultural and artistic approach. The actors gained new insights into their own craft through bringing Shakespeare's text alive and interacting with the Globe audience. When a production is mounted in the arena of cultural exchange and on a touring circuit under normal circumstances, however, any deep reflections on one's craft seem inevitably to be ensconced amid discourses on cultural representations and exchanges.

ENDNOTES

1   'Richard III from China to Perform in Shakespeare's Globe', National Theatre of China Press Release, March 2012.

2   'An Alternative Interpretation of *Richard III*: English Story, Chinese Expressions', National Centre for the Performing Arts Series, Phoenix TV, 6 August 2012.

3   'Richard III Invited to Perform in London will be Imbued with Chinese elements', *Dong Fang Daily*, 24 April 2012.

4   *San Cha Kou* (三岔口)is a famous short *jing ju* (Peking Opera) performance that tells the story of a banished *Song* dynasty general who had to spend a night in an inn. A fighter who was secretly protecting him got into a misunderstanding with the husband of the couple in charge of the inn, and the two started fighting in the dark. This fighting in the dark was, of course, performed on a lit stage.

5   Xu Bing is noted for his work *Tian Shu* ('Book from the Sky'), a large installation featuring precisely laid-out rows of books and hanging scrolls filled with written 'Chinese' texts. First presented in Beijing in 1988, the work challenged people's very approach to language through the artist's move to design and print over 4,000 characters that looked Chinese but were completely meaningless according to standard Mandarin.

6   'An Alternative Interpretation'.

7   Ibid.

8   Ibid.

9   The Capital Theatre houses the premier Beijing People's Art Theatre company, an important artistic and cultural icon of modern China.

10 Zhang Qiang, 'Shakespeare's Globe Chief Executive Neil Constable Visits NTC', NTC Communication News, www.ntcc.com.cn/news4_detail/newsId=397767b0–6791-4285-b695–4e3a4809cccf.html, 10 October 2012.

11 'Wang Xiao Ying's Chinese *Richard III* Returns Home and Premières in China', Sina Entertainment, 5 July 2012, http://ent.sina.com.cn/j/2012–07-05/04533676582.shtml, 10 October 2012.

12 Zhang Jian, 'Shakespeare and China, Classic and Modern, *hua ju* and *xi qu* – Richard III Seminar a Success', NTC Communication News, www.ntcc.com.cn/news4_detail/newsId=397767b0–6791-4285-b695–4e3a4809cccf.html, 10 October 2012.

13 Ibid.

14 Zhong Yi Ling, 'Watching Theatre in London: Chinese *Richard III*', *Nan Fang Daily*, 30 May 2012, http://epaper.nfdaily.cn/html/2012–05/30/content_7088785.htm, 10 October 2012.

15 Xu Cheng, 'Interpretation and Adaptation, Borrowing and Copying: NTC's *Richard III*', Xu Cheng Kyle's blog, 8 July 2012, http://blog.sina.com.cn/s/blog_667c86c5010163yj.html, 10 October 2012.

16 After its run at the Beijing Capital Theatre in early July 2012, the production was staged at the Beijing National Grand Theatre in late August. It was then performed as part of the Shanghai International Arts Festival in early November 2012 at the Shanghai Art Theatre, followed by runs at the HangZhou Theatre and at the National Theatre Theatre (*sic*).

CHAPTER EIGHT

'A GIRDLE ROUND ABOUT THE EARTH'

Yohangza's *A Midsummer Night's Dream*

Adele Lee

This delightfully entertaining 'brand production', which has been touring the global festival circuit since 2002, opened with the twin spirit Duduri (Puck) urging the audience, in English, to 'Have fun!' (see Colour Plate 4). Disregarding *A Midsummer Night's Dream*'s dark undertones, the company presented a colourful, light-hearted production which reflected both the director's interest in comic strips[1] and the aesthetic of cute, rooted in the Japanese cultural phenomenon known as *Kawaii* which currently pervades Korean popular culture. The production also reflected the three main trends, identified by Hyon-u Lee, in Korean theatre since the 1990s – a decade when the country entered a period of increased freedom and democracy. These trends are the Koreanization of Western drama (in particular, Shakespeare),[2] the growth in popularity of music and musical forms, and the centrality of the theme of feminism.[3]

Drawing on and experimenting with traditional Korean theatre conventions such as *Talchum* (mask dance) and *Cocdoo Nolum* (puppet dance), the Yohangza Theatre Company offered a simplified version of Shakespeare's comedy, focusing only on the relationship between the four lovers and the fairy queen and king. All the scenes, therefore, were set in the fantastical world of the forest, and the play in general favoured the mischievous but charming fairies or, as they were known in this, the *Dokkebi* (Korean forest goblins). Wearing hessian (rustic sacking) over plain tunics, the either masked or heavily made-up *Dokkebi* were country figures who belonged to a bygone Korea, and their popularity is arguably indicative of the nostalgia prevalent in the technologically advanced, hyper-consumerist 'New Asia'. In the opening, fog-filled scene, they formed a circle and danced to the beat of percussion instruments, freezing to strike momentary poses of the grotesque. Recalling Shakespeare's fairies' custom of 'danc[ing] ringlets to the whistling wind'

I am grateful to Hyon-u Lee for his help and advice.

(2.1.86), this dance, like all Korean folk dances, originated in ancient shamanistic rituals and was the first of several carefully choreographed sequences. Indeed, typical of traditional Korean theatre, which is not plot driven, this production can be regarded as less narrative drama and more a series of performative presentations, including mime, acrobatics, martial arts and slapstick.

Traditional Korean drama is known for relying on visual storytelling, so it is not surprising that language was secondary in this production – as perhaps it was in all the Festival productions. The script was written by Yang Jung-Ung whose adaptation was loosely based on Lee Kangsun's translation of the play, and there was little attempt to stay faithful to, or capture the cadences of, Shakespeare's poetic language. This led one harsh critic (rather alarmingly) to disparage the cast for speaking 'jibber jabber'.[4] Yohangza's *Dream* also included a substantial number of phrases in English (despite Festival Director Tom Bird cautioning against such a practice): Duduri delivered the prologue entirely in English; the philanderous fairy king, Gabi, asked an audience member 'Would you like some drink with me?'; and Ajumi (Bottom) requested from *her* doting lover 'fish and chips' and 'mushy peas' – a witty inversion of Bottom's request for 'dried peas' (4.1.34) that almost 'brought the house down'.[5] Signalling an attempt to endear themselves to the predominantly English-speaking crowd, the troupe's use of colloquial English also highlighted the linguistic imperialism of the English language in Korea which, in the words of Yeeyon Im, has 'had a devastating impact on Koreans' sense of cultural identity'.[6] English has become almost 'a fetish' in Korea, and its dominance signifies Korea's postcolonial status.[7] On the other hand, Yohangza's use of everyday English phrases underlined the *disregard* for Shakespeare's language within the Korean education system, which subscribes to the belief that Renaissance verse is 'intrinsically archaic' and which advocates the need for 'reductive strategies' when it comes to the Bard.[8]

Certainly, Yang Jung-Ung and his company's approach to Shakespeare is reductive in several ways – most notably, in terms of the number and complexity of characters and scenes – but the production was also deceptively multifaceted. The reversal in gender roles is probably the most notable and interesting aspect of this production as well as of other twenty-first-century Korean Shakespeares, such as Park Jae-wan's *Trans-Twelfth Night* (2002), which attempted to offer a feminist twist on the original too. In Yohangza's *Dream*, it is Oberon (Gabi) who is punished by Titania (Dot), and it is a female herb-collector, Ajumi, rather than the rude mechanical, Bottom, with whom Gabi is tricked into falling in love. Ajumi (Jeong A-Young), whose name is slang for Ajumoni, meaning 'a married woman',[9] was old and vulgar and the complete opposite of the pretty shepherdess, Phillida, with whom Oberon is accused by Titania of having an affair in the source material (2.1.66–9). After urinating on stage and smearing the liquid over her face to repel the *Dokkebi*, Ajumi is transformed into a pig instead of an ass and arguably humiliated to an extent that a male Bottom rarely is. Even though in Korean culture the pig is a symbol of good fortune and Ajumi's transformation into this auspicious animal can be interpreted as the director's way of suggesting that physically unattractive women have a right to love and be loved, it is difficult to view this as radically 'turning conventional concepts of femininity on their head'.[10] Ajumi, although loveable, is ultimately made a laughing stock in the way women past their prime and seeking male affection usually are. Alexandra Coghlan's interpretation of the rare plant (Ginseng) with which a delighted Ajumi is presented at the end of the play as 'an age-defying flower?' or 'Herbal Viagra?' further suggests that conventional/negative concepts of femininity were often far from being successfully challenged.[11]

Likewise, despite the fact that Titania, metamorphosed into the character of Dot, was granted the chance to manipulate and debase Oberon, she was simultaneously stripped of the sexual assertiveness that makes her role provoke patriarchal enmity. With the exception of Eeck (Helena), the female characters were denied the opportunity 'to fight for love as men may do' (2.1.241), and the play, as a whole, seemed to uphold the old-fashioned view that women 'should be woo'd, and were not made to woo' (2.1.242). Indeed, this is apparently the opinion maintained in Korea today. Furthermore, by playing the role of the scolding wife, Dot – whose name means fire – perpetuated the anti-feminist view that powerful women must necessarily be the castrators of men, while the transformation of Puck into her naughty little brother, Duduri, implied that a woman can only exert authority over male members of her own family, and that thus her power is limited to the domestic sphere.

The impish Duduri, played brilliantly by the charismatic actors Kim Sang-bo and Jeon Jung-Yong, embodied the festive elements of the *Dream* and enchanted the cast and audience alike. This dual figure, like Korea itself – a country comprised of two halves – also constituted a physical manifestation of the production's central concern with doubles and duality. As Brian Singleton points out, 'the overriding focus of the production appeared to be on binaries'.[12] The play's interest in exploring several binary oppositions – old and new, humans and fairies, male and female – ultimately highlights Korea's own condition of being in a transitional phase and caught between two worlds: old Asia and new Asia.[13] This liminality is similarly evident in the other Festival production by one of the so-called 'four Asian dragons':[14] the Cantonese *Titus Andronicus*.

ENDNOTES

1 Maria Shevtsova, 'Cross-Cultural Fields: Korean Shakespeare Productions in Global Context', in Hyon-u Lee, ed., *Glocalizing Shakespeare in Korea and Beyond* (Seoul: Dongin Publishing, 2009), pp. 157–78.

2 For a brief history of Shakespeare in Korea, see Kim Jong-hwan, 'Shakespeare in a Korean Cultural Context', *Asian Theatre Journal*, 12.1 (1995): 37–49.

3 Hyon-u Lee, 'The Dialectical Progress of Femininity in Korean Shakespeare since 1990', in Richard Fotheringham, Christa Jansohn and R. S. White, eds., *Shakespeare's World/World Shakespeares: The Selected Proceedings of the International Shakespeare Association World Congress 2006* (Cranbury: Associated University Press, 2009), pp. 273–91.

4 Tim Walker, '*A Midsummer Night's Dream* at Shakespeare's Globe – *Seven* Magazine Review', *Telegraph*, 11 May 2012, www.telegraph.co.uk/culture/theatre/theatre-reviews/9259876/A-Midsummer-Nights-Dream-at-Shakespeares-Globe-Seven-magazine-review.html, 10 September 2012.

5 Brian Logan, '*A Midsummer Night's Dream* – Review', *Guardian*, 2 May 2012, www.guardian.co.uk/stage/2012/may/02/midsummer-nights-dream-review, 10 September 2012.

6 Yeeyon Im, 'The location of Shakespeare in Korea: Lee Yountaek's *Hamlet* and the Mirage of Interculturality', *Theatre Journal*, 60.2 (2008): 257–76 (272).

7 Ibid. 273.

8 Youglim Han, 'Korean Shakespeare: The Anxiety of Being Invisible', in Sukanta Chaudhuri and Chee Seng Lim, eds., *Shakespeare without English: The Reception of Shakespeare in Non-Anglophone Countries* (Delhi: Dorling Kindersley, 2006), p. 56.

9 Daniel Gallimore, 'Inside Out: Dreaming the Dream in Contemporary Japan and Korea', in Lee, ed., *Glocalizing Shakespeare in Korea and Beyond*, pp. 225–41.

10 Lee, 'The Dialectical Progress of Femininity in Korean Shakespeare since 1990', p. 286.

11 Alexandra Coghlan, 'Globe to Globe: *A Midsummer Night's Dream*, Shakespeare's Globe', *The Arts Desk*, 1 May 2012, www.theartsdesk.com/theatre/globe-globe-midsummer-nights-dream-shakespeares-globe, 10 September 2012.

12 Brian Singleton, 'Intercultural Shakespeare from Intracultural Sources: Two Korean Performances', in Lee, ed., *Glocalizing Shakespeare in Korea and Beyond*, pp. 179–98.

13 Ibid.

14 The four Asian dragons refer to the highly developed economies of Hong Kong, Taiwan, Singapore and South Korea.

CHAPTER NINE

INTERCULTURAL RHYTHM IN YOHANGZA'S DREAM

Yong Li Lan

Introducing the Yohangza Theatre Company's production to their audience at Shakespeare's Globe, the actors playing Duduri (a re-creation of Puck as twin brothers) presented it in English with its informal title, 'A Midsummer Night's Dream from the East'.[1] On its numerous tours around the world,[2] reviews of the production's infectious and unusual style suggestively fused its origin with the notion of a dream: for instance, '*Dream* from the East', 'A Korean Midsummer Night' and 'To Korea to Dream of Shakespeare'.[3] Yet although the production's performance style strongly conveys the impression of belonging to South Korean theatre cultures or at least of having an Asian aesthetic, apart from the language spoken by the actors its Korean-ness or Asian-ness is not readily isolated or classified. Yohangza eclectically combined elements from Korean traditional performances without adopting any to a dominant or definitive extent.

More importantly, it transformed these traditional elements in a synthesis with elements from non-Korean genres, as well as some components that are entirely unique to this production. While contemporary intercultural productions that take this mix-and-match approach have been disparaged as opportunistic plunderings of traditions that put together a cultural buffet aimed at the festival market, this production's stylization and integration of its varied influences are so advanced as to create a single whole in which it is often difficult to establish with certainty that a particular element was drawn from one particular source. The signature image of the production is the elaborate, brightly coloured facial paint on a white base that distinguished the *Dokkabi* (golins who emerge at night) from the mortals. This make-up generically recalls the masks and facial paint that are an essential, prescribed part of many pre-modern theatre forms in Asia, like Beijing Opera or Kabuki. But its striking colours – details like the black lines drawn on the brow and cheekbones – and overall composition did not resemble the faces of any other form. Quite unlike the formal head-dresses of traditional performance, the electric blue hair worn by the male *Dokkabi* and crimson hair of Dot, the queen of the *Dokkabi*, was casually tousled, set with woven straw decorations, a material associated in Korea with rustic accessories, and topped by large, flat paper flowers that seem universal. The *Dokkabi* habitually contorted their faces in exaggerated, comic-grotesque expressions that this distinctive hair and make-up helped to emphasize. Together with their songs, dancing and acrobatics, the total effect the *Dokkabi* made was of theatrical beings born fully formed on the stage. This production performed like a true global child.

Yohangza's *Dream* can be understood as a rather special kind of intercultural structure whose disparate elements cohere primarily through their rhythmical organization. In broad terms, this structure resembles Shakespeare's separate groups of characters, in that the *Dokkabi* and mortals sustained a detailed performative contrast and complementarity in their respective appearances, behaviour and vocal delivery. However, Yohangza's adaptation had no equivalent of Shakespeare's Athenian court, and the entire action was contained within the world of the *Dokkabi*. Their introduction is remembered by one viewer as 'tearing the roof off' at the Edinburgh Festival (2005),[4] and described thus by another this time:

The opening tableau showcased Yohangza's exquisitely mannered style, and with the first transition into a dark, catchy drum beat that was to be a signature mood, I actually felt my flesh creep a little: this was foreign theatre, in the best possible way. I had no idea what might come next. A touch of the otherworldly stole over the audience as the circle of actors began rhythmically, vividly, to dance.[5]

A substantial portion of the expressiveness of the *Dokkabi* was highly enjoyable in itself but could not be understood in terms of plot. For instance, it was unclear whether there was any significance in the twin Pucks, Duduri, entering with their bodies interlocked, one suspended upside down from the other by hooking his legs around the other's shoulders (see Colour Plate 4), at the point when they enchanted Hang (Lysander). Dot, watching the four lovers' fight from the balcony, drank a mouthful of liquid and spat it in a spray over them to a single strike on the gong; her action was understood only in retrospect, by its effect of putting the lovers into slow motion and bringing the fight to a close. The *Dokkabi* world gave the impression of performing according to its own logic, which was partly in shadow.

A small but important distinction signalling the production's own version of the *Dokkebi* of Korean folklore is that they were called *Dokkabi*, a word which the names of their king and queen, Dot and Gabbi, combine to form. As against the constantly surprising behaviour of the *Dokkabi*, in their world at least the lovers' action was clearly patterned symmetrically. Each was initially dressed in a single-colour tunic and white underskirt, their colours of red, blue, green, yellow and white together representing the five directions. They came on in pairs with a dance-mime of their current relationship, switched to melodramatic acting punctuated by slapstick, then exited in a dance-mime again. The short, verse-like lines concentrated their emotions in poetic images – Ick (Helena) told Loo (Demetrius) as she pursued him, 'They say it takes a special karma just for the hem of my skirt to brush by yours.'[6] The lovers spoke naturally, as opposed to the stylized delivery of the *Dokkabi*, which swooped up and over a high pitch. Speech was accentuated and punctuated by sharply timed movements, and during their extended quarrel the choreography of the blocking depicted the ironies in their conflict as they changed groupings and re-formed in 2–2 or 3–1 tableaux across the diagonal.

While productions of the *Dream* invariably employ at least a visual contrast between the otherworldly and human beings, the performativity of that contrast in this *Dream* was not of a symbolic order (representing a netherworld of consciousness, for instance) but an aesthetic one. The interplay between segments of the action, and individual beats within one segment, combined many kinds of physical movement. An example could start at the entrance of Byock (Hermia) and Hang into a wood made up of *Dokkabi* striking odd-angled poses. The lovers struggled past the bodies of the *Dokkabi*, who changed positions with each beat of the lovers' progress. Settled in a clearing, Hang made advances on Byock, to which Gabbi (from the musicians' area) reacted on the kazoo after the manner of silent movies, while the *Dokkabi* imitated their kiss. She ran behind them and re-emerged, while Hang, following her, was caught between the legs of one *Dokkabi* 'tree'. When he rejoined her, she gave him a surprisingly strong shove as his body sprang back in the slapstick manner. Alone stage left, he was mocked by the Dokkabis' sexual gestures, one even baring his bottom, causing Hang to back away, still seated, into Byock. In successive switches of mood they apologized, upset; declared their love quietly; then a ripple of the Mark tree bar chimes shifted the scene into a gentle traditional dance set to a Pansori song accompanied on the Kayageum (a Korean stringed instrument). After they danced and fell asleep at opposite corners of the stage, more ripples on the bar chimes marked a new scene. Preceded first by notes on a flute, then a contraption resembling a single eyeball from which the magical flowers dangled at the tops of long staffs, Duduri entered, their bodies intertwined in a reverse image of the other half. While the lovers slept, Duduri pranced around first Byock, then Hang as they enchanted him, taking their time in a moment meant to be savoured for its mischievous whimsicality in their movements and facial expressions. As Duduri exited, the flute melody reached its finale, and Loo and Ick entered, quarreling in dance-mime.

In this richly articulated pattern of sounds and movements there was a spectrum of moment-by-moment shifts between physical theatre, naturalism with varying degrees of exaggeration, mime, slapstick, Korean martial arts (Taekkyon) and graceful traditional dance, as well as comic-grotesque dance, lyrical song and tableaux. These developed the scenes' detail, and invoked a corresponding variety of audience responses that were constantly changing and held in balance. Repetition was employed throughout in both movement and musical effect, and coached the audience in the vocabulary of the performance. Comic effect was also accumulated with each repetition.[7] The dramatic progression was shaped and paced in segments that elongated and abbreviated the plot moment, and varied and counterpointed one another. Correlatively, the spectator was taken through an experience of difference, balance and completion in each segment. Shakespeare's play was restructured according to a physical and aural rhythm that added aesthetic pleasure and emotional texture to the content of the story, and which was indeed our primary experience of that story.

This virtuosity of the actors can be compared to the wit, rhyme, images and wordplay of Shakespeare's verse at this point in his play: both Yohangza's physical theatre and Shakespeare's poetry treat the plot as a premise for elaboration that, as an art in itself, produces pleasure and admiration in the audience. The virtuosity in Yohangza's performance was not merely technical. Defining its use of the diverse elements that it brought together are two aesthetic principles characteristic of Korean performance. The first is called *shinmyoung*, which refers to the release of high spirits, and is especially evident in the dances and music of Yohangza's *Dream*. *Shinmyoung* was combined with the second principle, which is a high level of audience interaction. The Yohangza actors threw glow-in-the-dark armbands to the audience right at the beginning of their performance, igniting a high level of excitement in them and building up a shared mood of interactive festivity, before they launched into the performance proper. The same strategy after the interval brought the audience back into the performance, as Dominic Dromgoole quipped in his speech at the post-show reception: 'We now know that if we have a production that's in trouble, we can start the second half by throwing cheap garbage at the audience.' The actors often directed their gestures and remarks in asides to the audience, made ad hoc substitutions of the Korean lines with English phrases aimed at the English-speaking audience, and received roars of hilarity when Ajumi, the equivalent of Bottom in a gender-reversal, named 'mushy peas' and 'fish and chips' as her favourite food. The performance as a whole, according to one comment on Twitter, was 'the closest I've seen to a rave in the theatre'.[8] Thus the Korean-ness of Yohangza's performance lay not in its forms but its spiritedness, as is appropriate for *A Midsummer Night's Dream* from the East.

ENDNOTES

1 The words 'from the East' were part of the production's name in its previous tour of the UK (London, Bristol, Cardiff, 2006), at the Neuss Globe (2006) and in Singapore (2008).
2 The production has played at over eighty cities (at the last count) since 2003.

3 Rivka Jacobson, 'Jung-Ung Yang – Dream from the East', *The British Theatre Guide*, 2006, www.britishtheatreguide.info/otherresources/interviews/Jung-UngYang.htm; Joseph Simon Mutti, 'Un sueño coreano de una noche de verano', *La Jiribilla*, 20 September 2005, www.lajiribilla.cu/2005/n229_09/229_09.html; Cultural Centre Macau, 'A Coreia a sonhar com Shakespeare', *hojemacau*, 17 July 2008, www.hojemacau.com/news.phtml?id=29612&today=17-07-2008&type=culture. All accessed 12 October 2012.

4 David Cottis, 'Globe to Globe – The Second Week', David Cottis, 13 May 2012, http://davidcottis.blogspot.sg/2012/05/globe-to-globe-second-week.html, 12 October 2012.

5 Megan Murray-Pepper, 'Globe to Globe Week 2: *A Midsummer Night's Dream*', *Stet: An Online Postgraduate Research Journal*, 22 May 2012, www.stetjournal.org/blogs/theatre/globe-to-globe-week-2-a-midsummer-nights-dream/, 12 October 2012.

6 English translation by Alyssa Kim of the original Korean script written by Yang Jung-ung, courtesy of the Asian Shakespeare Intercultural Archive (A|S|I|A), http://a-s-i-a-web.org, 12 October 2012.

7 This essay is indebted to discussions with the data editors of A|S|I|A: Hwang Ha Young, who researched the data for this production, and Lee Chee Keng, who watched the performance at Shakespeare's Globe with me and made this point about repetition.

8 Cited in David Cottis, 'Globe to Globe'.

CHAPTER TEN

ART OF DARKNESS

Staging *Giulio Cesare* at the Globe Theatre

Sonia Massai

The choice of commissioning a young Italian company based in Rome to stage a production of *Julius Caesar* during the Globe to Globe Festival seemed informed by the same logic that led the organizers to select the National Theatre of Greece to perform *Pericles*. But, in fact, Andrea Baracco and Vincenzo Manna's *Giulio Cesare* pre-existed the Festival, at least as a 50-minute-long studio workshop inspired by the first two acts of Shakespeare's tragedy and provisionally entitled *Ventitrè*, as in the twenty-three stab-wounds inflicted by the conspirators on Caesar's body. And, as it turned out, Caesar's Rome and any reference to the historical setting within which Caesar's murder took place were cut in the pared-down, modern-dress version skilfully performed by six actors (with little doubling)[1] at the Globe Theatre on 1 and 2 May 2012.

Baracco's *Giulio Cesare* was not as far removed from Shakespeare's play and its classical setting as Societas Raffaello Sanzio's *Giulio Cesare*, which was performed in the capital as part of the London International Festival of Theatre (LIFT) 1999. However, Baracco's production did catapult Shakespeare's main characters into a world where their innermost fears and desires have effectively obliterated the outside world, the public sphere, and any remnant of functional social interactions. Baracco's take on Shakespeare's play was instead firmly focused on the disjointed inner lives of characters pushed to their psychological and moral limits by the extreme circumstances and events that eventually destroy them. Instead of representing *Julius Caesar* as a tragedy set in classical Rome or even in twentieth-century Rome, as several productions in English have done by casting Cesare as a fascist dictator,[2] Baracco opted for an original and exciting journey into the play's 'heart of darkness', effectively suggested through the heavily symbolic language of physical theatre.

Baracco's boldest directorial intervention was the excision of Caesar. Granted that the play is named after a character who speaks a mere 5 per cent of the lines in

Shakespeare's play, the realization that Caesar was never going to materialize on stage came as a shock to me when I saw the opening performance at the Globe. And yet cutting Caesar does make sense, both in relation to the play, where, to misquote Hamlet, 'nothing', including the elusive character of Caesar, 'is good or bad but *telling* makes it so',[3] and in relation to this production, where the killing of Caesar was nevertheless effectively executed. At this pivotal moment in the play, Bruto smoothed down his hair, straightened his tie, and marched slowly downstage with Cassio and Casca as if on a catwalk to the sound of Kraftwerk's *The Model*. They then proceeded to slash a bottomless chair with red chalk, the same chair which featured prominently throughout the production as the symbol of an all-consuming desire for absolute power.

The bottomless chair – in which Bruto and Cassio got suggestively and awkwardly stuck before killing Caesar, thus suggesting a desire to emulate as much as to destroy him – was the focal point of this production, which foregrounded a few other distinctive visual elements suggested by Shakespeare's dialogue. Central to Baracco and Manna's re-interpretation of the play were three large doors, occasionally left to stand on an otherwise empty stage or more often supported by the actors, who used them both as an extension of the tiring-house and as a liminal space behind which their characters cowered or skulked as the main action unfolded on the stage. The doors worked best when the actors used them to suggest absent characters or even states of mind, as in the forum when caps and flowers tied to long poles were held up to signify the throng of plebeians listening to Brutus and Cassius' orations, or in Brutus' house on the night before the killing of Caesar, when one hand protruding from behind one door supported Brutus' head, trying to lull him into sleep, while another hand clicked its fingers to wake him up every time he dozed off. Also effective was the way in which Calpurnia's obsessive writhing as she first entered the stage was echoed by three pairs of wriggling, squirming hands sticking out from the doors behind her.

When interviewed at the Globe, Giandomenico Cupaiuolo (Brutus) talked eloquently about the use of the three moving doors as a visual counterpart of Shakespeare's exploration of the inner lives of his characters, or, in Cupaiuolo's own words, 'of what normally happens behind closed doors' ('la vita oltre la porta'). At the same interview, Baracco more generally explained that the use of recurrent stage images, symbolic props or gestures inspired by the dialogue is one of the company's distinctive trademarks. An Italian reviewer has suggestively compared this technique to the sophisticated visual and physical theatrical language deployed by Lithuanian director Eimuntas Nekrošius.[4] The two black dustbins used in the second half of this production functioned as an explicit reference to Samuel Beckett's *Endgame*, another powerful model that clearly influenced Baracco's artistic vision. The two dustbins were first used to support the temporary podium from

Fig. 5 Brutus (Giandomenico Cupaiuolo (Bruto)), *Julius Caesar*, 369 Gradi/Lungta Film in collaboration with Teatro di Roma from Rome, Italy; director Andrea Baracco.

where Bruto and Antonio delivered their orations in the forum, but later on, when the action moved to Sardis, Bruto stacked them and sought shelter inside them, challenging Cassio while crouching down, almost in a foetal position, and thus visually reminding the audience of the sense of paralysis and helplessness conveyed by Beckett's talking heads in *Endgame*.

The elegant fluidity of the Italian translation-adaptation of Shakespeare's text relieved some of the sense of hopelessness and unease so forcefully represented through the actors' actions and body language. Portia's challenge to Brutus, 'Abito solo i sobborghi del tuo piacere?' ('Dwell I but in the suburbs / Of your good pleasure?' (2.1.285–6)), and Antony's curse, 'Che siano maledette le mani sporche del tuo nobile sangue!' ('Woe to the hand that shed this costly blood!' (3.1.258)), struck a chord through their beautiful simplicity. Also worth noting is that allusions to the deplorable state of Italian politics under former Prime Minster Silvio Berlusconi emerged, subtly but eloquently, from Baracco and Manna's script. A good example came in the first exchange between Bruto and Cassio, when Cassio remarked that 'Roma è ora soltanto una stanzetta' (loosely translated from 'Now is it Rome indeed, and room enough, / When there is in it but only one man' (1.2.156–7)).

Similarly memorable were the female characters, who have notoriously limited roles in a play that explores the impact of stifling and corrupt power structures on the lives of strong male individuals. This production gave Calpurnia (Ersilia Lombardo) and Porzia (Livia Castiglioni) more space and new lines. Calpurnia was visibly torn apart by her inability to give Cesare a child, a successor, and sought shelter from the public scrutiny and shaming she is exposed to during the Lupercalia by knocking on doors that not only remained shut but also repulsed her, sending her crashing down, repeatedly, on the floor. Baracco and Manna added a new scene to show Porzia's suicide, only reported in Shakespeare's play. Blood-red stains on Porzia's hands and face, as well as the violence inflicted on Calpurnia's body, functioned as stark reminders that the type of power so forcefully critiqued by Bruto and Cassio affects the public as well as the private lives not only of those who crave it but also, and tragically, of those who resist it.

This imaginative and original reworking of *Julius Caesar* had, as noted, first opened in Italy as a shorter studio workshop in January 2011 and later as a fully fledged adaptation of the play in July 2011 to great critical acclaim. Italian reviewers singled out the actors' formidable physicality and the arresting moment when the conspirators, instead of knocking on or walking around the doors signifying Brutus' house during the night before Caesar's assassination, nimbly climbed and sat on them, suggesting the sense of stealth and apprehension they all share.[5] Baracco's use of 'a theatrical language rich in complex and layered stage images and symbols'[6] was also hailed as original and exciting, the very best that a young and vibrant company could possibly offer to represent contemporary Italian theatre at the Globe to Globe Festival.[7] Above all, though, most reviewers praised Baracco and Manna's 'political instinct',[8] as they honed their translation to capture the mood of 'a generation who', in Baracco's words, 'can no longer endure the status quo and could overturn it but cannot imagine a different future'.[9] I would agree that Baracco and Manna's haunting translation and radical adaptation of Shakespeare's text proved unsettling without being overly topical. As Baracco was at great pains to explain when he was interviewed at the Globe on 1 May, Cesare is not former Italian Prime Minister Silvio Berlusconi. Even so, it is probably worth stressing just how prophetic Baracco's take on *Julius Caesar* has proved to be, given that the opposition parties finally gathered enough political momentum to force Berlusconi to resign in November 2011 after nearly twenty years of a more or less uninterrupted and stultifying regime, which another reviewer aptly referred to as 'Italy's social and cultural dark years'.[10] Inspired by Shakespeare, who, as Baracco put it during the same interview, wrote 'transversally' and not 'locally' or 'as a journalist' about his own time, this young Italian director undoubtedly created a haunting lesson in how not to try and get out of a political crisis. The human cost of acts of violence, even when justified, was one other important aspect of Baracco's *Cesare*, which was positively noted by some reviewers in Italy.[11]

The reception of this production at the Globe to Globe Festival was warm and enthusiastic among the crowds of Italian expatriates who filled the galleries and the courtyard on both dates (1 and 2 May). But reviewers interestingly expressed diametrically opposed views, the more positive ones focusing on specific moments in the production rather than on its overall vision or style, which was openly critiqued in the negative ones. Melissa Danes in the *Guardian*, for example, read the symbolic language of Baracco's dramaturgy and the physical style of the action as 'heavy on the silliness', but praised Cupaiuolo for giving 'a committed and increasingly layered performance, allowing [the audience] to see the moral conflict within "the noblest Roman of them all"'. Even within a production which she found was often 'bathetic' rather than 'unsettling', she went on to stress that '[Cupaiuolo's] suicidal rebel is a compelling mix of goodness, ambition, remorse and pragmatism, and the ending, when it comes, is measured and not without pathos'.[12] Reading the production more generally as stuck in the past, as opposed to experimental and ground-breaking as Italian reviewers had done, William Ward voiced a sense of alienation which was shared by some of the non-Italian members of the audience I happened to talk to on the opening day: 'Going to almost any contemporary production of Italian theatre (for anyone raised on the English language canon and its main schools of interpretation) is to hit a very hard wall of cultural dissonance. We go for grades of naturalism', he adds, while 'our Italian cousins are still deeply wedded to the rhetorical, declamatory style that went out in the late 19th century.' Ward ends with a final remark on his sense of temporal and spatial dislocation: 'Indeed, to witness a standard *produzione scecspiriana* in Italy is often like being projected in a time capsule to a faraway distant land.'[13]

Having seen most productions during the Festival, I can understand why this one felt somehow out of place, jarring and at odds with the performance space offered by the Globe stage. Interestingly, I sensed the same tension between the artistic vision informing other productions and the setting in which they were performed: worth mentioning in conjunction with Baracco's *Giulio Cesare*, especially in light of shared elements in their style and their reception during the Festival, is Nekrošius' long-travelled and internationally renowned production of *Hamlet*, performed over the weekend of 2nd and 3rd June, right in the middle of the Jubilee celebrations. Michael Billington, writing in the *Guardian*, noted that 'while I'm always happy to see Hamlet reimagined, [some of] Nekrošius [sic] notions seemed to me absurd'. Billington found Nekrošius' 'series of striking visual tableaux' and 'its unbroken chain of surreal images . . . eccentrically memorable', but ultimately missed 'any sense of developing character' and 'the polychromatic diversity of Shakespeare's indestructible play'.[14] While I am not assuming that Ward's and Billington's responses to Baracco's *Giulio Cesare* and to Nekrošius' *Hamlet* would be more positive if they had seen these productions in a different type of theatre, my contention is that the performance space offered by the Globe is not neutral and that it clashes with the aesthetic and more generally artistic principles that inform the theatrical language and approach shared by directors like Baracco and Nekrošius. I myself had a visceral sense of dislocation when I first saw Baracco's *Giulio Cesare* there, partly because I had not seen any Shakespeare in Italian in London for quite some time, but mostly because a theatrical language which had originated in a very different type of theatre, where light and sound thoroughly inform the artistic vision of those who work within it, clashed with the performance space offered by the Globe stage. My first impression of alienation was followed by a slower sense of recognition and memories of other shows I had seen in London and the UK, as well as overseas, where language is no longer the dominant element of the *mise-en-scène*.

One strikingly common response among the Italian reviewers who enjoyed *Giulio Cesare* was their appreciation of the darkness enfolding the stage action, which manifested itself both as an absence of light and the failure of reason. Significant in this respect were Bruto's attempts to nurture two light bulbs preposterously planted in a pot and Porzia's handling of some more lightbulbs, which she flicked on and off and then placed in her mouth as she took her own life. The flicking on and off of the lightbulbs must have been quite stunning in the black-box theatres where *Giulio Cesare* played before transferring to the Globe, and Baracco's heavy use of symbols must have seemed quite natural in venues like Teatro India in Rome, which has for some time now been associated with radical experiments and pioneering research into new ways of signifying through performance. Baracco's preference for an expressionist rather than a naturalist style of theatrical representation was recognized by Italian reviewers as belonging to the 'here and now' of a refreshingly experimental theatrical culture that is thriving among younger generations of theatre artists, in stark contrast to Ward's association between Baracco's style and a remote theatrical past.

Interestingly, several Italian reviewers linked the darkness against which Baracco's complex symbols and stage images stand out as if in high-definition, like crystal-clear and bold statements, to the young age of the company and the radical quality of their work. Andrea Cova wrote about 'the vocation for experimental work at the forefront of dramaturgical research and innovation associated with

Teatro di Roma', within which Teatro India represents the most iconic venue, and singled out Baracco's choice to present his *Giulio Cesare* as a 'disquieting journey in/into the night'.[15] Patrizia Vitrugno similarly evoked darkness as the defining element of this production: 'Darkness is everywhere, enfolding the fictive time arranged around the plotting and the planning'; 'and then there is [more] darkness. Rome, fallen, corrupt and intrinsically filthy, is darkness itself'; and, once again, linking Baracco's artistic vision to the youth and experimental qualities of his company, Vitrugno adds, 'there is a perfect balance among the characters, who bring to the stage their supple, light, athletic bodies', while 'the dark setting lends a fearful strength to the doubts that grip them as they wait to act'.[16]

Darkness is the one special effect that is impossible to achieve at the Globe Theatre. Whether playing in natural light during the afternoon or under the constant, uniform light coming from the several powerful spotlights nested under the eaves, the actors who play on the Globe stage are never surrounded by darkness. As I mentioned above, I was fascinated by the obvious disconnect between the unifying artistic vision underlying this production and the space within which it was being played at the Globe. Even more revealing was the fact that Baracco had removed the very lines that Shakespeare uses to evoke darkness in the play, because these lines belong to exterior, chorus-like moments which are extraneous to Baracco's relentless focus on the characters' ravaged inner mental landscapes. Hence the omission of lines like the ones between Cicero, Cassius and Casca in Shakespeare's Act 1 scene 3, when Casca reports his strange sightings while walking the street of Rome in the dead of night: 'what night is this!'; 'But never till tonight, never till now, / Did I go through a tempest dropping fire'; 'And yesterday the bird of night did sit, / Even at noonday, upon the market-place, / Hooting and shrieking' (42, 9–10, 26–8). Cicero's remark on Casca's description of nocturnal 'prodigies' shows how Shakespeare links the ominous night described by Casca with a darkness of the mind: 'Indeed it is a strange-disposèd time. / But men may construe things after their fashion, / Clean from the purpose of the things themselves' (1.3.33–5). These typically Shakespearean lines, Shakespeare's very own signature 'art of darkness', where language plays a key role in evoking setting and mood, had no place in a production where the same function belonged firmly to the realm of the visual.

When asked if he had adapted his production in preparation for the Globe to Globe Festival, Baracco candidly answered that he had not changed it at all. As I slowly realized while trying to unpack my own response to this production, he could not have adapted his production, which relied so heavily on the conventions of performing in a black-box theatre, without altering the very fabric of his artistic vision. Baracco's journey into the 'heart of darkness' of Shakespeare's *Julius Caesar*, exciting and auspicious as it turned out to be for Italian audiences and reviewers who hailed it as a sort of guiding light showing them the way out of the dark ages of Berlusconismo, could not, and should not have attempted to, emulate Shakespeare's 'art of darkness' which is thoroughly inscribed in the material conditions of performing in an early modern amphitheatre. What proved revealing for me was that what I have called Shakespeare's 'art of darkness' in this chapter is utterly antithetical to the conventions informing the type of physical theatre practised by so many contemporary theatre artists, ranging from well-established directors like Nekrošius to radical emerging companies like Baracco's. Their Shakespearean productions move seamlessly and to great critical acclaim between venues on the international festival circuit but do not seem to have found a 'natural' home at the Globe. The distance travelled by these imaginative and radical reworkings is not to be regretted, though; on the contrary, it should be celebrated, especially for plays which, like *Julius Caesar*, had already started to dream of their own afterlife in 'states unborn' and 'accents yet unknown'.

ENDNOTES

1 Bruto was played by Giandomenico Cupaiuolo, Cassio by Roberto Manzi, Casca and Ottaviano by Lucas Walden Zanforlini, Porzia by Livia Castiglioni, and Calpurnia and Caesar's Ghost by Ersilia Lombardo. All six actors played minor roles, including Brutus' army in the final scene. They also acted as stage hands by taking turns to move the three doors used as props and minimal setting throughout this production.

2 Examples have ranged from Orson Welles' 1937 acclaimed, but also hugely controversial, production set in fascist Italy, to John Barton's 1968 RSC production, revisited by Trevor Nunn, still for the RSC, in 1972. I am grateful to Bridget Escolme for reminding me of this strand of productions, which drew on the visual and ideological markers of Italian fascism in order to 'up-date' the play for mid to later twentieth-century audiences.

3 This line of interpretation is popular among recent Shakespearean scholars who have re-read the play in light of post-structuralist theorists, like Jacques Derrida, who have championed a notion of language as informing rather than representing extra-linguistic referents, thus querying the epistemological foundations of knowledge itself. See for example John Drakakis, '"Fashion It Thus": *Julius Caesar* and the Politics of Representation', *Shakespeare Survey*, 44 (1991): 65–73. He points out that the play lacks a figure of absolute authority and power and, by the same token, an epistemological centre from which its audiences can judge motive and characterization.

4 Rodolfo di Giammarco, 'Il bello della congiura nel *Giulio Cesare* di Baracco', *La Repubblica*, 11 March 2012.

5 See, for example, Claudio Ruggiero, in the newspaper *Latina Oggi*, 4th March 2012: 'una performance di notevole impatto fisico, tutti giovani gli interpreti che si muovono con grande padronanza in una scena efficacemente miminale, dominata da un eloquente e simbolico gioco di porte contro il quali sbattono i cospiratori'.

6 'L'originalità di Baracco più che nel taglio del testo sta nel linguaggio drammaturgico, composto di simboli scenici densi . . . e parlanti', Manuela Sammarco, www.teatroteatro.it/recensioni_dettaglio.aspx?prvz=1&uart=3445&idrap=5746, 28 January 2013.

7 Manuela Sammarco's review quoted above is suggestively headed 'Italian theatre will make us proud at the Globe to Globe Festival 2012' ('La drammaturgia italiana farà al "Globe to Globe 2012" una bella figura'). She then goes on to refer to Baracco's company as 'deserving competitors' at the 'Theatre Olympiad' organized by Shakespeare's Globe ('degni competitori delle olimpiadi teatrali . . . del Globe to Globe 2012').

8 A reviewer in *Il Manifesto* (G. Cap., 'Bruto, moderno liquidatore della politica', 28 April 2012), one of the more vocal left-wing national newspapers in Italy, used the phrase 'fiuto politico', which loosely translates as 'political instinct' (or, in Baracco and Manna's case, the current mood of hopelessness and despondency in Italy).

9 Quoted in Natalia Distefano, 'Giulio Cesare: La rivolta nei versi di Shakespeare', *Corriere della Sera*, Roma, 26 February 2012.

10 'Gli anni di oscurantismo sociale e culturale che ci troviamo ad attraversare': Andrea Cova, 'Giulio Cesare', www.saltinaria.it/recensioni/spettacoli-teatrali/giulio-cesare-teatro-india-roma-recensione-spettacolo.html, 7 February 2013.

11 In the same review in *Il Manifesto* quoted above, Baracco's Rome, 'taken over by rioting crowds and conspirators, more or less set on achieving their aims', is compared to 'European capital cities, caught up in the grip of a recession that seemingly has no end' ('Come oggi nelle capitali europee stremate da una crisi di cui non si vede l'uscita, anche la città in scena è attraversata da folle in tumulto e cospiratori più o meno decisi').

12 Melissa Denes, '*Julius Caesar* – Review', *Guardian*, 3 May 2012, www.guardian.co.uk/stage/2012/may/03/julius-caesar-globe-review, 7 February 2013.

13 William Ward, 'Globe to Globe: *Julius Caesar*, Shakespeare's Globe', *The Arts Desk*, 3 May 2012, www.theartsdesk.com/theatre/globe-globe-julius-caesar-shakespeares-globe, 7 February 2013.

14 Michael Billington, '*Hamlet*' – Review, *Guardian*, 3 June 2012, www.guardian.co.uk/stage/2012/jun/03/hamlet-review, 7 February 2013.

15 'Il Teatro di Roma conferma la vocazione espressa negli ultimi anni per la sperimentazione e le nuove frontiere drammaturgiche'; 'un approccio decisamente innovativo e sintetico, un inquieto viaggio notturno', Cova, 'Giulio Cesare'.

16 'Intorno è buio. Le tenebre avvolgono il tempo della macchinazione e dell'ideazione'; 'E poi c'è il buio. Il buio è Roma: decaduta, corrotta, intimamente sporca'; '[p]erfetto l'equilibrio tra i personaggi, che portano in scena corpi leggeri e atletici . . . le atmosfere cupe danno forza al dubbio che assale nell'ora dell'attesa': www.ilgrido.org/teatro/schede/giulio_cesare.htm, 28 January 2013. See also 'Giulio Cesare e la follia omicida' by Anna Concetta Consarino, who writes for *Agenzia Radicale* and uses almost identitical words to describe the dominant mood set by the absence of light in Baracco's production: 'Tutto intorno è grigio' ('Grey [darkness] is all around'): www.agenziaradicale.com/archivio/index.php?option=com_content&task=view&id=13649&itemid=66.7, February 2013.

CHAPTER ELEVEN

NEO-LIBERAL PLEASURE, GLOBAL RESPONSIBILITY AND THE SOUTH SUDAN CYMBELINE

Kim Solga

The origin story of the South Sudan Theatre Company's (SSTC) *Cymbeline* is by now quite well known. It began with a dream: 'I used to lie in the bush under the stars reading Shakespeare's plays, not thinking about the killing that would take place in the morning', the South Sudan Culture Minister wrote to the Globe Theatre Tom Bird as the SSTC sought a place in the Globe to Globe Festival, instantly hooking Bird with his 'compelling and irresistible' narrative.[1] *Cymbeline* was assigned, and suddenly the world's newest nation – South Sudan was officially formed in July 2011, six years after the official end of the Sudanese civil war – became responsible for creating a piece of theatre that could speak to new freedom; represent its capacity to make world-class performance at the heart of Western culture; honour its ravaged history; and announce its arrival on the world stage as successful, joyous, invigorating, inspiring.

That's a tall order.

In this chapter, I am going to be deliberately cynical in order to tease out some of the ideological and political challenges that can arise when a show like the SSTC's *Cymbeline* appears at a venue like Shakespeare's Globe. Using a cultural materialist approach, I will argue that the South Sudan *Cymbeline* – despite its indisputable emotional power for audiences and actors alike, and despite the real potential it holds to help launch a formal theatre culture in South Sudan – functioned at the Globe primarily as a neo-liberal social good. To put this another way: the SSTC's *Cymbeline* was anticipated in the London press as a piece of work that staged the triumph of the African spirit over extreme adversity, rather than as a performance event that brought into collision two extremely different experiences of living under a globalized reality (in post-industrial, tourist-centred London; in physically ravaged but oil-rich Sudan). The show was largely received as a way for spectators to connect with the tenacity of artists from a war-torn nation and to rejoice at their achievements; the subtext here implies that we can assuage the (quite radical) differences between 'Global North' and 'Global South' merely by coming together to see the SSTC's show. Looking at *Cymbeline* as an almost mythical achievement by an extraordinary group of artists, however, risks giving audiences permission to look *away* from the profoundly mundane and absolutely criminal disparities between 'North' and 'South' that neo-liberal ideology works to obscure and that the SSTC's journey to London brought forcefully to the Globe's stage.

To create theatre under the circumstances that faced the South Sudan artists is an achievement indeed, one for which audiences at the two performances I witnessed showed enormous respect and admiration, as well as a frankly thrilling willingness to go along on the actors' journeys, language and cultural barriers aside. What, then, provokes my cynicism here? Despite the pleasures of the show, I have been disappointed by its anodyne celebration in the press – responses that have lauded its rough-and-tumble comic appeal and the true grit of its artists[2] without also being willing to engage with the most obvious, and arguably most essential, aspect of *Cymbeline*: that compared with many of the other shows on offer at the Festival, *Cymbeline* felt thoroughly amateur, utterly shoestring, and in most ways visibly impoverished. In other words: it was poor theatre from a *very* poor place, a place very much unlike 'global' London. By not spending time unpacking the crucial material disparities revealed by *Cymbeline*, reviewers and commentators missed the opportunity to create a much larger conversation about the many kinds of cultural difference on display at Globe to Globe: differences of resources, access and cultural capital; different levels of national support for the arts; differences of training and experience among companies; differences between working artists and those performing bare survival. At the same time, they missed the opportunity to consider the productive and illuminating collisions among difference that this particular show held the potential to generate for spectators and producers alike.

I would like to explore some of these collisions now: moments when material rather than cultural or racial differences came into relief during and around the SSTC's work at the Festival (see Colour Plate 5). First, this chapter addresses some of the ways in which the SSTC negotiated *Cymbeline* – one of Shakespeare's least coherent plays – on the Globe's iconic stage, focusing specifically on their opening set piece and its shifts from the first to the second performance. Next, I consider two promotional trailers for the production and examine the ways in which, together, they may have complicated spectators' viewings of *Cymbeline*. The chapter ends with a look at the SSTC's remarkable curtain call, as I advance a reading of its political potential. Throughout, I argue that even as the media (and, to some extent, the Globe itself) lauded the arrival of the SSTC artists as a cultural triumph of radical individual fortitude, those same artists were putting subtle pressure on some of theatrical London's most closely held assumptions about how 'global' theatre gets made, for whom it gets made, what it should look like and who should benefit from it.

AN OFFERING TO SOUTH SUDAN

'Romantic antics, warring dynasties, poison plots, nation-building myths, randy wagers, skulduggery in bedrooms, banishment, ill-gotten "proofs" of things, treachery, jealousy, man-love, clever servants, witch-doctors, the ghosts of dead fathers, cross-dressing, transparent Italian pseudonyms, divine intervention – you name it, *Cymbeline*'s got it'[3] – and *Cymbeline*, despite its elite pedigree, could probably use a dramaturge. Shakespeare's plays have been mythologized in their own right, of course, but this does not mean they are all equally remarkable. The SSTC's comparatively amateur production – staged with no set, very basic props, and a group of actors not trained to find the emotional backstory in even the most maddening characterizations and plot twists – clearly and cleverly showed the Bard to be not without flaws, even as it took his raw material in fresh directions. Faced with few resources and a problem of a play, the SSTC artists used *Cymbeline* not as an opportunity to genuflect to the power of Shakespeare, but rather as a chance to do their own thing.

For me, the most exciting parts of the SSTC's two performances were the ones that the company brought to Shakespeare from their own performance traditions in order to help manage the play's obvious challenges. In this respect the company's addition to the beginning of the play, a roughly ten-minute call-and-response summation of the story that took the form of an energetic oral history, was especially noteworthy, acknowledging the difficulties of performing across the language barrier between Juba Arabic and English on one hand and winking slyly to Shakespeare's horrifically complicated plot on the other. In the SSTC's first performance, this telling went badly: the surtitles failed to match up with the actors' affects and gestures, and I could sense the artists' frustration as they struggled to communicate with the audience despite the choppiness. My first reaction to these problems was to wonder if the whole show was going to be a technical mess punctuated by awkward acting; my second was to recognize that the surtitle problems were probably due to radically curtailed rehearsal times – in other words, to circumstances imposed on the SSTC by the complex framework of this Festival, the sheer scope of which created both tremendous richness and, as in this case, moments (ironically) of material lack. Watching the actors manage the emerging chaos, I realized that the SSTC and the Globe were in this technical difficulty together, and that the problems I was witnessing were very much shared.

On day two, the opening storytelling was much tighter, the surtitles both more accurately timed and more detailed. Something else was new, too: on this second day the surtitles clearly framed the actors' performances 'as an offering' to South Sudan. As I wrote on my blog post about the production for the Globe, '[t]his notion of performance as offering' set the tone for the rest of the piece 'as a gift given *first* to the absent and unfinished nation, and only *then* shared amongst the spectators in the global capital'.[4] Naturally, the SSTC wanted to present their best work in London and to leave proud of their achievement; hence they had worked the show overnight, solving problems and expanding their repertoires of communication. At the same time, though, their second performance made crystal clear for all spectators that they did not undertake this work *for* the Globe or its audiences. They did it *first* for South Sudan and only then brought it *to* the Globe, to us in the yard and the galleries. This distinction strikes me as crucial: as the actors carried on with *Cymbeline*'s complicated politics and ridiculous buffoonery they invoked the place none of us could see but many of us probably imagined (thanks to the show's press) we already knew; further, they raised the spectre of South Sudan not only as a place of war and struggle but also as one of laughter and pleasure, of joy.

READY OR NOT, HERE THEY COME

Web-savvy spectators looking for more information about *Cymbeline* and the SSTC will doubtless have seen both the Globe's 'official' trailer for the show (available on the Globe's website) as well as the SSTC's own promotional one (available through the company's home site).[5] The Globe trailer foregrounds the SSTC's difficult national context and celebrates the work of translator and director Joseph Abuk; the SSTC's foregrounds the disparities in experience and resources between the SSTC and the Globe team assigned to help them. Together, the two promotional spots capture a much more complicated image of both the company and its mythic struggle than the majority of media reports offered.

The Globe's official trailer begins with an aerial view of Juba, quickly replaced by a mid-range shot of bodies chanting and dancing in the street. Next, we see one of the SSTC team members on a street corner, flanked by roaming oxen; he tells us he is 'waiting for the script, so that I can make copies to distribute to the actors'. It's a 'big project', he says, as a mototaxi pulls up with the goods strapped on the back. The message is clear: this 'big project' is almost too big for this place; will the actors be able to pull it off? As we follow the script in a car to a photocopying machine, words fade up on screen: 'the newest country in the world ... takes on its most ambitious cultural challenge yet'.

The camera then focuses on Buturs Peter, who will play Jackimo. 'The language is so difficult', he says in Juba, smiling broadly as he flips through his photocopied script, before exclaiming, 'If anyone can translate this, that's Joseph Abuk.' Next, we see Abuk in his small dirt garden, sitting on a plastic chair next to a transistor radio; again, the cut seems designed to raise just a bit of doubt. But then, moments later, we see a close-up of Abuk, his laptop in the shot, as he references 'the new beginning from page three . . . '. He sounds poised and confident, and he speaks clear English. Perhaps our assumptions about this man, this place, need checking.

The beginning of the Globe trailer is all about setting us up for a fall: yes, these people *can* do this; no, this place is *not* so very far from the Globe. It's a smart way to encourage audiences to 'get into' the story of the production by reminding us of the SSTC's lack of resources but then encouraging us to dwell on its assets instead. The piece goes on to celebrate Abuk as a great, inspirational South Sudanese writer, to be set perhaps alongside Shakespeare as the inspirational force behind the Globe to Globe Festival. In its second half the trailer introduces the Sudanese war, and we learn that Abuk was persecuted at that time; he explains the parallel between those war experiences and Pelarius' in the play. The soundtrack becomes thoughtful as we hear that Abuk was very active before the war, and that this project 'is *bringing him back*'. We see Abuk's face break into laughter, and then loud, joyous music returns to round out various close-ups of individual performers.

The Globe's trailer honours the work of Abuk and his actors and serves as a generous introduction to them, but it also, crucially, reminds us that Shakespeare – his 'light' and his universal appeal, if not his specific words – will be the agent of their transport to London, bringing their story to the Globe in a way not possible *without* Shakespeare. Abuk is the hero of the official trailer, but the Bard is his muse; in this way, the Globe trailer creates a familiar and comforting narrative in which one great artist supports another while the power of music, song and dance does the rest of the work to bridge the gaps between them.

The SSTC's trailer, meanwhile, is whimsical, charming and in places self-deprecating; it also conveys a quite different experience of making *Cymbeline* from that presented by the official video. It opens and closes with Shakespeare's (amused) face – the Droeshout portrait as it appears in shots of the banner affixed to the Bankside wall of the Globe – but it begins in earnest on the Globe stage, as Abuk receives a lesson in Elizabethan public theatre structures from the Globe's Associate Movement Director, Glynn MacDonald. MacDonald points to the 'heart', 'gods' and 'belly' of the auditorium as Abuk follows with his eyes, looking uncertain. His perplexed expression subtly undercuts the somewhat exaggerated import of the information on offer. Soon, both he and MacDonald break into laughter at the idea of 'the big god up there' (Abuk points at the sky), and cheery guitar music takes us to Juba. Next, we see the actors' living quarters, bodies curled in low beds with very basic dressings, but these spaces are not presented as strange or mean; the soundtrack is cheerful, and we watch an actor fold his bedding, gather his things neatly and leave the room with a smile. Shakespeare is not a muse to be revealed here, as he is, to some degree, in the official video; he is not up there, in the gods, but down here amid the bedclothes and the mundane practicalities of getting the show on its feet. He is the devil in the (material) details.

The heart of the Globe's trailer is marked by the appearance of Abuk as protagonist; the heart of the company trailer, by contrast, is marked by the appearance of Raz Shaw, a London-based director the British Council sent to Juba to assist the company as they prepared to mount the show. His role here, unlike that of Abuk's, is complicated. 'I'm worried', he says, as the camera moves amid resting actors slouched in the rehearsal room, 'I'm worried about this whole thing.' His body too is slouched, his hand over his head; he looks irritated and despondent. The next shot features him seated with the SSTC's Nichola Franco Lado in a courtyard, work papers strewn between them. When he speaks, his frustration is palpable – but so is his distance from the lives, experiences and working methods of those he has been sent to supervise:

SHAW: Can we make sure that *all* these people are available tomorrow? So that we can have one day, it would be great to have *one whole day*, where we do some *normal work*. Just so that we get some . . . *fucking discipline* into this room. (*Sighs*)
FRANCO LADO: But the situation here in Juba is different, different than in any other place –
SHAW: I know, I understand that, I understand that it's a different culture. But if they can't do that, then they can't do this thing!
FRANCO LADO: They will do it.

No soundtrack plays beneath this exchange, although parts of it are intercut with sounds and images of the actors in the rehearsal room. The mood in the quiet courtyard is tense, although Shaw is never less than respectful. The first time I saw this scene, I felt truly uncomfortable; trailers don't typically reveal tension or anger. On the contrary, they tend to celebrate creation as a largely seamless, linear process of challenge-and-overcome. Just as significantly, the tension this moment exposes is not dismissed (as it might be in a story told with less nuance) as 'racism': Shaw is very clearly struggling to reach across the cultural barrier he has encountered in Juba. He understands his job as managing actors from 'a different culture', but the banal emptiness of that phrase very clearly cannot account for what he and the actors working with him are facing as their radically different ways of being and knowing, their substantial disparities of training and professional resources, collide with one another in the process of *Cymbeline*'s creation. In this way, the trailer shows us just how hard, for both the Sudanese team and the English team, that process is, and what a significant role the lack of professional resources in Juba plays in the attempt to make work 'worthy' of Shakespeare's Globe.

The hard moment between Shaw and Franco Lado passes and the focus shifts to Margaret Kowarto (Innogen) and Francis Paulino (Posthumous) rehearsing in front of a house. They come together as Kowarto speaks her lines; suddenly a passer-by moves into the shot. 'Excuse me, we're in the middle of a performance',

Kowarto says to him, matter-of-fact, 'What are you thinking? Can't you see they're filming?' The passer-by largely ignores her and moves on. 'That's typical!' she says, frustrated. The soundtrack keeps the moment cheeky, light, but the link with Shaw's outburst in the previous scene is nevertheless clear. Like him, Kowarto is frustrated; like him, she wants things to run more smoothly, more professionally. Lest we imagine the story we are viewing is one of 'us' versus 'them' – Shaw/the British Council versus the actors, South Sudan or Africa itself – Kowarto reminds us that the lack she and her fellow actors face is not somehow culturally innate but very much material, political, economic. The SSTC actors are not mythic heroes, and they are not stereotypical, lazy 'others': they are working actors in a place that lacks infrastructure, proper wages and a host of other basic resources many London audience members take for granted. They are doing their best under tricky circumstances, and, as Franco Lado says, 'they will do it'.

The screen splashes the words 'Ready or not'. The trailer's punchline has to wait, though, as we see an intervening shot of a van racing down a dirt road. 'We're going to get our passports!' the actors shout excitedly, reminding viewers one more time of the stakes of this production for them, of the material difference their work on *Cymbeline* (might) make to their futures. Then we read: 'Here they come' – as in, whether the show is ready or not, here they come. As in, whether the Globe is ready or not, here they come. It's one more bit of whimsy, but it is also an emphatic statement of this company's human right, ready or not, to occupy the space at the centre of Western culture that Globe to Globe has offered them. The trailer ends back in London with a view across the Thames, followed by a shot of Abuk alone on the Globe stage. 'Hello', he says, 'Hello, gentlemen and gentle ladies.' He opens his arms expansively, gesturing at the imagined groundlings, and then laughs expansively as the video lands once more on Shakespeare's face. Abuk's laughter colours in the Droeshout grey.

SENSES OF ENDINGS

The SSTC's trailer demonstrates the specific infrastructural challenges the company faced in making *Cymbeline*, and also the significant differences in context between Juba and London, sites of its creation and reception. These differences were also evident in several of the company's staging choices. Because only a handful of South Sudanese community members attended each show, the SSTC faced the added challenge of making themselves understood across the Globe's large open-air stage without a language base among spectators to cue non-speakers' reactions. The default solution in such situations is to play for outsized, easily recognizable moments of laughter, which many of the SSTC actors did and on which the reviews picked up, but more interesting for me were those performances that sought neither comedy nor pathos but more complicated emotions that referenced the charged world(s) in which this production was created and ultimately took place. Victor Lado was exemplary as Belarius, an old man fighting an ancient enemy from whom he bears virtually no difference, as was Dominic Gorgory as Cloten. While Cloten is often singled out in productions of *Cymbeline* as comically oafish, Gorgory's was a wronged man, misunderstood and in desperate search of justice, genuinely furious with Innogen and deeply hurt by her lack of respect. His heartfelt anger during their confrontation referenced his bare need in that moment, a need unrecognized by the privileged princess and perhaps by spectators as well: he was seeking not just sex, but an unbreachable alliance with the king's daughter, a measure of political power not otherwise accessible to him. His rage was so palpable that almost no spectators laughed during this scene; the contrast he offered to the broad comedy elsewhere on stage placed the stakes of his struggle into high relief, momentarily making tangible the high stakes of this performance for the SSTC as well.

Cymbeline ended (like many of the Festival's performances) with a curtain call that gestured at the groundlings and celebrated our collective pleasure in the actors' work. But the SSTC's was a call with a difference: in the spirit of making Shakespeare raw, materializing the otherwise mythical bard, and in the wake of their hard working-through of their own material challenges between Juba and London, the SSTC actors barely paused to bow, beginning almost immediately to ululate, sing and dance. From the back of the stage they moved forward in formation, sliding effortlessly from the end of *Cymbeline* into a South Sudanese jam. They reached for spectators' hands, yes, but also handed us noisemakers, invited us to join in, to play their music with them. They pulled friends from home and from the London Sudanese community on stage to join in, too. Actors hugged each other while more boisterous dancing broke out on the lip of the thrust; the crowds remaining (and that was most of us) clapped, cheered and grooved along.

This improvised celebration could easily be read, like the haka performed in the yard following the Māori *Troilus and Cressida*, as an example of the profound links between and across cultural communities forged by the Festival. In other words, it can easily be read as a moment of differences overcome. Neo-liberal ideology prefers this reading: it is fun, it is inspiring, and it lets us off the hook for future work, for the labour yet required to make the SSTC a sustainable enterprise, South Sudan a truly live-able nation and home for the arts. Instead, I'd like to propose a reading of the *Cymbeline* curtain call as both less utopian and more material, more provocative.

For me, the South Sudanese performers' pit party hummed with the focus on material difference and material need that I saw in their opening 'offering', in their discordant trailer, and in their production's thoughtful juxtaposition of urgency and laughter – a light-hearted but still insistent pushback against mainstream accounts of who they are, how they got here, how they will go on, and whom their performances are for. At the curtain call, instead of standing apart from us to 'stand for' their work, the performers asked us to meet them in celebration. What were we celebrating? Their achievement and our pleasure in it, yes, but also, implicitly, their extended gift to the ever-absent referent – South Sudan. Finally, the SSTC used Shakespeare's *Cymbeline* not as muse or (simply) as inspiration, and certainly not as that 'big god' in the Globe's heavens, but as raw material, as improvised infrastructure, as prologue to an intensely performative, personal, extended performance of their new country and of the work that lies ahead of them as South Sudanese artists and citizens. Most importantly, they sang and danced and cheered that work as a collective undertaking, inviting us, urging us to join them.

ENDNOTES

1 Quoted in Erin Sullivan, 'Year of Shakespeare: *Cymbeline*', 8 May 2012, http://blogging shakespeare.com/year-of-shakespeare-cymbeline, 27 July 2012.

2 For examples see A.S.H. Smyth, 'Globe to Globe: *Cymbeline*, Shakespeare's Globe'. *The Arts Desk*, 4 May 2012, www.theartsdesk.com/theatre/globe-globe-cymbeline-shakespeares-globe-0, 27 July 2012; and Matt Trueman, '*Cymbeline* – Reviews'. *Guardian*, 4 May 2012, www.guardian.co.uk/stage/2012/may/04/cymbeline-globe-review, 27 July 2012.

3 Smyth, 'Globe to Globe: *Cymbeline*'.

4 'The South Sudan *Cymbeline*', 3 May 2012, http://blog.shakespearesglobe.com/the-south-sudan-cymbeline-reviewed-by-kim-solga/, 18 September 2012.

5 Trailer for *Cymbeline* (*Juba Arabic, South Sudan*), Shakespeare's Globe 2012, Youtube, www.youtube.com/watch?v=9ZxWOKa4MyQ, 27 July 2012, and *Shakespeare in South Sudan*, Trailer for *Cymbeline*, by the South Sudan Theatre Company, Banyak Films 2012, http://vimeo.com/channels/southsudantheatre, 27 July 2012.

CHAPTER TWELVE

TITUS IN NO MAN'S LAND

The Tang Shu-wing Theatre Studio's Production

Adele Lee

Frequently dubbed a 'cultural desert', Hong Kong is not typically associated with high art or theatrical experimentalism. Better known for its shopping malls and skyscrapers, the former British colony – and one of the 'four Asian dragons' (see p. 86, note 14) – is primarily a world financial centre, and finding cultural opportunities there can be challenging. In regards to Shakespeare, who constituted an important component in the colonial education system, the territory equally has not been known for its avant-garde proclivities. Approaches to Shakespeare, first performed in 1867 for the purpose of entertaining the expatriate community, have tended to be highly conservative/canonical, and theatre companies have usually shied away from political or theatrical radicalism and, indeed, from adapting the plays for local appreciation.[1] And even though more recently (that is, post-1997), thanks largely to the efforts of directors like Daniel S. P. Yang and Law Ka-ying, there have been growing attempts to localize Shakespeare and to adapt his works in a more bold and progressive manner, Hong Kong, in cultural matters, continues to 'manifest itself officially in the most hidebound and reactionary terms'.[2] It is not surprising, then, that Shakespeare in Hong Kong – which is positioned on the fringes of two Asian giants (China and Japan) – is on the sidelines of Shakespeare in Asia studies. It is not surprising, either, that the announcement that a Cantonese theatre troupe would be performing *Titus Andronicus*, one of the less critically acclaimed Shakespeare plays (Edward Ravenscroft notoriously described it as 'a heap of rubbish'),[3] at the Globe to Globe Festival did not inspire high expectations.

The Tang Shu-wing Theatre Studio, however, offered an understated, thought-provoking and reasonably effective version of Shakespeare's Roman tragedy. It also, in general, successfully captured both the horrific and comic elements of the play, although one suspects the director intended the production to be taken a little more seriously than it was. In fact, some of the laughter – such as that in reaction to Titus' reappearance on the stage after having chopped his own hand off which was due to the unnecessary surtitle 'Titus re-enters with his hand chopped off' – was clearly unsolicited. Similarly unsolicited, I presumed, was the laughter that attended: the rape scene, comical due to the miscasting of the baby-faced Eric Tang Chi-kin in the role of Chiron; the scene involving Aaron's killing of the nurse made absurd by the playing of the latter role, for no obvious reason, in drag; and the scene in which Quintus and Martius fall into the pit, likened by Josh Spero to something from the TV sitcom *Men Behaving Badly*.[4] By contrast, puns supposed to provoke laughter, like the infamous one regarding hands in Act 3 Scene 2, were met with stony silence. All of this emphasized the production's occasional problems with tone – a criticism that has, however, long been levelled at the source material.

According to the Globe website, 'the hybrid culture of Hong Kong informs this production', suggesting that Hong Kong's oft-commented-upon liminality[5] – its condition of being caught between two worlds, East and West – is evident in this adaptation. Certainly, the production seemed to promote both Eastern collectivism and Western individualism, while the acting style oscillated (rather incongruously, at times) between Eastern stylization and Western realism. Thus, in terms of style *and* content, the production revealed the hybrid identity of the former colony and this theatre troupe which had been appropriately called 'No Man's Land' when it was first formed in the year of the 'handover'.

The Andronici, broken in spirit from the very outset, also seemed to occupy a kind of no man's land in this production. Caught in the middle of the divide between the Goths (dressed, predictably, in black) and the Romans (dressed in white), they were suitably attired completely in grey – a colour that also underscored their moral and ethical dubiousness. Furthermore, the Andronici's ambivalent stance towards the Goths and Romans, and their subsequent shifting of allegiances, could be said to mirror Hong Kong Chinese ambivalence towards mainland China and Britain, and the sense of uncertainty in the territory as to which country represents the lesser evil.[6] The monochrome clothing meant, however, that Titus (Ng Wai-shek) and family often seemed to lack character and, at times, unfortunately, even presence.[7] Moreover, the cast sometimes appeared ill at ease with and even overwhelmed by the venue, and did not always manage to successfully fill the playing space. One notable exception to this, though, was when Quintus and Martius passed through the yard bare-chested, with their feet shackled and their outstretched arms tied to wooden planks (this is rumoured to be a common form of torture in the People's Republic of China), on their way to execution. They were followed by their distraught father – who dropped right to the ground at one point – pleading to the crowd for their lives and thereby achieving what was arguably the most dramatically hard-hitting moment in the whole production.

Of course, it was the intention of the director – known in some circles as 'the alchemist of minimalist theatre' – to present the play in as understated a fashion as possible, and the cast's plain costumes and restrained performances were in keeping with the bare stage and lack of special effects. However, as stated, it resulted in the characters lacking individuality, and, for this reason, it was difficult to empathize with them or get any real sense of the horror of their situation. Even Lavinia, whom Lai Yuk-ching played (intentionally?) as rather prim and spoilt, failed to elicit much sympathy from the audience. And the covering of her clenched fists in red silk gloves was too neat and stylized to convey adequately the atrocities afflicted on her body. As is often the case in stage representations of Lavinia, her body is aestheticized to the extent that the audience can forget her suffering. In a way, the identities of Titus and family were not so much hybrid or even 'floating'[8] as non-existent. This is apt, given Shakespeare's play's central concern with the annihilation of the individual in the service of the state (notably, some members of the Andronici wore the 'Mao suits' associated with Communist China), but also given, as Ackbar Abbas has pointed out, Hong Kong's peculiar lack of identity due to its being 'not so much a place as a space of transit' whose inhabitants regard themselves as transients and migrants on their way from China to elsewhere.[9]

The overall colourlessness of the Andronici allowed the distinctively clad and psychologically complex Aaron, played brilliantly by Chu Pak-hong, to stand out as the most intriguing and charismatic character in the production. (Though Tamora, played with gusto by Pang Ngan-ling, it should be mentioned, similarly 'sparkled' – and this wasn't just because of her sequined outfit.) 'Edgy' rather than racially 'Other', Aaron wore a leather jacket, had long hair, and sported several tattoos and body-piercings. This is not surprising, since Chinese directors of Shakespeare tend to ignore the issue of race and rarely cast foreign actors of the same race as the characters.[10] What was surprising, however, and somewhat ridiculous, was the retaining of the lines relating to Aaron's blackness and the use of a plastic black doll to represent his and Tamora's baby – a 'prop' that, again, led to considerable, inappropriate giggling. Surely translator Rupert Chan should have revised the original in order to accommodate the fact that this production's 'Moor' did not have a 'fleece of woolly hair' (2.3.34); nor was he 'of another leer' (4.2.101) to the other characters. Instead, Chan remained unflinchingly faithful to Shakespeare's text, thereby highlighting Hong Kong Chinese conservatism and their reluctance to change or, more accurately, 'Cantonize' revered English classics. Ultimately, it was this lack of daring that resulted in Tang Shu-wing's *Titus Andronicus* being potentially, rather than actually, wonderful.

ENDNOTES

1 Dorothy Wong, '"Domination by Consent": A Study of Shakespeare in Hong Kong', in Theo D'haen and Patricia Krüs, eds., *Colonizer and Colonized* (Amsterdam: Rodopi, 2000), pp. 43–56.

2 M. Ingham, '"Bottom, thou aren't translated": Shakespeare in Asian English-Language Productions', in Tam Kwok-kan, ed., *Shakespeare Global/Local: The Hong Kong Imaginary in Transcultural Production* (New York: Peter Lang, 2002), p. 30.

3 E. Ravenscroft, 'From his Adaptation of *Titus Andronicus* 1678', in Brian Vickers, ed., *William Shakespeare: The Critical Heritage: 1623–1692* (London: Routledge, 1974), pp. 205–13.

4 Josh Spero, 'Globe to Globe: *Titus Andronicus*, Shakespeare's Globe: The Cantonese take on internecine Roman slaughter', *The Arts Desk*, 8 May 2012, www.theartsdesk.com/theatre/ globe-globe-titus-andronicus-shakespeares-globe.

5 See Chan Kwok-bun, ed., *Hybrid Hong Kong* (London and New York: Routledge, 2012), for instance.

6 The appropriation of Shakespeare in Hong Kong to explore the triangular relationship between Hong Kong, China and Britain is discussed in A. Lee, '"Chop-Socky Shake-speare?!": The Bard Onscreen in Hong Kong', *Shakespeare Bulletin*, 28.4 (2010): 459–80.

7 Andrew Dickson. '*Titus Andronicus* – Review', *Guardian*, 10 May 2012, www.guardian.co.uk/ stage/2012/may/10/titus-andronicus-shakespeares-globe-review, 28 January 2013.

8 This is a term that director Clara Law and others often use to describe Hong Kong and its population.

9 Ackbar Abbas, *Hong Kong: Culture and the Politics of Disappearance* (Minneapolis: University of Minnesota Press, 2002), p. 4.

10 Alexander C.Y. Huang, *Chinese Shakespeares: Two Centuries of Cultural Exchange* (New York: Columbia University Press, 2009), p. 180.

Fig. 6 Titus Andronicus (Ng Wai-shek), Lavinia (Lai Yuk-chin), Lucius Andronicus (Cheung Ming-yiu) and Martius Andronicus (Leung Ka-wai), *Titus Andronicus*, Tang Shu-wing Theatre Studio from Hong Kong; director Tang Shu-wing.

CHAPTER THIRTEEN

TANG SHU-WING'S TITUS AND THE ACTING OF VIOLENCE

Yong Li Lan

While the Globe to Globe Festival had been conceived as Shakespeare in many languages, its role and timing in the 2012 London Olympics prompted audiences and companies to assess a production's efficacy as representation of the nation of native speakers. Of the thirty-seven productions in the Festival, *Titus Andronicus* was one of the few that could not be regarded as a national performance, because it came from Hong Kong and was performed in Cantonese. In contrast, a few days earlier, the National Theatre of China had played *Richard III* in Mandarin, and the company's representation of China had surfaced the more strongly during the sense of crisis that the actors performed under, owing to their elaborate set and costumes failing to arrive.[1] In a coincidence that might be read as a sequel to their enforced bare-bones style, the actors of *Titus Andronicus* (titled simply *Titus* in Cantonese) came on dressed in basic white, grey or black T-shirts and leggings. They performed Scene 1 sitting on a long row of chairs at the edge of the stage facing the audience, suggesting a rehearsal of their individual parts. Only after this scene did they put on the costumes that were placed folded in front of each chair, to embody their roles in a more naturalistic interaction. These costumes were formal, Western-style coats and dresses that indicated character types, in the same monochromatic shades. The director, Tang Shu-wing, states that this monochromy was intended to make each group of characters symbolic: 'white for royalty, black for darkness [the Goths], and grey for Titus' family who are in between – they have something evil, but also something pure'.[2] The actors of *Richard III* had been forced by shipping delays to perform without the ornate visual support that the company had designed as a display of Chinese cultural heritage, and to rely fully on the acting skills that, superb as they are, conventionally depend on costume to articulate them. On the other hand, *Titus* was conceived in a minimalist aesthetic that metatheatrically communicated the acting of the play by a non-English company, positioned at an angle to naturalist conventions of English Shakespeare performance. Not bearing the burden of a national performance, Titus also manifestly resisted putting on a cultural performance, defined by Milton Singer as an exhibition that manifests a cultural tradition to both those outside and inside it.[3]

Seen together, the two Chinese performances mutually illuminated the question in each other: what is Chinese, or intercultural, in a performance of Shakespeare without the spectacle of Chinese theatre traditions? Consciously or not, the gestural, aural, musical and visual virtuosity of classical Asian theatres (some dating from Shakespeare's time) is the difference that Asian performance is expected to make to his plays. Tang said of his experience at Globe to Globe, 'A Western audience looks for symbolic and easily identifiable cultural markers, and when these things are not there they feel dissatisfied and feel anyone can do it. They want to see how you represent your culture.' Yet the association of Asian theatrical traditions with beauty and spectacle is also problematic when brought to bear on Shakespeare, because the Western (and specifically Shakespearean) metaphysical tradition posits visual spectacle and show as external, and therefore superficial, and often deceptive, as opposed to the inner reality of consciousness revealed through language. If these performances are not reducible to Shakespeare in another language – that is, a foreign language – how might a spectator who doesn't follow that language engage their cultural identity when the visual exhibition is dialled down?

I argue that instead of a cultural performance exhibiting a holistically imagined tradition, the politics of an historical relationship to Shakespeare were crucially, and more interestingly, performative in the theatricality of Titus. A production of Shakespeare in Hong Kong, a British colony until 1997, necessarily negotiates parallel theatre histories and audiences of English and Cantonese Shakespeare productions.[4] Tang Shu-wing's Titus has its own history in two earlier versions he directed,[5] whose trajectory may be seen as a passage between several theatre cultures. Drawing on the naturalism conventional to English Shakespeare performance, traditional Chinese storytelling and modernist acting theory, the different versions experimented with how to position a relationship to Shakespeare in an ex-British colony, now an offshore part of China, in the twenty-first century. Tang says he moved from violence as a 'subject of representation' to a 'subject of investigation'.[6]

All three versions followed Shakespeare's story with the sustained intensity that marks Tang's work on this play, but they employed different acting approaches, and thereby presented differing treatments of the human subject in extreme violence. The first Titus, in 2008, used a commissioned translation of the play (by Rupert Chan) to set itself apart from the staging traditions of English productions. The bare set stringently avoided cultural, historical or social reference. The actors were dressed in generic formal Western costumes, each in one symbolic colour – red for Titus, black for the Goths, pink for Lavinia – and the sparse props were also symbolic. Inflected by this minimalist and symbolic staging, the naturalistic conventions of verbal and bodily expression took on an abstracted effect, as of a drama out of time and place. The actors' entrance in track suits for the first scene, after the intermission and the curtain call, created a distinct transitional space between Shakespeare's play and the acting of it.

Tang developed this approach in *Titus 2.0* in 2009:

I wanted to break through the dramatic constraints: release the actors and myself from space, time and representation tied to realism. This was the reason for *Titus 2.0*. I was interested in the potential expressive power of an actor and narrator at the same time, who is an organic human being. Around the time I created *Titus 2.0* I identified five key human expressions: voice, facial expression, breathing, gesture, and spatial displacement or movement. Strangely speaking, there is another key language, which is percussion, which depends on an object, hence I call it marginal. The five I call key are created by the human being himself and are realized in his body. I wanted to explore how to use these key expressions to tell a story. In doing so I found it phenomenal that each key expression has an impulse behind it that can be transformed into another form. You can use one single expression to tell the story, or combine several, or combine them with other forms. The pretext for creating *Titus 2.0* was not *Titus* itself, but to experiment with how to use these five expressions.

Titus 2.0 used an original script (by Cancer Chong) in more literary Cantonese than Chan's translation, which precisely followed Shakespeare's plot but in which narration of the action in the third person slipped in and out of direct first person speech. The actors took turns speaking both the direct and indirect speech, and while a specific actor was distinctly associated with one character, he or she did not always speak that character's lines and could also assume the role of a narrator. This movement between first and third person in the dramatization of the story and the acting created changing reflections, correspondences and dissonances between role and actor, *as part of* the feelings expressed and actions described by their words. Structuring the rhythm and development of the action, sequences of repetitive movements that expressed emotion in an economic manner were performed by the actors individually, in groups of two or three, and as an ensemble.

Tang's own acting method produced a way of relating to the characters and events that altered the company's return to naturalism in *Titus* 2012 at the Globe to Globe Festival. First, it made the gap visible between Shakespeare's play and the performing of it by actors from a non-Anglophone country, in a language other than English. Chan's translation was heavily edited, and its verbal delivery emphasized the aural character of Cantonese – for instance, by slowing to a deliberate word-by-word pace during the key or closing line of a speech. Much more formalized movement was introduced, creating the effect of an obsessive-compulsive emotion outside reason. Paradoxically for a play of terrible physical violence, the actors' bodily articulation in both their movements and speech expressed the psychological state of violence by avoiding the actual staging of physical violence. Thus, second, the characters were not, strictly speaking, fictional or individuated, but resembled archetypal dramatizations of a psychological condition. They gave the impression of being in the grip of a precise, articulate and immutable force individually generated and distinct in each of them. Inevitably, they were also presented more in terms of independent, complex pathologies of violence than as changing individuals or in interaction. For instance, the change in Lavinia after her rape was not dramatized in her ravaged appearance. Instead, appearing as neat as before except for her stark 'stumps' bound in red cloth, she contained violent emotions in decisive physical movements and sounds. As an ensemble, their physical force was tremendous and at the same time measured by the tableaux into which the action repeatedly resolved for a few seconds during its progress. Third, then, by these means of de-linking the actor and character to distil the psychological dimensions of the drama in physical terms, the performance of violence in this *Titus* partly emerged from the fiction as emblematic: this production was not about a set of people in any particular context but instead infused naturalism with formalism to depict states of violence in the mind.

The interaction of Chiron and Demetrius with Lavinia (Act 2 Scene 3) offers one example among many that can be compared across the three productions. In the first version, she was dressed in a light pink skirt and blouse and the brothers in dark striped jackets. They moved freely and spontaneously as they taunted and grabbed her, while she was tearfully frantic. Their manhandling of Lavinia was a preparation for their subsequent violence towards her, but it remained quite decorous in actual terms. In the second version, four actors, Kin, Qing, Ivy and Andy, who were identified with the characters and all dressed alike, took turns to speak the mixture of narration and first person speech. They stood in front of their chairs, moved towards and away from the audience, and performed tense, contorted movements that expressed the feelings of their lines. The rape was depicted with Qing (Lavinia) lying on the stage on her back, her legs bent at the knees and pointing away from the audience, her back arched, and arms and head stretched out behind her, while Kin and Andy (Chiron and Demetrius) panted heavily in turn. The actors did not touch or face each other at all. In the third version, Chiron and Demetrius, wearing black, stood at left and right down stage, holding their daggers pointed phallically at Lavinia in a grey dress who knelt by Bassianus' body dressed in white at centre stage. Tamora and Lavinia held their stances quite statically between definite movements at intervals during their dialogue. The lines were heavily cut and delivered with an intense yet measured force. The brothers walked quickly off and on stage again in unison in reaction to certain lines. They did not touch Lavinia until the end of the scene, when they dragged her off, but expressed their menace to her the more effectively for the lack of bodily contact. Chiron watched Lavinia plead with his mother with an intent look on his face, moved his left hand in a suggestive manner near his crotch and twitched his right leg with rough, jerky movements.

The differences in the treatment of this scene between the three versions show the evolution that Tang's approach to *Titus* has undergone. From a naturalism that projects Lavinia's rape as a realistic interaction between the characters, and which has limits in its capacity to portray an act as physically and psychologically violent as this; to an intense violence expressed in the body, but paradoxically depicted as experienced in the mind of individual characters; and, last, to a more formalized presentation in which the actors' raw physical expressions remained barely cushioned within the fiction. Interpreted in terms of the geo-cultural politics of generic conventions, these three productions of *Titus* can be understood as delineating a movement from some degree of alliance with the stage tradition of English Shakespeare, to a radical break with that tradition and its cultural embeddedness, and then a return to that tradition to synthesize it with an individual approach, that, fittingly, was occasioned by the company's return of their Shakespeare to the Globe. Precisely because none of Tang's versions of *Titus* displayed Chinese or Cantonese theatre forms or culture in features of the stage presentation, his *Titus* requires one to reconsider current understandings of interculturality. In particular, his experiments in how actors enact and express a story in the latter two productions re-engaged the conception of the human subject that is central to a common understanding of Shakespeare's significance. Tang recounts that in working on his method of acting for *Titus* 2.0, he was reminded of Brecht's alienation effect and was also influenced by Gao Xing Jian's 'tri-partition of the actor': the person, the neutral actor and the character. This tri-partition radically reconfigures the binary of actor–character so fundamental to Western critiques of role, character and the individual subject in Shakespeare's plays. As opposed to this binary, according to Tang, 'there are overtones of the actor playing the character in the narrator. These transitions between actor, character and narrator are crucial for the human being, and this is also part of Eastern philosophy and religion.' Reducing the demands of the spectacle on our attention may be necessary in order to recognize what might be called a metaphysical interculturality. This can be seen in *Titus* and may well be true of other productions that draw on non-Western belief systems.

ENDNOTES

1 See Lee Chee Keng's 'Performing cultural exchange in *Richard III*: Intercultural display and personal reflections', Chapter 7 in this volume, pp. 75–82.

2 Personal interview in English with Tang Shu-wing, 29 July 2012. Unless otherwise indicated, all quotations from Tang Shu-wing are excerpted from this interview.

3 Milton Singer, *Traditional India: Structure and Change* (Philadelphia: American Folklore Society, 1959).

4 For an account of an English-language production of *A Midsummer Night's Dream* in 1992, see Mike Ingham, 'Shakespeare in Asian English-Language Productions', in Kwok-Kan Tam, Andrew Parkin and Terry Siu-han Yip. eds., *Shakespeare Global/Local: The Hong Kong Imaginary in Transcultural Production* (Frankfurt: Peter Lang, 2002), pp. 29–42.

5 Full-length videos of the two earlier versions are archived at the Asian Shakespeare Intercultural Archive (A|S|I|A), http://a-s-i-a-web.org, which also contains the production scripts, translations and a scholarly apparatus that I have drawn upon for this chapter.

6 Chan Fai Kin, ed., '*Taitesi jinhualun: Zuotan Taitesi* 2.0 [On the Evolution of *Titus Andronicus*: An Informal Discussion of *Titus Andronicus* 2.0]', *Artism* (October 2009): 19–23, 22.

CHAPTER FOURTEEN

'A STRANGE BROOCH IN THIS ALL-HATING WORLD'

Ashtar Theatre's *Richard II*

Samuel West

Before the death of Steven Pimlott, for whom I played Richard II at the RSC, he and I discussed filming the White Box production that we'd done at The Other Place in 2000. We thought long and hard about a proper space for this modern-dress version that could encompass the White Box's triple identity as laboratory, operating theatre and madhouse. Eventually we decided it would be exciting to film it after hours at the National Portrait Gallery (NPG), with Richard standing before pictures of his Tudor successors before wandering down the uncluttered corridors of the twenty-first century to look at photographs of Kate Moss and muse on the nature of celebrity and kingship. I'm sorry we never got to do it, partly because it's a good idea, antidotal to the BBC *Hollow Crown* which (good though it was) presented a fairly conventional view of *Richard II* as a play of pageantry, spectacle and divine right, and partly because our NPG version might have been a worthy pendant to this one by Ashtar Theatre, which was aggressively secular and political at every turn.

The original Globe was named at a time when theatre wasn't embarrassed to trumpet its significance; perhaps the greatest achievement of this Globe to Globe Festival is to remind us of that. The Greeks thought life on stage was useful while we decided how best to live our lives off stage. Now we name our theatres after actors or monarchs. Now is the summer of our Diamond Jubilee. What, today, is the global significance of *Richard II*? The play has been many things to many people: a hymn to the divine right of kings, an exploration of what it means to be mortal, fuel to those about to attempt a coup. Inevitably with this production the last of those looms largest. On 7 February 1601, supporters of the Earl of Essex paid the Chamberlain's Men to stage a performance of *Richard II* the night before their armed rebellion. Where did they stage it? At the Globe, of course.

The quotation in the title is from *Richard II* 5.5.66.

Palestinian company Ashtar are based in Ramallah, in the West Bank. The company has daily experience of performing and rehearsing (or trying to rehearse) under occupation. Their tale of the toppling of a dictator throws up countless echoes of life beyond the walls of the theatre. It began like a nightmare: an elderly man, who we are told is Gloucester, is brought out of his prison in the earth. He checks his face for deeper wrinkles; he's offered water by his hooded captors. He is allowed to shave. They slit his throat with his own razor.

Richard (a detailed, witty performance from Sami Metwasi) enters, shakes hands with the front row, then wipes his hand with a handkerchief, an item which Richard is sometimes credited with inventing. *Richard II* is often overlaid with lazy reverence for the semi-divine job of kingship, and in this country it would be almost impossible to find a production that so completely eschewed religious imagery as Ashtar's did. There are no candles, no incense, no singing; it's hardly like the 1980s RSC at all. There's little debate about the king's two bodies; Metwasi seems happy enough in one. He's not the Messiah, he's a very naughty boy: neither divine nor right. In place of religion we get factionalism and family. In Ramallah I once bought a book of Arabic sayings illustrated with cartoons. It's called *The Son of a Duck is a Floater*; the English equivalent is 'Like father, like son'. By the end of Ashtar's *Richard II* I thought an idiomatic translation should be closer to 'Blood is thicker than water.' Because family matters, in these family matters.

In staging the factions, some people always wear uniform (Bolingbroke, Percy), some always wear suits (Gaunt, York) and some, like Richard, switch. Metwasi's Richard seems happier in civvies – and looks sharper. As soon as he can he removes his tie, and Greene gives him a mirror to check his reflection. For his visit to the dying Gaunt he puts on another, even brighter tie – the opposite of mourning. He's moody and mercurial; when York (a nuanced, funny George Ibrahim) gives him both barrels after Richard confiscates Gaunt's estate, Richard whistles and checks his wife's nails while he holds her hand against his cheek.

The Globe's painted stage isn't particularly helpful, except to make the dictator's palace look gaudy – the theatrical equivalent of Donald Trump's malachite hand-basins. On it, the play sounds great: a muscular, mouth-filling meal. The performance was advertised as being in Palestinian Arabic, but I'm told by an Arab friend that the translation was pretty much Standard – apart from one extraordinary scene. The Welsh captain's news that his men have left the tardy Richard and allied with Bolingbroke is usually taken as a sad blow to the king's fortunes; here it was flipped on its head. A few lines of Salisbury's testimony from Act 3 Scene 2 were shifted backwards; after the captain's catalogue of ominous signs, the surtitles told us 'The people are crying out for Bolingbroke' and suddenly the outside world came banging in: the stage was filled with people shouting slogans (these *were* in Palestinian Arabic), an unmistakable Arab Spring uprising full of bloodstained flags and screamed revolt against the absent king. It was also hard not to think of Hamas/Fatah infighting, each tribe out to better the other; I'm told that Arabic can reflect this diversity – a vast array of dialects, each with its own constituency. I wish I were able to hear that. One of my other favourites from *The Son of a Duck* is 'For lack of horses they saddle dogs.' If Metwasi's regime is broken, should the people have faith in Nicola Zreineh as his successor, Bolingbroke? But he seems equally earth-bound, equally tainted. Will the revolution turn out like Tunisia's, or Syria's? On 4 March, Ashtar's first night in London, two people were killed and several hundred injured in protests in Egypt. Levantine power struggles were being played out beyond the walls.

And in whose name is this power exercised, anyway? The people aren't friendly: when Richard is led through the street they throw fruit from the balconies and in return he spits at them. The women's lamentation, in headscarves and in black, is powerful, clamorous, reaching upwards into the clouds. It reminds us of countless others we've seen on the news where beloved sons or husbands have been lost to terror. This was one of the few times I've been pleased that the Globe has no roof; another was in the deposition scene, when a helicopter flew over just as Richard said 'here cousin, seize the crown', and he and Bolingbroke paused to watch it pass.

This is a play in which the word 'earth' occurs twenty-nine times and 'ground' another twelve, and they both have prominent parts in some pretty famous speeches. In Ashtar's version this connection is implied, not stated. It's there in the rooted connection with the stage that the best actors have. It's there in the fine stillness of the actresses. And it's highlighted by its absence in the king. He claims a special relationship to the dust of the country, but it's just talk. On his return from Ireland, greeting his estranged daughter England from whom he's been absent too long, Richard pats the stage, proprietary but patronizing. He doesn't speak for the trees. He's out of touch. The seesaw of Act 3 Scene 2 is big and fast; for this scene to work, Richard's effort to drag himself out of despair must be genuine, and ultimately successful. He begins by taking the metaphor of himself as the sun and with evangelical certainty running with it for eighteen lines. In the past, doubt about his relationship with God has nearly upset him; he comes back from Ireland with mad certainty. Much better to allow himself the belief that he is God's anointed, and should behave that way. Metwasi is terrific here. He meets the scene's rushing disappointments with speed and depth. As the seesaw heads downwards, an access of self-knowledge, a quick rush of almost-euphoria, takes him to the edge of the stage; he hangs his legs over the front to tell the audience of the 'death of kings' (3.2.156), only to recoil from his own vision on 'farewell, King!' (3.2.170). It's simple and touching. Elsewhere, there are moments of brilliant unsentimentality – the second gardener, thinking the queen's tears foolish, sends them up and sweeps away the seeds the first one has planted. Show me a British production that would risk republican sideswipes like that.

This production hurtles to its conclusion. It is never afraid to embrace comedy, which makes the decision to cut the Aumerle/York frontcloth business quite odd, but no less welcome. By the time Richard finds himself in prison, the production's speed and avoidance of the inner had made time for reflection. But we got very little of his great 'I have been studying' soliloquy (5.5.1–66); I wanted more. Most of Irish director Conall Morrison's decisions are helpful. His production is not deep or especially complex, but it's clear, fast and muscular. There's a recurring motif of someone sprinkling blood on a murdered character's eyes; they wake and become a witness to what follows. It's a good idea, which brings home just how much spying and how many murders there are in this extremely bloody play, and subtly sharpens the political teeth of the production. When Bolingbroke, in the play's final speech, promises to wash the blood from his guilty hand by making a pilgrimage to Jerusalem, the audience's laughter is bitter and plentiful. Nicola Zreineh said in a post-performance discussion that while his character could plan to go to Jerusalem, over 2,000 miles from London, as a Palestinian living in Bethlehem he was unable to visit a city only 6 miles away.

Fig. 7 Members of the company waving flags as the rebels, *Richard II*, Ashtar Theatre from Ramallah, Palestine; director Conall Morrison.

CHAPTER FIFTEEN

'WE WANT BOLINGBROKE'

Ashtar's Palestinian *Richard II*

Tamara Haddad

Ashtar Theatre's *Richard II* opened with a scene not found in Shakespeare's original text but one that is crucial to the action of the play: the murder of the duke of Gloucester. Two jailors gave Gloucester (George Ibrahim) a mirror and a razor, and, as he cautiously began to shave his face and look at himself in the mirror, his throat was cut by one of his captors. With his forehead covered in blood and a look of confusion on his face, Gloucester then watched from the background as the opening scene of Shakespeare's play unfurled on stage. In choosing to begin the performance with this scene, Irish director Conall Morrison brought to the fore the turmoil surrounding the reign of a humorously narcissistic Richard (Sami Metwasi). The powerful image of the captors – faces covered to avoid recognition – became quickly juxtaposed against the rich military attire of Henry Bolingbroke (Nicola Zreineh) and Thomas Mowbray (Ihab Zahdeh) as they accused each other of Gloucester's death. Each threw down his gage in anger and challenged the other to a duel; Richard exiled both from England for their behaviour and seized Bolingbroke's inheritance to fund battles in Ireland. Bolingbroke returned to reclaim his inheritance, and the Welsh abandoned Richard's cause to join Bolingbroke. The stage was then taken over by actors with covered faces carrying flags in Palestine's national colours and shouting 'We want Bolingbroke'; Palestinian flags were unfurled by some in the audience and remained on display until the end of the show.

The clever doubling of Gloucester and York (George Ibrahim) served to remind those who are familiar with the text of the subplot of Aumerle's treason against the king, although this part of the action was omitted because of time constraints. It would have been interesting to see how this would have played out and whether the duchess of Gloucester (Iman Aoun) would also have doubled as the duchess of York, recasting herself as the mother of a traitor. In addition to the doubling, the use of the playing space was also especially effective, allowing the earl of Northumberland (Edward Muallem) to move back and forth through the audience to convey messages between Richard and Bolingbroke, articulating the divide between the two characters on stage while they negotiated the terms of Bolingbroke's inheritance (see Colour Plate 6).

The characters were mainly dressed in contemporary and military attire, not signalling a specifically Palestinian cast except for the characters of the gardener and his wife (Raed Ayasa and Iman Aoun), both dressed in traditional Palestinian garb with cross-stitched designs. The costumes were immediately brought to the fore since the only major addition to the Globe's stage in its basic form was the throne. After the gardener revealed Richard's imprisonment to the queen (Bayan Shbib), in a moment of humour the gardener's wife kicked the plants he had just put in the ground, scattering the herbs he had planted for the queen's sorrow. Richard later crowned Bolingbroke as the new king, and as he placed the crown on Bolingbroke's head it slid down to his ears, lightening the mood during perhaps the most serious part of the action.

Richard was then given a mirror which he looked into before throwing it to the ground, a mirror that no longer reflected a king. He shattered the glass with his heel, reminding the audience of the mirror that Gloucester looked into just before his own death. In another attempt at bringing the play full circle, the queen met Richard as he made his way to Pontefract with her head covered in a black shawl, the same shawl worn by the duchess of Gloucester while she mourned her husband's death at the beginning of the play. Unlike Gloucester's jailers, however, Richard's captors were not disguised by scarves, although, like each of the other characters who are killed on stage, Richard's forehead was also anointed with blood. Bolingbroke then took the stage briefly and, in an addition to the original text, poured more blood on Richard's forehead to signal his role in the king's deposition. Like Gloucester, too, Richard got up in a state of confusion after he was killed and wandered to the front of the stage for the closing scene.

Aside from the later use of traditional Palestinian dress for the gardener and his wife and the figures waving flags in the national colours, there was little besides the language to suggest a particular association with Ashtar's homeland. In keeping with Shakespeare's use of formal English – the play has a marked lack of prose in the dialogue – Ashtar cautiously chose to present the play in Standard Arabic, a dialect associated with newspapers and official documents, rather than in the colloquial Palestinian dialect. The dialogue was heavily edited and modernized by Palestinian poet Gassan Zaqtan (based on Mohammad Anani's original translation of the text) and uses a language more widely accessible to those with knowledge of Arabic beyond the Palestinian borders. In approaching the performance in this way, Ashtar was able to keep the dialogue formal (though not adhering to a rhyme scheme or set rhythm). Nevertheless, it would have been interesting to see the play performed in a colloquial Palestinian dialect, perhaps even assigning the gardener and his wife a regional village dialect to convey their status.

Bolingbroke's vow to go on pilgrimage to Jerusalem at the end of the play would have been less effective, too, if the performance had already been set in Palestine – he would not have to suffer the hardship of travelling all the way from England for penance. In choosing to portray the setting and characters in a locale that is not clearly visible on stage, the broader themes of kingship and resistance remained easily accessible to an audience perhaps unaware of the nuances of Palestinian politics or culture that would have been present in a more nationalistic performance. This performance shows one way of adapting *Richard II* for audiences outside the English-speaking world and how Shakespeare remains relevant beyond the historical context of the Elizabethan stage.

CHAPTER SIXTEEN

O-THELL-O

Styling syllables, donning wigs, late capitalist, national 'scariotypes'

P.A. Skantze

Productions marked by nation, as in the Globe to Globe Festival, trigger expectations for the audience, expectations sometimes based on the slimmest amount of information about the country presenting Shakespeare. But as I walk into the yard for an early Sunday evening performance of *Othello* by the Q Brothers, a company from the USA, my native country, I am anticipating what 'our' offering might be like. Where in the Festival booklet words like IsiZule, SeSotho, Māori, Russian, Swahili, Juba Arabic and Palestinian Arabic appear before the '/' followed by the name of the theatre company, tonight it reads Hip Hop. If a shut-in who never listened to radio or television wandered into the Globe this night, you might forgive him or her for thinking they were about to hear a play in 'bunny' by the National Rabbit Theatre.

One quick glance around the space confirms, however, the popularity of the Globe's decision to host a hip-hop production: the theatre is packed – at least one-third more people tonight in the theatre than in any of the productions I have seen thus far. As with the Russian production of *Measure for Measure*, I am immediately aware of the curse and blessing of Globe acoustics. The blessing is how good they are; the curse is that with artificial amplification having been added for the first time at this Festival, sound now blasts out in odd jagged spurts because of both the placement of the speakers in relation to where one is standing – in a packed yard it is easier to manoeuvre from the side but the sound on the side is much louder – and the uneven nature of recorded sound in relation to where bodies are on stage.

Above the stage on the balcony we have a DJ already entertaining the audience, a beginning very in tune with original practices where music often signalled preparation and was followed by blasts of a trumpet to open the action. Faux curtains hang at the doors allowing graffiti, the visual equivalent of the contemporariness of hip hop, to appear as if spray-painted on the walls. Perhaps this is the first moment of many to come where I wonder to myself what real risk might have meant for this production. Imagine really spray-painting the sacred space of the Globe.

Four guys enter in overalls: one white (Jackson Doran), one tall, dark and Othello-ey looking (Postell Pringle), two with less easy to define physical racial characteristics (JQ and QQ, the creators and directors).[1] For a while I watch, expecting women to enter. Slowly I understand that there are, and there will be, no women. Desdemona is a disembodied voice making sounds without words from above, at the back of the upper gallery. Necessary only when Othello addresses her, needs her, berates her, kills her. An early modern scholar might suggest that this renders the Q Brothers' production even more 'authentic', because boy players, and all-male companies such as Propeller, bring us Shakespeare as he was meant to be: all boy, all the time. However, even this early on in the Festival, several of the companies have instructed me about the elasticity of cross-dressing and gender-swapping. So the amplified, loud 'girlness' in the production when the actors 'do' the women, combined with the extraordinarily loud absence of Desdemona, un-embodied, suggest a deeper problem about women (see below).

Disembodied or embodied, voice projects race; the sound of hip hop itself might be considered a racial sound, even when it is cross-voiced by white boys doing a 'black thing', or their idea of a 'black thing'. Stew, creator of the musical *Passing Strange*, might remind us that white *and* black boys often do a 'black thing', or their idea of a 'black thing' too.[2] Added to the racial information in the hip-hop cadences comes the actual sound of Desdemona's voice, which undoes a primary plot device of the prominent and successful soldier Moor or African courting a young white Venetian. From the little we hear of Desdemona's voice making noise if not sense, she 'sounds' black, though in the commercial music moment in which we are living this could be a girl trained to sing black from a young age, in the style of many young white successful singers who imitate the Queens of soul.

All of these components suggest this production may be the most truly 'global' offering in the Globe to Globe Festival, because its language – easily digestible hip hop – comes from the global zone of corporate land, of those truly transnational entities like Shell, Coca Cola and Apple. The adaptation of the play follows the late capitalist logic of the marketable commodity that is hip hop: the stakes are reduced to a kind of banality we know well from stage and screen. Desdemona's claim to disembodied fame is that she lives in a house with a lot of 'stuff'. The duke's political and cultural power as a nobleman in Venice dissolves into that of a record executive obsessed by tennis and tennis stars.

Fun, likeable, witty, these will be the adjectives I hear when others describe the production. This might strike the theatrical spectator as a bit at odds with *Othello* the play which in teaching I refer to as a new form of 'revenge tragedy', not because Spaniards go to great lengths to avenge deaths but because the playwright skewers the spectators who should, to use a contemporary notion, be dialling 999 long before Desdemona's breath is stopped. Loathe as I am to join in the too easy notion of all of us being complicit when we see a performance of violence, in this play it seems clear that we (might) stand between a woman and disaster.

Instead, with the pacifier mikes at their mouths, the four actors turn the play into a babyish story. The most the Moor will lose is celebrity, and having no female bodies on the stage absolutely turns Othello into a sympathetic hero – importantly his is the *only* body we *see* suffering. In an interview the actors confirm the outcome of these choices, suggesting they wanted to 'highlight' the comic bits of the tragedy.[3] Dead women, dead protagonists, dead soldiers: all fodder for hip-hop couplets.

HIP HOP, LATE CAPITALISM AND JAMES BALDWIN

Let me return to what was obviously not my experience – the fun, likeable, witty part. To have chosen hip hop as a language in a Festival offering specific manifestations of language (Mexican Spanish, Brazilian Portuguese among them) would imply hip hop as a 'dialect' of English, particularly US English. Such a choice also has race embedded in it as surely as Swahili does. The tradition of Shakespeare in the USA is as varied as that in the UK, from nineteenth-century all-Black troupes to the Wooster Group's revelatory *Hamlet*.

Asking an English-speaking country to send a play in 'another language' already marks the offering as odd; even stranger, I eventually came to believe I was hearing a separate language or at least a global dialect. This safe and bland form of hip hop takes its place in our time as an *idiom* of late capitalism. In the interview on the Globe website the creators suggested that 'Every theme is relevant to hip hop; hip hop is just a lens through which we see it.'[4] This is the level of critical engagement possible in a global art industry: making things relevant to all and therefore challenging to no one. Every theme being relevant to hip hop translates to art made 'accessible', a value taken for granted in cultural discussions of performance-making, art and audience. In these discussions I would suggest 'accessible' veils its true meaning of 'consumable'.

Consumable it certainly was, since all three performances of the Q Brothers were sold out. While for many of the productions I stood in the yard with groups of students, the number of students attending this production with their teachers seemed to insist on the hip-hop access nexus of a Shakespeare 'relevant' to student audiences. As with any question of why and how an audience attends and responds the way it does, my assumptions remain approximations. What concerns me here, however, is the certainty with which arts councils and other funding bodies give money to productions that 'appeal' to a particular group as if we knew what such performances were, or who those groups are, or whether the easy assumption of 'hip hop = happy engaged students' can stand.

'A language comes into existence by means of brutal necessity, and the rules of the language are dictated by what the language must convey', writes African American playwright and essayist James Baldwin in his fierce interrogation 'If Black English Isn't A Language, Then Tell Me What Is?'[5] Ironically sounding as if he had been attending the Globe to Globe Festival, where wet and cold were the physical conditions of almost every production, Baldwin focuses for a moment on nation, race and voice:

The range (and reign) of accents on that damp little island make England coherent for the English and totally incomprehensible for everyone else. To open your mouth in England is (if I may use black English) to 'Put your business in the street': You have confessed your parents, your youth, your school, your salary, your self-esteem, and, alas, your future.

No one knows this better than an ex-pat teaching in London; to open your mouth is to be received as an American first and foremost. No matter that I have chosen to live in Europe for years. But Baldwin's excoriating and lucid argument about how we use language suggests an important corrective to the easy-listening hip-hop tune:

There was a moment, in time, and in this place, when my brother, or my mother, or my father, or my sister, had to convey to me, for example, the danger in which I was standing from the white man standing just behind me, and to convey this with a speed, and in a language, that the white man could not possibly understand.[6]

There is something Shakespearean about Baldwin's description of stakes and risks and language here that applies particularly to *Othello*. Othello himself cannot afford to understand Iago's manipulation of him. And sadly he listens not to his wife or his friend and comrade-in-arms to 'hear' as they offer a sort of language and representation other than that of the white villain standing always insidiously at his side. If he listened, he might hear what the audience hears in Desdemona's speech, her satisfied love in her confident play with him about Cassio, her wooing by his affection for the officer disaffected. In performance her exaggeration in her suit for the return of Cassio to Othello's favour ('His bed shall seem a school, his board a shrift / I'll intermingle everything he does / With Cassio's suit' (3.3.24–5)) heightens her seizing of the sudden power a young maid might feel over her besotted new husband.

Instead of being a clandestine creation moving outside the 'master's language' (to use an old race and gender term), the Q Brothers' muted hip hop turned any judicious language from Cassio 'whiny' (of course Desdemona cannot speak for herself or, much more importantly, speak to Othello about himself, speeches essential for an audience to hear even if Othello's ear is now tuned to Iago's frequency). In the process of 'translation' the production squandered the noble political tradition of hip hop as critical intervention. (Have a listen to Soweto Kinch's 'Love of Money' where he smuggles the names of every pirate-banking corporation – RBS, Sterling, Mastercard, Natwest – into the lyrics of a love song.) Rather, Cassio's entrée to Othello's 'crew' requires him to pump up the b-boy bits and play the white dude as good rapper. When very quickly this sours due to Iago's playing him for a drugged, drunken fool, his voice makes almost exactly the same cadence as it does when he dons Emilia's wig, a why-does-everything-have-to-happen-to-meee American sitcom wail.

Where Baldwin offers an adapted language, a language for use in situations that theorists of performance would undoubtedly call performative, the hip-hop couplets of the Q Brothers smooth over most differences – differences that Baldwin articulates by exposing the embeddedness of nation and race in language, here particularly the nation of the USA and the race of Black Americans, two components inseparable from the hip-hop Othello:

Now, I do not know what white Americans would sound like if there had never been any black people in the United States, but they would not sound the way they sound. Jazz, for example, is a very specific sexual term, as in *jazz me, baby*, but white people purified it into the Jazz Age. *Sock it to me* . . . has been adopted . . . along with *let it all hang out* and *right on!* *Beat to his socks*, which was once the black's most total and despairing image of poverty, was transformed into a thing called the Beat Generation, which phenomenon was, largely, composed of *uptight*, middle-class white people, imitating poverty, trying to *get down*, to get *with it*, doing their *thing*, doing their despairing best to be *funky*, which we, the blacks, never dreamed of doing – we *were* funky, baby, like *funk* was going out of style.[7]

Antiquated as the specifics of borrowed language sound, it is easy to replace 'let it all hang out' with the far more linguistically lazy 'whatever' or the coy rhyming that invites the listening audience to complete trigger with n . . . – thus have your racist cake and eat it too.

Writing in 1979, Baldwin cuts through to the complex longing underpinning race relations in the USA, whites 'imitating poverty' to 'get down' transformed into its mirror opposite in the global adoration of hip-hop stars that sits cheek by jowl with the huge gulf between the world's predominantly white male haves and millions of multicoloured – including white – female and male have-nots.[8]

ACOUSTICS, SOUND AND MICROPHONES

If for Samuel Taylor Coleridge in the nineteenth century the reception of theatrical performance depended on the spectator's 'willing suspension of disbelief', the twenty-first century moves this suspension from the visual to the auditory realm.

In many, many contemporary theatrical settings, we the audience agree to believe we are hearing the actors speaking or singing even though the sound does not travel from their bodies to our ears but from one or two sources beside or above the stage. The give-and-take between players and audience changes radically in a miked production: you can sit back and hear from anywhere, no work required on your part to direct your ears to where the players speak, no change in volume according to their position on stage, no physical effort manifested in the breath as they strain the body to gather volume since they never need to project their voices by air.[9]

In early discussions with Festival Director Tom Bird about potential productions for the Festival – we met because I have been seeing a great deal of European Shakespeare these last years in Italy and France – I suggested that one of the most innovative parts of the Festival to my mind would be the demand on directors and companies to adapt their often very technical productions to the Globe stage. Particularly I remarked on the need to create soundscapes and to speak with the body and with unamplified instruments. Between the time of planning and the actual Festival, the Globe team decided to add amplification. As Tom Bird suggested in a question-and-answer session, companies were told that song and instruments worked really well in the space, and later the Globe installed a sound-speaker system for the Festival because they felt it would be an imposition to prevent companies from using recorded music.[10]

From this spectator's perspective not one production that used either recorded music or microphones used them to good effect, and this includes productions I loved, such as *Timon of Athens*. Either the sound was too loud or the music sounded as if suddenly a film soundtrack was directing our ears and perhaps our emotions towards the next scene – music that erased how, in the plays, Shakespeare already uses metre and rhyme to indicate just such shifts: couplets at the end of scenes provide acoustic closing doors, a shift of tone, or a move to blank verse moves us to the street or the throne room. 'Imposition', I would argue as both a director of performance and theatre and as a scholar of theatrical practice, is a gift. Only a challenge will be a catalyst for challenging work. In the global performance economy, the difficult part of deciding to stick to your rules – no sound system – is that you will need to withstand the pressure of the National Theatre of China or a hip-hop production when they push. And leaning towards the accessible and thus the consumable too often results in missing an opportunity to do something really interesting, to make sound differently, to have recorded music but to restrict its blanket effect by playing it off one source on stage, a boombox (antique as they are) or a CD player.

What would this production have been like if the Globe had insisted on natural acoustics? All the jumping, circling, adjusting of dicks, but with none of the 'in-your-earpiece' volume effect? Now that would have been risky and might have demanded a very different physical practice on the part of the actors and the spectators.

WOMEN AND SCARIOTYPES

In the original abstract for this chapter, submitted before I had an idea of what the *Hip-Hop Othello* would be like, I posed these questions: What then about the ex-colony's presence dressed, at least metaphorically, in bling, backward caps and baggy pants? Will the overwhelmingly male form of hip hop and its consumption of female bodies as image, idea and commodity, its consumption of language as commercial code, reinforce European stereotypes of the USA and reinforce the patriarchal nature of the play?

And so it came to pass that not only did the genre import a patriarchal attitude but the creators of this production decided that female actors were superfluous, even though there were women in their 2011 production *Funk It Up About Nothing* (a 'hip-hoptation' of *Much Ado*).[11] I can believe this might have been an unwitting choice in that inexorable way all racism, sexism and homophobia sewn into our attitudes exist uncritically examined until challenged. Thus, to play Emilia and Bianca the boys don women's wigs and bits of dressy things to 'do' the women as stereotypically as possible. Why can't men who are cross-dressing conceive of doing women subtly? Are they so afraid a subtle embodiment will betray the very little distance between the sexes, how good we are at being each other? This was fully true in the Georgian and the Swahili productions, to name just two – little was necessary to make a transition, and when the grand and vulgar cross-dressing moment happened in *Merry Wives* with Falstaff, who appeared enormous in ridiculous pantomime clothes, its vulgarity worked *because* it was in direct contrast to the everyday ease of the other gender exchanges happening actor by actor.

The Q Brothers' Bianca and Amelia sound like a Latina princess and a valley girl milktoast. The desperately girly turns deflected any of the homoerotic possibilities implied throughout *Othello*. During the interval I heard two young women talking, as one of them complained in a minor key: 'I like it, but in not having any women they give up one of my favourite parts of the play when Emilia and Desdemona talk about the behaviour of men.' In fact the only acknowledgement of Emilia's articulate assessment of the condition of women and class in the world that she inhabits is a faux Supremes, girly, breathy turn of James Brown's 'It's a Man's World'. The complexities of that song get wigged and jiggled and karaoke-ed out of existence – make no mistake, the Godfather of Soul is troubled in spirit over the relations between the sexes, even if he has no difficulty with a patriarchal prerogative.

Fig. 8 Emilia (Jackson Doran) with Gregory Qaiyum (GQ) and Jeffrey Qaiyum (JQ) as back-up singers, *Othello*, Q Brothers/Chicago Shakespeare Theater/Richard Jordan Productions from Chicago, USA; directors JQ and GQ, developed with Rick Boynton.

As the men prowled the Globe, mimetically making the circles that the short rap rhymes and the stage itself inspires, I was reminded of the emotional contract of patriarchy that great writers like Shakespeare, George Büchner and Toni Morrison represent, whether in sympathy with the power structure or at the mercy of it.[12] Keep your women still – faithful, domestic, subordinate in speech – the world is in order; but if a woman moves out of any of those categories, even in the imagination of her lover, inevitably she will have to die so as to restore order to the world by being removed from circulation, by not being in motion without permission. If things have changed, they have changed only in consequence: now perhaps women don't have to die, but they damned well have to suffer – think of any, and I mean any, woman in public office and the scrutiny she undergoes. This observation is not in any way outside the sphere of global hip hop; the number of hip-hop artists who are female is tiny – the majority of the women in the record executive's office are still there serving coffee and Coke.

So I would argue that the removal of Emilia's autonomy and Desdemona's presence does not just constitute a particular take on the play but follows out the late capitalist logic shot through this production. If you have no women, then the disaster in this tragedy, rather than being sinister, inevitable and quite truly breathtaking for the audience and the character, occurs in the strangest of lands, between one hammered-out line and another lost in the global, commercial order. Men donning bling, women cooing as they shake booty to get some booty. It would not have been so difficult for female players to follow out Emilia's logic in 4.3.84–94 in the key of hip and hop:

> But I do think it is their husbands' faults
> If wives do fall. Say that they slack their duties
> And pour our treasures into foreign laps,
> Or else break out in peevish jealousies . . .
> Yet have we some revenge. Let husbands know
> Their wives have sense like them. They see, and smell,
> And have their palates both for sweet and sour,
> As husbands have. . . .

Into

> Dudes are bad
> They make us mad
> Just like our Dads
> They all are Cads
> But we got power
> Charge 'em by the hour
> Then they will see
> They can't get it free
> Specially in this E-con-o-Me.

ENDNOTES

1 Throughout this Festival the faulty faculty of sight will prove to be a bad discerner of race and nation. In the Swahili *Merry Wives* an actor offers a bottle of beer to the audience. A young, blonde-ish woman responds to her in Swahili, and she and her white male companion accept the beer. Thus the easy assumption 'all people of colour in the Globe must understand Swahili and all those who are white must not' is undermined in practice and reception.

2 The musical *Passing Strange* takes its own name from *Othello* and the word 'scariotype' in my title comes from the libretto. The musical began at the Public Theatre in New York and then moved to Broadway; Spike Lee has made a film of it called *Passing Strange*. Directing an actor playing his young self from the vantage of what he knows now, Stew creates a musical from a sung narrative, propelling the story the four actors inhabit from LA to Amsterdam to Berlin, assumptions stated and undone, stereotypes employed and discarded.

3 Jo Caird, 'Q Brothers: Hip-Hop Othello', *Ideas Tap: The Creative Network*, 3 May 2012, www.ideastap.com/IdeasMag/the-knowledge/q-brothers-interview, 20 October 2012.

4 JQ and GQ, '*Othello*: International Insights', audio interview (interviewer Amy Kenny), Shakespeare's Globe London (2012), http://globetoglobe.shakespearesglobe.com/plays/othello/interview, 20 October 2012.

5 James Baldwin, 'If Black English Isn't a Language, Then Tell Me What Is?', *New York Times*, 29 July 1979: E19.

6 Ibid.

7 Ibid.

8 Eric Lott's *Love and Theft: Blackface Minstrelsy and the American Working Class* (Oxford University Press, 1995) brilliantly analyses how imitation results in a history of violent tensions between white American men towards African American men; in the lyrics of *Passing Strange* we hear a more contemporary critique of how race is performed, consumed and presumed across the binary of black and white.

9 Some companies do 'act' with microphones, taking into account the loss of the physical consequences of making unamplified sound: the Wooster Group, for example, play to and with the microphones. Like surtitles, small mikes have inspired creative companies to be creative, but for the most part the mikes are used to make actors and audiences feel more secure and to reproduce a flat, solid volume very like that of earphones.

10 Tom Bird, 'Globe-to-Globe Festival Q & A', Intercultural Shakespeare Symposium, the Globe Theatre, London, 19 May 2012.

11 The description is from the Chicago Shakespeare Theater website, www.chicagoshakes. com/main.taf?p=2,19,3,29,1,32, 26 October 2012.

12 Toni Morrison provided a very different adaptation of *Othello*, entitled *Desdemona* and staged as part of the World Shakespeare Festival (Barbican Theatre, July 2012), which takes on the very challenges the Q Brothers eschewed.

WEEK THREE

CHAPTER SEVENTEEN

POWER PLAY

Dhaka Theatre's Bangla *Tempest*

Christine Dymkowski

The Tempest is arguably the most protean of Shakespeare's plays, and yet what makes
its openness possible is its intense focus on issues of power without dictating how
they should be theatrically presented. Productions of the play over the past 400-
odd years, particularly in English-speaking countries, have made it a vehicle to
celebrate or to condemn colonialism, to endorse or to contest gender ideology,
to display the magic of theatre or to mine the human condition via the magician
Prospero, who might struggle to forgive or find it easy, be confident or inadequate
in his interactions with others, revel in his supernatural powers or give them up
with relief.[1] While, for an English-speaking audience member, Dhaka Theatre's
Bangla adaptation of the play, performed at Shakespeare's Globe on 7 and 8 May
2012 as part of the Globe to Globe Festival, at first glance appeared to sidestep
many of the issues with which Western productions have engaged, a more nuanced
understanding of its elements reveals its own sensitive approach to the issue of
power, particularly in relation to questions of national identity.[2]

National identity is clearly a crucial consideration for the company. Dhaka Theatre, established in 1973 and directed by Nasiruddin Yousuff, is:

one of the pioneers of the neo-theatre movement in [Bangladesh]. Its members believe that
theatre should depict the life of the people and therefore endeavour to find a theatrical
expression which will truly depict the country and its people. To achieve this goal, the group
emphasises the traditional performing art forms and has tried to mingle old forms with
modern ideas and technologies. The group's productions have been appreciated for their
artistry as well as their portrayal of Bangladeshi themes.[3]

In an interview recorded for Shakespeare's Globe Library and Archive, Yousuff
explains that tragedy is more popular than comedy in Bangladesh, and that the
play he really wanted to direct for the Globe to Globe season was *Macbeth*, his

other choices being *Julius Caesar*, *A Midsummer Night's Dream* and *The Comedy of Errors*. However, as Imogen Butler-Cole, the British producer of the production, explains in the same interview, she chose *The Tempest*, on the basis that the company should perform something 'light' (sic), that the importance of water in the play gives it a natural affinity to a country disproportionately affected by flooding and that the magic in the play reflects an 'undercurrent of magic' in Bangladesh, with Prospero reminiscent of a *Baul*, or Sufi mystic. It is ironic that, in an era when postcolonialist readings of *The Tempest* prevail, this particular production from a developing country should have so colonialist a genesis.

Despite what would seem an inauspicious start, Yousuff nevertheless managed to find meaningful resonances between *The Tempest* and his country's recent history and present situation. Originally a British colony as part of India, it became East Pakistan at the time of independence and partition (1947), winning its own independence from Pakistan in the 1971 war of liberation.[4] Although a republic, its history since then has been marked by assassinations, military coups and martial law; despite the relative stability obtaining for the past twenty years or so, when Bangladesh became a parliamentary democracy, its politics continue to be subject to violent power conflicts.[5] Besides noting his country's parallels with the colonized Caliban and the play's actual and intended usurpations, Yousuff instructed the play's translator, Rubayet Ahmed, to adapt the play to popular Bangla theatre forms; after an unsuccessful first try, Ahmed managed to transform Shakespeare's text into a type of traditional performance called *panchali*, a combination of verse, dialogue, song, music and dance, often used to portray folk tales.[6] Much of the play's dialogue became songs set to the tunes of 'traditional Bangladeshi folk songs',[7] and Yousuff also had his company of actors trained for seven months in Manipuri *natapala*, a dance style in which the foot lands with the toe rather than the heel; Nil Moni Singha and Bidhan Chandra Singha, the two non-company members who did the training, joined the production to play the traditional drums called *pungs*.

Even to the uninitiated, it was immediately apparent that the production would be a celebration of Bangla culture. The front of the stage was set with vividly painted boxes arranged in a multilevel semicircle, their fronts decorated with images ranging from ships to horses to a dinosaur and their sides with floral patterns; a helpful member of the audience told me they resembled the folk art paintings seen on rickshaws, particularly in Dhaka.[8] The Globe's three doors were covered with large, similarly brightly painted cloths, all of them showing ships at sea: their bowsprit figureheads looked like cartoon faces and sported big red clown-like noses, suggesting the comic tack the story would take. The cloth nearest me, over the stage-right door, also had a generic goddess floating above the ship, a white-winged horse with a female face that could possibly bring to mind al-Buraq (or Burak), the mythical mount on which Mohammed ascended to heaven.[9]

The play began as the thirteen actor-musician-singers, dressed in traditional clothes, entered and each picked up one of the painted boxes by its handle; retreating to the back of the stage, they sat cross-legged on red and blue rugs in front of their now opened boxes, which contained props and instruments. The storm started as one of the actors – later revealed to be Prospero – lifted the large conch shell set downstage centre and blew a long note on it;[10] then five dancers with small white ships on their wristbands gracefully danced the storm. Leading them was a female figure draped in a floor-length flimsy blue veil, who might have been the sea but was in fact Ariel: a nice conflation of identities in this scene.

The gentleness of the tempest in this production was matched by what followed: Prospero sang as well as spoke some of his exposition in Act 1 Scene 2, the folk song sounding as cheery as the storm dance had been graceful. Similarly, Caliban smilingly sang a song after entering in that scene, Prospero looking perplexed rather than angry during most of their interaction. For those brought up on a diet of Western *Tempests*, this approach was disconcerting: as London reviewers noted, the 'emotional resonances of the play seemed muted in the first half', and 'the relationship of Prospero and Ariel . . . felt underplayed', as did that of Prospero and Caliban, the latter seeming 'a hail-fellow-well-met sort'.[11] The tension we had come to expect in Prospero's interactions with the play's other characters was virtually absent, making it easy for us to miss just how deeply the production's 'strikingly modern message of power-sharing and toleration' replaced the more usual 'focusing on Prospero's individual journey to understanding'.[12]

While this message was embodied in the very marrow of the production, going well beyond how it handled the play's diegesis, the extent of its embodiment could easily be missed by those not conversant with Bangla culture. For instance, as I earlier mentioned, the actors were dressed in what I took to be traditional clothing, but Taarini Mookherjee was surprised that what she saw on stage was 'not mainstream' Bangla: she would have expected the women to be dressed in richly beautiful Dhaka saris and the men in dhotis, but instead they wore clothing 'closer to what I imagine is Manipuri . . . [or] some other tribal influence'.[13] The Manipuris, whose dance style the actors learned especially for this production, comprise one of Bangladesh's (and India's) minority tribes, with their own language and culture; unlike the Bengali Muslim majority, they are also overwhelmingly Hindu. In fact, according to Mookherjee, the production's elements were 'Hindu through and through', with 'no Islamic elements' that she could discern.[14] As she explained, the conch shell that was to feature so prominently in the action is in fact the most important part of Hindu daily worship; kept in the sanctum and blessed with holy water, it is sounded at weddings and other celebrations.

To explore this inclusive aspect of the production further, I want to focus on the presentation of Caliban and Ariel, two of the characters whose interpretation radically affects the play's ultimate meaning. As I have written elsewhere,

> most contemporary productions emphasize Caliban's status as victim and portray him as essentially human, albeit grotesque or deformed in some way, rather than as an out-and-out monster. Although still often played by black actors, . . . whatever the race of the actor playing the part, its overall interpretation continues to serve as an accurate index of which groups in society are at present alienated, disadvantaged, and vulnerable, and, for that reason, threatening to and threatened by those with more power.[15]

In the Dhaka Theatre production, Chandan Chowdhury's Caliban was in no way monstrous, either in form or behaviour. Although he was hunched over and the fingers of both of his hands were clenched, he was not an 'other', but a human being who resembled Prospero. At the end of the play, Prospero approached him, holding out the conch shell that began the storm and the play proper, while Caliban cowered in response. When it became clear that Prospero was offering it to him, Caliban took hold of it, accompanied by dramatic drumming, growing erect and unclenching his fingers as he did so. Greeting this change with a triumphant laugh, he blew a long note on the conch, laughed again, and then he and Prospero bowed respectfully to each other.

Given the resemblance between Prospero and Caliban, both in physical appearance and in dress, I read this moment as symbolic of the Bangladeshi war of liberation, with Prospero as West Pakistan and Caliban as East Pakistan, the latter escaping oppressive rule to emerge, erect and whole, as Bangladesh. The actual words spoken at this point strengthen the impression made by the physical staging. As Mookherjee explained in response to my query:

> Right at the end, Prospero does have a 'farewell' speech for Caliban. He tells him that he is going back to his own land and therefore Caliban now has the island to himself. Caliban can now live in a manner of his own choosing and is free to roam around and do what he wants. Prospero then holds out the conch shell and says: 'Caliban, you're free, independent' (still using the derogatory/informal form of you). But right at the end (after the boat dance) Prospero shouts out 'Caliban, farewell!'[16]

The final image of the production celebrated Caliban's being granted the 'rule of the island', as the surtitle proclaimed: beaming and wreathed with flowers, he stood enthroned on a pile of brightly painted boxes while the rest of the company danced around him to the beat of the exuberant drums.

While this reading of Caliban is perhaps the most accessible for a non-Bangla speaker, there are other, richer layers to his presentation. As Mookerjee explained to me, the Bangla language has three levels of address: the very formal, used for complete strangers, teachers, and those senior to oneself, sometimes including parents; the semi-formal for everyday speech; and the intimate, used between very close friends and by masters to servants. Prospero spoke to both Ariel and Caliban in this intimate way, with his tone more condescending to Caliban than to the spirit. However, Caliban's own speech was very disrespectful to Prospero, making a number of jokes at his expense and using the semi-formal rather than formal 'you' to address him. In confronting Prospero in Act 1 Scene 2, he was also self-confident, moving freely about the stage as Prospero stood guiltily rooted to the spot, reversing their expected statuses: this was a Caliban with dignity and belief in his own worth.

Ahmed's rewriting of Caliban's 'You gave me language' speech was also pointed:

Besh bariye bolle kintu (You have really exaggerated)

Shotto she ami-o jani tumi-o jano (Both you and I know the truth)

Ja shikhiyeccho she to tomar reeti tomar-i aadesh (What you have taught me has been by your custom/practice and your decree)

Aamar bhasha kere nile, tomar bhasha ja shikhale she-o tomar nirdesh (You carried away my language and what you taught me of yours was also your decision)

Tomar kacche aamar bhashar ki dam acche? (What value do you place on my language?/Do you place any value on my language?)

Maa-er bhasha, Maa-er buli, Matribhasha jaake boli. (The mother's language, the mother's speech, that which we call the mother-tongue)

She-i bhashake kere nile jano kina, porinoti bhalo noi (That was the language you carried away, don't you know, the consequence isn't good).[17]

Whereas Shakespeare's text is ambiguous – did Caliban know no language when Prospero and Miranda arrived on the island, or did he simply not speak their own? – Ahmed's text makes explicit that colonization deprives people of their native tongue, just as English became the dominant language of the Indian subcontinent during British rule. However, as Mookherjee points out, the lines are also relevant to the present-day situation, where Bangla has displaced many of the country's tribal languages.

This acknowledgement of the difficulties minorities can face may also be reflected in the casting: not only was Chowdhury the only member of the cast with a Hindu surname, apart from the two Manipuri drummers drafted in for this production, but he was also the darkest-skinned member of the company and, as such, could be seen to represent the lower-caste members of Bangla society. Caliban's re-written speech continues in a way that makes this idea about prejudice explicit and also powerfully asserts their shared humanity:

Borno niye dondo tomaar, aami kaalo dhobol tomaar (You have a problem/quarrel with colour, I am black, yours is grey/white)

Shirai shirai bohe je dhara, ki rong taar, ki chehara? (That which flows through our veins, what is its colour, what is its character/ appearance?)

She rong ektai- laal (It is one colour – red)

Nirbodh, tomarta ki neel? (Fool, is yours blue?)[18]

Yousuff's treatment of Ariel was similarly rich. In the West, Ariel has been played by both women and men, but in England the trend has been to use the spirit's gender 'as a way of legitimizing or of questioning the power of Prospero, be it domestic or political': that is, portrayals of female Ariels have tended to validate Prospero's authority, and those of male Ariels to challenge it.[19] As already noted, Shimul Yousuf's first appearance as Ariel was not immediately identifiable as such: in her floor-length blue veil, leading the ships in the tempest dance, she could easily have represented the power of the sea, an idea that director Yousuff thought significant for a Bangla production of the play;[20] after the actor was revealed as Ariel, her association with the sea remained.

The staging further enhanced the sense of Ariel's power: when she entered in response to Prospero's summons in Act 1 Scene 2, she did so dancing to the driving beat of the two spirit-drummers who initially accompanied her. Prospero seemed to be in thrall to the spirit: looking at her with a rapt expression on his face, he was eventually drawn in by the music, dancing to her beat rather than vice versa. Nevertheless, he did 'torment' Ariel with the memory of Sycorax, performing his magic by doing two huge circular jumps, forcing Ariel to perform four of the same jumps in unison with him, an athletic display that elicited the evening's first round of applause.

More specific cultural references bear out this sense of contradiction in their relationship. Ariel used the very formal 'you' to address Prospero, but, as already noted, Prospero used the intimate form of 'you' to address her. However, at one point Prospero told Ariel '*ami tor bhokto chhilam*', 'I was a devotee/worshipper of yours'; as Mookherjee explained, the word '*bhokto/bhakti* is generally used with reference to a god or higher ideal', and Hindu Bengalis worship only women, so anyone who could understand the language and recognize the production's Hindu frame of reference would have been aware of the complex relationship between Ariel and her ostensible master.[21] In addition, to Mookherjee, Ariel's initial appearance was not only very powerful but frightening: an older woman with long loose hair extending below her waist, dancing in a slightly manic way, she was reminiscent of a *daini* or witch. The position of women in Bangladesh is as complicated as it is anywhere else in the world and outside the scope of this chapter: just as in Britain and the USA, laws may give equal rights but the reality is often very different.[22] Yousuff's handling of the Ariel–Prospero relationship not only pointed to such inconsistencies but also avoided the gendered dichotomy that English productions so often reproduce:[23] although she had to serve him, there was no way in which this Ariel was inferior to Prospero, nor was there any sense that she would miss that service. As British reviewers noted, her liberation was a 'climactic' moment in which she 'reache[d] up, stretching towards the infinite sky, poised to take flight, and laugh[ed and danced] for joy'.[24]

At the end of the performance, when the company came out for a second curtain call, one of the actors brandished a Bangladeshi flag. While the whole production was certainly a celebration of Bangla culture, this celebration, as I hope is clear by now, was as far from crude nationalism as is possible. Yousuff is known in Bangladesh for developing a 'theatrical ideology for Dhaka Theatre known as "post-colonial narrative"',[25] and the far-reaching nature of this ethos was evident throughout his production. Not only did the design use 'mythical motifs and attire from [Bangladesh's minority] Manipuri culture' but even the title role of Prospero went to 'guest actor' Rubol Noor Lodi, a member not of Yousuff's Dhaka Theatre but of the Bogra Theatre company.[26] Similarly, this predominantly Muslim company replaced Shakespeare's masque with Miranda and Ferdinand's traditional Hindu wedding (see Colour Plate 7), complete with the exchange of garlands and celebratory ululations, and Yousuff created more opportunities for women actors in this production than are usual: not only was Ariel played by a woman, but Samiun Jahan Dola's energetic and engaging Trinculo created a powerful and comic rapport with the audience, giving her character a real prominence. This emphasis on inclusivity embodies the kind of integration that *The Tempest* itself dramatizes: just as Shakespeare's Prospero, prompted by Ariel, acknowledges the common humanity he shares with his erstwhile enemies (5.1.17–24) and reminds us in the closing lines of the epilogue (19–20) that the need for pardon is not a simple one-way matter, so Yousuff's production of the play demonstrated that national identity can be as 'rich' as Alonso's supposed sea-changed bones (1.2.396–401): it is not necessary to create a 'them' so that an 'us' can exist.[27] Although the Dhaka Theatre production, like all theatre, has now 'melted into air, into thin air', the way 'this insubstantial pageant' was created can teach the real world an invaluable lesson (4.1.150, 155): power can be generous, letting other people 'be themselves', although all too often it is, as Prospero recognizes, 'The rarer action' (5.1.32, 27).

ENDNOTES

1 See Christine Dymkowski, ed., *The Tempest*, Shakespeare in Production (Cambridge University Press, 2005), pp. 1–93.

2 I am enormously indebted to Taarini Mookherjee, an Indian national of Bangla extraction, who interned at Shakespeare's Globe in 2012 as part of her MA in Shakespeare Studies offered by King's College London in conjunction with the Globe Education Department. Besides translating some of the Bangla text for me, she helpfully illuminated many cultural references that lay outside my understanding. We met on 18 June 2012 to discuss the production and subsequently exchanged e-mails that gave me further information and clarification.

3 Ataur Rahman, 'Theatre Groups: Dhaka Theatre', National Encyclopedia of Bangladesh *Banglapedia*, www.banglapedia.org/ http/HT/T_0146.HTM, 16 June 2012.

4 For background information, see Syeda Momtaz Sheren, 'The War of Liberation', *Banglapedia*, www.banglapedia.org/HT/W_0020.HTM; Md Mahbubar Rahman, 'History: Pakistan Period', *Banglapedia*, www.banglapedia.org/HT/H_0136.HTM; Aksadul Alam, 'History: Bangladesh Period', *Banglapedia*, www.banglapedia.org/HT/H_0136.HTM, all 16 June 2012.

5 Yousuff mentions these points about Bangladesh's erstwhile colonial status and its continuing bloody power conflicts in his interview; see also Sirajul Islam, 'Constitution', *Banglapedia*, www.banglapedia.org/HT/C_0335.HTM, 16 June 2012.

6 Yousuff interview; see also Sambaru Chandra Mohanta, 'Panchali', *Banglapedia*, www.banglapedia.org/HT/P_0059.HTM, 16 June 2012.

7 Globe to Globe *Tempest* website, Shakespeare's Globe London (2012), http://globetoglobe.shakespearesglobe.com/plays/the-tempest/english-103.

8 For a fuller explanation and example of rickshaw art, see Niaz Zaman, 'Rickshaw Art', *Banglapedia*, www.banglapedia.org/HT/R_0201.HTM, 16 June 2012.

9 Internet sources vary in their descriptions, some claiming a male and others a female face, but all agree on Burak's white body, wings and human face. One of the most informative and illustrated websites is 'Burk-E-Albani / البُرَاق / Al-Burāq: The Mythological Steed of Mohammed the Prophet', www.harekrsna.de/artikel/islam-al-buraq.htm, 16 June 2012.

10 In his interview, Yousuff notes that he started with the image of the seashell because the sea's power is so important to Bangladesh. Besides this large conch shell that figured in the action, many of the characters, including Prospero, Miranda, Ariel and Caliban, wore smaller seashells as decoration and jewellery.

11 Respectively, Peter Culshaw, 'Globe to Globe: *The Tempest*, Shakespeare's Globe', *The Arts Desk*, 9 May 2012, www.theartsdesk.com/theatre/globe-globe-tempest-shakespeares-globe; Imogen Tilden, '*The Tempest* – Review', *Guardian*, 8 May 2012, www.guardian.co.uk/stage/2012/may/08/the-tempest-review, Culshaw: both 16 June 2012. See also Christine Dymkowski, 'Blog: *The Tempest*', blog.shakespearesglobe.com/the-tempest-by-christine-dymkowski-royal-holloway/, for my initial naive response to the production, 16 June 2012.

12 John Farndon, 'Global Shakespeare: Dhaka Theatre Stages Indigenous Tinged *Tempest* in London', *Daily Star* (Dhaka), 10 May 2012, www.thedailystar.net/ newDesign/news-details.php?nid=233441, 18 June 2012.

13 E-mail, 29 June 2012.

14 Bangladesh's population is 88.3 per cent Muslim, 10.5 per cent Hindu, 0.6 per cent Buddhist, 0.5 per cent Christian, and 0.1 per cent other; see Masud Hasan Chowdhury, 'Bangladesh', *Banglapedia*, www.banglapedia.org/HT/B_0141.HTM, 16 June 2012.

15 Dymkowski, *The Tempest*, p. 71.

16 E-mail, 19 June 2012.

17 Mookherjee's transcription and translation, e-mail, 10 July 2012.

18 Ibid.

19 See Dymkowski, *The Tempest*, pp. 34–48; quotation from p. 48.

20 See n. 10.

21 Mookherjee further noted 'that religious terminology is extremely prevalent' in Ahmed's adaptation: 'Prospero is referred to as god, Ferdinand wants to be a devotee of Miranda, she thinks he is one of the gods and so on.' E-mail, 19 June 2012.

22 See 'Women', *Banglapedia*, www.banglapedia.org/HT/W_0067.HTM (16 June 2012), for a series of essays by different authors on the past and present position of women in the country.

23 In England, Ariel was treated as a 'gossamer female fairy' for over 100 years; see Dymkowski, *The Tempest*, p. 37. Mookherjee notes that the Hindu equivalent of such a sprite-like figure would have been a *pori*.

24 Respectively, Culshaw, 'Globe to Globe', and Tilden, '*The Tempest* – Review'.

25 Jamil Mahmud, 'Theatre: Tempest Set to Go to Global Shakespeare Fest', *Daily Star* (Dhaka), 29 April 2012, www.thedailystar.net/newDesign/news-details.php/nid=232028, 2 July 2012.

26 Ibid. Shyamal Bhattacharya, 'Theatre Groups: Baguda (Bogra) Theatre', *Banglapedia*, www. banglapedia.org/HT/T_0146.HTM (16 June 2012), notes that the company was the 'first group in Bogra who subscribed to the ideals of the group theatre movement. This group believes that plays reflect not only human life, but also indicate ways how a life should be lived.'

27 Ahmed's adaptation further makes explicit this idea of relinquishing power in order to achieve equality: Caliban ends his long speech to Prospero in Act 1 Scene 2 with '*Sha-hosh thake jaadubidya chhere esho, koro dekhi lorai*' ('If you have any courage, leave your knowledge of magic, let's see if you can fight without it'); Mookherjee's transcription and translation, e-mail, 10 July 2012.

CHAPTER EIGHTEEN

LOCATING MAKBET/LOCATING THE SPECTATOR

Robert Ormsby

How does one place a production like the Teatr im. Kochanowskiego's Polish-language *Makbet* at the Globe Theatre in 2012? Was it, strictly speaking, Polish? Did it embody aspects of global London and the internationalized Globe or a post-Communist pan-European dystopia? Was it Shakespeare? Perhaps the question should be: how did *Makbet* place its audience members? Polish culture and politics, multicultural London, the Globe's theatrical traditions and Shakespeare's play all became points of orientation in *Makbet*, leaving individual spectators to discover where they stood in relation to the production.

Director Maja Kleczewska located the play's action in a Mafia demi-monde; the characters inhabited a clannish environment, the closeness of which led only to wretchedness. The men looked like members of a lower-order crime family in ugly athletic gear, speedos and gaudy suits. These were nasty specimens always on the edge of brutality, and their savage world was even more misogynistic than Shakespeare's (see Colour Plate 8): while Lady Macbeth (Judyta Paradzińska) chastised her sometimes insecure husband, Macbeth (Michał Majnicz) was quick to rough her up. Two of the witches, meanwhile, were transvestites who had no power over the mortal men in the play but, like the other women, were the bullied sexual playthings of the clownishly violent males. Narrow as this world was, it was also globalized in that its gruesome inhabitants swayed to the rhythms of modern popular music; the actors often danced and sang along to internationally chart-topping tunes of the twentieth century. Paul Prescott has argued that *Makbet*'s costuming, cruelty, soundscape and its 'disillusioned, anti-heroic and shop-soiled' aesthetic align it with a specific form of globalized Shakespeare, 'the sub-branch of stage Esperanto that we might affectionately call EuroShakespearean'. Yet, while *Makbet* may have 'spoken' a theatrical vernacular that mixes traditions in order to be understood across cultures, a vernacular that 'many continental European directors' have employed 'for some time', there were other forces at work that localized this production.[1]

At one local level, aspects of *Makbet* appeared to redeploy Globe performance conventions. The witches' campy performances, for instance, could be seen as an instance of the theatre '[d]emocratising the audience'.[2] When Witch 'Lola' (Maciej Namysło) had an audience member lift her/him onto the stage from the yard at the play's start and then flaunted her/his buttocks to the appreciative crowd, that crowd arguably witnessed what Christie Carson calls Globe Theatre performances' usual 'lack of reverence for the texts' that 'can also be recognised as an approach to the text which assumes the development of mutual understanding' between pit and stage.[3] While Namysło's display established overt rapport with the crowd, a certain kind of 'purist' might well perceive the display as an excessive pandering to theatre-goers with simplistic titillation. As in traditional Globe performances, the music, too, was often used to draw the audience into the spectacle's titillating 'fun', such as when Duncan (Grzegorz Minkiewicz) tackily stripped off to Michael Jackson's 'Billie Jean' or the witches belted out Gloria Gaynor's upbeat disco-gay anthem 'I Will Survive' directly to the groundlings.

If the company *was* consciously playing with Globe traditions, they elsewhere put these traditions to some squalid uses. The music, in particular, created an ugly ironic counterpoint; 'I Will Survive' was repeated as most of the company callously danced around Macbeth's corpse, the whole scene looking suspiciously like the Globe's customary crowd-pleasing post-show cast dances. Similarly, by staging Lady Macduff's (Aleksandra Cwen) vicious rape far downstage on the apron, Kleczewska reframed the convention of playing directly to the audience. The excruciatingly lengthy rape scene was accompanied by the melancholy pop ballad 'Bang Bang', earlier lip-synched by one of the witches while Macbeth murdered Duncan. Here, spectators were 'co-opted into a relationship with the narrative', though one unconnected to the 'playful ratification of the authenticity' of the Globe's architecture and early modern-ish aura.[4] Instead, by thrusting Cwen's contorted face up close to the crowd, by having them watch as her screams were muffled, all accompanied by a song about 'shooting down' a lover, the director enjoined spectators to reconsider their earlier participation in the songs sung from the same place downstage, including Lola's show-opening licentious 'amusements'. Kleczewska seemed implicitly to ask theatre-goers, 'What is your place in this violence? Are you typical Globe "participants"? How would you like to be part of this stage action, developing a mutual understanding with us?'

But the production was not only about Globe traditions, and perhaps the merely intermittent impression of *Makbet*'s 'Globe-ness' resulted from the show appearing in this particular theatre because at other times the production, first performed in 2004 at the company's venue in the city of Opole, looked very much like it was designed to play in a black-box space. Specifically, certain moments and images, such as Macbeth's pale flesh covered in blood or the sequined silver shoes that Malcom (Adam Ciołek) held up as the absurdly ostentatious symbols of his kingship once Macbeth was dead, would have been far more compelling artificially lit in a darkened theatre. So, too, did the acting frequently seem better suited to an indoor space. The power of the many shrieked lines dissipated in the Globe's open space, and even the songs would have carried more weight in cabaret-like surroundings, surroundings that the witches' modern drag costumes evoked.

What specifically Polish signification did *Makbet* entail, then? Did it, as Prescott suggests, have topical force as a commentary on gangsterism in Polish politics? Perhaps this is how the ex-pat Poles in the theatre understood the performance, although I do not have the knowledge to say so with certainty. Indeed, the production forced me to confront my own place in the theatrical experience, and my identity as a Canadian academic tourist witnessing a performance that was often impenetrable to me because of its and my mutual alien-ness. As a non-Polish speaker, I failed to grasp the nuances of the acting, a fact that affects my perception that the production was not ideally suited to the space. My outsider status was driven home to me by the attentive Polish-speaking theatre-goers who understood the jokes that I did not and who seemed to represent the majority in the packed house.

My own particularized understanding aside, was this production really foreign? Why, for instance, would spectators (Polish and non-Polish) not read *Makbet* as a comment on the shabby criminality of politicians in many places? To return to the action's globalized world, the songs served to reach beyond a local, London-based, Polish-speaking audience to one familiar with international popular culture, most of which was made in the USA. 'Bang Bang', for example, was a hit for Nancy Sinatra in the 1960s, and re-popularized in Quentin Tarantino's 2003 film *Kill Bill Volume One*. The music, like Shakespeare's play, might thus have provided a common denominator for at least some non-Polish speakers to connect to the production, but such popular-culture intertextuality also contributed to the sense that this production is far from international Shakespeare that 'writes back' to the Bard from an easily identifiable postcolonial position. *Makbet* might have decentred Shakespeare and its English-language audiences while momentarily coalescing a Polish community in London, but it is also part of a broader, well-established global Shakespeare that marries the plays to cultural forms that do not necessarily belong to any one nation, despite their mostly Hollywood origins.

Makbet did not necessarily locate critics according to their misunderstanding of its codes, although published response does reflect the production's dense signification at the Globe. One consistent motif in the reviews was a declared uncertainty about the production's meaning: 'Grasping for overarching metaphorical unity to tame this sensory riot produces empty hands';[5] 'while this version...has a reckless, pop-culture vitality, it is hard to grasp its point';[6] 'It is hard to place where D'Insane [Dunsinane] might be'.[7] *Makbet* did place critics according to whether they embraced and enthusiastically unpacked its pop-cult allusions[8] or considered it not to live up to Shakespeare.[9] Like the Globe to Globe Festival of international performance, the production tried to make contact across cultures, but its cross-cultural resonances were, inevitably, localized diversely, in ways that were simply not possible at Opole in 2004. Playing it during the 2012 Festival meant that precisely where, or to whom, it belongs is a matter of spectators' location and perspective.

ENDNOTES

1 Paul Prescott, 'Year of Shakespeare: *Macbeth*', 11 May 2012, http://bloggingshakespeare. com/year-of-shakespeare-macbeth, 16 May 2012.

2 See Christie Carson, 'Democratising the Audience?', in Christie Carson and Farah Karim-Cooper, eds., *Shakespeare's Globe: A Theatrical Experiment.* (Cambridge University Press, 2008), pp. 115–26.

3 Ibid., p. 122.

4 Rob Conkie, *The Globe Theatre Project: Shakespeare and Authenticity* (Lewiston, NY: Edwin Mellen Press, 2006), p. 49.

5 Catherine Love, 'Macbeth', 10 May, 2012, http://exeuntmagazine.com/reviews/macbeth-4/, 8 July 2012.

6 Michael, Billington 'Macbeth – Review', *Guardian*, 9 May 2012, www.guardian.co.uk/stage/ 2012/may/09/macbeth-shakespeares-globe-review, 8 July 2012.

7 Peter Culshaw, 'A Druggy Punk Polish Version of the Scottish Play with Transvestite Witches Wows the Globe', *The Arts Desk*, 10 May 2012, www.theartsdesk.com/theatre/ globe-globe-macbeth-shakespeares-globe, 8 July 2012.

8 See Culshaw, Love, Prescott and my 'Macbeth', 10 May 2012, http://blog.shakespearesglobe. com/macbeth-by-rob-ormsby, 28 January 2013.

9 See John Morrison, 'Globe to Globe: Macbeth', 9 May 2012, http://blackpig.typepad.com/ john_morrison/2012/05/globe-to-globe-macbeth-teatr-im-kochonowskiego.html, 8 July 2012, and Billington, 'Macbeth – Review'.

CHAPTER NINETEEN

'WHO DARES RECEIVE IT OTHER'

Conversation with Harriet Walter (9 May 2012) following
a performance of *Makbet*

Harriet Walter

I thought the performances on the whole were very charismatic. What I saw presented was a society where everybody was ambitious, everybody was decadent, everybody's hands were dirty and everybody knew what was going on in the mind of somebody like Macbeth because they were all (even including Duncan and Banquo) as bad as one another. I began with an open and excited mind, but fairly soon I began to feel let down.

Macduff, I thought, was set up to be a sort of dissident intellectual type standing against the Mafioso, grease-ball decadence of the rest of this world. This was reflected in his dress, but I didn't think the idea was followed through. His wife was a kind of bimbo on a housing estate with a cigarette and a pram, and I just didn't see how the two of them were connected . . . and we never witnessed his grief for her, which is such a driving force in his revenge at the end of the play.

The great asset of *Macbeth*, the greatness of that play, lies in the step-by-step relentless logic of the downfall of a man of some kind of moral nobility, the step-by-step disintegration of a man through his lust for power. That journey is so brilliantly charted. It's one of Shakespeare's shortest plays. It's so spare and its psychological accuracy is terrifying. Every building-block in the wall is timed at the right point, so why, please, in this production is Macbeth haunted by the ghost of Macduff before he learns that he's been killed? Why, please, is Lady Macbeth pregnant and then suddenly not pregnant? The whole point is this is a barren couple who are very paranoid and jealous about a man for whom it has been prophesied that his progeny will be kings. This feeds Macbeth's need to kill Banquo.

So where I started out being open to a very Polish take on the play – the current political system in Poland being, as we hear, pretty decadent in lots of ways – and while I tried to hold back judgement and tell myself that I'm in another world and this is a Polish response to the play, I ended up thinking that if you do that play without any kind of psychological journey, then I'm not interested in Macbeth after the interval. I didn't want to see any more, because it had lost any kind of logic or complexity. Where were the paradoxes within the play? Macbeth is a warrior, and yet he's so out of his mind with guilt when he kills the king. He's not frightened of blood, he's not frightened by death, but he's frightened when he kills someone he admires, someone under his roof, because he's broken all the codes of conduct he can think of, because what is noble in war is ignoble in peace, and this contrast is so fascinating and spins him off into everything that happens afterwards.

If you have an awful, decadent King Duncan in the first place, you just make the point that one sleaze-ball succeeds another sleaze-ball (see Colour Plate 8), and, right at the end, Malcolm is yet another sleaze-ball, which is certainly true of many political situations, but if this production wanted to make that point it seems to me they had hitched themselves to the wrong play. That is not the message of Shakespeare's *Macbeth*, which is less of a political play and more of a moral and psychological play. It is also a great philosophical play – 'tomorrow and tomorrow and tomorrow': where was that speech?

The brilliant psychology of the character of Lady Macbeth was missing, too. Her subtle knowledge of her husband's mind, her ability to tap his own ambition but give him licence to do the unthinkable act by taking on a lot of the responsibility herself, all this was summed up by the inadequate surtitle, 'Lady Macbeth persuades him to kill the king.' Encouraging your husband to follow his innermost ambitions is different from putting the idea in his head and corrupting him singlehandedly, and besides, in this production Macbeth was far from the noble soldier who is corrupted. He was pretty decadent from the outset. No need for Lady Macbeth, then!

What Shakespeare brings out is the question, 'Are you guilty when you just think you are going to do something or want to do something, or only when you actually carry out the act?' For me, that is what makes the dynamic between the couple so fascinating. Neither would do the deed without the other. There is also the whole issue of their barrenness, which gives them a kind of desperate motivation and makes the play so poignant and frightening. I wasn't frightened by this production – and what might have frightened me was treated too frivolously.

My heart sank when I saw the witches were men dressed as women, because it denied the whole idea that there might be wise women. Lady Macbeth is very perceptive, and some people think of the witches as an aspect of her or her as an aspect of the witches. I know I sound like I'm saying 'don't mess with Shakespeare', but these things are intrinsic to the play's greatness. Having said all this, I thought some of the character actors were fantastic – that sort of freedom physically, that full-bloodedness. And I liked Lady Macbeth's whole atmosphere. I thought she was lovely; I was quite transfixed by her in many ways. But, as I said, my engagement started to fizzle out because connections, character, language, the plot's momentum and its coherence, a lot of these were missing. After a while I had to give up and look at it as a degenerate cabaret.

As to the whole idea behind the Festival (as with the RSC's Complete Works Festival (in 2006) and their World Theatre season back in the 1960s), to me these are thrilling events and demonstrate Shakespeare's complete universality. Whatever one thinks of any individual production, it is a wonderful thing that every culture has their own response to this same guy's body of work that speaks to all of us. I think it can be set in any period; it can be done in any way so long as you remain true to the essence of the play, why the play was written. The stakes were very high in Jacobean England, and I thought moving into Eastern Europe we'd have something with similarly high stakes that perhaps our current English world doesn't really experience. I hoped to learn something about their world and have something added to my understanding of the play, but I have to say that this production did neither for me.

CHAPTER TWENTY

TWO GENTLEMEN OF VERONA FOR/ BY ZIMBABWEAN DIASPORIC COMMUNITIES

Sonia Massai

This production of *The Two Gentlemen of Verona* pre-existed the Globe to Globe Festival, having been first staged in London (at the Oval House Theatre in November 2008) and then in other venues across the UK and overseas, including, most crucially, at HIFA (the Harare International Festival of Theatre) in 2009, as well as in high-density suburbs in Harare. Denton Chikura and Tonderai Munyevu, the two actors playing fifteen roles between them, including Crab the dog, moved to London from Zimbabwe just over ten years ago, while Arne Pohlmeier, the German-born director and co-founder of Two Gents Productions, was raised in Cameroon and lived in South Africa before settling in London. The personal backgrounds and the self-consciously intercultural mission statement that informs the work of this extraordinarily talented young company have had a palpable impact on their magnificent reworking of *The Two Gentlemen of Verona*, which opened as part of the Globe to Globe Festival on 9 May. Within seconds of entering the stage via its trap-door, Chikura and Munyevu had gripped the audience's attention through their unique style, which draws from South African township theatre as much as from Shakespeare, to offer a phenomenally entertaining, fast-paced version of Shakespeare's early comedy.

By the time it opened at the Globe to Globe Festival, this production had changed in some obvious and in some more subtle ways. Generally speaking, as director Pohlmeier explained when I asked him how he would define his approach to this play, the work he had done with Chikura and Munyevu to adapt their production to the Globe stage still relied primarily on the conventions first used in *Woza Albert!*, which has become the best-known example of South African township theatre worldwide since its première at the Market Theatre in Johannesburg in 1981. Pohlmeier added that Bertolt Brecht and the Berliner Ensemble had also had a considerable influence on South African theatre in the second half of the twentieth century, either directly, as their work became renowned internationally, or via other theatre artists and practitioners, including Peter Brook, who favoured a presentational over a representational approach to theatre-making. Still, according to Pohlmeier, South Africans found that Brecht and Brook validated the way in which local traditions foreground storytelling over characterization.

The main change prompted by their participation in the Festival was a switch from performing mainly in English to performing exclusively in Shona. Like all of the companies who played at the Festival, Two Gents were asked to use no English. I wondered whether they felt that switching to Shona proved inspiring or hampering, given that English is the dominant language in which they normally perform and that a hybrid of English and Shona is currently spoken in most areas of modern-day Zimbabwe. Pohlmeier confirmed that using a specifically commissioned translation of Shakespeare into an archaic, elevated version of the language currently spoken in Zimbabwe proved a wonderful opportunity to make changes that in turn clarified and fine-tuned some of the staple features of their production. Most important among these features is their use of a theatrical language which, by drawing on songs, set gestures, minimal props and accessories, signifies alongside the dialogue, or, for non-Shona speakers who watched the production at the Globe, without relying on language. 'When directors and actors can rely on language to reach their audiences', as Pohlmeier put it during an informal conversation we had at the Globe soon after the Festival had ended, 'they can get away with paying less attention to visual and acoustic signifiers other than language itself. As a result', Pohlmeier added, 'the visual or acoustic features in productions where the directors and the actors and their audiences share the same language can come across as redundant if they are not carefully thought through, but they are essential in productions conceived with touring or international festivals in mind.'

Other subtle changes found their way into their well-travelled show in preparation for its opening at the Festival. Many pre-existing details in this production are references to how middle-class Zimbabweans experience everyday life in large cities like Harare. Among such references, most memorable is the domestic setting for the first exchange between Julia and Lucetta (Act 1 Scene 2), when Julia groans with pleasure as Lucetta helps her slip into the trunk that features throughout the production, in this instance signifying a warm bath. New references to modern-day Zimbabwe were added, the most prominent being the duet that Julia and Proteus sing as the latter prepares to leave Verona (the leave-taking scene, Act 2 Scene 2). Apparently, the songs in this sequence are very popular in Zimbabwe. The sequence of scenes in Act 2 had also been rearranged, the action jumping from the end of Act 1 to Act 2 Scenes 2 and 3 (there is one other leave-taking scene, where Lance tells off his 'cruel-hearted dog' (2.3.7), Crab, played with extraordinary aplomb by Munyevu, for failing to empathize with his owner and the rest of his family as Lance prepares to follow his master Proteus to Milan). This change was prompted by the

Fig. 9 Silvia (Tonderai Munyevu) and Eglamour (Denton Chikura), *Two Gentlemen of Verona*, Two Gents Productions, from London/Harare, Zimbabwe; director Arne Pohlmeier.

fact that the narrative thrust of the production had to be reinforced, especially with a non-Shona-speaking audience in mind. As a result, all the scenes that take place in Verona before the action moves to Milan were played sequentially.

The response Two Gents enjoyed at the Globe was overwhelmingly positive. Pohlmeier was delighted to report that performing in Shona at the Globe had become very much part of the journey of self-discovery that they had started as intercultural, diasporic practitioners when the production first opened in 2008. In Pohlmeier's words:

the combination of four years of hard work and the feedback we have received since playing at the Globe before a very mixed audience, made up of non-Shona-speaking theatre-goers but also of members of Zimbabwean communities in London, has helped us realize just how strong cultural (rather than merely national) affiliations have become for us since moving to London.

At least for this young, London-based company, the Globe to Globe Festival proved a thoroughly enjoyable and professionally exciting experience.

CHAPTER TWENTY-ONE

INTER-THEATRICAL READING

Theatrical and multicultural appropriations of 1–3 Henry VI
as a Balkan trilogy

Aleksandar Saša Dundjerović

Shakespeare's plays are some of the most frequently produced works in the national repertoire in Serbia, Albania and Macedonia. His work came to the Balkans at the end of the nineteenth century, translated and adapted from the German, as part of the European-wide Romantic Movement. The plays have been part of a growing national consciousness that arose in different Balkan nations at different times throughout the nineteenth and early twentieth centuries. Nations recently liberated from the Ottoman empire appropriated Shakespeare as a way of connecting themselves with the wider framework of European culture. Moreover, in translation Shakespeare's iambic pentameter sounds like epic heroic poetry, which dominated the oral tradition in Serbian, Macedonian and Albanian cultures. This greatly helped to localize Shakespeare within people's experience, making the plays sound like the stories from their national cultures.

By bringing Serbian, Albanian and Macedonian national theatres and their directors' visions together through the three parts of Henry VI, the 'Balkan trilogy' worked as an intercultural mini-festival within the Festival proper. I came to these productions interested in how the first plays about England's civil wars would be seen through the experience of recent civil wars in the Balkans. I wanted to know how Shakespeare's plays would be used for a collaboration between three well-established national theatres. However, I was to discover that this was an organizational grouping initiated by the Globe and based on national contexts (some might say prejudices) that suggested which nations could best understand Shakespeare's 1–3 Henry VI; this was a marriage of expedience that inadvertently produced a number of inter-theatrical connections once the three quite different interpretations had been seen at the Globe. Ideas of closeness, misunderstandings and the domestication of Shakespeare in response to the realities of history helped to unite these three quite disparate performances.

The national theatres involved in this Balkan trilogy share a similar theatrical approach founded on the centrality of the director's concept, permanent members of an acting company, the text as a starting-point, and a willingness to mould textual interpretation to specific cultural and social circumstances. Once the *Henry VI* trilogy had been commissioned, the companies began to edit the texts according to their cultural, political and theatrical visions, in this way constructing an inner production framework that spoke to their local audiences. However, there was an implicit awareness that the London performances would also have to speak to a more international audience as part of the Festival. The productions as they were performed at the Globe appeared, then, within a more complex cultural/political/artistic outer framework.

Although recent productions of *Henry VI* in Britain – the landmark Wars of the Roses adaptation by the English Shakespeare Company in 1989, and Michael Boyd's RSC production of the full trilogy in 2000 and 2006 – place the three parts within a single theatrical context, the Balkan trilogy comprised quite separate productions by different national theatres and produced quite different outcomes. Not only were the performances in three distinct languages, but their directors approached Shakespeare's trilogy as three individual plays. These theatre companies were not in contact with each other before the opening of their productions at the Globe. Each group worked independently, aiming to produce the best possible show for their individual opening nights at the Festival. It was not until all three productions were performed together in the final performance on Sunday 13 May that the trilogy could be viewed as a whole and as one inter-theatrical narrative. Each of the productions was just over two hours long, a running time mandated by the Festival, making a total playing time of approximately seven hours. The demand to trim the plays from their usual running time of around three hours each appears to have been critical in determining the emphasis and focus of the directors' visions.

The first promotional material designed by the Globe before these three productions were created used images from recent wars: for the Serbian part, a Yugoslav army tank out to crush Croatian independence; World War II bunkers in Albania served as reminders of Enver Hoxha's dictatorship which closed the country off from the rest of the world for the latter part of the twentieth century; and a line-up of military boots on the Macedonian flyer illustrated the growing tension between the country's Macedonian and Albanian populations. London audiences might easily assume they would see performances with very contemporary settings and a clear, shared, conceptual framework. Such a collaborative production would have been (and would be) a phenomenal cultural encounter; however, these respected national theatres have yet to agree to perform for each other's audiences, although they are geographically only a few hundred miles apart. The fact they all came together on the Globe stage is in itself one of the great success stories of the Festival.

1 HENRY VI – THE NATIONAL THEATRE BELGRADE, SERBIA

In Serbia, it was the famous and controversial poet Laza Kostić who first translated the Sonnets and *Romeo and Juliet* into Serbian in the style of national epic poetry in 1859, and the first part of the *Henry VI* trilogy reflected that same epic tone. Part 1 set up the life of King Henry VI (Hadzi Nenad Maricić) from the death of Henry V, the subsequent loss of England's French lands and the political machinations that contributed to the dynastic feud which led to the Wars of the Roses. It is arguably the weakest part of Shakespeare's trilogy, with its plethora of names, jump-cuts to various locations and lengthy battle scenes. It might have seemed at first glance that the Serbians had drawn the short straw, but this was not true. When asked which of Shakespeare's plays he would like to tackle, Nikita Milivojević (the director) said that he would most like to stage 1 *Henry VI*, because it was not about Shakespeare – 'it is the story about us'.

By focusing on political spin and augmenting the descriptions of the battles through physical, often slapstick, humour and non-verbal commentary about what is taking place delivered by two very funny messengers (Pavle Jerenić and Bojan Krivokapić), this production both set up the action and introduced the conflicts that would be developed in Parts 2 and 3. Both Milivojević's adaptation and directing were comically brilliant because they focused on group improvisations, non-verbal physical expressivity and the inter-theatrical interplay between different characters in situations which subtly mimic those that led to the break-up of Yugoslavia and the civil war that ensued. Thus, in Milivojević's version the English have become the Serbians and the French the Croatians. Talbot (Nebojsa Kundacina) has become one of the many Serbian heroes produced by the civil war, and the bishop of Winchester (Predrag Ejdus) turns into a manipulative and power-driven local Serbian oligarch. Joan of Arc (Jelena Djulvezan) became a key character in this environment. In the trial scene Joan was delusional because she believed in a cause that was not supported by the main council, mirroring all those people who believed in independent states in the former Yugoslavia. There was a great deal of meaning in all of these characters for a Serbian audience, who reacted to these resonances sometimes with laughter and sometimes with sadness, recognizing their local experiences of the civil war in Yugoslavia. The UK, and in particular London, became home for thousands of Serbians escaping war and military conscription in the 1990s. Live music, created both by actors drumming on metal chairs and by three musicians accompanying the performance from the balcony above the main stage, amply underpinned the local references to Serbian national sentiment and were used to support the action.

In the words of the translator, Zoran Paunović, 'we wanted to create our very own Serbian *Henry VI* in which we can recognize ourselves'.

For Milivojević, the main theatrical prop was a big round metal table that served multiple uses and was made up of components that could be moved around. The table was evocative: it suggested a disintegrating body politic, a decision-making body like the UN or the Hague War Tribunal, but also local politicians embroiled in endless discussions about the peace process and postwar settlements. The key decisions, which determined the action of the play, were communicated through group chanting, repetitive rhythms and drumming on the metal chairs around this central round table, a stage metaphor that made sense to the Serbian contingent in the audience. For the past twenty years, all political decisions there have been made by some group of people sitting around some round table and talking in what have become repetitive clichés, full of soundbites without passion or purpose.

The Festival audience that understood Serbian (in my estimate about half the auditorium) vocally responded in real time to comments and to the very local Serbian context built into the performance and received the production very enthusiastically, clearly taking in all the political nuances and references. This was especially evident in the instance of the Serbian translator adding the word 'bridge' as an afterthought following the word 'tower' which occurs in Shakespeare – 'they prepared an ambush on the bridge . . . no, I mean, in the tower' (1.3) – thus alluding to the first assassination attempt on the late Premier Zoran Djindjić, an event that is still part of what is considered a national conspiracy, with suspects ranging from paramilitary units to crime cartels and the CIA.

2 HENRY VI – THE NATIONAL THEATRE OF TIRANA, ALBANIA

In Albania, Shakespeare was first introduced in the early part of the twentieth century. Translations by Skënder Luarasi, Vedat Kokona and Alqi Kristo were mainly driven by the political situation, and particularly during the Communist period (1944–90) they were used as a propaganda tool to elicit national pride. The Albanian production, arguably the most dated staging of the three, had a very specific set of references for its native audience. The notion of revenge at the centre of this play is rooted in blood feuds in Albania, where whole families are involved and where people are eliminated across generations in acts of retribution. This desire for revenge dominates the future in Albania and Kosovo today. Moreover, the reference to political power in this production was founded on political oligarchy, and its theatrical representation of ridiculous and infantile political behaviour was clearly recognized by the Albanian audience watching the production at the Globe.

2 Henry VI is, of course, to be defined more in terms of plot structure, involving a weak king who, as the focus of intrigue, provokes dissent. It begins with the marriage of King Henry VI (Indrit Çobani) to the young and dowry-less Margaret of Anjou (Ermira Hysaj) brought over from France as a trophy by Suffolk, who will use her as a gift to the young king, and in return for which he is given a dukedom. Gloucester, unhappy with this promotion and fearing Suffolk's new influence on the king, starts plotting against Suffolk. This establishes the power struggle that dominates this play. In this Part, Richard positions himself as rightful heir to the throne, while Jack Cade starts a peasant rebellion and popular revolt against the King.

The game of power, in director Adonis Filipi's version, which saw twenty-two members of the National Theatre on stage, was conceptualized as a child's game. However, with some of their leading actors in the ensemble adopting a very old-school style of performance, the playfulness was lost. This production of *2 Henry VI* was met with considerable criticism in subsequent blogs and in official reviews.[1] I found it to be the least accomplished of the trilogy. Different parts of the production were disjointed, such as the style of acting, the director's vision, the set and the costumes. The most glaring problem involved costumes that were a cross between nineteenth-century opera and *Star Trek*; they did not suit the daylight, the open-air stage or the replica sixteenth-century building. The music was electronic, pre-recorded and, for the most part, mixed with some live acoustic moments and live drumming, but added nothing to the performance itself, as it was rather undefined and understated. The interaction with the audience was effective, but it was more of an add-on to the action than something integral to the production.

I could not understand why the director had chosen this dated approach. The *Guardian* critic situated this production in the 1950s, and other bloggers somewhat insultingly referred to it as 'The Eurovision' and 'Borat-like moment of the Festival'.[2] However, on reflection, I think that Filipi may have deliberately created a theatrical style that found its starting-point in children's games and in dark dreams of being in power, where everyone wants to be a king one day. The opening scene showed three children on scooters playing around the stage and wearing paper crowns from party crackers. The closing scene, which showed one of those same paper crowns on an empty throne moved by remote control, perhaps indicated what the director's concept was supposed to be, but these moments were not consistently developed within the main action throughout the performance. Rather, they functioned precisely as dramatic moments, even dramatic flashes, in their own right. This was a very slow and static performance whose intention was, as Filipi told me after the production, to show 'children playing with history, where anything can happen'. Indeed, from costumes to props, which looked like they had been taken from the story of Peter Pan, the staging represented a vision of a world both infantile and dangerous at the same time.

I could see how on a proscenium stage and perhaps in an indoor theatre this production would have worked much better. Having developed the production for a proscenium stage in Tirana's National Theatre, Filipi's theatrical expression relied on lights, recorded sound effects, a revolving stage and different playing areas. As a result, the production faced numerous obstacles, chief among which was to adapt the production to the space, with its Elizabethan thrust stage. The physical space of the stage, therefore, worked against the director's vision. The fact that the Globe's stage does not support any technical machinery and that the companies were given a mandate to keep both set and costume to a minimum did not allow the director any interplay with key features of set or props, such as the over-sized bed or the throne. All of the stage effects were lost, because the production was played in broad daylight. On this thrust stage, without décor and with the very specific requirement for strong vocal projection, the actors were pushed into overacting.

Actor Bujar Asqeriu, who played the rebel Jack Cade, brought new energy on stage and made a drifting audience more engaged, but unfortunately the unfocused group performance by the other rioters did not support his performance. The very static, monumental *mise-en-scène*, coupled with a dull, classical, declamatory style of acting and statesman-like movements from Henry's court, worked against Filipi's vision but oddly in favour of the space. The Globe stage best supports an actor centre stage declaiming a great text for an audience listening attentively to the words. In that sense the chosen theatrical approach was not inappropriate, but it failed to move, leaving a non-Albanian-speaking audience in confusion as to why it was staged in this style. The Albanian-speaking audience, however, responded incredibly well to the production. At the end, the performance moved from the stage into the auditorium and the outside courtyard, where the actors greeted, and talked to, the audience, while at the same time playing the national drum (the 'goc') and dancing. Thus the end of the production turned into a communal celebration interrupted only by the house manager and the ushers, as the next show was scheduled for shortly afterwards.

3 HENRY VI – THE NATIONAL THEATRE OF BITOLA, MACEDONIA

The first theatre productions of Shakespeare in the Macedonian language did not take place until after 1944. The city of Bitola perceived itself as the cultural capital of Macedonia, where the National Theatre was founded after World War II, performing both regionally and internationally. The ensemble of the National Theatre of Bitola joined up with the established American director John Blondelle, who was invited to stage *3 Henry VI*. In making this invitation, the Bitola theatre demonstrated an openness towards international and world theatre. As a result, this Festival performance seemed in some ways to be the most free from a dependence on language and the most contemporary of the three. It was an excellent group performance, driven by visual theatricality. This part of the trilogy was founded on musical numbers and choreographed dance scenes, reminding the audience, through symbolic movements, of the beheadings and war atrocities that took place in the Balkans in the 1990s.

Part 3 starts with a struggle over the throne after Henry's escape from recent battles and as York takes his place, although temporarily. Henry (Petar Gorko) is now older and tired of fighting but is pushed to continue by those around him, especially his wife, Margaret (Gabriela Petrushevska), who is now very powerful and aggressively seductive. This play contains several battle scenes in which war is in full swing, increasingly placing Richard (Martin Michevski) at the centre of the action. Blondelle had previously staged a version of it in California with his own theatre company, casting his wife as Margaret of Anjou. The Bitola production, however, was not a copy of the one staged in the USA.

Blondelle's Part 3 was generally considered by many commentators the most interesting of the Henry trilogy, and it has been praised for its modern interpretation of the battle scenes.[3] He found theatrical solutions for numerous battles through stylized acting and choreography. The pallet of blue costume, accentuated with bursts of colour that drew attention to the particular emotional state of a character, worked especially well. These costumes were inspired by a hybrid representation of military uniforms and the Macedonian national costume, and were subtly accentuated with colour and with such details as Queen Margaret's red stiletto shoes, or a brooch that distinguished whether a character belonged to the House of York or Lancaster. Imaginative and highly symbolic use of music and dance with live drumming composed by Miodrag Necak was particularly effective. For example, a dance using sticks represented one of the numerous battle scenes. Like the Albanian production, the Bitola performance used the national drum (the 'goc') located centre stage.

There was a considerable difference between the two halves of this production. The first was very slow-paced, consisting of fragmented scenes reminiscent of a soap opera, with its various twists and turns in family life and relationships. However, the second opened up at a fantastic pace and with clear images rapidly built one upon the other, as if it was a different production. I felt like I was watching the second half of a football game where the players had been told by their coach to change their game completely. The most impressive choreographic numbers took place in this second half, and I was left quite moved by the end of the production, feeling the futility and madness of the never-ending complexity of war. Talking to the director after the performance, I understood that he deliberately wanted the first part to develop slowly in order to allow the audience to absorb the atmosphere of the play. This allowed him to conceive the second part as a distinct contrast, immersing the audience in a whirlwind of battles.

The strongest part of the production was its representation of the women. Blondelle focused on Shakespeare's dramatic portrayal of Margaret of Anjou. Indeed, the best scene in the production came in the second part when, through physical movement and implied intrigue, the marvellously powerful Queen Margaret meets Sonja Mihajlova's Warwick and Kristina Hristova Nikolov's Louis of France cast as women. This cross-gendering was informed by the context of the Balkan wars, where women played not only a crucial but also an ambiguous role. On the one hand, women were among the most vocal opponents of the war, army conscription and violence in general. On the other, women also occupied prominent positions within the regime that generated the conditions for violence or were directly involved in it. One such powerful woman was Mirjana Marković, wife of the former president of Serbia, Slobodan Milosević. Another woman associated with militantism was a popular folk music singer married to Zeljko Raznjatović Arkan, one of the most powerful and menacing warlords of the paramilitary groups. Long after the production was over I could still see the images and the brilliant directorial solutions in this production. Blondell's theatricality was effective and image-driven, involving live sound, physical expression and the use of colour to accentuate meaning. It also interlaced physical movement with inter-theatrical connections between the political and the aesthetic, communicating strongly with the audiences. This powerful ending to the Balkan trilogy engaged different senses, turning the trilogy into a kind of meta-narrative, or an overarching affective framework for the Balkan wars of the 1990s.

ENDNOTES

1 See Matt Trueman, 'Henry VI (Parts 1, 2, 3) – Review', Guardian, 16 May 2012, www.guardian.co.uk/stage/2012/may/16/henry-vi-parts-1-2-3-review, 28 January 2013; Craig Melson, 'Globe to Globe: Albanian Henry VI is Henry the Terrible', PlayShakespeare.com, 12 May 2012, www.playshakespeare.com/henry-vi-part-ii/337-theatre-reviews/6053-globe-to-globe-albanian-henry-vi-is-henry-the-terrible; Ivan Toronyi-Lalic, 'Globe to Globe: Henry VI, Parts 1, 2 and 3, Shakespeare's Globe', the Arts desk, 14 May 2012, www.theartsdesk.com/theatre/globe-globe-henry-vi-parts-1-2-and-3-shakespeares-globe; Peter Orford, 'Year of Shakespeare: Henry VI Part Two', 15 May 2012, http://bloggingshakespeare.com/year-of-shakespeare-henry-vi-part-two, all 13 October 2012.
2 Toronyi-Lalic, 'Globe to Globe'.
3 See Trueman, 'Henry VI', Melson 'Globe to Globe', Toronyi-Lalic, 'Globe to Globe' and Orford, 'Year of Shakespeare'.

Fig. 10 Joan of Arc (Jelena Đulvezan) with members of the company, 1 *Henry VI*, National Theatre Belgrade in association with the Laza Kostic Fund from Belgrade, Serbia; director Nikita Miliojević.

CHAPTER TWENTY-TWO

'THIS IS OUR MODERN HISTORY'

The Balkans *Henry VI*

Randall Martin

SERBIA

Watching Shakespeare performed during the Festival in half a dozen languages I don't understand has made one thing clear: the most successful productions have used physical expression and non-verbal modes of communication to connect the locally transformed plays to Globe audiences. That's not to say the spoken text in translation hasn't mattered. Far from it. One of the delights of this festival has been seeing the theatre globally transformed every day, as London's multicultural communities have turned out to watch Shakespeare in their home languages. But these spectators have also appreciated an emphasis on showing the story, since most are presumably unfamiliar with plays like 1 *Henry VI*. The powerful visual telegraphing of this early, multi-authored and eclectic drama of England's loss of its medieval French conquests and back-story to the Wars of the Roses was just one of many impressive aspects of Nikita Milivojević's brilliant National Theatre Belgrade production.

Peter Hall and John Barton's influential RSC production of *The Wars of the Roses* (1963–4) ditched the traditional staging of Shakespearean history as heraldic pageantry, reverence for kingship and martial heroism. Instead, they offered audiences a sceptically updated reading of Shakespearean politics shaped by brute force, political opportunism and self-destructive ambition. Milivojević's boldly conceptual staging was reminiscent of *The Wars of the Roses* in several ways. One was the continual use of a large central table. In Hall and Barton's production it served as historical council-board, political arena for contending egos and factions, and focal point for the beleaguered ship of state. Milivojević's table captured all these functions. But because it was multi-sectioned it also evolved theatrically as soundscape,

The quotation in the chapter title comes from Nikita Milivojević, director of the Serbian production.

metadramatic set, and natural and built environment: a polyfunctional stage within a stage.

The actors lay motionless on the table-top as the play began. Upstage centre, a medieval-style reliquary containing the remains of Henry V sat on one of the high-backed chairs. It remained on stage throughout the action, silently bearing witness to both medieval and modern imperial overreach and collapse. Slowly the actors awoke to quiet Serbian music – history rising into contemporary life the way Thomas Nashe described Edward Alleyn reviving the play's tragic hero, John Talbot, on the Rose Theatre stage in 1592. Winchester slowly paced around the table, brooding and menacing, joining the rest after they had seated themselves, but remaining a scheming insider-outsider. Here and in the early scenes of squabbling and sieges, the atmosphere was often matey and jokey, aggression masked behind comic insults but steadily accumulating in beautifully paced waves of rancorous violence.

Milivojević used the continually metamorphosing table to represent the kind of siege warfare Elizabethan England was involved in. When Joan of Arc recaptured the city of Orléans from the English, for instance, she crawled up from beneath the divided table and slowly pulled the sleeping English soldiers down to the floor before climbing on top, victorious. With the exception of Joan (Jelena Đulvezan), this production's emphasis was not on martial heroism or family sacrifice (the operatic deaths of Talbot *père et fils* were cut) but on national and international group dynamics. Lords and soldiers on both sides were dressed similarly in a medieval-modern mix of rough, earth-tone fabrics. The French were distinguishable by their blue-ish coats, and Joan by her long country braids. She was the only female character in this adaptation. That freedom in reshaping the text – not just by cuts but by means of local allusion and intelligent re-organization that would speak to modern audiences' political consciousness through sharpened historical analogy – was another way in which Milivojević's production recalled the imaginative audacity of Hall and Barton.

Joan's controversial spirituality was suggested by inward conviction rather than militant religiosity, her charisma by the power to galvanize French resistance rather than by erotic or demonic connivance. When she defeated Talbot in combat, she wielded the production's one and only sword, with the help of a dozen Frenchmen lined up behind her, joining their arms to hers with the awesome force of a steam-engine piston (see Figure 10). By way of compensation for cutting the countess of Auvergne and Margaret of Anjou, Joan's expanded trial became a highlight of the production's second half. Starting within the table's removed centre section she was cross-examined by the English, first calmly, then hysterically when they failed to gain any incriminating purchase on her shrewd and level-headed answers. Milivojević told me about this scene after the performance. He wanted to make Joan's trial less one-sided, so he inserted French historical reports of Joan's trial which he had seen dramatized in Luc Besson's 1999 film, *Jeanne d'Arc*. The additional dialogue counterbalanced Joan's crude condemnation in 1 *Henry VI*, establishing her rather than Talbot as the production's tragic hero, while also strengthening topical associations with Serbia's recent political history.

Another typical moment of visually adept storytelling was King Henry's ennobling of Talbot. This followed the signature Temple Garden scene (Act 2 Scene 4), in which Shakespeare imagines the Wars of the Roses growing out of an after-dinner argument in which adversaries pluck white or red roses to signify their allegiance. Here the country's break-up was suggested by rivals pulling apart table sections and weaving maze-like to the centre piece, where they smeared their foreheads with red or white paint hidden beneath it. The table's curved segments were then re-formed into a serpentine diagonal on which all the English lords stood lined up behind Henry to greet Talbot at the downstage end. Talbot announced himself with the long list of heraldic titles that, in the original text, Sir William Lucy boasts of to the French when he comes to retrieve Talbot's dead body. In this temporally contracted moment, Talbot seemed to pronounce his fly-blown destiny at the pinnacle of his worldly fame. While this was going on, Vernon and Basset, supporters of York and Somerset, traded factional shoves at the back of the line; humorously, Henry and Talbot were oblivious to their commotion. This was emblematic of the way Milivojević heightened the Shakespearean technique of irreverent juxtaposition to de-centre the play's privileged English viewpoint and to suggest the tragi-comic fractures of contemporary Serbian and Eurozone politics.

Earlier, Vernon and Basset had helped the audience negotiate Mortimer's genealogy of York's dynastic right to the throne by visually mimicking its tangled story of births, inheritances and betrayals. In the play's final scene they reprised this kind of pantomime, but now in a playfully serious tussle over Henry V's funeral urn, which they ended up fumbling, spilling its ashes. A mock-embarrassed Vernon and Basset tried to sweep these under a section of the now completely upturned table, whose metallic legs suggested the natural and political thickets through which the coming civil wars would be fought.

ALBANIA

Although, chronologically, Part 2 of the *Henry VI* trilogy follows events dramatized by Part 1, contemporary evidence suggests Part 1 was written after Parts 2 and 3 as a prequel. So Part 2 marked Shakespeare's debut in the genre of secular dramatic history that he largely invented himself. The play's experimental circumstances explain its three episodic templates: a tragedy of court intrigue centred on Humphrey, duke of Gloucester, and his wife Eleanor (Acts 1–3); the comic-destructive popular rebellion of Jack Cade (Act 4); and the outbreak of the Wars of the Roses between Lancastrians and Yorkists in the First Battle of St Albans (Act 5). To its credit, Adonis Filipi's National Theatre of Albania's production did not attempt to flatten this challenging diversity but used its strongest actors to give each phase a distinct representational mode and tone.

Eleanor and Humphrey's downfalls have an air of fatalistic inevitability that this production conveyed through formalized classical presentation. Body language was physically closed, and the actors' facial reactions, when they were not speaking, tended to be inscrutable. Henry VI (Indrit Çobani) was appropriately a bit of an exception. His visible passions underlined his conflicted inability to impose his authority on his subversive lords. Margaret of Anjou (Ermira Hysaj), on the other hand, was coolly statuesque. When she and her banished lover, Suffolk, parted, their lips came close but did not touch, suggesting their passionate affair was non-sexual. Yet it wasn't enduring either (her scene cradling Suffolk's head was cut), since Margaret later expressed silent interest in a macho Lancastrian substitute, Somerset.

These presentational choices created a wooden performance by today's standards. The drama was carried by the spoken text, making it more challenging for non-Albanian, and possibly also native, speakers, most of whom were presumably encountering this early Shakespeare play for the first time. In addition, the script consisted mainly of cuts to Shakespeare's play to arrive at the preferred Festival running time of two and a quarter hours, rather than a combination of trimming and adaptation. This is arguably a more respectful approach to Shakespeare's work, and the overall ethos of the Albanian production suggested that cultural homage was one of its goals. But here, as in other Globe to Globe Festival performances I saw, in practice straight cuts without reshaped dialogue and visual re-invention made telling the story and expressing character psychology more restricted. It also tended to produce a script that was less agile in making Shakespeare a vehicle for an intercultural exchange of ideas and identities.

Nonetheless, performances by Gloucester (Kristaq Skrami) and Eleanor (Yllka Mujo) showed that a 'neo-classical' sensibility was not simply bloodless. In the opening scene Gloucester stifled his anger at hearing the humiliating terms of Henry's marriage to Margaret. Aided by a commanding voice, he remained steely and measured in response to outlandish accusations by Margaret, Somerset, Suffolk and Winchester, who were seeking his death to advance their personal agendas. Eleanor was especially effective in expressing a sense of tragic decorum. Her banishment for necromancy evoked stoicism rather than pathos. Wearing a flowing white gown, she walked with grave dignity down the stage and centre steps into the yard. There Globe spectators spontaneously collaborated with the production's courtly sensibility by

Fig. 11 Jack Cade (Bujar Asqeriu) with members of the company as the rebels, 2 *Henry VI*, National Theatre of Albania from Tirana, Albania; director Adonis Filipi.

respectfully opening a lane for her to exit at an unbroken, self-possessed pace, in contrast to the cruel ridicule of the mob that Eleanor describes at the beginning of the scene.

Jack Cade (Bujar Asqeriu) burst this restraint with broad comic bluster and narcissistic appeals to the audience to chant his name. When he invoked the utopian language of freedom and equality, he tossed out small oranges to ragged followers (supplied by his puppet-master, York?), suggestive of huckstering demagoguery. One orange went to a Blind Woman who was left to wander precariously when the crowd went off to savage the gentry. When Henry's agent, Lord Clifford, arrived to persuade the rebels to submit to the king, the Blind Woman listened carefully and led the crowd's reversal against Cade. His encounter with the self-satisfied country landowner Alexander Iden was cut, thus depriving the play's topical but still politically resonant protest against rural displacement, poverty, and hunger of a final, memorable voice.

Trimming of the original text meant that Cade's compressed narrative shifted quickly into the play's civil-war phase, dominated by a splendidly forceful and splenetic duke of York (Vasjan Lami) and his lame brat of a son, Richard (Roland Saro, who had earlier played a cleaver-wielding Dick Butcher). But the climactic battle of St Albans was represented by stylized choreography in great-coats, a wardrobe choice which inadvertently seemed to restrict the ensemble's anti-heroic presentation of epic combat. A final ambiguous touch came by way of an up-for-grabs throne, rolled centre stage on hidden casters as a wordless epilogue, with a paper crown on its empty seat. This detail took us back to the production's prologue, where three children, one of whom was presumably meant to represent the boy-king, wore paper crowns and raced around the stage briefly on scooters. Driven by a sharp breeze on the afternoon I attended, the throne resumed rolling a bit further around the stage in an open, wandering arc.

MACEDONIA

3 Henry VI depicts the brutality and suffering of civil war as a series of agonized battles and death scenes, punctuated by blasted or ironized hopes of peace. In less imaginative productions the fighting and dying begin to look and sound the same. Inspired ones, such as John Blondell's National Theatre of Bitola production in Macedonian, creatively differentiate these moments as historically specific but always sadly contemporary human calamities.

Part 3 stretches any company's material and personal resources by calling for four major battles to be staged. Historically these represent the downward national spiral of the late medieval Wars of the Roses, human fragments of which are still being dug up today. Blondell individualized each battle with stylized images of modern warfare familiar from today's media, and with locally evocative details such as Macedonian songs and dances. Each battle therefore told a different story but built up a typology of war. Blondell also internally unified the sequence of battles through recurring circular actions and repeated movements that suggested the wider Balkans history of endemic retaliation. In the first conflict (Wakefield), slow-motion soldiers wielded long wooden pikes like ancient hunters sticking wild pigs, while Clifford viciously revenged his father's death (in Part 2) by slicing the throat of York's youngest son, Rutland, with a red-gloved hand. National culture turned schizoid during the second battle (Towton), as a trio of girlish Fates sang an upbeat folksong while muscle-shirted thugs mimed killing-field atrocities. The third battle (Barnet) juxtaposed the 'king-maker' Warwick, disrobed in a whirling Dance of Death, with black-hooded killers and victims relentlessly swapping roles in rapid execution scenes. Eventually they gathered to sing a chorus-line lament until, after one by one imaginary bullets had been fired in to their heads, the final voice was silenced. Soldiers danced around an exhilarated Queen Margaret for the final battle (Tewkesbury) before shoving her down stage to watch the York brothers, Edward, Clarence and Richard, impulsively slaughter her son, Prince Edward. Throughout these battles not a single broadsword, banner or suit of chainmail appeared.

These briskly paced ensemble-narratives alternated with skilfully nuanced and energetic individual performances. The Lancastrian King Henry (Petar Gorko) signalled his conflicted rejection of royal authority by contemplating his doffed crown in the opening stand-off with the Yorkists. His philosophical bent continued in

Fig. 12 Margaret (Gabriela Petrushevska) with members of the company, *3 Henry VI*, National Theatre of Bitola from Bitola, Macedonia; director John Blondell.

the Towton-field vision of symbiotic natural and human creation. But shadowed by choric grief for fathers and sons blinded to human attachments by the predatory instincts of war, it exploded into angry frustration when Margaret (Gabriela Petrushevska) entered to disturb his pacifist reverie. Henry gave the queen his crown and displayed his one violent impulse of the production by briefly lunging at her throat.

Margaret's tragedy of thirsting vengeance unfolded with her wardrobe. Wearing crimson high heels and a tailored blue uniform, she mimed lapping up blood with her hand during Rutland's death, sending the first of many deliberately mixed signals about women in power. She veiled her thirst socially in the amusing transition scene at the French court. Sporting a fashionable red top, she downed several glasses of vodka while pleading for King Lewis' support to restore her deposed husband to the throne. As she became more tottery, Lewis (Kristina Hristova Nikolova, one of several cross-castings) dallied with the lips of a suddenly vulnerable but booze-befuddled Prince Edward (Nikolche Projchevshi). The French farce deepened further when Warwick arrived to broker an arranged marriage between a fizzy Lady Bona (Valentina Gramosli, later doubling as Lady Grey) and the new Yorkist King Edward. Margaret miraculously sobered up as news of Edward's marriage to Lady Grey made her and an enraged Warwick instant allies. Prince Edward awoke from his alcoholic stupor to find himself betrothed to Warwick's daughter.

Learning later of Warwick's death (a scattering of red petals), Margaret's deep desires were revealed through a blazing scarlet dress as she licked her wrists in anticipation of full-blooded revenge at Tewkesbury. She had taken in nothing from York's agonized curses after taunting him with a cloth dipped in Rutland's blood, and not seen any danger in Prince Edward gleefully setting up York's severed head on the city of York gates (i.e. the Globe balcony – one instance of this production's full and inventive use of the Globe Theatre space). Margaret's devastated lament for her murdered son was nonetheless deeply moving, even if not redemptive. The beautifully sad music which accompanied her was typical of greater Macedonian detailing in the play's second half. In a thrilling reversal, the dying Warwick (Sonja Mihajlova) transformed the inward-looking focus of Shakespeare's contempt-for-ambition speech into the resentment of a modern Balkans soldier addressing the audience: 'This death isn't just mine, it's yours too,' she seemed to say, '*you* are also responsible for these wars!', before exiting defiantly.

The physically contrasting duo of Edward and Richard mirrored psychological opposites. At 6 ft 4 in., Edward (Ognen Drangovski) strutted the width of the Globe stage in about three paces. After bluntly propositioning the widowed Lady Grey, ruttishness compounded his political dimwittedness. By contrast, his compact and loyally deceitful brother Richard of Gloucester (Martin Mirchevski) furiously bobbed and limped. When he revealed his fratricidal ambitions in mid-play soliloquy, the white heat of his psychopathic anger needed no translation. It culminated in a full-frontal assault on a shakily righteous Henry via a jar full of blood thrown twice at the king's white nightgown.

The socially versatile Lady Grey, destined to outfox even Richard III and survive into the Tudor regime, was the capstone of this exuberant, visually inventive production. Normally her principled resistance to Edward's advances turns into defensive reserve after she becomes Queen Elizabeth, when she then fades into the theatrical background in this male-dominated world. But here her unabashed sexuality as Edward's consort gave him the self-confidence to throw off his temporary un-kinging by Warwick and bounce himself back into power as a kind of overgrown toy-soldier, pounding a regimental drum. Queen Elizabeth was next seen heaving into a bucket with morning sickness. News of Edward's capture shifted her priorities to saving her unborn child and her husband's political future by fleeing independently to France. She shifted roles again in the final ironic scene of Yorkist triumph. In contrast to Edward's red boots, she was dressed spotlessly in white, cradling a white rose on a pillow and tendering it a lullaby. It was perhaps the only moment of real innocence in the still unravelling national yarn of blood and death.

WEEK FOUR

CHAPTER TWENTY-THREE

SHAKESPEARE 2012/DUCHAMP 1913

The global motion of *Henry IV*

David Ruiter

In May 2012, with the help of the Compañía Nacional de Teatro Mexico, Argentina's Elkafka Espacio Teatral, the two parts of Shakespeare's *Henry IV* and the Globe Theatre in London, suddenly I was transported back to discussions surrounding the Armory Show in New York City in 1913, including Marcel Duchamp and his painting *Nude Descending A Staircase, No. 2*.

In 1912, Duchamp submitted the painting for inclusion at the Salon des Indépendants in Paris, but a fairly 'progressive' and intellectual hanging committee, including his brothers Raymond Duchamp-Villon and Jacques Villon, essentially rejected the painting for a variety of reasons, including the fact that Duchamp had painted the title on the canvas and that nudes do not traditionally descend staircases but rather recline. Upon hearing this criticism, Duchamp took a taxi and picked up the painting straightaway. Following a couple of European showings, *Nude Descending A Staircase, No. 2* came to the Armory Show in New York City in 1913. There it caused considerable outrage: one *New York Times* critic labelled the piece 'an explosion in a shingle factory';[1] another critic renamed it *Rude Descending a Staircase (Rush-Hour at the Subway)*;[2] and a magazine sponsored a contest for anyone able even to find the nude in the painting.[3] Without question, *Nude Descending a Staircase, No. 2* made a number of impacts, and became hugely influential on modern and contemporary artists. Today, the painting is considered a classic, hanging in the Philadelphia Museum of Modern Art.

So, over time, something changed. Duchamp was hardly the first to have toyed with the tremendous canonical expectations surrounding one of the most traditional of art subjects, the female nude: Édouard Manet had created at least equal shock and dismay fifty years earlier with both *Olympia* and *Le déjeuner sur l'herbe*. In those instances, part of the concern centred around the fact that the nudes were looking directly at the audience, challenging it to come to terms with the women in the paintings, as well as with present realities and politics. In this way, both Manet and Duchamp were inviting the audience not simply to gaze but to participate. And in this participation, there needed to be a certain recognition of tradition and a certain willingness to see that the traditional might not fit the current moment. That fact, rejected by some, welcomed by others (including many of their fellow artists), required translation, a movement out of one historical perspective and into another – learning a new language for artistic expression, as it were. And this translation from the past to the here and now entailed a real sense of loss: a certain canonical, or contained, perspective had been lost. But another had been found.

Something similar to Duchamp and the Armory Show in New York City in 1913 happened ninety-nine years later with two Spanish-language productions of Shakespeare at the Globe to Globe Festival in London.

GLOBE TO GLOBE

No matter what the circumstances, it would be hard to see a performance of Shakespeare's *Henry IV* at the Globe Theatre as a real break from tradition. The Globe is a traditional piece of architecture, built as a contemporary reconstruction of Shakespeare's own sixteenth-century playhouse. Shakespeare is the heart of the English literary canon. The four parts of the Second Henriad, culminating in the nationalist *Henry V* – the one play performed in English in the Festival series – are perhaps the most English of Shakespeare's works. So these performances of *Henry IV*, even if produced in Spanish by Mexican and Argentine companies, can hardly be seen as parallel to the presentation of *Nude Descending a Staircase, No. 2* at the Armory in New York, even if both use traditional subjects in traditional locations – Shakespeare at the Globe and the nude at the Armory art show – to do something new. And, indeed, I am not trying to force a parallel, except to say that sometimes, with the right production at the right time and place, with the right audience, something special happens in cultural life that allows paintings or music or theatre to become more than artistic entertainment and to take on a meaningful urgency found outside of the expected, the traditional, the canonical, or, in this case, even the language. In these moments, the works become rediscovered in the special circumstances of the moment – found, in effect, in translation.

Nowhere in my theatre-going experience has this idea of 'found in translation' been more evident than in the staging of 1 *Henry IV* by the Compañía Nacional de Teatro Mexico, and, to a lesser extent, in the staging of 2 *Henry IV* by Argentina's Elkafka Espacio Teatral during the Globe to Globe Festival at Shakespeare's Globe in the spring of 2012. The plays, the translations, the direction, acting and audiences brought into focus the idea that the global diversity of Shakespeare productions is truly the health and future of Shakespeare performance in the twenty-first century.

Fig. 13   Falstaff (Roberto Soto) and a Traveller (Gabriela Núñez), 1 *Henry IV*, Compania Nacional de Teatro from Mexico City, Mexico; director Hugo Arrevillaga Serrano.

To elaborate this point, I will first reflect on each performance individually before considering their collective accomplishment.

1 *HENRY IV*: WHAT GLOBAL THEATRE CAN DO

Under Hugo Arrevillaga Serrano's exhilarating direction, the performance of 1 *Henry IV* by the Compañía Nacional de Teatro Mexico managed possibly the best of what theatre can do: break down the barriers between actors and audience and induce participation in the provocative realities of our shared and disparate histories. There was no doubt of such accomplishment at the Globe Theatre with this production: witness the no fewer than four curtain calls the company received for each performance. Amazing. So the first question is simply: how did they do it?

First, it was technically a bravura performance: from the full, lively and expanded use of stage space, to the woolly costumes and dynamic costume changes, to the sparkingly vivacity of Gabriela Núñez as the only female actor but one playing more than five roles, to the deft use of tuba, trumpet, clarinet, trombone and percussion, to the beautifully choreographed battle scenes and the fine and fast-paced use of Latin American Spanish, we bore witness to the finest of articulations of dramatized history, British and Mexican, both from the past and in the present. Like the stage itself, with its additional construction literally and figuratively adding new avenues into the audience, the play grew from the soil of its robust past and flourished anew in the London rain.

Of course, as with any performance, technical finesse can as easily build the fourth wall as break it down, keeping the audience at an austere distance or pulling them into the centre. The real magic of this performance came from the finely woven fabric of interaction with the audience, including the light use of direct address from the actors and culminating in the whole crowd being momentarily transformed into the rag-tag royal army, mere mortals ready to be the food for powder of yet one more cannibalistic economy, as those with power use those without it for their own dehumanizing and violent discourses. The audience – global in its own right – was often amused, sometimes worried, and always and in all ways engaged.

The anxious passion of the former criminal rebel Henry Bolingbroke, now made the certified King Henry IV (Marco Antonio Garcia), here inspired the aggression of the next generation – particularly Hotspur (David Calderón) and Hal (Constantino Morán) – and created a sense of induction to violent political histories that is necessary to ensure the prospect of equally vicious political futures. Ideas of honour and heroism revolve, as Falstaff (Roberto Soto) makes clear, around a nonsensical death-wish that will come to all who pursue it, even while the common people, the necessary raw material to these ventures, would much prefer a laugh and a glass, a good story and a chance to live outside the fray.

For this play, Arrevillaga Serrano reveals that the poignancy of such politics is not the sole possession of medieval English kings and rebels, or of early modern playwrights, but rather the real stuff of the present moment. In a Mexico ravaged by violence which the media is keen to exploit, where both the government and the rebels appear to vie for supremacy in events that bloody rather than build the common weal, and borders and territorial boundaries are protected or challenged with little consideration of human cost, the play strikes home with the disturbing hyper-masculinity that binds most cultures of terror. In Henry and Falstaff's England, the nation is ravaged by the whims of ambitious men, by strong class division, thievery, double-dealing and tavern excess. The present Mexico has its own problems of state, marked by continued exploitations of various colonizers, destructive economies from within and without, strong class divisions and the drug wars. As Arrevillaga Serrano and artistic director Luis de Tavira state:

Our reality in Mexico today is violent; it's very disturbing. And to bring that to the universal themes that Shakespeare presented is very current – the themes of this play with what we are living in our country today . . . [In the play] they are rebelling against their government; there's a lot of corruption, problems that speak to Mexican society. The character of Falstaff in the middle of all of this – he just wants to stay alive. And that was one of the points that drew [the actors] to this project of *Henry IV*.[4]

In both settings, all manner of violence – against the poor, the local, women and each other – is propagated by the 'manly' few who control or wish to control territories, access and overall identity. But, as this production of 1 *Henry IV* makes evident, that dream of the powerful few is also fraught and whimsical, as those of us good enough to provide cannon fodder might well prefer not to go to war. We might, instead, wish to stay alive and work collectively to find a new, transnational, transhistorical consciousness framed by cultural openness, understanding and a different, life-embracing brand of heroism and global life.

Finally, there is also the matter of the language, nation and culture of Mexico, here so beautifully able to bring new life to an old story, but also to bring new audiences to the Globe itself. After the show, I had the opportunity to discuss the play with members of the audience from Mexico, Columbia and Spain. All had a profound appreciation for what the troupe had done: in bringing Spanish to this most English of locations; bringing a superior performance to a large and active crowd, many of whom had never been to the Globe before but who were drawn in for reasons of their own linguistic and cultural histories; and bringing a real solidarity to that crowd and space for nearly three hours. In all of this, the Compañía Nacional de Teatro Mexico showed that this is what theatre can do – reach across time and space, through cool assumptions of nations and cultural birthrights, and do something better: engage us as cosmopolitan agents in an historical process that inevitably binds us all in a community of actors and spectators, encouraging us to step out of the passive role and take up together the possibility of forging histories of a new type. This new cultural and historical making and remaking could still offer the opportunity to create and share a cultural bigness that is less violent, more constructive and indeed more globally honourable.

2 *HENRY IV*: PLAYING POLITICAL HISTORIES

Rubén Szuchmacher and the Elkafka Espacio Teatral's Argentinean production of 2 *Henry IV* had a hard act to follow. The performance of 1 *Henry IV* by the Compañía Nacional de Teatro Mexico created a brimming vivacity that heartily engaged cast and audience in an increasing solidarity of purpose and action. So when Part 2 of the history of Prince Hal (Lautaro Vilo) and Plump Jack (Horacio Peña) hit the stage with the pre-intermission action bent on delivering the Boar's Head gang in full and drunken depravity, some air came out of the balloon. The staggering and clown-suited Falstaff was no longer fun and lovable, but merely a loser (see Colour Plate 9).

Prince Hal's time with the gang became less than small beer, more shameful, and all in all simply ridiculous. Indeed, the first half played not as a pendulous competition between the gravity of state politics and the competing warmth (along with politics) of local tavern life, but merely as farce.

There was, however, a first-half moment that set the stage for better things to come. When King Henry IV (Horacio Acosta) made his brief appearance, weak with insomnia and fretting over past actions, we saw the consequences of histories and behaviours on nations and their legacies, from time immemorial. Opportunism on the part of Henry Bolingbroke had led to the destabilized throne and nation, a problem difficult to set right again and a pattern for those with the imagined strength and ambition to reach the ladder's top rung. After the intermission, the tone changed dramatically, and now we were drawn into the high stakes at hand. The archbishop (Szuchmacher) and the rebels entered into a compact of surrender with the prince's deadly serious brother, John of Lancaster (Julián Vilar), only to have him immediately renege on the terms of surrender by arresting the archbishop and the rest of the rebel leadership. King Henry collapses at the news of victory, only to have his crown temporarily stolen by the ambitious and unready Hal. Henry's stern rebuke and worry over Hal's future leadership become most serious, and the Prince's promise of reform met with all due scepticism. At this point, we see that Falstaff's concern from Part 1 has come to full reality: there is no honour here, not even among political thieves.

In the end, we find that gravity, at least temporarily, wins out: Hal does appear reformed and becomes united strongly with Prince John and the chief justice. Some shifting of high and low occurs in these moments, but the old gang's viability in the coming world is largely repelled. The rejection of Falstaff appears, here, not just good politics, but a generally good and necessary idea, and the new and more martial future of Hal aligned with his always-uniformed brother is seen as the right and only move to make. The disgusting delinquency of the many – see Shallow and Silence, all the everyday troops, as well as the gang, and maybe us, as audience – will be reformed by the passionate intensity of the few. And whether we align with one side or the other, Falstaff or the chief justice, this historical back and forth may rock us all to present nightmares of war, disenfranchisement and restriction. As a history lesson, it is one that we may well find in the midst of Shakespeare's work, but if this production took some of the joy of life out of the Falstaffian legend, it did serve to remind us, quite starkly, that a shift to the liberal and festive side of the ledger has historically often received its corrective by an excess of powerful regimentation on the other. And those in power, whether in medieval England or modern Argentina or the USA, may or may not be well suited to find or establish any domain other than the one that fully extends their own version of the haves and have-nots, the free and the chained, those who make the history books or those who, like Falstaff, we attempt to disappear.

Found in translation

Overall, the Mexican and Argentine directors and actors were amazed by the experience of place and of audience at the Globe. Szuchmacher stated: 'I have never been here before, and the Globe was a picture, like I say, a metaphor, or something like that, but not a real space. And I am a director who tries to understand the place, to understand the spaces.'[5] He went on to label the experience there as 'incredible', and Arrevillaga Serrano and de Tavira called it 'magical'. But in the case of both performances this amazement derived even more from audience than from physical space. The Mexican directors said: 'Two factors came together that are very difficult to find in the same place in the same play. Often there's a very good theatre group; often there's a very good audience. Not very often are they at the same level at the same time.'[6] Vilo (Argentine's Prince Hal) saw the audience as 'doing' the play with them, as true partners in the enterprise, as in a dance. And all were at pains to emphasize that people had come to see the play not in English but in their first language (Spanish), in London, at Shakespeare's Globe. In other words, it was the fact of the translation that made the situation so memorable.

And, in fact, the directors began their post-performance interviews on the topic of translation. For their work, what had to be done first was to translate the play into Mexican or Argentine Spanish and then to adapt the play for performance with their actors and in the space of the Globe. In this they made clear that Shakespeare's plays as they found them had to be moved from one time period to another, from one language to another, from one place and nation to another. Everything, then, had to be translated. The English *I Henry IV* travelled to Mexico, and then the Spanish *I Henry IV* travelled to England. A sixteenth-century Shakespeare play came to Mexico City and a twenty-first century Shakespeare play came to London. These performances were not just a matter of Shakespeare done in Spanish, which has happened innumerable times before; rather, these performances were all about what is found in translation, in the 'into' and 'out of' motion: into the present and out of the past; into Spanish and out of English; out of England and into Argentina and Mexico, and out of Argentina and Mexico and into England. What these plays came to be and mean resulted from the motion.

To return to the introduction and Duchamp, it's important to recollect that *Nude Descending a Staircase, No. 2* was moved out of Paris and into New York in order to find that special space and time and audience synchronicity that the directors mention above. At the right moment, in the right place, the painting arrived under conditions that allowed for its impact to be felt most fully by the art world, including the audience, critics, collectors and fellow artists. The 'magical' moment happened, the past of the nude and the present nude of Duchamp came into new conversation, and indeed started a new dialogue. But this did not happen in isolation. Duchamp was not on solo exhibit at the Armory, but was instead surrounded by a stunning collection of American and European artists, including Cézanne, van Gogh, Hopper and Cassatt. Kandinsky and Picasso, along with Duchamp, were experienced by American audiences for the first time. Native American art, including basketry, was also part of the show, challenging traditional boundaries between art and craft. And, with *The Blue Nude* and *Luxury, II*, Henri Matisse caused nearly as much concern and public criticism as Duchamp. The Armory Show, in fact, contained over 1,200 artworks, and whatever impact Duchamp had was surely highlighted through his work's conversation with all those around it.

The same is true of the productions of *Henry IV* within the Globe to Globe Festival. The concept of bringing together thirty-seven plays from thirty-seven countries means that what many have assumed as fundamental to Shakespeare work – the language – has, like the art at the Armory, been put into new conversation. As with Duchamp's *Nude*, growing out of a vast and rich art tradition, the Globe to Globe concept pricks the reclining object, Shakespeare in the original English, and puts it in motion, translates it into a new cross-cultural dialogue that has the capacity to relieve a certain near-stasis and to move all of us, as critics, audiences, players, directors and truly partner participants, to new understandings of new possibilities of dramatic activity and meaning. Returning, in conclusion, to the Globe to Globe Festival's Mexican and Argentine productions of *Henry IV*, the potential impact of such new motion becomes clear: the plays are rejuvenated in this enterprise, the global audience becomes both more inclusive and more vast, the inheritance of Shakespeare becomes cosmopolitan in its articulation in the present moment, the language and meaning and performance can challenge artistic and political boundaries in newly creative ways, the dialogue expands, the past and traditions are honoured not for what they were and meant but for what they are and can still become in our lively, current, crossing cultures. These two plays, within the context of the Festival as a whole, show in microcosm the un- or under-discovered territories still available for Shakespeare and literary and artistic endeavours. And these discoveries will be found – in new places and spaces and languages and cultures – in translation.[7]

ENDNOTES

1 Julia Street, quoted in Milton W. Brown, *The Story of the Armory Show* (New York: Abbeville Press, 1988), p. 137.

2 J. F. Griswold, *New York Evening Sun*, 20 March 1913.

3 *American Art News*, 11.21 (1 March 1913): p. 3, and 11.22 (8 March 1913): p. 3.

4 Arrevillaga Serrano and Luis de Tavira, 'Henry IV: Part 1: International Insights', audio interview (interviewer Amy Kenny/translator unknown), Shakespeare's Globe London (2012), http://.bloggingshakespeare.com/year-of-shakespeare-henry-iv-part-one, 29 October 2012.

5 Rubén Szuchmacher, 'Henry IV: Part 2: International Insights', audio interview (interviewer Amy Kenny/translator unknown), Shakespeare's Globe London (2012), http://bloggingshakespeare.com/year-of-shakespeare-henry-iv-part-two, 29 October 2012.

6 Serrano and de Tavira, 'Henry IV: Part I'.

7 I would like to express my gratitude to Margarita Cabrera for many thoughtful discussions about and insights into ideas of art, migration and politics contained in this chapter.

CHAPTER TWENTY-FOUR

FOREIGN SHAKESPEARE AND THE UNINFORMED THEATRE-GOER

Part I, An Armenian *King John*

Michael Dobson

Accounts of Shakespearean productions produced by academics fall into two main categories: reviews written soon after a performance, incorporating varying proportions of evaluation and contextualization but largely consisting of eyewitness testimony; and more detailed analyses produced much later, which supplement the writer's first-hand experience of the show in question, if any, with information drawn from other sources – promptbooks and partbooks, published reviews, practitioner interviews, theoretical and theatrical manifestoes, and so on. What the two categories usually have in common is a claim to possession of all the relevant knowledge. Academic theatre reviewers generally position themselves as securely belonging to a production's target audience, so fully competent in its codes and its context that if they haven't understood it, nobody will; while academic analysts of productions from the recent or distant past similarly lay claim to an understanding of their full aesthetic and historical significance, a grasp of everything they sought to mean at the time, everything they succeeded in meaning and everything they have come to mean since. The opportunity to return to the Globe to Globe Festival's *King John* and *Antony and Cleopatra* some four months after seeing them, by contrast, offers me the chance to write something which is neither fully informed eyewitness reportage nor meticulously researched historical reconstruction. Instead, it constitutes a reflection on what may be left in the memory and the understanding of a theatre-goer who knew much less than usual about what he was seeing at the time, and has since learned that much of what he thought he knew was wrong.

It isn't that I am unaccustomed to seeing Shakespeare performed in languages other than English, or to seeing translated Shakespeare without the line-by-line surtitling which the Globe to Globe Festival eschewed in favour of (sometimes tendentious) scene-by-scene summaries. I suspect, for instance, that the production I will remember best from 2012 will be Silviu Purcărete's haunting *Furtuna* (*A Tempest*), which I saw performed in Romanian in Romania, so that it lacked surtitles altogether. As this circumstance suggests, though, when it comes to understanding Purcărete I have at least been to Romania, and although this production has since toured extensively outside Romania I had the privilege of seeing it in the auditorium for which it was originally rehearsed. But as a spectator at the Globe to Globe Festival I instead saw productions from two countries with which I am much less well acquainted, Armenia and Turkey. It is true that I used to go to an annual Armenian diaspora street festival in the district where I lived in Chicago, from which I dimly remember folk dancing and some very solid ethnic baking, and I once visited Istanbul for five whole days; but before seeing this *King John* and *Antony and Cleopatra* I had seen no theatre from either country, and my Turkish vocabulary consisted almost entirely of the word *sutluk*, a kind of milk pudding nowhere mentioned in Shakespeare.

I chose to see these two productions regardless because I originally intended, in a transparent instance of buck-passing, that my contribution to the Festival's blog should not be reviews at all but should be transcripts of post-show interviews with a trio of favourite RSC actresses, whom I planned to take to see plays in which they had themselves performed with conspicuous success. Kelly Hunter, a fine Constance for the RSC in 2001, would come to *King John*; Harriet Walter, one of the best Lady Macbeths in recent memory (in Gregory Doran's production of 1999), would come to the Festival's Polish *Macbeth*; and Janet Suzman would come to *Antony and Cleopatra*. In the event, Kelly had to be in Ohio while the *King John* was running, and I was sent to Chicago during the Polish *Macbeth* (so that I instead saw an excellent *Timon of Athens* that night, directed by Barbara Gaines at the Chicago Shakespeare Theatre), and the only interview I was able to record was with Janet Suzman. I was very much aware at the time, as I recall, of a temptation to make each show into some sort of allegory about what little I knew of the current situation of its country of origins. Of Armenia, for instance, I knew what everybody knows: that the boundaries of Armenianness and the boundaries of Armenia have never corresponded very comfortably; that terrible genocides and mass emigrations took place when the diverse Ottoman empire was forcibly reshaped into the less diverse Turkish nation state; that Iran and Azerbaijan haven't always been very comfortable neighbours to have, either; and that, as with other nations emerging from provincehood, Armenia early on sought to add prestige and international status to its native language and drama by translating and cherishing Shakespeare. Of present-day Turkey I knew rather more, having taught some Turkish students over the years, and having read much more in the Anglophone press in recent years about the country's relations with the European Union and with its neighbours in the Middle East. One of my principal memories of both productions, however – and in this respect the two are liable in retrospect to blur into one another – is of a generalized impression of mid Asian folksiness: leather coats with no sleeves, kaftan shapes, russet scarves, something emphatically and deliberately rustic about the acting.

Just as the costume design of one of the resident company's productions at the Globe may produce only a broad impression of Elizabethan-ness or the olde-worlde by opting to perform for a present-day audience in re-created clothing of a long-lost period, so a visiting foreign company may produce a similarly vague effect by playing in clothing styles only partially readable by local theatre-goers. While the trunks and suitcases brought onto the stage by the thirteen-strong Armenian troupe, as they arrived out of character and one by one, which were variously used as furniture, scenery and props thereafter, were clearly a particular trademark of this show (or of this company), their fawn and brown costumes, usually made of coarse, non-urban-looking cotton, seemed generic, and they seemed the more so after I had seen some very similar clothes used in the Turkish *Antony and Cleopatra*. All the customary impulses of the academic reviewer at the opening of a production, as he or she makes a start on decoding a production's design choices by interpreting the period or social register or aesthetic of the costuming, were thus blocked by sheer ignorance. The economics of the Festival, moreover, which, with so many companies giving so few performances each, could not possibly support the provision of full-scale programmes for each production, denied us would-be authoritative reviewers even the faint hope of simulated expertise offered by programme notes – notes of exactly the kind I habitually supply myself when overseas companies bring Shakespeare to the Edinburgh Festival. At the time I saw these productions, with the exception of knowing something of who Haluk Bilinger (Antony) was, I knew practically nothing about the two companies or the circumstances under which the two shows had come into being. When it came to enjoying and evaluating them (and, however pejoratively donnish the notion of evaluating live theatrical events may sound, the pleasures of critical judgement and discussion have always been a major part of the pleasures of drama), I was alone with my knowledge of the untranslated scripts on which, to an unknown extent, they were based – that and whatever assumptions I was prepared to make about how far the theatrical languages these productions were deploying corresponded to any I was myself competent to read.

The only respect in which I was not thus stranded in unassisted ignorance was that the Globe's full-daylight performances meant that I could at least observe the behaviour of those Armenian-speakers and Turkish-speakers who had been drawn to this *King John* and this *Antony and Cleopatra*. The responses of a small but attentive matinee audience of London-based Armenian expatriates, for instance, soon convinced me that the governing aesthetic of the National Academic Theatre of Armenia – essentially one of playing as broadly and narratively as though telling a story beside a camp fire – is eminently comprehensible outside Armenia, since their compatriots elsewhere in the auditorium were clearly following exactly the same

Fig. 14 Constance (Alla Vardanyan) and Queen Eleanor (Nelly Kheranyan), *King John*, Gabriel Sundukyan, National Academic Theatre from Yerevan, Armenia; director Tigran Gasparyan.

moves and moods as I was. Two reed players and a percussionist, on stage most of the time, explained the emotional timbre of successive scenes (their range including some wonderfully shrill discords for the battles), and the only problems anyone in the house may have had in following the story were the fault of the surtitles rather than of the players. The scene-by-scene summaries appeared to be based on a full, literal translation of the play rather than on the adaptation the company was in fact using: surtitles occasionally appeared, fleetingly, describing scenes which had in fact been cut. A summary of the Bastard's closing speech appeared, similarly, despite the fact that only a fragment of it remained, reassigned to Hubert: he, without any comment from the title boards, assumed the dead John's leather coat and leather crown and, repeating the play's opening word, 'Chatillon . . . ', seemed to be on the verge of repeating its entire story. Nor did the surtitles acknowledge that this production treated Arthur not as a child but as an immature and increasingly alcoholic adolescent, played rather well by Gnel Ulikhanyan. Actually, the surtitles wouldn't always have supplied a very reliable gloss to an unadapted text either: the Bastard's famous speech decrying the kings' pragmatic and selfish pursuit of political advantage, 'tickling commodity' (2.1.573), for instance, was summarized as his marvelling that kings should be so 'interested in commodities', which isn't the same thing at all. But no such problems of translation applied to the histrionic style of this production. Whatever other misfortunes have happened to Armenia, method-acting does not seem to have been among them: Armen Marutyan was a big, loud, tragi-comic Ubu-esque King John, Alla Vardanyan an operatic Constance (her grief for her abducted son a fine set-piece mad scene, complete with a suitcase full of flowers), Nelly Kheranyan an unfunnily caricatured old battleaxe of an Eleanor, complete with walking stick and rubber bald wig. As the Bastard, Tigran Nersisyan lacked ironic comedy (and the cuts robbed him of both his half-brother and of Austria as stooges), but he made up for it in sheer bass-baritone attack, and the Armenians in the yard evidently loved him.

Is it a matter of sheer interpretive laziness that the Turkish *Antony and Cleopatra* ten days later produced, for me, such a similar effect of broad, rustic, un-nuanced storytelling? I shall continue to reflect on my experience of both of these productions a little later in this volume (see Chapter 33).

CHAPTER TWENTY-FIVE

THE RIGHT TO THE THEATRE

The Belarus Free Theatre's *King Lear*

Keren Zaiontz

On 4 July 2012, the skies over Ivyanets – a small town 70 kilometres outside Minsk, the capital of Belarus – changed unpredictably. Brown teddy bears attached to parachutes canopied the streets and demanded the attention of the locals. The bears clutched protest signs in English and Belarusian between their paws: 'You cannot silence us' and 'Free speech now'.[1] The airdrop, initially bound for Minsk, was meant to scatter free-speech signs over the presidential palace of dictator Alexander Lukashenko. Since 1994, Lukashenko has maintained his grip on power through such repressive tactics as censorship, vote-rigging and state violence. He operates as if the Iron Curtain that divided east and west Europe during the Cold War had never been lifted, and continues to run the country like a Soviet state. This includes the use of military and police – including the secret KGB service – to silence citizens who question his regime. At the hands of Lukashenko, Belarus' most prominent opposition leaders, journalists, political activists, lawyers, academics and artists have faced imprisonment and torture, 'disappeared' without warning and 'committed suicide' on the eve of presidential elections. The unlikely campaigners of the more than 800 teddy-bear airdrop were not, however, Belarusian citizens. They were Studio Total, a Swedish advertising firm, who describe their action as 'a performance to support democracy in Belarus'.[2] This performance from above prevented a direct encounter with the despotic regime from below. It was at street level that a Belarusian journalism student, 20-year-old Anton Suryapin, did what young people just about everywhere do and posted the images online. This banal act of post-and-circulate resulted in the forced detention of Suryapin by the KGB, who now accuse the student of 'assisting illegal entry'.[3] Studio Total had illegally crossed into Belarusian airspace to campaign for Charter 97, an online organization that reports human rights abuses from inside Belarus, and the authors of the country's 1996 'Declaration of Resistance against Belarusian Dictatorship'.[4] Both Charter 97 and Studio Total demonstrate political resistance by embattled journalists from within and privileged campaigners from without. But there are also groups who work between the borders of Belarus and Western Europe to confront the despotism of the Lukashenko regime. These are Belarusian citizens and exiles who aim to address the concerns of those situated inside Belarus, as well as to capture the attention of those 'outside' whose experience of dictatorship is limited to news headlines. It is this cross-cultural work that describes the artistic practice of the Belarus Free Theatre, a company whose performances grapple with and condemn human rights abuses in Belarus.[5]

Since 2005 the Belarus Free Theatre have devised and staged plays that put them in direct opposition to the Lukashenko regime, which the company frequently describes in their press materials as 'the last dictatorship in Europe'. And yet it is this very opposition that has made them a recognizable voice of, and for, Belarus. Their participation in the Globe to Globe Festival with a performance of *King Lear* reinforced the status of the company as a politically resistant symbol of national culture. The company reused the celebratory markers of nationhood such as language, poetry, costume and song to critique the authoritarianism of present-day Belarus. Significantly, they adapted and performed *King Lear* in Belarusian. On the surface, this choice appears completely traditional and reproduces the means by which nations organize and promote themselves as autonomous from other nations.[6] However, Belarusian is not the primary language spoken daily by the majority of people in the country, nor is it the official language used in government and state institutions. That language is Russian, and its dominance is the result of a contested history of Soviet incorporation and occupation. This imperialist protocol continues under Lukashenko, who speaks only Russian in public, and who secures his power from the finances and oil incentives of the Russian government with whom Belarus shares its eastern border. No one in power, or no one who wants power (or even upward mobility), speaks Belarusian.[7] The denigrated position of the Belarusian language has made it a point of relation for activists who reclaimed the language in the years before the fall of Communism and present-day Belarusians who want to audibly demonstrate their opposition to the Lukashenko regime.[8] It is for this reason that the Belarus Free Theatre's performance of *King Lear* in Belarusian does not signal the promotion of national cohesion but national rebellion.

When a language is denigrated or repressed it can be made a symbol of counter-nationalism. Writing in a condemned tongue, artists can shift the 'discourse surrounding the nation'[9] in a new direction. In addition to performing *King Lear* in Belarusian, the Belarus Free Theatre used the poetry of Andrei Khadanovich in the final act of the play when the ensemble performed one of his pieces in the style of a folk song. Khadanovich is a poet and academic based in Minsk, and the current president of the Belarus centre for PEN International.[10] His poetry is not taught in Belarusian classrooms, and his collections are more readily found in bookshops in

Kiev than Minsk.[11] Speaking with Ales Kudrytsky, Khadanovich states: 'Coming to events such as a literature reading or artistic performance becomes some kind of protest. People use it to demonstrate their critical position, to interact with the like-minded.'[12] Cultural activities in Belarus are a crucial meeting-point to collectively, and performatively, re-imagine the nation as a democratic space.

THE BELARUS FREE THEATRE

It is under these unauthorized conditions, where assembly is a political act, that the Belarus Free Theatre was formed. Founded by producer Natalia Kaliada, playwright Nicolai Khalezin and director Vladimir Shcherban, the company started by producing the work of postdramatic playwrights such as Sarah Kane and Mark Ravenhill, playwrights not permitted on the stages of Belarus' state theatres, the only licensed or authorized theatres in the nation. Kaliada and Khalezin, who are married and share the title of artistic director, turned to the theatre after the three independent newspapers where Khalezin, one of the founders of Charter 97, worked were shut down by authorities. Theatre was viewed as one of the last public domains in Belarus not heavily censored by the state or KGB. Denied the right to officially register the theatre, and thus cut off from public funds and private donations, the company worked underground devising plays about human rights and their abuses in Belarus.[13] While the company toured works to festivals in the USA and Western Europe, as well as to benefit events for PEN and Index on Censorship where supporters, activists, spectators and reviewers freely assembled, US scholar Catherine Coray, in an interview with the *New York Times*, describes how spectators in Minsk assembled to watch shows in secret:

They do their pieces in this tiny studio, with no publicity whatsoever, for an audience that is reached through text messages . . . And that audience never comes directly to the theater. They are met at another location and escorted to the theater by a cast member. When you come, you are advised to bring your passport, because you never know when the police are going to show up and haul everyone off to jail.[14]

The taken-for-granted of free assembly, an assumed right of theatre spectators in democratic countries, also extends to the right of free association. Our attendance at a theatre in London or New York City does not risk being 'informed' on by someone to the authorities; in fact, we willingly post our whereabouts and associations on online platforms such as Twitter and Facebook. In Belarus, however, there can be consequences. Most of the artists and theatre students who worked for the Free Theatre evaded the authorities by performing underground but felt the effects of violating the censors through police intimidation and threats to their livelihoods. Between 2005 and late 2010 ensemble members were systematically isolated from their network within the official theatre community – who were clearly being sent a message – when members were fired or otherwise expelled from their positions in the state theatre, including the National Academic Theatre, the Belarusian Young Spectator Theatre, the Belarusian Army Theatre and the state university.[15] Some ensemble members were prohibited from applying for jobs (*any* job) because of their association with the company. But it was the days that followed the December 2010 presidential elections, condemned by international observers as neither free nor fair, that the company faced profound new political pressures. The Lukashenko regime systematically suppressed the opposition movement, jailing dissidents, including former presidential candidates (many of whom remained imprisoned during the 2012 elections) and the editor-in-chief of Charter 97, Natallia Radzina.[16] Kaliada was among hundreds of people forcibly detained in the mass protest staged in Minsk immediately following the elections; by bureaucratic error she was released fourteen hours following her arrest. Living and performing in Minsk now proved impossible for Kaliada and Khalezin, who fled the country with one of their daughters in early 2011. Today, they and Shcherban, as well as actor Aleh Sidorchik (who played King Lear at the Festival), live as political refugees in London.

The Free Theatre is 'homeless', working in exile, and its artistic directors fear returning to Belarus where they risk persecution. But it is precisely the company's politically tendentious existence that has proved so remarkably productive within the contemporary London and UK theatre scene. Their narrative as censored artists and political exiles is not only present in the topics they dramatize but constitutes the bulk of the press coverage that circulates about them. In addition to theatre reviews, they are referenced in mainstream journalism about the political struggle in contemporary Belarus and, uniquely, have accrued testimonials by such high-profile playwrights and actors as Tom Stoppard and Jude Law, who have protested on behalf of the company on YouTube and on the streets.[17] These testimonials are inextricable from the identity of the Free Theatre, who actively enjoin their supporters to a compelling narrative that places them in opposition to the company's state oppressors.

THE 'HOME' STAGE

Following both the matinee and evening performances of *King Lear*, Natalia Kaliada appealed to the audience to donate money to the company on their way out of the theatre – the only company to do so in all of the Festival.[18] The aim was to raise much-needed funds, but the appeal also reproduced the narrative of the company as rootless and marginalized, showing it to be inseparable from the horizon of expectations of seeing the show. And yet, while critics were familiar with this narrative, it is difficult to tell whether spectators identified this gesture as a sign

9 *Falstaff* (Horacio Peña), centre, with Mistress Quickly (Graciela Martinelli) and Doll Tearsheet (Irina Alonso), 2 *Henry IV*, Elkafka Espacio Teatral from Buenos Aires, Argentina; director Rubén Szuchmacher.

10 *Goneril* (Yana Rusakevich), *Lear* (Aleh Sidorchik) and *Regan* (Maryna Yurevich), *King Lear*, Belarus Free Theatre from Minsk, Belarus (now exiled in London); director Vladimir Shcherban.

11 *Phoebe* (Tamar Bukhnikashvili) and Rosalind (Ketevan Shatirishvili) in the forest of Arden, *As You Like It*, Marjarnishvili Theatre from Tbilisi, Georgia; director Levan Tsuladze.

12 *Coriolanus* (Dai Ishida), centre, with Yohei Kobayashi, Saki Kohno, Shie Kubota and Satoko Abe, *Coriolanus*, Chiten from Kyoto, Japan; director Motoi Miura.

13 *Antony* (Haluk Bilginer (Antonius)) and Cleopatra (Zerrin Tekindor (Kleopatra)), *Antony and Cleopatra*, Oyun Atölyesi from Istanbul, Turkey; director Kemal Aydoğan.

14 Antonio (Alon Ophir) bound in the court scene with Shylock (Jacob Cohen) about to stab him, *The Merchant of Venice*, Habima National Theatre from Tel Aviv, Israel; director Ilan Ronen.

15 *Katherine of Aragon (Elena González (Catalina of Aragon), centre, kneeling, with Henry VIII (Fernando Gil (Enrique VIII)) and Anne Bullen (Sarah Moraleda (Ana Bolena)) standing behind holding the baby Elizabeth, Henry VIII, Rakatá from Madrid, Spain; director Ernesto Arias.*

16 *Timon* (Michael Meyer), centre, *Timon of Athens*, Bremer Shakespeare Company from Bremen, Germany; director Sebastian Kautz.

of the company's nomadic status and underground conditions in Belarus. The summary about the group 'holding secret performances' and 'suffering every form of intimidation and harassment' was printed in the larger festival booklet but not in the programme note distributed to audiences. Moreover, signs warning that there would be nudity and violence suggested that the Belarus Free Theatre's explicit aesthetic was not common knowledge to Globe spectators.

However, the question of expectation marked both sides. Despite the company's well-ensconced position on the London stage, performing Shakespeare at Shakespeare's Globe was viewed as a stage apart. Vladimir Shcherban called it an invitation to a 'guest house', which marked its distinction from the 'home' stages they occupied in London.[19] The international frameworks of the World Shakespeare Festival and London Cultural Olympiad meant that, in addition to 'contemporary' and 'political', the company was now read as 'classical' and 'national'. Andrew Dickson attests to these shifts in his review of *King Lear* for the *Guardian* (one of a handful of reviews by a major UK daily):

A gaunt and arthritic king totters on stage, his head a thatch of matted white hair – then, grinning, he springs up like a jack-in-the-box and whisks off the wig. This is, we gather, one of Lear's dangerous little jokes: one of many in a production that teases constantly at our expectations. Instead of treating the play as it's so often done in Britain, as Shakespeare's attempt at a PhD in epistemology, Vladimir Shcherban and a young, energetic Belarus Free Theatre company offer instead a Lear returned vividly to its roots: as a comic folktale that shatters into tragedy.[20]

The company retains its standing as an ensemble that tests 'our expectations', but they also uncover *King Lear*'s 'roots' by rendering the tragedy as a 'folktale'. The implication here is that the Belarusian production accesses Shakespeare's authenticity in a way that British productions cannot, bound as they are by a pedantic tradition that is corrosive because it is intellectual.[21] The Belarus Free Theatre renews the play and, in doing so, gives *King Lear* back to its British audiences at the site of Shakespeare's 'natural' home.

Dickson's review of the production – and what it does for Shakespeare – expresses a familiar binary in the 'reception economies' of *King Lear* rooted in the oppositional markers 'authentic' and 'radical'.[22] Susan Bennett, in her analysis of late twentieth-century UK productions of *King Lear*, engages with the public discourse of theatre reviews to identify how essentialist and constructivist distinctions exemplify a drive to achieve an original staging of *Lear* that reproduces the transcendent value of the tragedy. The claim to access the foundations of the tragedy through language, or to (re)imagine it through experimental performance practice, effects its 'greatness' and supports our cultural capital as artists, audiences and reviewers. Whilst Dickson's review redeploys both distinctions, the markers 'authentic' and 'radical' support, in this instance, something other than the status of Shakespeare's tragedy. The Free Theatre puts *King Lear* in the service of performing a dissident Belarusian nationalism on the Globe stage. The very context of the Festival confirms the possibility of an alternative nationalism because the performances are read in light of (and contained within the grammar of) national 'folk' authenticity.

NOT BELARUSIAN ENOUGH?

The Free Theatre knew they would not be performing to the same audience base as their usual 'homes' at the Young Vic or Soho Theatre. But they also did not know who exactly would be in the yard or the galleries during their two-day run. Their hope was that Belarusians would respond to and rally around the show. Initially, Festival organizers insisted that the group perform in Russian, appealing to a more populous subset of communities in London. The Free Theatre resisted this mandate; they fought and won the right to perform in Belarusian, but, in the end, few Belarusians attended the production. Yuri Kaliada, brother of Natalia and one of the company's producers, described the poor turnout by Belarusians as a combination of 'distance' and 'indifference'. He believes the company is unfavourably looked upon by the Belarusian diaspora because they are not perceived as Belarusian *enough*, performing the majority of their works in Russian.[23] While the company's place in the Festival confirmed a national authenticity for its British supporters, this was not necessarily the case for Belarusians living in London. The core group of spectators consisted then of festival-goers, many of whom were just as new to Shakespeare's Globe as the Free Theatre.

POSTDRAMATIC LEAR

The company placed Shakespeare in the grips of their postdramatic theatre style. This marked their first time with a classical text after having exclusively devised and staged contemporary work. The Free Theatre mapped their self-consciously political dramaturgy onto their two-hour adaptation of *King Lear* (a time limit imposed by the Festival organizers) by bringing Shakespeare into the heart of contemporary Belarusian society. Shcherban called the company's adaptation a 'blueprint' of Belarus on stage. Performing this national model revealed three adaptive strategies: (1) a 'multilingual theatre text' defined by the contradictory use of official and unofficial languages; (2) an emphasis on visual *gestus* that summarized the relations of abuse that permeate the stage world; and (3) an explicit body performance style that revealed the malevolence of totalitarianism by showing how citizens are physically brutalized. Woven into all three strategies were the protocols of banal violence anchored in falsified truths spun by the state and internalized by the family. *King Lear* became a way to witness a traumatic political reality that could not be represented in contemporary Belarus.

Hans-Thies Lehmann argues that '[m]ulti-lingual theatre texts dismantle the unity of national languages',[24] a process that describes the Belarus Free Theatre's approach to their translation and adaptation of *King Lear*. Jostling alongside Khadanovich's contemporary verse, which was adopted into the devising process, was the performance of state-sanctioned songs and unsanctioned Belarusian folk songs. In the opening scene, these mix with Shakespeare's verse (voiced as an official and therefore untrustworthy language), a veneer that thinly disguises the abuses that underpin society.

In the 'love test' (Act I Scene I), the ensemble enters practising scales and vocal techniques, as if having just completed a routine warm-up, and seat themselves on long benches on either side of the stage.[25] The Fool assumes the role of a piano player, and Kent takes up an accordion. In anticipation of Lear's announcement it appears as if everyone has rehearsed the parts. Spectacle is revealed to be what binds court and family. The daughters will not only demonstrate their bond to their father through speech, but will soon try to outdo one another through song and dance numbers. They will have to earn their inheritance through their performing bodies. Even Cordelia gleefully partakes in this display; her aside to the audience – 'What shall Cordelia speak? Love, and be silent' (1.1.57) – is excised from the script. She claps along and appears to revel in her sisters' filial gestures, now adapted into raucous court entertainments. The contest for the king's affection references those dictatorial regimes where citizens perform their fidelity to a megalomaniacal leader through demonstrations of mass weeping or applause. The daughters' performances are no different; their bodies labour to prop up their father's greatness. The rehearsed quality of these performances suggests that their speeches, songs and dances are part of a 'typical plot' in which spectacle is used to reproduce the power of a tyrannical leader (see Colour Plate 10).

That official discourse of tyranny, pulled off with 'Soviet flair' by the ensemble, is brought into dialogue in *King Lear* with *trasyanka*.[26] A hybrid of Russian and 'peasant' Belarusian, *trasyanka* is not a 'proper' or specialist language but, for many Belarusians in rural and urban regions, the language of everyday life. This ordinary language is used to perform a scene in *King Lear* that is traditionally reported: the hanging of Cordelia. The British camp near Dover is remade into a prison in Belarus that enacts the typical protocols of arrest, search, seizure of belongings, interrogation, contrived allegation and sentencing.[27] The authorities are riot police masked in balaclavas. Their masks deny the possibility of an ethical face-to-face encounter with inmates – they can punish with impunity – since they cannot be identified. It is a state apparatus inhabited by nobodies who can act against anybody.

The guards itemize Lear and Cordelia's belongings: his armoured glove, her pearls, high heels and hat. Layered over this display of prison bureaucracy in *trasyanka* are redacted lines from Shakespeare's text that Lear recites to Cordelia in Belarusian. Shakespeare's language now flips from falsified claim to familial tenderness. Father and daughter sit on top of the piled benches from the opening scene, their backs turned to each other, watching the police play with their belongings. Under Edmund's supervision the authorities invent crimes. Cordelia is convicted of inciting state instability, economic instability, for committing terrorism – the list goes on. 'Lear and Cordelia are accused of *everything*', says Shcherban. He notes that the protocol of inventing false offences was designed to mirror Belarus' own penal system: 'It is our daily reality.'

The hanging itself illustrates a radical visual *gestus* that operates in the post-Brechtian tradition. Cordelia stands atop a stool, which is kicked out from under her by the police. They hold out her spreadeagled arms as she convulses in their grip, a visual sign of sacrifice. But it is a sacrifice without any higher purpose. Overlaying prison violence is sexual violence, as Cordelia's convulsions in the arms of police result in her dress riding down her body. Half naked and restrained, she connotes through her movements the possibility of a double brutality, rape and murder at the hands of the state. The Fool bears witness by setting Cordelia's death to his own music. He plays the saxophone during her execution until he, too, is hauled off by the riot police. Jill Dolan, quoting from Brecht's canonical essay 'Alienation effects in Chinese Acting', notes how 'Brecht's freeze-framed, demystified narratives quote the social moment as *gestus*, which "demonstrate a custom which leads to conclusions about the entire structure of society in a particular (transient) time"'.[28] Dolan goes on to discuss how feminist theatre refocused *gestus* as an illustrative strategy: 'Rather than a textual illustration, the *gestus* is a visual sign. Since it occurs within the theatrical moment, it prompts consideration of events and relationships drawn out in space.'[29] The Free Theatre not only draws out an event that is traditionally elided from theatrical space but also maps onto the hanging of Cordelia state abuses prevailing today that operate behind closed doors.

In an interview following the run at the Globe, and in preparation for *Minsk, 2011*,[30] Natalia Kaliada observed: 'When you live in a suppressed society, many things happen, but one is that a culture of sexual violence develops and grows very fast and this is what we explore [in our work]. The whole country is isolated, freedoms are suppressed and violence is one of the things that grows out of that.'[31] The company uses an explicit body performance style to demonstrate the systemic nature of sexual violence in Belarus. Coterminous with the use of their bodies as a physical site of violence is the use of their personal experiences as performance material. It is a dramaturgy that fully implicates itself within feminist and civil rights movements rooted in the conviction that 'the personal is political'.[32] To testify to this adage in the context of staging human rights abuses is to show how citizens internalize state abuse as performative models of conduct in their daily lives. For the Free Theatre, a key entry point into *King Lear* was exploring instances of intergenerational violence. Before working with Khalezin's redacted version of the play, the company devoted the first two weeks of rehearsal to excavating their own experiences of family trauma. One of the images (another visual *gestus*) to emerge from the devising process was staged in the false letter scene between Gloucester and Edmund (Act 1 Scene 2).[33] Gloucester, who moves around in a wheelchair, reacts to the contents of the letter by repeatedly whipping his military belt on the floor. Yuri Kaliada and Shcherban claimed that spectators from the former Soviet Union and Soviet bloc nations would have recognized this moment of rage – and the military belt itself, outfitted with a five-pointed star buckle, and a hammer and sickle in the centre – as a common instrument that fathers used to 'discipline' their children. Shcherban states: 'We wanted to question why Shakespeare completes his tragedy with total annihilation [of the family]. We found our answer lay in domestic abuse. The oppression of one person over another.' Violence can take place in, and between, families and thus illustrates that oppression can happen in the most intimate of institutions. Those who know us best can commit their worst by transforming familial intimacy into a point of abuse. When it concerns the denial of basic rights, domestic spaces can be as lawless as any anonymous house of torture. And it is this consciousness that the company brings to their production of *King Lear* at Shakespeare's Globe.

THE NOMADIC CONSCIOUSNESS OF *KING LEAR*

Staging *Lear* from the perspective of sexual violence did not go unnoticed.[34] In a review for the 'Year of Shakespeare' blog Sonia Massai discusses how the Almeida Theatre's production of *King Lear* pivots around an autocratic Lear who sexually exploits his daughters and observes 'interesting similarities with the Belarusian *King Lear*', including 'a similarly radical re-reading of Lear's character, which turned out to be uncannily similar to the sexually abusive Lear portrayed by Aleh Sidorchik in the Belarusian production'. The tyranny of the father is reused but applied for psychological effect rather than to explore, as the Belarus Free Theatre does, 'the experience of homelessness at the hands of a despotic regime'.[35] Does this reduce the contestatory potential of the Free Theatre's production strategies to that of character treatment? I would emphasise, as Massai and others do, that the company's political struggle is what invests the tragedy with new meanings.[36] By deterritorializing the location and language of the play so that it 'speaks' Belarusian and possesses its current political realities, the Free Theatre brings an emergent ethics to the tragedy. Relinking *King Lear* to scenarios of abuse that cannot be represented in their place of national origin links the audience to the violations 'over there'. We are made aware of our globalized link to the other, and it is this nomadic consciousness that constitutes the Belarus Free Theatre's greatest contribution to *King Lear*.

ENDNOTES

1 Articles documenting the bear-drop include Vital Tsyhankou and Ron Synovitz, '"Teddy-bear Airdrop" Takes Aim at Belarus Denials', *Radio Free Europe/Radio Liberty*, 13 July 2012, www.rferl.org/content/facing-denials-sweden-group-releases-full-video-teddy-bear-airdrop-belarus/24644267.html, 20 July 2012; David Landes, 'Swedes launch Teddy Bear "Assault" on Belarus', *The Local: Sweden's News in English*, 4 July 2012, www.thelocal.se/41816/20120704/; and Louise Nordström, 'Belarus KGB Summons Swedish Teddy Bear Stunt Team', *Guardian*, 12 August 2012, www.guardian.co.uk/world/feedarticle/10390681, all accessed 8 November 2012.

2 Studio Total's teddy-bear airdrop declaration, 'Why we did it', is available on their website.

3 Suryapin was detained by the KGB from early July until 17 August 2012. The images on his citizen journalism website, www.bnp.by, were still online as of February 2013. For details about Suryapin's detainment, see Andrev Serada, 'Lukashenka Fires Top Officials over Teddy-Bear Drop', *Belarus News*, 1 August 2012, http://naviny.by/rubrics/english/2012/08/01/ic_articles_259_178670/, 10 October 2012; and Maria Grechaninova, 'Belarus Journalist Detained for "Airlifted Teddy Bears" Pictures', *BBC News Europe*, 24 July 2012, www.bbc.co.uk/news/world-europe-18958520, 8 November 2012.

4 Charter 97 maintains an active news feed at http://charter97.org/en/news/. An English translation of the charter can be found on the *Nasha Niva* website opinion pages, 'Charter 97' – 27 June 2012, nn.by/?c=ar&i=75965&lang, 15 July 2012.

5 The Belarus Free Theatre used to run a multilingual (Russian-, English-, and French-language) website, dramaturg.org, that aggregated many of the press articles about the company and provided information about the mandate of the company. The website, sadly, no longer exists.

6 As Steven Grosby (in *Nationalism: A Very Short Introduction* (Oxford University Press, 2005)) notes: 'Those who speak one language understand themselves to be different from those who speak a different language. *The nation is a social relation of collective self-consciousness*', p. 10 (emphasis in original).

7 To publicly state 'Long live Belarus' (*Žyvie Bielaruś*) in Belarusian is considered an anti-state slogan.

8 For Belarusian activists and artists on the Left – particularly those opposed to proposals for 'reunification' in the late 1990s – the marginalized status of the Belarusian language is a human rights issue. For a critique of the Left's politicization of the Belarusian language, see Elena Gapova, 'The Nation In Between; or, Why Intellectuals Do Things with Words', in Sibelan Elizabeth S. Forrester, Magdalena J. Zaborowska and Elena Gapova, eds., *Over the Wall/After the Fall: Post-Communist Cultures through an East–West Gaze* (Bloomington: Indiana University Press, 2004), pp. 65–87.

9 Nadine Holdsworth, *Theatre and Nation* (Basingstoke: Palgrave Macmillan, 2010), p. 26.

10 PEN is an organization that 'campaigns on behalf of writers across the globe who are persecuted, harrassed [sic] and attacked for what they have written or simply for being a writer' (http://pen-international.org/campaigns/current-campaigns/).

11 Ales Kudrytsky, in an article for the Brussels-based NGO. Office for a Democratic Belarus, 'Poetry on Tiptoes', *Belarus Headlines* 23 (January–February 2008): 7–8, writes:

> Surprisingly, the very first book by Andrey Khadanovich (*Letters from under the Blanket*) was published in Kyiv [Kiev] – in Ukrainian. His another [sic] book *From Belarus with Love* was a bold experiment – printed in Ukraine in Belarusian (!) language, it was actually sold in Ukrainian book shops. Books printed in Belarus followed, but they are not always easy to find in the country. Andrey Khadanovich is one of those writers whose books are allowed to be printed by private publishers, but are often prevented from being disseminated in Belarus. (Exclamation mark in the original)

12 Ibid.

13 They also founded an underground art school, Studio Fortinbras, which teaches students how to organize political performance interventions.

14 Larry Rohter, 'Escaped from Belarus, Actors Raise Voices', 4 January 2011. *New York Times*, nytimes.com/2011/01/05/theater/05company.html?pagewanted=all, 8 November 2012.

15 This information about the ensemble members was published under each of their names in the *Minsk, 2011* programme note in place of their stage credits. *Minsk, 2011: A Reply to Kathy Acker* is a devised piece that explores the sexual politics of living in present-day Minsk. The company dig into their own lives, which they use as stage material, for accounts that focus on sexual violence. The Free Theatre also represents public moments of crisis in Minsk that range from the 2011 subway bombing to the arrest of activists during the city's Gay Pride parade. These flash-points mix with how sex is accessed in underground clubs and state-authorized strip clubs. First presented at the Edinburgh Festival Fringe, *Minsk, 2011* was staged at the Young Vic in London and co-produced with Fuel as part of the London International Festival of Theatre (LIFT) 2011.

16 See Tom Parfitt, 'Belarus Election: Opposition Leaders Beaten as Lukashenko Declares Victory', *Guardian*, 20 December 2010, www.guardian.co.uk/world/2010/dec/20/presidential-candidate-dragged-from-hospital, 8 November 2012.

17 For articles that reference and link the Free Theatre to the political crisis in Belarus, see Nick Cohen, 'The Fine Art of Making Drama out of a Crisis', *Guardian*, 18 July 2010 www.guardian.co.uk/commentisfree/2010/jul/18/belarus-theatre-nick-cohen, 8 November 2012; A.A., 'The Election that Wasn't', *The Economist*, 27 September 2012, www.economist.com/blogs, 10 October 2012; Sirgrid Rausing, 'Belarus: Inside Europe's Last Dictatorship', *Guardian*, 7 October 2012, www.guardian.co.uk/world/2012/oct/07/belarus-inside-europes-last-dictatorship, 3 February 2013. For a sample of articles and videos that feature the involvement of high-profile UK artists, see 'TEDxObserver – Jude Law', 29 March 2011, www.youtube.com/watch?v=HDMmIrvmdMs, 8 November 2012; and Roland Oliphant, 'Tom Stoppard Takes on Europe's Last Tyrant''', *Independent*, 7 July 2010, www.independent.co.uk/arts-entertainment/theatre-dance/news/tom-stoppard-takes-on-europes-last-tyrant-2020123.html, 8 November 2012.

18 The Free Theatre ran a crowd-sourcing campaign on *sponsume* that aimed to raise £7,000 to cover the costs of the ensemble during the run of *King Lear*. They also received material

support (for this and other productions) from the Old and Young Vic Theatres, which have held Index on Censorship fundraisers, been a stage for the company's contemporary work and supplied rehearsal space, including for *King Lear*.

19 All direct quotations of Vladimir Shcherban and Yuri Kaliada are from an interview I conducted with them on 10 September 2012 at the Young Vic Theatre in London. Kaliada acted as translator as well as an interlocutor, relaying my questions to Shcherban in Russian.

20 Andrew Dickson, 'King Lear – Review', *Guardian*, 23 May 2012, www.guardian.co.uk/stage/2012/may/23/king-lear-review, 8 November 2012.

21 Dickson's review includes a tongue-and-cheek link to Robert J. Bauer's 'A Phenomenon of Epistemology in the Renaissance' *Journal of the History of Ideas*, 31.2 (April – June, 1970): 281–8.

22 See Susan Bennett, *Performing Nostalgia* (London: Routledge, 1996). In the chapter 'Production and Proliferation: Seventeen Lears' Bennett reveals how both authentic and radical distinctions are constructs:

> Authenticity, we know, is impossible: we cannot *reproduce* (since we do not *know*) the original conditions of Shakespeare's stage or text, and all performances, by virtue of the genre itself, are necessarily different. And, in the case of radical interpretation, this seems at best dubiously radical, since theatre critics, and not only that specific viewing community, are always able to align a particular revision with one which has gone before. (p. 46, italics in original)

> In opposition to these hegemonic Lears, Bennett examines productions that re-evaluate *King Lear* through intercultural and feminist strategies, and brings the tragedy into conversation with identity politics in their historical moment. I would argue that the Belarus Free Theatre maps (and adapts) the strategies of identity politics onto a *Lear* that addresses the representation of human rights and their abuses.

23 What Kaliada may not have fully admitted to here is that potentially more Belarusians would have turned out had the production been performed in Russian. National affinity and belonging in Belarus do not universally operate on the level of the Belarusian language.

24 Hans-Thies Lehmann, *Postdramatic Theatre*, trans. Karen Jürs-Munby (London: Routledge, 2006), p. 147.

25 The cast of *King Lear*: King Lear, Aleh Sidorchik; Goneril, Yana Rusakevich; Regan, Maryna Yurevich; Cordelia, Victoryia Biran; Duke of Albany, Yuri Koliada; Duke of Cornwall, Alex Shyrnevich; Earl of Kent, Dzianis Tarasenka; Earl of Gloucester, Pavel Garadnitski; Edmund, Aliaksei Naranovich; Oswald, Yuliya Shauchuk; Fool, Pavel Arakelian.

26 'Soviet flair' is Yuri Kaliada's colourful expression and was articulated during our interview with Shcherban.

27 Shcherban claimed these protocols are a daily reality for many young people in Belarus who are often victims of police brutality.

28 Jill Dolan, *Feminist Spectator as Critic* (Ann Arbor: University of Michigan Press, 1991), p. 108.

29 Ibid.

30 See the description of *Minsk, 2011* in note 15 above.

31 See Carole Cadwalladr, 'Natalia Kaliada: "In Belarus it's Very Simple – Everything's Repressed"', *Observer*, 3 June 2012, www.guardian.co.uk/theobserver/2012/jun/03/natalia-kaliada-belarus-free-theatre-interview, 8 November 2012.

32 See Rebecca Schneider, *The Explicit Body in Performance* (London: Routledge, 1997). Schneider examines how US feminist performance artists put their own bodies to work and 'combined their art with a blatant feminist activism' (p. 38). She goes on to say that: 'The body of the artist was implicated in the body of the artist's work in particularly personal – which is to say political – ways' (p. 39).

33 Gloucester is played by a young actor, Pavel Garadnitski, who is a contemporary of the actors who play Edmund and Edgar. A cheap grey wig is the only sign that he is senior to his sons.

34 See Rosi Braidotti, *Nomadic Subjects: Embodiment and Sexual Difference in Contemporary Feminist Theory* (New York: Columbia University Press, 1994).

35 Sonia Massai, 'Year of Shakespeare: King Lear', 28 September 2012, http://bloggingshakespeare.com/year-of-shakespeare-king-lear-at-the-almeida, 10 October 2012.

36 In Andrew Haydon's review of *King Lear* for his theatre blog, *Postcards from the Gods*, he notes: 'It doesn't feel as if [the] Belarus Free Theatre have taken the play and used it to say anything about the situation in their own troubled country. Instead, the political act here is the fact of their being here at all.' Clearly, Haydon did not evaluate the production as a 'blueprint of Belarusian society' (see Shcherban's comments in this chapter). I believe his reading reflects a missed opportunity on the part of the Festival organizers to highlight the cultural semiotics of specific stage elements such as costume, props and music. This information could have been included in the press release for reviewers like Haydon. And yet, despite not reading Belarus into the tragedy, Haydon still aligns the way the company reinvents the play with their political status as an exiled company. We do not go to see *King Lear* but how the Free Theatre stages (reinvents) *Lear*.

CHAPTER TWENTY-SIX

'PLAYING' SHAKESPEARE

Marjanishvili, Georgia's *As You Like It*

Katie Normington

In *Star Trek: New Voyages*, 'Blood and Fire: Part One' (2008), the aptly named Russian agent, Lieutenant Pavel Chekov, remarks: 'Somebody didn't know their Shakespeare very well. A Russian wouldn't make that mistake.'[1] This popular culture reference shows the degree to which Russians are seen as having adopted Shakespeare as part of their heritage, particularly since the fall of the Soviet Union some twenty years ago. It is against this background that the Marjanishvili Theatre from Tbilisi, Georgia, presented their version of *As You Like It*. Similarly, they drew upon another part of their heritage, most specifically their Russian theatrical lineage, with its interest in physical embodiment and depth of character, to inform a production that meshed Shakespeare and Chekhovian styles to great effect.

The Marjanishvili State Drama Theatre, named after Kote Marjanishvili, their founding director, was first established in Kutaisi, Georgia, in 1928 and moved to its home at the Zubalashvili's Public House, Tbilisi, in 1930.[2] Marjanishvili, of Georgian birth, worked for over twenty-five years as a director in Russia alongside such innovators as Stanislavsky, Nemirovich-Danchenko, Meyerhold and Vakhtangov. Of particular note is that Marjanishvili worked as an assistant to Edward Allen Craig on his production of *Hamlet* in 1911 at the Moscow Art Theatre.[3] It was a production which dangerously recast the relationship between theatre, visual design and acting. By the 1920s Marjanishvili had returned to Georgia, and in 1925 he staged an acclaimed version of *Hamlet* for the Rustaveli Theatre. Since then, Shakespeare has been a central feature of the repertoire of the Marjanishvili company. The theatre's profile was significantly developed internationally through a 1984 performance of then director Temur Chkheidze's *Othello* at Weimar, Germany, to mark the Shakespeare International Conference held to celebrate Shakespeare's birthday. The production later toured to Bulgaria in 1987 and in 1990 was invited to the Glasgow International Theatre Festival. Further internationalization of their

Shakespeare productions was achieved in 1996 when *King Lear* toured to the Edinburgh International Festival, Prague, Russia and Poland. Levan Tsuladze, director since 2006, produced *The Merchant of Venice* and *A Midsummer Night's Dream* for the company, and the latter toured to the USA and Armenia. His production of *As You Like It* for the Globe to Globe Festival thus spoke to the heritage of Shakespeare within the company.

A penchant for Shakespeare productions is shared with other Georgian theatre practitioners. Robert Sturua, who trained at the Tbilisi State Theatre School and became director of the Shota Rustaveli Theatre in 1979, has done much to cement the relationship between Georgia and Shakespeare through international productions of *Richard III* (London and Edinburgh, 1979–80) and *King Lear* (New York, 1990). He has staged seventeen of Shakespeare's plays, including *Hamlet* (1986) for the Riverside Studio in London with Alan Rickman as Hamlet. The Georgians feel a strong affinity with Shakespeare: as Nico Kiasashvili notes, 'Shakespeare always helped us when we saw him as part of world culture and even more so when my nation went through the tragic stage of its history.'[4]

This empathy for Shakespeare is not something that Russians have always held. From the time translations of his work appeared in Russia in the nineteenth century there has been awareness of his plays. It is an interest sparked by the likes of Catherine the Great, who translated *The Merry Wives of Windsor* and *Timon of Athens*. However, his popularity waned until the mid 1930s: 'the first view, dominant in Soviet studies before 1930 and reminiscent of Tolstoy, was that Shakespeare's works had an aristocratic tendency and that their author despised the common people and held reactionary feudal views'.[5] Despite this reservation, Georgia has had a particular affinity with the playwright; indeed, one of the earliest productions of Shakespeare in Russia can be traced to an amateur performance of *The Merchant of Venice* in Cholchis, Georgia, in 1873.

It is against this background that the Marjanishvili Theatre produced *As You Like It* for the Globe to Globe Festival. Their approach, described by critics as Chekhov meets Shakespeare, brought together facets of Russian theatre, namely embodied physical expression, wrought with detailed human observation.[6] The metaphor of the world as a place of 'play' dominated the production, established from the first entrances by the company as they explore the stage, hide in large trunks, open others to reveal dressing-room-like pods and create percussion sounds from glasses, saucepans and the like. The notion of play filled the 'stage' (a raised platform which is reminiscent of a travelling pageant stage) but also permeated the 'offstage' space, that which is not the platform but still forms part of the Globe stage.

It is perhaps easiest to capture a sense of the production through the contradictory concepts that underlined the staging ideas. These are best exemplified in the worlds of the court and the country, and through Jacques as a figure who mediates between these worlds and values. The world of the court was created as much by what happens on the raised-stage platform as the activities that take place around it. Here the men played chess, the women adjusted their hair and make-up, or sometimes just watched the action intently, caught somewhere between their stage personas and real selves as actors. It was here at the court that the embodiment of a Chekhovian world could be found. The shabby-chic, salmon-pink world of Edwardian dress created a sense that nothing was stable or trustworthy at the court. This was enhanced by the fact that Duke Frederick had little authority and was undermined by the offstage prompter, who fed him his lines and turned him into a puppet-style leader. Even at the court the sense of 'playing' escaped onto the stage like some jack-in-the box unable to remain contained. There was a fabulous wrestling match between Orlando and Charles where the latter was replaced with a life-sized dummy that hurtled across the stage, while Le Beau took out salt and pepper and ate his sandwich centre stage. It was touches like these that constantly reminded the audience that *As You Like It* is about playing, role-playing and shifting identity. In fact, the production explored identity further than many other versions of the play by having women play the roles of Adam and Jacques. The increased presence of women in the ensemble created an easiness about the playing of gender on stage since a whole gamut of 'femaleness', from the cross-played older masculine characters of Adam and Jacques to the youthful femaleness of Rosaline and Celia, was explored.

Arden, in contrast to the court, was a delightful place, created by air-blown silk leaves that increasingly filled the acting podium. It was here that the visual richness of the stage married with the physical embodiment of the actors in the space. One scene melted into the next, and an increasing sense of play was released (see Colour Plate 11). This was embodied in such incidents as Audrey's milking of a stuffed sheep, in the choral ditty 'As You Like It' sung as a refrain by a chorus of actors, Touchstone fishing and helium balloons that sailed into the open skies of the Globe bearing Orlando's written declaration of love. But it was to Jacques that the production belonged. It was this actor who nosed her way first onto the stage as the actors got ready to perform, and it was Jacques whose haunting, passionate speech opened the Arden scenes. Here she (read by spectators as 'he') appeared not so much a melancholic presence, as in some representations, but instead seemed to caution reality against the playfulness of the world we saw. And it was here that the deep, passionate Georgian language found full resonance for the spectator. In this delightful Marjanishvili production we were made aware of the full significance of Jacques' speech that 'All the world's a stage' (2.7.139) as the entire stage, and by implication the world, became a place of play.

ENDNOTES

1 *Star Trek: New Voyages*, Andy Bray (2008), 'Blood and Fire: Part One' (Episode 1.4), USA: Paramount Pictures.

2 Further information about the company is at www.marjanishvili.net/eng/history

3 Lorna Hardwick, 'Antigone's Journey: From Athens to Edinburgh, via Paris and Tbilisi', in Erin B. Mee and Helene P. Foley, eds., *Antigone on the Contemporary World Stage* (Oxford University Press, 2011), p. 402.

4 Nico Kiasashvili, 'The Martyred Knights of Georgian Shakespeariana', *Shakespeare Survey*, 48 (1996): 190.

5 George Gibian, 'Shakespeare in Soviet Russia', *Russian Review*, 11.1 (January 1952): 27.

6 The Chekhovian approach is identified in the review in the *Guardian* newspaper. See Kate Kellaway, '*As You Like It* – Review', *Guardian*, 22 May 2012, www.guardian.co.uk/stage/2012/may/22/as-you-like-it-globe-review, 3 July 2012.

CHAPTER TWENTY-SEVEN

ROMEU E JULIETA (REPRISE)

Grupo Galpão at the Globe, again

Jacquelyn Bessell

This chapter is a reflection on my personal experience of attending *Romeu e Julieta* at the Globe on two occasions separated by a dozen years. I am an advocate of this production, and therefore its critic.[1] Objectivity is sometimes thought necessary in criticism, but my responding motivation for this particular production arises precisely from an experience of powerful involvement in it. And any insight I have to offer derives from that same involvement. When I first saw *Romeu e Julieta* at the 2000 Globe to Globe Festival, I was a member of staff at the Globe. I remember sobbing uncontrollably at more than one point during that performance, and the wry smiles on the faces of favourite former colleagues I spotted in the same audience twelve years later told me that others remembered this too. Indeed, the return to the Globe of *Romeu e Julieta* in 2012 was for me a real reprise, a return to a beloved space, a pilgrimage to the scene of a cherished memory. And *Romeu e Julieta* is a production which understands and trades openly on the theatrical value of such feelings of nostalgia; it is a remarkable production in dialogue with the ghosts of its own past.

Grupo Galpão's work on *Romeu e Julieta* began in 1991. David S. George, who saw this production at the 1993 Festival de Curitiba in southern Brazil, praised the way the production 'resurrected Shakespeare's play from the dust of accumulated romantic clichés to the delight and fascination of audiences and critics alike'.[2] The same show has been in and out of production for nearly twenty years since that review, and with the 2012 World Shakespeare Festival/Globe to Globe season production coinciding with Grupo Galpão's thirtieth anniversary as a company, I wondered whether the UK press would this time hail Galpão as global theatre veterans, or dismiss them as yesterday's news. Maddy Costa's generally positive review for the *Guardian* had a single reservation: 'There is much to admire in this production, but it is let down by a fundamental flaw. At no point does it achieve the seriousness of tone that might provoke emotional resonance: the laughter never admits the possibility of tears. Perhaps the fault lies with a cheerful audience, who laugh at the unlikeliest of times.'³ And Costa's reservations chime with her *Guardian* colleague Michael Billington's review of the troupe's first visit to the Globe in 2000. While Billington's assessment was also generally positive, he too complained that 'Grupo Galpão, a populist group whose origins lie in street theatre, never gets to grips with the tragic elements of the story.'⁴ Accusations of this kind are surely an occupational hazard for any troupe that makes a habit of playing tragedy in clown make-up and red noses. But never mind the greasepaint, here's the roar of the crowd: if the wider reception of this production may be gauged by either of the capacity crowds at the Globe of which I have been a part, this production has been a roaring success for a very long time.

SOUNDS

Scholars and voice coaches are fond of reminding us that Shakespeare's first audiences went to 'hear' a play, and the same premise seems to guide much of Grupo Galpão's production. We hear the company before we see them, as a motley band strikes up on the Globe piazza before the doors to the yard swing open. Once inside, the troupe seizes the first available opportunity to recruit its audience, strumming, drumming, tooting, fluting and snaking through a packed yard of excited groundlings who clap them to the stage like a returning battalion of clown soldiers. Eduardo Moreira's blog records his memory of the same moment, in language that suggests an altogether different relationship: 'Let's go. It's time to confront the beast. The theatre's doors open and we surprise the audience from behind, as if we caught an army from the rear. A "war" starts in which actors and the audience must play together.'⁵ Music's ability to soothe savage breasts of all shapes and sizes is, of course, well documented, but in this production music can do more than simply please or appease large, excitable crowds. In fact, much of the narrative itself is carried by music. The production's soundscape is founded on popular Brazilian serenades in dialogue with the text, and underscoring it in places. Grupo Galpão's actors are accomplished musicians and impressive multi-taskers. Some of them – notably Moreira's sad-faced Romeo – can sing, play an accordian and walk around on giant stilts at the same time. Sung refrains return again and again, like tiny sonnets, and a lot of narrative work is done with relatively few notes.

Moreira describes one collection of songs – Chiquinha Gonzaga's 'Lua Branca' ('White Moon'), André Filho's 'Cinzas' ('Ashes') and 'Última estrofe' ('Last stanza') by Cândido das Neves – as 'compositions of the "belle époque" of Brazilian music in the early twentieth century . . . heavily influenced by European salon music, especially waltzes'.⁶ These songs use the same instrumentation as a second strand of compositions taken from the *mineiro* folklore of the state of Minas Gerais, home to Grupo Galpão. These *serestas* and *modinhas* such as 'É a ti, flor do céu' ('Are you the flower of heaven') and 'Amo-te muito' ('I love you too') are typical of a folk tradition associated with the city of Dimantina, sung in the dialect of the *sertão*.[7] Grupo Galpão incorporate both musical idioms in a richly contrapuntal exchange, marking the development of the narrative over the production's one-hour and forty-five-minute life-span and also presenting a microcosm of Galpão's practice over the last thirty years. This production uses a series of transactions between both European and Brazilian musical traditions to respond to the formal and rhythmic considerations of the script. The musicology of the production is aligned to other aspects of the company's practice in that it draws equally from European and Brazilian traditions of composition and performance.

Two musical themes emerge with particular structural and narrative significance. The first, in a major key ('Flor, minha flor' or 'Flower, my flower') belongs to the Brazilian folk tradition;[8] the second, in a minor key, is the well-known Romanian waltz 'Waves of the Danube' (or 'Ondas do Danúbio' in Portuguese) by Iosif Ivanovici. These two themes remain in dialogue with each other throughout the performance. The effect is of ongoing reflection, development, recollection and recapitulation, with music that is a kind of shared reference point in the collective memory of the audience, as Moreira noted in his blog post: 'As soon as the show starts we feel strong vibrations coming from the audience. The Brazilians react emotionally and express nostalgia for their childhood and native land, which is induced by the soundtrack.'[9] Tonal variation and orchestration matter, of course, but what perhaps matters even more for Grupo Galpão's audience is the unmistakable sense that one has heard all this somewhere before. Repetition is therefore central to an understanding of *Romeu e Julieta*, and, by association, Bogart and Landau's 'Viewpoints' system[10] – of which repetition is a key element – provides an apt technical vocabulary to read Grupo Galpão's work within the context of twenty-first-century American devised theatre. The Viewpoints system uses the idea of repetition to generate and recycle original, devised material with theatrical potency. And, as Shakespeare uses repetitions and variations on the sonnet form for both narrative development and dramatic effect, so Grupo Galpão uses repetitions of phrases and musical sequences to achieve the same ends. When these repetitions are added to one's own memory of the much-loved performance of a dozen years ago, the effect is overwhelming. Short- and longer-term memories cross-pollinate, collate and clash in interesting ways, and blur the distinction between immersion in the present moment and nostalgia for the same place, long ago.

So how does this work? It is the major-key instrumental iteration of 'Flor, minha flor' which opens the piece, as the company wind their way through the groundlings towards the stage. This song surfaces again at the Capulet's ball. The refrain, sung this time by the whole company, underscores Romeo's speech 'O, she doth teach the torches to burn bright' (1.5.43–52) but cuts out abruptly for the famous lines of the 'shared sonnet' (1.5.92–105); striking up again immediately, the music highlights the narrative and stylistic significance of the shared sonnet form in the script.

'Ondas do Danúbio' is a familiar minor-key waltz, frequently used to underscore transitions between scenes or travelling steps danced by the company on their feet or on stilts, but it emerges first through a flute solo by the clown 'Shakespeare' and underscores the Nurse's prose speech to Juliet extolling Romeo's physical attributes (2.5.38–44). The effect here is to problematize the otherwise comic stylings of the Nurse (we've already seen her conducting the research which informs this speech, taking a good look under Romeo's tunic). The same tune is played by Romeo on his piano-accordion as Juliet dons her bridal veil, and again as the couple descend to the stage level to be married by Friar Laurence. The same waltz underscores both Tybalt's and Mercutio's pantomimed deaths, the former involving the slow removal of Tybalt's stilts by a grief-stricken Lady Capulet, the latter being an extended, broad and bawdy comic physical routine that could be the climax of Bottom's performance in 'Pyramus and Thisby'.

It is at this point in the performance that the two central themes enter into real dialogue with each other. The bodies of Mercutio and Tybalt are carried off to the minor-key waltz played by Romeo, already banished, in solitary confinement under the stairs leading up to the first platform. What follows is a scene that simultaneously stages the business of Act 3 Scene 2 ('Gallop apace . . . ') on top of the car with that of Act 3 Scene 3 (Romeo banished in Friar Laurence's cell) below. Later, the ensemble sings a slow-tempo 'Flor, minha flor' serenade to accompany the couple's fleeting attempts at lovemaking just before Romeo leaves in the morning for Mantua (Act 3 Scene 5). The minor-key waltz does not return, but the major refrain ('Flor, minha flor') does, again at its slower tempo, to underscore the deaths of both Romeo and Juliet. Interestingly, the music is cut short in both these instances, as if failing to resolve. Within this scheme of musical repetition, the serenade 'E a ti, flor de ceu' doubles as the score for both the balcony scene and Juliet's funeral. Mercutio leads the ensemble in the latter iteration, which also incorporates the text of the Capulets' lament for their lost Juliet (4.4.41–122). Musically, the connection between love and death is consistent and unequivocal. Juliet dies as a swan, to music (and in pointe shoes), leaving the company to bring back 'Flor, minha flor' for one last time, at its normal up-beat tempo, for the curtain call, before they dance a jig and exit, progressing through the yard and picking up a train of groundlings behind them as they do so.

SIGHTS

The set draws on what George calls a 'mixture of itinerant medieval theater . . . commedia dell'arte, circus techniques, and the *mineiro* flavour of Guimarães Rosa'.[11] A Volvo estate plastered with floral window-stickers, looking like a limousine at a clown-wedding, is parked on the Globe stage. A dozen years ago, the arrival of the car on the Globe stage seemed a provocative intervention, given the then artistic directorate's experiments with 'original stage practices'. In 2012, parked on a stage that now bears the marks of many structural interventions in the more recent past, the car looks more quaint than radical. This car supports a small stage platform, and the platform supports a stepladder, as well as several bendy bamboo poles. On the end of the longest bamboo, a crescent moon dangles, like giant lunar bait. What the set does is to turn the Globe stage into a sort of giant's puppet theatre with a proscenium arch, inviting some interesting shifts in scale and perspective at various junctures. The first example is when the lines of the Prologue are preceded by a dolly-puppet show played out on the mini-proscenium of the car's downstage windows. As Lydia Del Picchia enters, wearing a ragdoll dress and make-up, she dances in front of the car like a giant dolly in an altogether larger puppet theatre.

Proscenium staging has also determined the gestural language of the production, with most of the communication happening *en face*, and with little or no attention paid to depth of field or to thrust staging. Instead, Grupo Galpão uses split-focus address: sometimes dialogue between performers is sent out over the heads of the groundlings, the response being bounced off the back wall of the house; elsewhere exchanges occur between two performers, one in hieroglyphic profile, one face on to the bulk of the audience. This suggestive manipulation of spatial relationships (another component in the Viewpoints system) also allows the company to play with multiple or inverted levels: prime examples of this technique are the simultaneously staged scenes in Act 3 mentioned above, and the 'balcony' scene (Act 2 Scene 1), in which Romeo lies on top of the car roof and speaks out to Juliet's 'balcony' below him, on the Volvo's passenger seat.

Moreira traces this performance style to Grupo Galpão's origins in street theatre, a performance tradition which 'values direct play between the actors and the audience. This often justifies the use of direct address to the audience, rather than the characters facing each other directly. I think it's a feature well suited to the popular theatre and the street.'[12] The stilts used by Romeo, Benvolio and Tybalt can be traced to the same tradition, of course. This being Grupo Galpão, the provenance of this street-theatre idiom is both local and international. Galpão actors Teuda Bara, Antonio Edson, Wanda Fernandes and Eduardo Moreira first met in 1982 at a workshop led by Kurt Bildstein and George Froscher from the Munich Free Theatre.[13] Moreira explains that the founding members of Galpão 'worked with them on the

Fig. 15 Romeo (Eduardo Moreira) and Juliet (Fernanda Vianna) with the company, *Romeo and Juliet*, Grupo Galpão from Belo Horizonte, Brazil; director Gabriel Villela.

street, and learned many techniques to work on the street, such as stilts, acrobatics, and circus techniques'.[14] Describing these workshops as 'the genesis of the group', Moreira notes that 'The street has forced us to seek the acquisition of different techniques and languages related to the popular theatre, for example work with the masks of the commedia dell'arte, music, melodrama, and epic narrative theatre, mime, pantomime, etc'.[15]

And, while emphasizing the significance of local and street performance conventions, Moreira also acknowledges the role that Peter Brook's writings have played in the development of the company, as 'he said that in today's world the only place that it would be possible to recreate Shakespeare's Elizabethan theatre audience would be the streets. This was essential to realize that we were on track.'[16] Brook's influence may also be traced in the rigorous physical training for this production and the way in which this was integrated into the company's approach to verse-speaking:

How might Shakespeare's poetry, written in the late sixteenth century, sound alive and vibrating in the actors' bodies? When Brook did *A Midsummer Night's Dream*, he put his actors to work with a trapeze, and their comments indicated how this training helped them to stop declaiming and start living the poetry. This was a fundamental observation. Then we read some research that called *Romeo and Juliet* the tragedy of precipitation. The characters don't think, they act. It is the tragedy of youth. This led us to create a system in which we were obligated to work the text and the songs on a very narrow plank about 2.5 metres above the ground. This meant that the words gained a nervousness, and a strong intensity. All the physical work is based on this premise: the characters are on the brink of a precipice, about to precipitate. The stilts and the ballet pointe shoes come from this too.[17]

Responding to the 2000 production at the Globe, W.B. Worthen used such connections with Brook's practice to argue that the production was 'deeply in dialogue with the First World theatrical avant-garde',[18] whereas Billington's critique of the same suggested that what might cut it in Belo Horizonte was no longer good enough in London: 'the circus metaphor is in danger of becoming an exhausted cliché. In Brazil it may still have resonance. But in the west we have seen too many people, from Fellini, Brook and Anthony Newley to every avant-garde group you care to name, colonise it for it to have any residual life.'[19] The use of 'colonise' in this context prompted Worthen to tear something of a strip off Billington back in 2003,[20] and so I don't need to repeat that exercise here. But as Rome, Paris and London (where one might place Fellini, Brook, Newley and Billington) all lie to the east of Belo Horizonte, I can't help wondering whether Billington is simply a weak geographer, or whether he – unlike Worthen – is rather uncomfortable with terms like 'First World' with reference to Peter Brook and theatre politics.

These days, I find Grupo Galpão's practice is in dialogue with Bogart and Landau as much as with Brook. In addition to the use of repetition I discussed above, the compositional element referred to by Bogart and Landau as 'revelation of space'[21] finds several expressions in *Romeu e Julieta* at the Globe. One example of this can be seen at the start of a dumb-show battle at the top of the show, as the feuding factions enter through, over or under the parked Volvo. Later, in a striking *coup de metathéâtre*, the discovery space at the Globe is itself discovered as the Volvo car-platform rolled off to one side, like a stone before a tomb, to reveal the mourners seated within the discovery space at Juliet's funeral. They advance to engage in a lament on the main stage, while Juliet herself lies on the Globe balcony, above. Graves marked out at the stage level allow for the interior and exterior to be revealed in a single moment.

Of course, the use of multiple simultaneous perspectives is not confined to modern theatre practice; the same compositional strategy may also be seen in artwork produced by small children, and Grupo Galpão incorporates the visual currency of childhood memories in a variety of interesting ways. A hilarious dumb-show shoot-out between rival clown-factions ends with the 'dead' victims frozen, their limbs held in rigid 'star' silhouettes, creating a tableau that could have been sketched by a 4-year-old witness to the crime; this lends a brilliantly simple resonance to Juliet's plea, 'Give me my Romeo, and when I shall die / Take him and cut him out in little stars' (3.2.21–2). The Nurse's job-description is manifested by the two enormous satin, tasselled cushions hanging around her neck as comically amplified bosom-pillows, and the same appealing logic determines that Mercutio's death and ascent into 'heaven' involves solemnly switching his red clown nose for a white nose, to become a 'ghost clown' version of his former self. Finally, and for me most movingly, the two lifesized chalk outlines drawn on the Globe stage to mark the lovers' graves also mark the spaces occupied by the younger Moreira and Fernanda Vianna twelve years before.

For Moreira, the production is the occasion for a profound and difficult dialogue with ghosts of his own. His original Juliet in 1992 was his wife, Wanda Fernandes, who was killed in a car crash in 1994. The production's return to the Globe prompts Moreira to reflect on the space Fernandes left in the troupe:

> There are moments in which it is difficult to control our emotions. The voice becomes choked. The speech stumbles. The show brings up many remembrances, and staging it again at the Globe Theatre, after almost twelve years, evokes a very emotional movie. It brings back rehearsals in Morro Vermelho, the presence and loss of Wanda, dreams, achievements, scars and losses over thirty years on tour.[22]

Comments such as these surely indicate Moreira's acute awareness of the 'tragic elements' in *Romeu e Julieta*, but equally the chalk outlines of bodies on the stage invite his audience to project their own feelings of presence and loss into the spaces provided.

In closing, I will return to the sound of this production, to say something about language and its capacity to move. I don't have a lick of Portuguese, but listening to this familiar story in this unfamiliar language strikes me as the aural equivalent of watching actors perform in neutral masks. Actors may use masks to develop a kind of precision in somatic storytelling; the mask prompts the spectator to refocus their visual engagement, to find meaning in the actors' movement and gestures, rather than in their facial expressions. Hearing this play in a language I do not understand similarly concentrates my ear on sounds rather than words. And, for the most part, the sounds I hear are vowels, which – as many voice teachers since Cicely Berry like to remind us – carry the emotional weight of the word. So I experience a song-stream of vowels, which takes me deeper into the grief and longing at the heart of this story I thought I knew so well. Listening to the groundlings join in a chorus of 'Flor, minha flor . . . ' as the actors exit through the yard for the final time, their progress impeded by countless impromptu embraces from both new and returning audience members, I consider how both the troupe and I have aged these past dozen years, before I decide to blame the vowels, or the music, or the occasion, or the ghosts for the lump in my throat as I leave.

ENDNOTES

1 Eduardo Moreira, artistic director of Grupo Galpão, has given very generously of his time and insights through a series of e-mail interviews with me. Senhor Moreira's observations were translated by Renato Rocha, artistic director of Os Inomináveis Theatre Company

(Rio de Janeiro) and director of *The Dark Side of Love* (for the World Shakespeare Festival and the London International Festival of Theatre (LIFT) 2012), and Paulo Henrique Da Silva Gregorio, a research student at the Shakespeare Institute; to them I am most grateful. I would also like to thank Aleksander Dundjerović, who helped me to make initial contact with Grupo Galpão.

2 David S. George, *Flash and Crash Days: Brazilian Theater in the Postdictatorship Period*, Latin American Studies, vol. xix (New York and London: Garland, 2000), p. 129.

3 Maddy Costa, '*Romeu e Julieta* – Review, *Guardian*, 22 May 2012, www.guardian.co.uk/stage/2012/may/22/romeo-and-juliet-review, 25 September 2012.

4 Michael Billington, '*Romeu e Julieta* – Review', *Guardian*, 15 July 2000, www.guardian.co.uk/culture/2000/jul/15/1, 25 September 2012.

5 Eduardo Moreira blog post, 'Notas dispersas da viagem de reestreia de "Romeu e Julieta" 5', 2 June 2012, www.grupogalpao.com.br/blog/, 19 July 2012. Translated by Paulo Henrique Da Silva Gregorio.

6 Eduardo Moreira, e-mail interview, translated by Renato Rocha, July 2012.

7 Ibid.

8 Ibid.

9 Eduardo Moreira blog post, 'Notas dispersas da viagem de reestreia de "Romeu e Julieta" 6', 4 June 2012, www.grupogalpao.com.br/blog/, 19 July 2012. Translated by Paulo Henrique Da Silva Gregorio.

10 For more on the Viewpoints system, see Anne Bogart and Tina Landau, *The Viewpoints Book: A Practical Guide to Viewpoints and Composition* (New York: Theatre Communications Group, 2005).

11 George, *Flash and Crash Days*, p. 129.

12 Eduardo Moreira, e-mail interview, July 2012.

13 Grupo Galpao website, www.grupogalpao.com.br/engl/historia/trajetoria.html, 19 July 2012.

14 Eduardo Moreira, e-mail interview, July 2012.

15 Ibid.

16 Ibid.

17 Ibid.

18 W.B. Worthen, *Shakespeare and the Force of Modern Performance* (Cambridge University Press, 2003), p. 166.

19 Billington, review of *Romeu e Julieta*.

20 Worthen, *Shakespeare*, pp. 160–1.

21 Bogart and Landau, *Viewpoints*, pp. 150–1.

22 Eduardo Moreira, 'Notas dispersas da viagem de reestreia de "Romeu e Julieta" 6'.

WEEK FIVE

CHAPTER TWENTY-EIGHT

BREAD AND CIRCUSES

Chiten, Japan and *Coriolanus*

Deana Rankin

Four people step onto the stage; one carries a fifth on his back. Two onstage musicians provide the soundtrack. There are echoes of Noh theatre about the scene – some of the actors are even carrying masks. But the costumes read differently: these are 'realistic' clothes, the blue *shibori* traditional tie-dyed cloth of the Japanese peasant. Once he steps down off his carrier's back, Martius, soon to be Coriolanus (Dai Ishida) does not speak; instead, he puts on his head a basket – the ego-effacing headwear of the Buddhist mendicant monk or Komuso (see Colour Plate 12). Is it there to evoke a military helmet? To suggest the beggar-monk seeking alms? Or is it both: the samurai warrior adopting a traditional disguise? Whatever the answer, the tone is set. This *Coriolanus* (it seems) is not about the irresolvable tragic conflict between the aristocracy and the plebians of Rome; this *Coriolanus* aims for comic subversion. It is a play about how the canny lower classes outwit the bombastic upper-class hero and get away with it. While Ishida's role as Coriolanus remains constant, the four other cast members who make up the 'chorus' (Satoko Abe, Shie Kubota, Saki Kohno and Yohei Kobayashi) are shape-shifters; they play senators and citizens, Romans and Volscians with a striking combination of equanimity and subversive playfulness. Shakespeare's scenes of riot and war in the long first act here become a series of childish games: the bugles do not quite work but instead produce Punch and Judy-style voices. Towards the end of the first half, those playground games return and escalate further as the chorus first follow Coriolanus, then play follow-my-leader, then further subvert that game with a mimicry that verges on bullying.

As Martius/Coriolanus laments his apparent imminent defeat, the chorus keep blowing out the votive torch he is trying to light; and this Roman hero is armed with . . . a baguette. It is a nice touch – *Coriolanus* famously starts with a bread shortage, a riot and a lot of talk about bellies. But as the baguettes multiplied across the show, as the chorus spoke the lines of both senate and citizens through flying crumbs, the hunger and discontent of Shakespeare's Rome were dissipated. As the bread turned into a circus, it was easy to forget that this is a play about the brutality of peace as well as of war.

Many of the productions in the Globe to Globe Festival went for the spectacular to entertain and win over audiences who do not speak their language. This Japanese production took the risky decision to trade on language: Coriolanus never stops talking. When, under heavy duress, he finally makes his speech to the citizens, he does so in a fake accent (rather than an insincere tone). The self-consciousness of the performer's play-acting of the leader risked being lost on those without any knowledge of Japanese. At Tuesday's performance a timely overhead helicopter aided and abetted the actor, suggesting the great leader had perhaps jetted in for some crowd-pleasing election speeches. When Coriolanus lets his hair down and leaves Rome as an exile to travel to the Volscian capital, his disguise fools no one: the chorus outdo each other in stealing his baguettes. The play moves steadily towards a monologue: Coriolanus is transformed from playground alpha male to incessant bore. At one point the chorus load him up again and carry him off stage, but still he does not stop talking. Indeed, he seems not to notice that his feet are no longer on the ground.

In the first act, there is a heavy price to pay for this focus on Coriolanus and his language. Little room is left for the women's voices to emerge. His wife, Virgilia, steps forward from the chorus only briefly. When Volumnia, his mother, emerges for the first time in the second half, she is voiced by her son in a strange sound-scape, an act of possession. It is a dangerous occlusion. The critical history of *Coriolanus* in performance suggests that to have a memorable production, you have to have, opposite the son, a memorable mother. And yet this disconcerting moment where son and mother are fused also signals a promising change of pace, a shift towards the kind of expressionist, almost operatic, style of theatre for which Chiten are renowned. When in the closing scenes the chorus, now playing Volumnia and her family, visit Coriolanus to plead for Rome's safety, Volumnia kneels, addressing her son in a swaying sing-song. It is a far cry from Vanessa Redgrave's berating of Ralph Fiennes while sporting full military regalia.[1] This static, keening Volumnia seems to hypnotize her son into submission, her erratically pitched pleading raised against Coriolanus' groans. It does not always work, but the moments when it did gave a glimpse of a much braver experimental version of *Coriolanus* struggling to get out.

Chiten, based in Kyoto and led by the visionary, award-winning director Motoi Miura, are known for their experimental work with classical theatre texts. Indeed, Globe to Globe Festival Director Tom Bird first saw their work not in Japan but in Moscow, where they were playing not Shakespeare but Chekov – an hour-long version of *The Seagull* complete with tea ceremony, video installation and klaxons.[2]

Miura's ongoing work on Chekov has won him the Toga Festival Directors' Competition for *The Seagull* and the Agency for Cultural Affairs New Director Award for *The Cherry Orchard*.[3] Bird's invitation to join the 2012 Festival was a welcome one, and it was the company who decided on *Coriolanus* as their first Shakespearean venture.

Rather surprisingly, Chiten's *Coriolanus* is the first Japanese Shakespeare production to be staged at the Globe. There is, after all – from the extraordinary epic films of Akira Kurosawa to the ground-breaking productions of Tadashi Suzuki and Yukio Ninegawa – a powerful tradition of Japanese Shakespeare. Within this tradition *Coriolanus* is also a hard act to follow: trading on the samurai resonances of the text, Yuko Ninagawa's 2007 production at the Barbican won great acclaim for its epic battle scenes, as well as for the extraordinary and intimate chemistry between Coriolanus (Toshiaki Karasawa) and Volumnia (Kayoko Shiraishi). British directors have also picked up on the Japanese resonances of the play: David Farr's 2003 RSC production pitted a sneering, muscular Coriolanus, driven by a fierce inner sense of Samurai honour (Greg Hicks), against the terrifying matriarch Volumnia (Alison Fiske): it was a very close contest. And in 2011 Ralph Fiennes, director and lead performer in the film *Coriolanus*, took inspiration from the fact that Coriolanus is a 'sort of samurai figure . . . He is not equipped to be a political animal.'[4] Chiten, with a cast of five, were never quite going to take on the legacy of the Samurai-Coriolanus, but did the weight of Japanese Shakespearean tradition perhaps take its toll in other ways?

Miura has acknowledged the huge influence of Suzuki on his work. A regular attendee at the Toga festival, he recalls the 'truly shocking experience' of seeing Suzuki's *King Lear*: 'I had seen many plays up until that point in time, but I got the feeling that with this play I was seeing true "theatre" for the first time.' Miura has also singled out two key aspects of Suzuki's work as inspirational: first, the use of the prop as a powerful theatrical device. It is not difficult to see Coriolanus' Komosu basket as reminiscent of the baskets used in Suzuki's *Ivanov* (his version of Chekov) which conceal and reveal the actors within. Second, there is the use of the dramatic pause 'ma' as it is exploited in both vocalization and movement in the Suzuki acting method.[5]

With these in mind, we can return to explore the possibility of that braver experimental production of *Coriolanus* mentioned above. We caught just one or two further glimpses of the experimental possibilities of this company's work when the chorus, now transformed from Coriolanus' family to Volscian soldiers, voiced their dissatisfaction with war through physical anguish: Suzuki-style impossible movements extended for unearthly lengths of time. Another such powerful moment came when those failed snorting bugles of the first act eventually sounded for Coriolanus' death, accompanied by a solo violin. Against this plaintive harmony, Aufidius and the chorus tried, again and again, to hoist the dead leader's body onto their backs;

they fought, they loved, they failed. Such glimpses left me wondering what if Chiten had chosen not to perform a full, text-based version of *Coriolanus*, but had instead, following their own theatrical practice, broken up, explored and reconstructed the text in their own powerful way to give their audience a truer account of Shakespeare's tragedy?

ENDNOTES

1 Ralph Fiennes, *Coriolanus* (2011), United Kingdom: Icon Entertainment International/BBC Films.
2 Victoria James, 'Shakespeare's Globe Hails a Japanese "Coriolanus"', *Japan Times*, 10 May, 2012 www.japantimes.co.jp/text/ft20120510a1.html, 10 October 2012.
3 'Chiten', EU–Japan Fest Japan Committee, 2010, http://eu-japanfest.org/n-english/n-program/2010/06/chiten-year-round-support.html, 11 October 2012.
4 J.S. Marcus, 'Ralph Fiennes's "Samurai" Coriolanus', *Wall Street Journal*, 11 February 2011.
5 For information on the Suzuki acting method, see 'Giving Expression to Dissected Texts: The New Possibilities of Compositional Theater Pioneered by Motoi Miura', 2010, www.performingarts.jp/E/art_interview/1002/1.html, 11 October 2012; Motoi Miura, *Omoshiro-kereba OK?* (Tokyo: Goryu Shoin, 2010); Tadashi Suzuki, *The Way of Acting: The Theatre Writings of Tadashi Suzuki* (New York: Theatre Communications Group, 1993).

CHAPTER TWENTY-NINE

'NO WORDS!'

Love's Labour's Lost in British Sign Language

Kate Rumbold

The Globe to Globe production of *Love's Labour's Lost* was billed as one of the more unusual acts of translation in the Festival: from Shakespeare's 'rich, pun-riddled text' into the 'physical language of BSL'.[1] Deafinitely Theatre, an 'independent, professional Deaf-led company'[2] based in London, set out to transform a play all about verbal excess into the visual medium of British Sign Language (BSL). Despite being one of the more local of the global visitors to the Festival, the company's language was foreign to many in the audience. Deafinitely's production was also billed as 'the first full-length Shakespeare play to be performed in BSL'. Video recordings of 1990s Arts Council-funded, small-cast BSL film adaptations of *The Tempest*, *A Midsummer Night's Dream* and *Twelfth Night* exist,[3] but more frequently reported is the BSL *interpretation* of hearing performances for Deaf audiences: 'the live interpretation of a spoken message in real time', as opposed to translation, or 'working with written source and target forms'.[4] In this fast-paced work, the interpreter focuses on 'understanding the intended meaning of the message', capturing 'the power of the plots, the nuances and sub-plots', and 'the richness of the characters', if not the form of the language.[5] Other studies have suggested how interpretations borrow from performance and gestural traditions to effect better 'cultural mediation'.[6] Proponents of American Sign Language (ASL) theatre have recently sought more rigorous techniques for the full translation of Shakespeare. Peter Novak, leader of the ASL Shakespeare Project established at Yale, suggests that merely asking actors to translate their lines from English into ASL 'mitigates against any linguistic, stylistic or historical continuity',[7] and that the ideal ASL translation does not remove sound or intricate rhymes, but 'searches for a new paradigm of communication that decodes Shakespeare's spoken text and reproduces it visually'.[8]

I am grateful to Gemma Rumbold, Sarah Tucker and Susan Hunston for advice about BSL, and to Andrew Muir for responding to my questions about the script.

Deafinitely Theatre had hitherto been outside this emerging tradition of sign-language Shakespeare translation. Tackling Shakespeare was a new challenge for the company, but tackling what 'Shakespeare' represented was perhaps of even greater significance. Company members had previously observed that for many Deaf people, 'English is the language of oppression, of being forbidden to use sign language'.[9] As children, some were forced to concentrate on learning to speak English rather than on learning to sign, and thus found it difficult to communicate either with hearing or Deaf people. Among the international companies visiting the Globe in 2012, the Deaf community would not be alone in experiencing, at least historically, the dominance of the English language over native forms of expression. For Deafinitely, that language could also signal exclusion from full participation in mainstream education. Shakespeare could seem the very embodiment of that exclusion, and one could read a defiant declaration of independence into the determination to find non-English 'equivalents' for Shakespeare in BSL. As Lyn Gardner noted, however, by 2009 Deafinitely was already shifting away from its issues-based, even angry, approach to drama, as represented in the 2007 production, *Playing God*, which railed against doctors' enthusiasm to 'repair' Deaf children by the use of cochlear implants, and was 'starting to develop a distinctive approach, combining the visual and physical', which could engage a wider, mixed Deaf and hearing audience.[10] Nonetheless, the director's hope that the Globe experiment might be a 'break' for some of the actors, helping them to cross over into the mainstream theatre from which they had been excluded, is a reminder of continued division;[11] and Deafinitely actor Matthew Gurney's determination to prove, through *Love's Labour's Lost*, that 'give us any script, and we can do it',[12] is as poignant as it is confident. Mastering Shakespeare seemed powerfully to represent both independence and inclusion for this company.

How did Deafinitely come to perform this play? According to Paula Garfield, Artistic Director of the company, they were offered by the Festival team a choice of two plays: *Love's Labour's Lost* or a play about gentlemen. She said that she chose the former because it sounded more romantic.[13] Translating *Love's Labour's Lost* into any language other than English is a significant linguistic challenge: the play is 'exhilarating as only a language comedy can be to a professional of language resources, exasperating for the sheer catalogue it provides of discursive patterns and of the flowers of *Elocutio*', with the additional demand that the translation represent in a new cultural setting the diverse cultural backgrounds of its characters.[14] For a Deaf theatre company, this linguistic challenge would only be increased, requiring the translation to convey a complex plot and to find 'equivalents' for the erudite, Latinate language of the play in a range of visual signs. Deafinitely were also required not simply to interpret an existing 'hearing performance' for a Deaf audience, but to construct a Deaf performance that would be accessible for Deaf and hearing audiences alike.

Having relatively little experience of Shakespeare herself, Garfield called on Andrew Muir, the company's Literary Associate, to translate the play into modern English. From there, Garfield and creative interpreter Kate Furby sought 'equivalents' for his words in BSL. As Furby describes, 'Andrew would explain the meaning of the text, then I would have to translate it coherently in BSL. We also had to explain the metaphors and what they meant, as well as some of the words' – including words with double meanings.[15] Furby admits that sometimes one had to 'choose one of the predominant meanings to go with;'[16] and Garfield suggests that, rather than get 'bogged down' in word-for-word interpretation, 'we decided that the content and the meaning was the same thing'.[17] The creative team worked on the text for several months: 'We made notes, made cuts, adapted for BSL and it was extremely hard, but it was worth it.'[18] Next, they and the actors moved into a two-week 'translation' process, during which time the team set out to 'explain, translate the text, get them to sign it back, check that it's correct, then film all of their lines'.[19] A several-week gap for the company to work on other projects – and to memorize their collaboratively produced lines – was followed by a final, short rehearsal period, including a brief opportunity to practise in the Globe space.

The resulting 'script' of this multi-stage translation process might seem to be several removes from the original text of Shakespeare's play – more so, perhaps, than many of the foreign languages presented at the Festival. Yet in other ways, the physical medium could be seen to add new layers, closing down some double meanings, but opening up new linguistic dimensions. Garfield did not want this to be a 'sign-supported English' production, dutifully interpreting every word of the play, but rather an 'equivalent' that was genuinely Deaf theatre.[20] Her creative team shared her sense that they could at once 'remain faithful' to Shakespeare and create 'an equivalent that was completely accessible to a Deaf audience'; and that while 'Deaf actors whose first language is actually English and not British Sign Language were very fearful of losing the Shakespeare' and 'moving . . . as far away from the script as we'd have liked to to create a British Sign Language equivalent', they eventually gained their 'trust that we were remaining faithful, we just had to go a different path in order to do so'.[21] This collaborative, creative translation process involved the innovation of everyone from director to actors in constructing the inventive translation of the lines. They shared the goal of 'trying to find the same beauty' in signs as in Shakespeare's language.[22]

During the Festival, the Deafinitely company were required to work without their normal repertoire of techniques for simultaneously engaging Deaf and hearing audiences. Deafinitely typically incorporate into their performances visual media such as Powerpoint and spoken English-language voiceovers. Because of the Globe to Globe Festival policy that no English should be spoken by the visiting companies, the company had to rely on the brief surtitles that summarized each scene to interpret the signs to a hearing audience. One of the few overt concessions to that audience was the folk band that played a jolly accompaniment to the opening scene and then proceeded to annotate every subsequent mood change of the play, in the manner of a silent film. The consistent musical backing brought warmth and continuity to the production, but was not, as the native instruments of an international visiting country might be, intimately connected to the culture of the performers, and one was sometimes acutely aware that the music worked in parallel, rather than in harmony, with the actors' movements.

When the performance began, and the cast staggered onto the stage to enact a crowd scene of wine-soaked debauchery, a likely response for both Deaf and hearing audiences was confusion: with so much visual noise going on, where should they look first? But as the king of Navarre signed down reproachfully from the balcony, and the 'text' of the play began, confusion slowly turned to clarity. The stage cleared, surtitles summarized Navarre's proposal of three years' sequestered study, and his lords lined up neatly to negotiate the oath, stepping forward one at a time to sign up for, or struggle with, its conditions. In these opening scenes, actors grappled with the choice between the clarity of presenting their signs straight ahead, and the need to communicate with a Globe audience arranged around three sides of the thrust stage; early in the production I noticed two women get up from their seats in the lower galleries to the right of the stage and move to the centre of the yard to better follow the performance. The actors had had to adapt rapidly to using the entire stage space, and to acquire the unnatural skill of not facing their interlocutor directly.[23] Straight-ahead signing, while potentially clearer for those directly in front of the stage to follow, could lead to the same loss of understanding that accompanied the static moments in other foreign productions in the Festival.[24]

Muir observed the need to act 'big' in this unusual theatre space, and noted how the actors' movements had grown larger even during the two-day run.[25] Rehearsing in a small studio, the actors were initially concerned that the exaggerated movements the Globe demanded would somehow be less 'true'. The resulting actions were somewhere between BSL (including finger-spelling) and large-scale theatrical gesture. One blogger noted the range of mimes used to engage the audience: 'the curve of a woman's body', 'food being placed into the mouth', 'the right hand being held aloft' in oath and 'the cutting of his own tongue', as well as the idiosyncratic use of 'grandiloquent' movements by Armado and 'coarse' ones by Costard.[26] Incorporating performance gestures has been deemed 'vital to a successful translation' in sign-language interpreting, creating 'equivalent textual access' for Deaf audiences;[27] in this production, both Deaf and hearing audiences benefited from these legible movements. Unmistakable gestures for 'not to see a woman in that term' (1.1.37) got a big laugh with every anxious repetition by Berowne, Dumaine and Longaville; and while the company were keen to stay on the right side of pantomime, these larger-than-life gestures seemed to engage the widest audience. In the set-piece scene when the lords overhear one another professing their secret love for the women, the physical comedy delighted the audience: one by one, the lords retreated behind stage pillars (or, in Longaville's case, turned himself into a tree in the absence of spare pillars) as another arrived on the stage to unburden himself of his secret; one by one, they emerged from their hiding-places to mock the lover they had overheard, only then to be exposed themselves as lovers, culminating in the delivery of the letter that triumphantly proved Berowne just as smitten as his friends. Later, on arriving at the French camp in the guise of Muscovites, they brought the house down when they enacted the imaginary trials of their journey, lying prostrate on the stage and swimming furiously.

It is tempting to draw connections between BSL and early modern and eighteenth-century traditions of gestural theatre, not least because John Bulwer, the author of *Chirologia: or The naturall language of the hand* (1644), the book of diagrams of familiar, codified 'speaking' expressions of the hand that is often taken to be a useful guide to the repertoire of movement in early modern stage performance, was also a promoter of education for the Deaf. It also has resonances with the codified eighteenth-century acting gestures made famous by actor David Garrick, whose prescribed stance of 'terror' defined that century's stage representation of Hamlet.[28] However, the gestural vocabulary used by Deafinitely was not, as it would have been to those earlier audiences, familiar to everyone present. As actor Donna Mullings observes, whether Deaf and hearing audience members understood the production would depend on their ability to 'visualize' and follow the actors' body language.[29] To ask these movements to stand in for words entirely is another kind of theatrical challenge.

Focusing exclusively on these larger gestures, however, would obscure the subtleties of the company's achievement. While the nuanced variations of 'hand-shape, location of the sign, movement pattern, and palm orientation'[30] used to create meaning in BSL were beyond the reach of this reviewer, the varying levels of 'energy and emphasis' the actors gave to these movements were visible to all. Deafinitely's translation process successfully achieved a distinctive register for each character. Matthew Gurney's Berowne infused his signs with audience-engaging urgency, sometimes bursting out in noises of surprise or indignation. Rosaline (Charly Arrowsmith) was wonderfully expressive both in her contempt for Berowne, and in the feelings to which that contempt finally gave way. Nadia Nadarajah, a less experienced actor with a background in presenting, made a gentle, retiring Princess, with more tentative signs, while, by contrast, Maria and Katherine doubled as

Fig. 16 Berowne (Mathew Gurney), *Love's Labour's Lost*, Deafinitely Theatre from London, UK; director Paula Garfield; translation team including Andrew Muir and Kate Furby.

Moth and Jacquenetta respectively, their body language switching into more or less overtly feminine registers. Brian Duffy's signs captured Boyet's harried, go-between status, while David Sands' Costard galloped around the stage gesticulating with barely contained energy. Most captivating of all was Adam Bassett's Don Armado, whose eloquent movements made him more sympathetic than ridiculous. The distinctiveness of each character's movements was accentuated by the musical riff played whenever they took centre stage: a romantic, samba-style shuffle for Berowne and Rosalind, and a Spanish lilt for Armado (thus meeting the challenge mentioned above of signalling cultural difference in translation). Individual characterization – including making sympathetic, emotionally engaging characters out of figures like Armado and the king of Navarre – was one of the strengths of the production.

At the end of the performance, Bassett's unusually expressive gestures became poignantly eloquent when his Armado, rather than Hiems and Ver, delivered the song of Spring and Winter. In beautiful, flowing movements, he captured with wonder the delicate growth of 'daisies pied and violets blue' (5.2.859) emerging from the earth, and the chill of 'birds' that 'sit brooding in the snow' (5.2.888). His movements evoked not just *images* of winter and spring but the sensations associated with those seasons. In BSL poetry, one cannot so easily detach the signer from the implied 'poetic-I' of the poem: 'the written form of English makes these poems less immediately related to the poet, compared to the live "embodied" performance of a signed poem'.[31] When Bassett signed the effects of warmth and cold on the different creatures – shivering tenderly, or impersonating an owl at rest and in flight – he seemed to embody each of them in turn, rather than simply narrating them in a detached, if mellifluous, third-person account more typical of hearing performances. The poem perhaps also profited from the anthropomorphic inventiveness of BSL poetry, in which objects from toothbrushes to volcanoes can be afforded personalities.[32] Muir's modern English translation thus provided tantalizing performance suggestions, glossing 'And Dick the shepherd blows his nail' (5.2.878) with '(*Blows on his fingernails*)'; and the production transformed third-person abstractions like 'When blood is nipped and ways be foul' (5.2.881) to movements that captured that coldness. Armado's poetic language was amplified when the rest of the company began to move in unison with him, empathetically shivering and signing along in a way that recalled the uplifting dance at the end of all Globe productions. The poem was the real moment of 'equivalence' in this sign-language production, evoking, and even enhancing, the lyrical beauty of Shakespeare's words with its 'visual poetics'.[33] It is unsurprising that the poem – described by one Facebook fan of the company as 'spine-chilling, heartbreaking and gorgeous when you performed it at the Globe' – was excerpted for performance in subsequent London festivals.[34]

The lyricism of the final moments of the play would have been welcome throughout. Glimpses of the rehearsal process, in which actors ask writers 'Am I supposed to be angry in this scene?',[35] and the director urges one character that 'You don't trust him. Is he really telling the truth?',[36] support the impression that this is an emotion- and narrative-led piece, rather than one that revels primarily in language. Yet while beautiful imagery and playful puns might not have been immediately apparent to hearing audiences, all audience members could gain a new appreciation of the play from the company's more emotional emphasis. Garfield's interest in the 'love' aspect of the title was evident in the way that the romantic elements of the plot were brought to the fore. After the Princess received news of her father's death, and she and the ladies planned to depart for France, the lords rapidly abandoned their exuberant gestures to the audience to share gentle, face-to-face signs with their beloved women. This switch, which in hearing productions can signal the beginning of a subdued ending, here represented a surge, rather than a drop, in emotional intensity. BSL signs, more strained in the round, found new expressiveness in the one-to-one conversations for which they were designed. These quiet, private exchanges, overheard, or rather seen, by the audience, made the final declarations of love seem particularly intimate. While other productions might use the verbal patterning of this final series of male–female conversations to exaggerate Shakespeare's disobedience of the conventions of comedy ('Our wooing doth not end like an old play: / Jack hath not Jill' (5.2.852–3)), Deafinitely's take on the ending was earnest, and moving. The company developed in rehearsal a sign to represent Love's Labour's Lost, comprising a gesture towards the heart, and a gesture of the heart following a departing loved one;[37] and they emphasized, accordingly, the lords' and ladies' tender feelings of separation, rather than the metatheatrical playfulness of the women's happy-ending-defying challenges.

The ending was greeted with rapturous applause, hands clapped and palms waved in unison. Within this memorable image of shared enjoyment, it is worth reflecting on the multiple communities that met in this 'amazing audience'.[38] Even before the production began, it was clear that London's Deaf community was a strong presence in the theatre, signing to one another in greeting across the yard in a manner evocative of the theatrical audiences described in eighteenth-century novels. Within that community was a smaller, tighter one, focused around Deafinitely: the company had 'a lot of friends' present,[39] and the way the actors lingered on stage, waving excitedly to individuals in the audience, showed what a personal achievement this represented for them. One should be cautious, though, about describing the event as a cultural capital conquest for all: as Mullings mentioned above, some gestures would be beyond both Deaf and hearing audiences; and the school pupils seen signing to one another throughout the production might have felt as disenchanted as any teenage group on a compulsory outing. Likewise, the hearing audience at this production included both enthusiastic Globe-goers (who are, as Muir and Furby perceive, 'up for anything, because they know their plays') and visitors unfamiliar with the plot of Love's Labour's Lost, making sense of the experience with more or less ease for all the absence of Shakespeare's language.

The warm and enthusiastic reactions from Deaf audience members outside the theatre, captured on The Hub and the 'Year of Shakespeare' website, evoke the conversion narratives of surprised pleasure often voiced by new hearing audiences for Shakespeare: 'I thought it would be like the Old English I had studied in my GCSE, which I hated. But I loved this!'[40] Deaf and hearing audiences can share the same anxieties about the cultural capital required to engage with Shakespeare, and a challenging, linguistically dense play like Love's Labour's Lost ironically promotes this sense of equality: Deafinitely's version reminds us how often hearing companies, too, gesture their way through this play in order to help hearing audiences make sense of less comprehensible stretches of language. If companies like Deafinitely – and the Globe – can resist the polarizing assumption that a hearing audience already understands Shakespeare and a Deaf audience does not, and embrace instead the liberating notion that 'Shakespeare is foreign to all of us',[41] this theatrical experiment might go a long way to show how Shakespeare could bridge persistent divides for hearing and Deaf actors and audiences.

ENDNOTES

1 http://globetoglobe.shakespearesglobe.com/plays/loves-labours-lost/english-79, 31 October 2012.

2 'Vision and Values', *Deafinitely Theatre*, www.deafinitelytheatre.co.uk/index.php?pid=9, 31 October 2012.

3 John Lee, dir., *The Tempest: By William Shakespeare in British Sign Language with Voice-over* (DVD, The Sign Language People, 2007).

4 Peter Llewellyn-Jones, 'Interpreting Shakespeare's Plays into British Sign Language', in Ton Hoenselaars, ed., *Shakespeare and the Language of Translation* (London: Arden Shakespeare, 2004), pp. 199–213 (p. 199).

5 Ibid., pp. 209, 213.

6 Lindsey Diane Snyder, 'Sawing the Air Thus: American Sign Language Translations of Shakespeare and the Echoes of Rhetorical Gesture' (PhD thesis, University of Maryland, 2009), p. 13.

7 Peter Novak, '"Where Lies Your Text?": *Twelfth Night* in American Sign Language Translation', *Shakespeare Survey*, 61 (2008): 74–9 (75).

8 Peter Novak, 'Shakespeare in the Fourth Dimension: *Twelfth Night* and American Sign Language', in Pascale Aebischer, ed., *Remaking Shakespeare: Performance across Media, Genres and Cultures* (Basingstoke: Palgrave Macmillan, 2003), pp. 18–38 (p. 18).

9 Lyn Gardner, 'Beckett in British Sign Language? Why Deaf Theatre is Coming of Age', *Guardian* 10 December 2009, www.guardian.co.uk/stage/2009/dec/10/deaf-theatre-deafinitely, 19 June 2012.

10 Ibid.

11 *The Hub 2: Programme 3*, April 2012, www.bslzone.co.uk/bsl-zone/the-hub-2-programme-3/, 31 October 2012.

12 *The Hub 2: Programme 6*, July 2012, www.bslzone.co.uk/bsl-zone/the-hub-2-programme-6/, 31 October 2012.

13 Globe Education Department 'Shakespeare Found in Translation' lecture at Shakespeare's Globe Theatre, 23 May 2012.

14 Rue Carvalho Homem, 'The Feast and the Scraps: Translating *Love's Labour's Lost* into Portuguese', in Hoenselaars, ed., *Shakespeare and the Language of Translation*, pp. 114–29 (pp. 114–15).

15 *The Hub 2: Programme 3*.

16 Globe Education Department, interview with assistant director and creative interpreter, http://bloggingshakespeare.com/year-of-shakespeare-loves-labours-lost, 31 October 2012.

17 *The Hub 2: Programme 3*.

18 E-mail from Andrew Muir to author, 20 July 2012.

19 *The Hub 2: Programme 3.*

20 'Shakespeare Found in Translation'.

21 Kate Furby, in Globe Education Department interview.

22 Andrew Muir, in Globe Education Department interview.

23 *The Hub 2: Programme 6.*

24 E.g. Pete Orford, 'Year of Shakespeare: *Henry VI Part Two*", 13 May 2012, http:// bloggingshakespeare.com/year-of-shakespeare-henry-vi-part-two, 31 October 2012.

25 'Shakespeare Found in Translation'.

26 '*Love's Labour's Lost* – Globe to Globe', *Margate Sands*, 31 May 2012, http://margatesands. wordpress.com/tag/deafinitely-theatre/, 31 October 2012.

27 Snyder, *Sawing the Air Thus*, p. 16.

28 See Dene Barnett, *The Art of Gesture: The Practices and Principles of Eighteenth-Century Acting* (Heidelberg: C. Winter, 1987).

29 *The Hub 2: Programme 6.*

30 Snyder, 'Sawing the Air Thus', p. 14.

31 'A Problem of Gender in BSL and English – The Poet, the Performer and "Poetic-I"', in 'More on metaphor', *Metaphor in Creative Sign Language Project*, University of Bristol, www. bris.ac.uk/education/research/sites/micsl/downloads/poetsandgender.pdf. See also Bruce R. Smith's discussion of the 'I' in ASL readings of Shakespeare's sonnets, in *Phenomenal Shakespeare* (Oxford: Blackwell, 2010), pp. 38–81.

32 Donna West and Rachel Sutton-Spence, 'Shared Thinking Processes with Four Deaf Poets: A Window on "the Creative" in "Creative Sign Language"', *Sign Language Studies*, 12.2 (winter 2012).

33 Novak, ' "Where Lies Your Text?" ', p. 75.

34 Sian-Estelle Petty, comment on a post on Deafinitely's Facebook page, 31 August 2012, 11.39am, www.facebook.com/#!/pages/Deafinitely-Theatre/38319916161?fref=ts, 31 October 2012.

35 'Shakespeare Found in Translation'.

36 *The Hub 2: Programme 6.*

37 'Shakespeare Found in Translation'.

38 Globe Education Department interview.

39 Ibid.

40 *The Hub 2: Programme 6.*

41 Dennis Kennedy, ed., *Foreign Shakespeare: Contemporary Performance* (Cambridge University Press, 1993), p. 16.

CHAPTER THIRTY

ENDING WELL

Reconciliation and remembrance in Arpana's *All's Well That Ends Well*

Peter Kirwan

Shakespeare's history on the Indian subcontinent is one of the ambiguous legacies of the country's colonial history. The late nineteenth and early twentieth centuries saw what Sukanta Chaudhuri refers to as the 'Indian Renaissance', during which 'Shakespeare provided the biggest single channel for not only literary or artistic innovations but the underlying transformation of values'.[1] From 1855, Shakespeare formed a core part of British recruitment for the Indian civil service, embedding the works into institutional discourse at the highest levels.[2] Since independence, however, the balance of the country's relationship with Shakespeare has shifted from the theatre into the study, becoming 'merely an occasional contributor to a theatrical agenda shaped by other themes, techniques and concerns'.[3]

Arpana Theatre's repertoire, typical of the modern Indian theatre, focuses primarily on contemporary Indian playwrights interspersed with a selection of modern and classical European dramas. In presenting the company's first take on Shakespeare, it is perhaps telling that Sunil Shanbag's production was set at the turn of the nineteenth century, evoking simultaneously Shakespeare's heyday in Indian culture and a period of ambivalence towards the cultural hegemony and control enjoyed by Britain. The setting was, perhaps, a light way of acknowledging the complex relationship of this non-Shakespearean company to the playhouse and festival within which its *All's Well That Ends Well* received its London performances; the joyous celebration of the invitation to participate and be invited onto the Globe stage was tempered by gentle jokes at the expense of British cultural dominance. Arpana's careful balance allowed the production to act simultaneously as a reaffirmation of the country's love for Shakespeare and an assertion of the company's own artistic and creative independence.

This was the first production of *All's Well* in the UK since the debate carried out in the pages of *The Times Literary Supplement* over the play's authorship, following Laurie Maguire and Emma Smith's claims of Middleton's collaboration on the

Fig. 17 Company dance at the beginning of the performance with the masks of Ganesha, *All's Well That Ends Well*, Arpana from Mumbai, India; director Sunil Shanbag.

play.[4] The debate that raged in the pages of the newspaper over subsequent weeks reinforced some of the age-old assumptions about the play – that this 'problem play' is structurally and tonally weak, that it preserves inconsistencies, that it is somehow inferior to Shakespeare's other comedies. Mihir Buhta's Gujarati adaptation, however, found coherence in the play that the Indian setting emphasized. As the early encounter between Heli (Mansi Parekh's Helena) and Parbat (Satchit Puranik's Parolles) made clear, this was a play about class. The avoidance of Heli by Chirag Vora's Bharatram (Bertram) was not so much a question of personal distaste as self-consciousness over Heli's low-caste status, a status that Parbat reinforced aggressively to Heli's face before leaving with Bharatram. The foregrounding of the status division in this context shifted a portion of the blame for Bharatram's actions to the conventions of the society at large, depicting Kunti (the Countess) as more progressive than her self-conscious son in her willingness to enable a match across caste boundaries.

Bharatram's concern for his public appearance made sense within the play's trade context, where the king figure – Utkash Mazumdar's Gokuldas – was an elderly opium trader, dependent on his underlings to negotiate and enforce agreements, particularly with Burma, where Nishi Doshi's Alkini (Diana) stood in for her mother and attempted to stand firm against the ruthless bargaining of Bharatram and Parbat. It was in this sequence that the play's most biting commentary emerged: Parbat pointed out to Alkini that the trade embargoes imposed by the British left her with few options for her surplus stock other than to 'allow' Parbat to take it off her hands, on condition that she slept with the enamoured Bharatram. With this seduction linked so closely to trade purposes, the bed-trick became not only Heli's means of fulfilling her husband's demands but also Alkini's of avoiding sexual coercion for the sake of her livelihood. In miniature, the drama was figured as two women's near-desperate attempts to assert self-determination under the oppressive conditions of class hierarchy and imperial rule.

Yet this was all implicit, an undertone to what was, fundamentally, a joyful comedy. The loss of obvious set pieces such as Parolles' kidnapping, which would have had no meaningful place in this context, was made up for by engaging, informal performances that kept the audience (dominated by Gujarati speakers) in hysterics throughout. The revelation here was Gokuldas, accompanied by his clownish servant Pandurang (Ajay Jairam, in the only role with no direct equivalent in Shakespeare). The double-act of grumbling master and playful servant undercut the pretensions of Bharatram, who donned a Western suit jacket over his native wear in Gokuldas' presence. Coughing with the unmistakable signs of late-stage tuberculosis, Gokuldas had no time for decorum and barked in irritation when he needed to be taken off stage to pee, or when complaining about the attentions of English doctors (to the biggest laugh from the Globe audience). A traditional patriarch, Gokuldas talked freely over Bharatram's interruptions, arranging deals and marriages with no interest in others' opinions. He was cured by Heli in a simple sequence that offered one of the production's occasional stylized moments: Pandurang assisted the old man in walking round the stage, and on each circuit Heli fed him another spoonful of medicine and his pace increased. When Pandurang finally let go of Gokuldas, who bent freely at the knees, the audience burst into spontaneous applause.

Gokuldas' performance was deliberately disruptive, creating an improvised comic mood that depended on familiarity with the figure of the cantankerous but kindly patriarch. These attempts at engagement pervaded the production, most notably in Laffabhai (Archan Trivedi as Lafew) who served as chorus, chatting to the audience and nodding or winking throughout the performance. The presentational aspect extended to the more serious elements of the performance, particularly Heli's songs. Heli's emotional range was privileged through the use of frequent musical interludes during which she articulated her losses (bereavement and abandonment) and fears in soliloquy, dancing as she did so. This particular convention of Indian performance provided a commentary on the comic action and placed Heli's private emotions in a different performative register that informed the main action of the play but also separated her from it, creating an affective relationship with the audience that operated at a level of personality rather than plot. This allowed the main plot to maintain its comic and occasionally ridiculous aspect while not sacrificing the sense of urgency that informed Heli's choices.

The balance accorded to Bharatram allowed for the possibility of genuine reconciliation throughout the play. In love with his status and role in trade, Bharatram was nonetheless a gentle and often sensitive youth, the more innocent foil to the more worldly-wise Parbat. In his wooing of 'Alkini', he treated the veiled girl gently, sitting with her on a bed and sliding a ring onto her finger, before she lay down on the bed in anticipation. His original marriage to Heli was carried out with similar grace, going through the motions of the marriage while sharing panicked looks with Parbat. The appearance of Heli in spectacular wedding robes drew another ovation from the audience, and the ceremony was performed with full pomp and a chorus of wedding songs. Yet it was the simplicity of their eventual reunion that was most effective. Bharatram's face on seeing Heli alive and wearing his ring was one of wonder, and he barely hesitated in moving towards her and taking her hand, finally shaken out of the systems of behaviour that had hitherto governed his actions. This was an awakening rather than a redemption, a realization that Heli transcended the class and professional distinctions he had prioritized. As such, the audience was allowed to invest in the hope of a happy ending, with the two finally able to greet each other on an equal level.

The speaking back of this Indian company to its country's colonial past acted to reclaim the play, situating the problems of the play in the imperial context that it evoked and resolving them in a modern, independent production. As English academics argued over the disintegration of the play's words, the Gujarati language version found a unity and harmony in the romantic comedy that made sense of a play so often the subject of generic and critical dispute. As such, this was one of many instances during the Festival during which the visiting companies were able to show the host nation how it can be done, offering up *All's Well* as an affecting, entertaining and often hysterical comedy of love conquering obstacles of class and money.

ENDNOTES

1 Sukanta Chaudhuri, 'Shakespeare in India', *Internet Shakespeare Editions*, http://internet shakespeare.uvic.ca/Library/Criticism/shakespearein/india1.html, 28 June 2012, p. 1.
2 See Andrew Murphy, *Shakespeare in Print* (Cambridge University Press, 2003), pp. 181 ff.
3 Chaudhuri, 'Shakespeare in India', p. 6.
4 Laurie Maguire and Emma Smith, 'Many Hands', *The Times Literary Supplement*, 20 April 2012, pp. 13–5.

CHAPTER THIRTY-ONE

CREATIVE EXPLOITATION AND TALKING BACK

Renegade Theatre's *The Winter's Tale* or Ìtàn Ògìnìntìn ('Winter's Tales')

Julie Sanders

There are no bears in Nigeria, or at least it seemed so from the opening moments of the Yoruba reworking of *The Winter's Tale* (Ìtàn Ògìnìntìn) by the Renegade Theatre Company of Lagos. In the opening sequences of this particular production it became abundantly clear to members of the very full audience that watched the evening show on London's Bankside on Friday 25 May 2012 that a number of keynotes of conventional British theatre interpretations of this late Shakespeare play would be joyously set aside and quite deliberately turned on their head. Renegade Theatre is, as a company, all about turning norms upside down.[1] They have continued to stage live theatre in Lagos, chief city in the south-western region of the country, where Yoruba is the dominant ethnic identity, at a time when the form has been under threat from state-level neglect and the competing attractions of television soap-operas and Nigeria's own version of the film industry, 'Nollywood'. There are very few purpose-built theatre spaces in Nigeria, and in Lagos the national theatre, constructed by the 1970s military regime in the suggestive if disconcerting shape of a military cap, today lies privatized and largely unused. The company has, then, a strongly recuperative ethos in its live performances (frequently staged at weekends) to make theatre take on new meaning for Nigerian audiences. Part of that recuperative ethos can be registered in the willingness of the cast of Ìtàn Ògìnìntìn – many of whom are notable celebrities in the world of television and film in their home country – to be challenged by the act of participation in traditional theatre performance and specifically in the culturally loaded space of the Globe performance of Shakespeare translated into a formal version of the Yoruba language that none of them deploys on a daily basis.

Renegade's patron is the playwright-poet-director Wole Soyinka, winner of the Nobel Prize for literature in 1986. The company has regularly performed Soyinka's work, and his theoretical writing on Yoruban mythical and ritual drama clearly informed their approach to Shakespeare for this commission. This production refracted the Shakespearean story of oracles and animated statues through a Yoruba cosmology. Unlike some contributors to the Globe to Globe Festival, Renegade did not bring to the commissioning table a ready-made production; following several months in development, the first performance of their show, a public rehearsal in front of upwards of a hundred people, had taken place in Lagos just days earlier, so it was a very fresh (and therefore comfortingly rough-edged) piece to which audiences were exposed.[2] It is worth noting that Renegade actively chose to perform *The Winter's Tale* and indeed to commission an entirely new translation. That work was undertaken by a retired Ibadan teacher named Tade Ipadeola; he produced 147 pages of formal Yoruban (distinct from the mix of colloquial Yoruba, English and pidgin spoken on the streets of contemporary Lagos). Director Olúwolé (Wole) Ogúntókun selected the late romance for his adaptation (despite the Globe's claim that they were working in the Festival with translations, not adaptations, it seems the correct term to apply in this instance)[3] precisely because it is not widely known in a country where Shakespeare is mostly encountered through his mandatory presence in an educational system still modelled on that of the UK through its A Level examinations; more obvious choices would have been *Macbeth*, *Othello*, *Romeo and Juliet* or *Julius Caesar*, although, even then, Ogúntókun referred to Shakespeare as being 'like Marmite' for most Nigerians, a reference to a British yeast extract product that tends to inspire either love or hate in its tasters. Much has been made of the Globe's insistence that this was not to be a season about national identities and the fact that it actively discouraged companies from incorporating flags, anthems or folk songs into their productions. While flag-waving nationalism was anathema to this assertively Yoruban production (Nigeria is in reality a highly complex mix of Yoruba, Hausa and Igbo cultures, complicated yet further by the traumatic legacies of colonial activity and missionary policies, and is, at the time of writing, facing deep internal rifts between the radical Muslim north and other regions), it would be equally false to claim that this was an interpretation of *The Winter's Tale* that turned away from the place, space and culture from which the performers had travelled. This was a working example of Yoruba culture and belief-systems, in which gods and ancestors are presumed to have an everyday presence in the world, and of the ways in which, as Soyinka has described, Yoruba theatre performances provide 'a multi-level experience of the mystical and the mundane'.[4] Shakespeare's eclectic 1611 late romance, in which oracles and tricksters are knowingly juxtaposed, and in which gods appear to intervene in personal relationships, provided the perfect vehicle for a theatrical meeting-place between the human and the divine.

Yoruba theatre collapses the worlds of humans and of gods; several of the chief gods in traditional storytelling have, according to the myths and narratives that have attached themselves to them, made the transition from a previously human existence. Eldred Durosimi Jones observes: '[In Yoruba culture] Human life itself is regarded as part of a continuum of life stretching from the spirits of unborn children through bodily existence to the spirits of departed ancestors';[5] key gods (there are 401 in all in the Yoruba belief-system) recur in plays across the centuries. Chief among these are Ogun and Ṣàngó, flawed hero-gods who, in the Renegade adaptation of *The Winter's Tale*, appear as repositionings of Polixenes and Leontes, those two monarchs 'trained together in their childhoods' (1.1.19) whose deep friendship is entrusted to the care of the heavens at the start of Shakespeare's play: 'The heavens continue their loves' (1.1.26–7).[6] By re-imagining the rulers of Bohemia and Sicilia as gods, Ìtàn Ògìnìntìn does not relocate the play's events to a higher level: rather, it grounds it in the complex mix of cosmology and personal responsibility that lies at the heart of Yoruban spiritual belief. Ṣàngó's paranoid jealousies, his faith in and then rejection of the oracle, all of which map the course of Leontes' passions in the Shakespearean source, can be comprehended through traditional frameworks; Ṣàngó is Leontes re-imagined as the god of lightning and justice, and some of the lightning-speed twists of thought that have troubled commentators on the play made more sense in this context. The decision to re-sculpt characters in these ways affects, furthermore, the plot trajectory of Hermione. Re-imagined here as Oya, this initially all-too-human and vulnerable character (the onstage trial of a pregnant queen who proudly asserts her tribal status – 'The Emperor of Russia was my father' (3.2.117) – lost none of its resonance) was, in perhaps the biggest *coup de théâtre* of the night, temporarily revived from her final-act condition of statue only to be snatched from Ṣàngó a second time and translated into the goddess of the whirlwind. The highly permeable line between human and deity, king and god, life and spirit-life, in Yoruba culture transported Shakespeare's tragicomic ending into a whole new ambiguous realm.[7]

Soyinka has written of the ability of mythologically based 'drama of . . . hero-god(s)' to 'travel' and suggested that subsequent interpreters of these stories can be understood to be 'creative exploiters' of what has come before.[8] The phrase is beautifully apt for the loyal, recognizable and yet radically re-imagined interpretation of *The Winter's Tale* that this production offered. The performance opened in attention-grabbing fashion with dance, drumming and song (including the remarkable voice of Motúnráyò Oròbíyi who played Ìgba or Time throughout as a chorus, framing, introducing and often directly engaging with the audience in her sung storytelling). A group of hide-wrapped mariners mimed rowing to symbolize the journey in a canoe of a Sicilian lord and the cast-off baby daughter of Ṣàngó (Leontes) to the dangerous Bohemian coast. There was to be no 'exit pursued by a bear'; this 'Antigonus' (here the programme listed the character only as a 'Sicilian lord') was attacked by robbers, and a very willing Globe audience was, in the process, primed for a show that intervened in Shakespeare's play in memorable ways.

Fig. 18 Time (Motúnràyò Oròbíyi (Ìgba)), *The Winter's Tale*, Renegade Theatre from Lagos, Nigeria; director Olúwolé Ogúntókun.

We had also begun the play at a different point. In an enlightening pre-show discussion with the director and four of his company, the team talked of the non-linear approach they had adopted and, tantalizingly, gestured towards their surprise ending. In this 'African reboot',[9] we began with the discovery of the baby Olúolá (Perdita) by the Darandaran (Old Shepherd) and his son, and then Ìgbà/Time quickly sang us through sixteen years to a festival of hunting (a trope that sits more readily within Yoruban tradition than classical pastoral sheep-shearing) where Olúolá (Perdita) and Foláwẹ̀wó (Florizel) were in full courtship mode. There is much to register about the ways in which Yoruban traditions were being interwoven with core aspects of the Shakespearean romance. In *The Winter's Tale* the archetypal figure of Time (often interpreted emblematically as Old Father Time with wings and/or a scythe) enters as a quasi-chorus at the opening of Act 4 to explain to audiences both the temporal shift of sixteen years:

> Impute it not a crime
> To me or my swift passage that I slide
> O'er sixteen years, and leave the growth untried
> Of that wide gap

(4.1.4–7)

and the geographical relocation to the kingdom of Bohemia that is involved in this transitional moment in the dramaturgy:

> [I]magine me,
> Gentle spectators, that I now may be
> In fair Bohemia

(4.1.19–21)

These quotations indicate the ways in which Time mediates between audience and stage as well as between time and place. Time was reconstituted as a professional female praise singer through the highly significant casting of Oròbíyi, a well-known singer rather than actor in Lagos circles. The significance of music and in particular of poetic praise songs or *oriki* to Nigerian culture in general and Yoruba practices specifically cannot be overestimated.[10] Oriki can be sung or drummed (this production made plentiful use of both) and are the central feature of festival culture; they therefore found a perfect home in this version of a play that has as one of its central scenarios a Bohemian sheep-shearing festival. Looking back at the Shakespearean text in the light of the Renegade interpretation, the Act 4 dialogue between Florizel and Perdita which juxtaposes the world of gods and humans is noteworthy:

FLORIZEL: These your unusual weeds to each part of you
Does give a life: no shepherdess, but Flora
Peering in April's front. This your sheep-shearing
Is as a meeting of the petty gods,
And you the queen on't.

(4.4.1–5)

At the newly imagined hunting festival Perdita distributed fruit rather than flowers, but the basic premise remained. Key Yoruban festivals take place around harvest time and betrothals, and feature feasting, drinking, dance and song; there are, then, lines of connection to the sheep-shearing festival of the source. In this confident restructuring of the play's events, the story of Ṣàngó's intensely jealous reaction to the affection he witnesses between his wife Oya (Hermione) and his oldest friend Ogùn (Polixenes) becomes an inset narrative told by the exiled Sicilian courtier Adéagbo (or Camillo, a crowd-winning comic performance by Olásúnkànmi Adébàyò). Events on the Bohemian coastline and at the hunting festival became the effective frame for the story of warring gods that followed. There was, however, as many reviewers felt compelled to note, something utterly West African about the Florizel–Perdita wooing scenes: Olúwatóyìn Alli-Hakeem as Olúolá (Perdita), herself a well-known Nigerian soap-opera actor, and Joshua Adémólá Àlàbì as Foláwẹ̀wó (Florizel) brought a considerable degree of 'sass' to the dancing between these two young lovers, much to the delight of an increasingly vocal and participatory audience.

One of the great encounters found in this cosmological reworking of *The Winter's Tale* was between Autolycus and the trickster figure of Yoruban culture and art, here brilliantly interpreted by Adékúnlé Smart Adéjùmò. Attired in leather trousers and an animal-hide waistcoat as Ikokò, she dominated the stage space, lithely moving around other characters as she picked their pockets and figuratively, and occasionally literally, stripped them naked. Her gender-bending, audience-challenging performance built quite readily on the significance of tricks and jokes in Egungan tradition, which itself reaches back to sixteenth-century court theatre in West Africa, yet another marker of a night in which this Lagos company truly owned the space.[11]

Ikokò is Yoruba for 'wolf', and the character's richly suggestive name operated as a direct equivalent to Shakespeare's Autolycus, who is named from Greek mythology after the son of Hermes and Chione and whose name means 'The Wolf Itself'. If Autolycus in his guise as a ballad-seller at the sheep-shearing festival is the veritable 'wolf in sheep's clothing' of animal fables, so Ikokò signified in plural ways; nineteenth-century missionaries, failing to find an equivalent for the devil in the Yoruban pantheon of gods, settled on Ikokò. This multiple signification told a wider story about the knowledge exchange that was taking place in this 'creative exploitation'. *The Winter's Tale* and some of Shakespeare's own practices of adaptation were remade by the encounter with Yoruba culture and theatrical practice, as much as Renegade's work was informed by the particular spatialities and experiences of the Globe. It is important to make this point when assessing any of the Globe to Globe productions: the publicity for the Festival was designed to bring out what the opportunity to perform Shakespeare in the Globe would 'give' to the international visiting companies, but, at least in the case of Ìtàn Ògìnìntìn, the story on that May night was as much about what the production did for regular Globe audience members and *Winter's Tale aficionados* to alter their understanding. Some commentators on the Festival have praised the decision to deploy English surtitles that summarized plotlines rather than offering line-by-line scripting of what was happening on stage.[12] Certainly this sparser approach to surtitling facilitated better focus for non-Yoruba-literate spectators on action and intepretation rather than the Shakespearean script, but in the case of this production a very particular decision appeared to have been taken (apparently with the consent of the theatre company) to retain the Shakespearean character names, so that we were told that it was Leontes and Hermione or, indeed, Perdita and Florizel on stage at a given moment, rather than Şàngó and Oya, or Olúolá and Foláwĕwó. The one-page programme did offer the Yoruba linguistic substitutions but no larger explanation of the adaptive impulses at play – the plot summary provided was, tellingly, that of the

Shakespearean drama, not this new story of Yoruba gods and of Oya's transition from human to statue to goddess of the whirlwind. Anyone who did not understand Yoruba and who had not enjoyed the benefit of the pre-show or post-show contextualization may have lacked the framework that enabled a richer purchase on the particular politics of the interpretation. As with many of the productions in this Festival, there were multiple audiences with different points of entry and levels of access to what was being staged.

Overall the production became on the night a story of audience participation of a very specific kind. It has become something of a given in writing about the Globe to pay tribute to its capacity for involving spectators in the production of the 'event', and, certainly, Renegade's actors had much to say on this subject in the pre-show talk, responding to the warmth they had felt in the matinee performance the previous day.[13] But audience participation is also central to Apidán theatre practice in Nigeria, where spectators are accorded the status of 'co-actors' and are frequently asked to fill in the gaps in retellings of traditional scenarios and tales, so the extent to which the atmosphere of participation was one that the company imported into the Globe needs to be considered.[14] Ogúntókun indicated as much in an interview when he said that he hoped the production would represent a re-energizing of West African theatre: 'We will tell our stories and not have our stories told to us all of the time.'[15] The 'creative exploitation' of Shakespeare's *The Winter's Tale* that the director, along with his company of actors, undertook to achieve was, then, less a hostile 'writing back' to the colonial centre than a celebration through imaginative and active appropriation of indigenous stories and practices within the wooden embrace of the Globe, and by extension a direct claiming of that space. Soyinka has written that 'Drama . . . exists on the boards; in the improvised space among stalls in the deserted or teeming market, on the raised platform in a school or a community hall', and he argues that 'It is necessary always to look for the essence of the play among these roofs and spaces, and not confine it to the printed text as an autonomous entity.'[16] My argument is that the Renegade *Winter's Tale* not only remade the printed text of the play as they received it but brought something fresh and challenging to the roofs and spaces of Bankside, and that it was through the medium of audience participation that the active claiming of space could be most clearly registered. As the Yoruba-speaking section of the audience warmed to their task on a pleasantly breezy London evening (south-east London has the largest Yoruba population outside of Nigeria),[17] the call-and-response rhythm of the production hit its stride. For anyone with practical experience of Nigerian culture and discourse, an all-too-familiar sound from the streets of Lagos, Kano, Calabar and elsewhere began to fill the wooden 'O'. Members of the audience began to 'talk back' to the production; spectators endorsed, questioned or quite openly dismissed some of the suggestions the actors were throwing out to them in lines that were frequently delivered as direct address (an indication in itself that a large percentage of the audience was following the play in Yoruba); they sang along with the songs, they knowingly feigned disgust at some of the bawdier jokes or gestures. Even the dignified figure of Ìgbà/Time began to take on an element of 'calling' in the audience members to participate in this way; and the avian life of London seemed happy to get in on the act as one particular blackbird settled himself on the Globe thatch in the first half to join in his own version of call and response as Motúnráyo Oròbíyi sang her glorious framing songs.

The Globe to Globe Festival as an entity has raised important questions about possession and presence on Bankside that we are all still, as theatre-goers and as academics, trying to absorb. The effects of watching Shakespeare in a language not your own in the presence of many who are completely absorbed in the equally compelling experience of hearing Shakespeare delivered in their language are visceral at times. Who owns the punchlines? Who is in on the joke? What are the stories about inclusion and exclusion, familiarization and defamiliarization, to be told here? What is the motive for attendance on the part of the spectators?[18] In the end, though, as I found myself standing in the yard that night and wanting to have eyes in the back of my head and be able to watch the audience at the same time as what was unfolding on stage, it was about call-and-response. Amid the generous applause afforded the company at the close, they caught sight of a notable dignatory in the gallery (an interesting throwback to 1611, when actors might well have acknowledged the presence of significant individual spectators, and perhaps patrons and commercial supporters, in this way) and began to offer a praise song to their watching patron, Wole Soyinka. This was a theatrical 'event', then, in the broadest sense of the term, an experience that stayed with my own company of friends as we headed for a bus back along Thameside; it left us full of energy and with a different kind of choreography in our bodies. Olúwolé Ogúntókun would put that in part down to what the Globe makes possible in terms of proximity – quite literally, the nearness of actors to spectators – but perhaps we were also being worked upon by Yoruban theatre practice, becoming co-actors and participants in new ways, bearing out what this Festival achieved in terms of enabling fresh theatrical encounters and knowledges. As Ogúntókun put it: 'If you are going to dance with us, you can't do that from far away.'[19] The Globe danced, sang and answered back quite willingly that night.

ENDNOTES

1 The company observed that it had 'turned *The Winter's Tale* upside down' through its non-linear approach in the Globe Education Department 'Shakespeare Found in Translation' lecture/workshop with the company held on 25 May 2012.

2 Information derived from 'Shakespeare Found in Translation' and also Nicholas Ibekwe, 'A Winter's Tale from Nigeria', http://naijainsightlondon.wordpress.com/?s=winter %27s+tale, 17 July 2012.

3 For a discussion of related terminology and the vexed issue of categorization, see Julie Sanders, *Adaptation and Appropriation* (London: Routledge, 2005).

4 Wole Soyinka, *Myth, Literature and the African World* (Cambridge University Press, 1976), p. 2. Eldred Durosimi Jones has written that Soyinka himself 'starts as a Yoruba' and explores the scholarly interest he has taken in his own culture and in making it available for a Western readership; Jones, *The Writing of Wole Soyinka*, rev. edn (London: Heinemann, 1983), p. 3. See also Mpalive-Hangson Msiska, *Wole Soyinka*, Writers and their Work (Plymouth: Northcote House, 1998).

5 Jones, *The Writing of Wole Soyinka*, p. 4.

6 Line numbers refer to the New Cambridge Shakespeare edition.

7 Raphael Lyne, *Shakespeare's Late Work* (Oxford University Press, 2007), usefully explores the ambiguous status of the playwright's late dramatic forays into romance and tragicomic form.

8 Soyinka, *Myth, Literature and the African World*, p. 7.

9 See the Associated Press article, 'Shakespeare's Winter's Tale Gets African Reboot'. www. cbc.ca/news/arts/story/2012/05/25/nigeria-shakespeare-winters-tale.html?cmp=rss, 14 July 2012.

10 Abiodun Awolaja, 'Yoruba Oriki: A Dying Cultural Genre?', *Nigerian Tribune*, Monday 15 November 2010, www.tribune.com.ng/index.php/features/13508-yoruba-oriki-a-dying-cultural-genre, 14 July 2012.

11 Gotrick Kacke, *Apidan Theatre and Modern Drama: A Study in Traditional Yoruba Theatre and its Influence on Modern Drama* (Stockholm: Almqvist and Wiksell International, 1984).

12 I am indebted to Sonia Massai for discussion of this element of the Globe to Globe Festival at the AHRC-supported workshop on the 'Year of Shakespeare' blog project headed by Erin Sullivan, Paul Prescott and Paul Edmondson, held in London, June 2012.

13 Christie Carson, 'Democratising the Audience?', in Christie Carson and Farah Karim-Cooper, eds., *Shakespeare's Globe: A Theatrical Experiment* (Cambridge University Press, 2008), pp. 116–26 (p. 117).

14 Kacke, *Apidan Theatre*, passim. See also K. Barber, S. A. McGrath and C. Fyfe, *Yoruba Popular Theatre as a Historical Object* (Edinburgh University Press, 1996): and Joachim Fiebach, 'Cultural Identity, Interculturalism and Theatre: On the Popular Yoruba Travelling Theatre', *Theatre Research International*, 21:1 (1996): 52–8.

15 'Shakespeare's Winter's Tale Gets African Reboot'.

16 Soyinka, *Myth, Literature and the African World*, p. 44.

17 Mark Hudson, 'Globe to Globe: *The Winter's Tale* Shakespeare's Globe', *The Arts Desk*. 'What's "Exit, Pursued by a Bear" in Yoruba? Problem Play Mythologised by Nigerian Company', 27 May 2012, www.theartsdesk.com/theatre/globe-globe-winters-tale-shakespeares-globe, 15 July 2012.

18 There has been discussion of the ways in which expatriate and second-generation ethnic audiences were encouraged to attend plays in their first language through websites and other publicity materials. It is clear that London's Nigerian community had been encouraging attendance – this was made clear anecdotally on the night from conversations

with fellow audience members on the part of the author but is also visible in comment threads on websites. One particular respondent on the naijainsightlondon site, when informed of the upcoming Yoruba language performance observed, 'Make wunna represent.' See comments thread to Nicholas Ibekwe, 'A Winter's Tale from Nigeria', http://naijainsightlondon.wordpress.com/?s=winter%27s+tale 15 July 2012.

19 The phrase was used in the 'Shakespeare Found in Translation' lecture/workshop.

CHAPTER THIRTY-TWO

A SHREW FULL OF LAUGHTER

Elizabeth Schafer

The Taming of the Shrew – of all Shakespeare's plays – is the one I love to hate. I have seen more productions of the play than is healthy: over twenty live performances in various theatres across the world. In addition, when I was writing a performance history of the play, I squinted at approximately fifteen archival video records of performances going back thirty years;[1] I watched feature films; I read promptbooks annotated by long-dead stage managers detailing stage business performed by long-dead actors and actresses. I experienced the play performed as a farce and as a tragedy; I watched Katherina being brutalized and I watched Katherina as a feisty feminist in lust with her Petruchio, who was going to give him hell over the submission speech. I saw directors stressing the misogyny, the romance, the sex, the violence, the farce, the class politics – and, depending on what was emphasized, Katherina's story came out completely differently. But seeing the play performed in Urdu, by Theatre Wallay, representing Pakistan in the Globe to Globe Festival, promised a whole new experience, and I was very curious to see what Theatre Wallay would make of this most infuriating of plays.[2]

I know little of theatre in Pakistan, but Omair Rana, the production's Petruchio, speaking in an interview, talked of the lack of government support for theatre in his country.[3] He also spoke of the wide range of theatrical traditions to be found in Pakistan, and how regional theatre is particularly grounded in storytelling. And a storyteller – in this case a lively, energetic woman, wearing a bright pink tunic covered with tiny mirrors, and a jingling coin headband – turned out to be crucial in Theatre Wallay's *Taming of the Shrew*. This storyteller, named Ravi, was partly a transmogrified version of Shakespeare's Christopher Sly, but she was also far more: a mistress of ceremonies, occasional bit-part player, shape-shifter and presiding genius. Played by Maria Khan, Ravi presented, framed and ultimately controlled the telling of Katherina's story.

Ravi was, in many ways, a logical extension of Shakespeare's dramaturgy. Shakespeare took the fundamental decision that the tale of Katherina and Petruchio would be presented as a play within a play, a comedy performed to entertain the drunken tinker Christopher Sly, who is the subject of a practical joke – tricked into thinking he is a lord being entertained by a troupe of travelling players. Although many theatre productions have cut the Sly framework, if Sly is cut, Katherina's story is transformed: *The Shrew* becomes theatrical rather than metatheatrical; normative rather than Brechtian; a story rather than a debate. Cutting Sly not only omits the only extant piece of writing by Shakespeare securely located in his home environment of Elizabethan Warwickshire, but it also changes the play's presentation of the act of taming: when Sly is retained, far more is open to question, simply because the audience sees Sly's reactions to the inner play of *The Shrew*. Sly palpably resists the play by falling asleep during Act 1 Scene 1, asking 'Comes there any more of it?' (1.1.240–1) when is he woken up, and then commenting 'Would 'twere done!' (1.1.243).[4]

Although one of Ravi's early manifestations was as a Sly equivalent, a beggar woman, cradling a black rag for a baby and being conspicuously ignored by Qazim/Lucentio and Mir/Tranio, in fact Ravi was very much in control. At the beginning, while the other actors stood posed, frozen on stage, Ravi wandered in through the audience, greeting and chatting with people as she passed among them.[5] Once onstage, Ravi checked the four musicians were ready, and finally gave a signal to the actors that they could begin;[6] it was only then the performers unfroze and launched into a lively and energetic dance. Ravi then turned up in a range of disguises; she was a comic priest, with a wild, white beard, at the wedding of Kiran/Katherina and Rustam/Petruchio, tumbling on the floor as Rustam did his man-behaving-badly act; Ravi played the pedant, dressed in walking-boots, a tweed jacket and a black beard, looking like some mad Englishman out in the midday sun; Ravi was a servant in Baptista's house, calling Bina/Bianca to get ready for Kiran's wedding; she became a streetseller with a tray of food strapped around her neck; she was a clothes-horse while Mir and Qazim swapped clothes, listening to and agreeing with their plotting. She applauded enthusiastically at the story of how Hasnat/Hortensio came to have a guitar smashed over his head. She was on stage almost all the time, and she was also a puppet mistress; occasionally, Ravi hauled characters on stage, miming the action of pulling them on as if they were attached by long ropes. Sometimes her swirling and twirling became distracting; and one device – having Ravi lie asleep on an otherwise empty stage to signal time passing after Rustam's arrival home – was theatrically dull;[7] however, in general Ravi's presence added a distinctive, as well as a politically charged, presence to this *Shrew*.

It was particularly significant that Ravi-as-narrator was onstage while Rustam explained his taming plan in his 'Thus have I politically begun my reign' speech (4.1.159). Indeed, Rustam addressed most of this speech to Ravi rather than to the audience.[8] Ravi listened and responded; she wagged her finger several times in disapproval, and she also signalled that she thought Rustam was mad. However, this staging generated a feeling that Ravi could stop Rustam at any stage in the taming process if she wanted to, and this suggested there was some kind of safety net for Kiran's taming. Certainly, when Ravi reappeared shortly after Rustam's speech, now in the role of the tailor, the fact that the tailor-as-Ravi had heard Rustam sketch out his plans added layering to the episode: instead of Kiran being humiliated in front of a complete stranger, there was a sense, for the audience, of Kiran being watched over by the all-knowing, ubiquitous storyteller.

Making Sly into a female figure who controlled the entire performance completely recast Shakespeare's tale of wife-taming and helped produce a very genial *Shrew*. In addition, this *Shrew* did not allow its heroine, Kiran, to suffer very much. For a start, Kiran made it clear that from the first moment she clapped eyes on Rustam she found him very attractive. Circling behind Rustam, who was facing front, Nadia Jamil's Kiran communicated a message of physical attraction that needed no translation for the non-Urdu speakers. The taming process was then presented very much as Rustam teaching Kiran how to play-act when the men of her society, who found it hard to deal with a strong, clever, educated and feisty woman, were around.

Overall Kiran did not seem terribly shrewish; she was more violent than Rustam, but her most energetic display of aggression was against her sister Bina (Act 2 Scene 1). Complexity was added to this moment, however, because the sisters' fight only erupted after Bina had ripped Kiran's beautiful Basant kite, damaging it beyond repair. At the beginning of the scene, the so-called shrew, Kiran, entered singing quietly and tenderly to herself while holding her kite. Then Bina entered, began teasing Kiran and inadvertently ripped the kite; before long both sisters were on the floor scrapping, while the audience laughed loudly. Once their father Mian Basheer/Baptista had restored calm, Bina first burst into tears, something which caused the audience to roar with laughter, and then repeatedly stuck her tongue out at Kiran behind their father's back. However, though it was clear Bina knew which buttons to press to wind Kiran up, the fact that the two sisters were dressed in similar clothes and looked similar was important: they were both strong-willed, educated women, and they faced similar challenges. They were certainly not arch-enemies, something indicated by the fact Bina moved to comfort Kiran when it seemed that Rustam was not going to appear for the wedding. And while Bina had learnt to play by the rules of patriarchy, and found her power in being manipulative, Bina's happiest moment was just before the lesson scene (Act 3 Scene 1) when she appeared to be, like Kiran just before in Act 2 Scene 1, happy to be alone, relaxed, playful and away from the irritating men.

Rustam's taming of Kiran was not unremittingly brutish; for example, after Kiran executed a mocking, over-the-top servile bow of thanks for the food Rustam had

Fig. 19 Katherina (Nadia Jamil (Kiran)) and Petruchio (Omair Rana (Rustam)), *The Taming of the Shrew*, Theatre Wallay from Islamabad, Pakistan; director Haissam Hussain.

prepared, she had time to devour a substantial amount of rice before the tailor arrived. And when Kiran was denied the dress and shawl brought by the tailor, and she stood on stage, dashing away the tears in her eyes, Rustam came over and tenderly wrapped her in his own shawl. Kiran stood stock-still, unresponsive, but the moment she was left alone on stage she hugged herself in the shawl, swirled around and sang, seemingly extremely happy at this development.

Kiran's various submissions – on what time it is, whether it is the sun or moon that shines so bright, and her final speech – were greeted with enthusiastic applause and much laughter, especially by the older Pakistani women in the audience. However, the fact that the clock struck two when Kiran was arguing that it was two o'clock and Rustam was insisting it was seven (4.3.181–9) reinforced the silliness of Rustam's game-playing; Kiran was learning to fool around, to play theatre sports. This was particularly clear in the sun-and-moon submission. Kiran threw herself enthusiastically into the game of treating Waqaruddin/Vincentio as a young girl but also made the most of the joke in the lines speaking of 'my mistaking eyes/ That have been so bedazzled by the sun' (4.5.45–6). The question marks Nadia Jamil inserted after her long-drawn-out 'the s-u-u-u-u-u-n???' made it clear that, if Rustam moved the goalposts again and made the sun the moon, Kiran would immediately catch the ball and run with it.[9] And when, at the end of Act 5 Scene 2, Kiran submitted by holding Rustam's hand in public in the street, she did this on her own terms:[10] first she point-blankly refused to hold his hand; then she called Rustam over; when he came she shoved his shoulder twice to get his full attention and then walked a short distance away, struck a pose and broke out into a song-and-dance routine, which ended with Kiran and Rustam both holding hands whilst the audience clapped and cheered.

The culmination of the taming process – Kiran's last speech – was a comic masterpiece, but, unusually, it was a two-hander, performed as much by Rustam as by Kiran. First, as the Begum/Widow complained about the prospect of having to listen to Kiran, Rustam and Kiran were clearly visible, standing down stage and close to most of the audience. As they bent their heads together, Rustam appeared to be letting Kiran know about the bet on her obedience. As Kiran began her speech, Rustam clapped loudly in front of the Begum's face to ensure she was paying respectful attention. Kiran then clicked her fingers and Rustam obediently ran over to her side. As Kiran began the speech, which speaks of the labour husbands undertake for their wives, she reclined lazily on a seat while Rustam rushed around fanning her or massaging her feet. Both Kiran and Rustam demonstrated marital conflict with energetic pushing, shoving and comic fisticuffs. They took it in turn to stand upon a low stool or pedestal as Kiran's address to the throng continued. And at the end, when Kiran lifted her hand high in the air, offering to place it under Rustam's foot, he quickly prevented her. The whole speech became a double-act, with Rustam making himself extremely attentive as he assisted in his wife's performance.

The geniality of Theatre Wallay's *Shrew* was also helped by the fact that Rustam was seen to be tamed during the action of the play; before meeting Kiran he had a roving eye; every time Ravi wandered past him Rustam had to be stopped by the men around him from following her. Rustam, a Pathan from Mianwali, was also presented as a rough clown compared with the sophisticates of Lahore/Padua, where most of the action was set. But when Rustam did his cave-man act, carrying Kiran off from the wedding, this emerged very directly out of Kiran's own domineering behaviour: as Rustam lay prostrate on his stomach on the floor, Kiran seized the chance to sit down and straddle his back. Omair Rana's Rustam was able then to stand up with Kiran perched precariously on his shoulders and holding on for dear life. After this impressive feat of strength Rustam then carried Kiran off in triumph.

The scenes in Lahore were played against a brightly coloured street-scene backcloth hanging down from the gallery. The Lahore backcloth included the image of a couple of kites flying above the city, and kites were an important motif in the production. At the opening of the play, Kiran, who had not joined in the general dancing, ran across the stage holding her kite. And when Rustam first saw Kiran she was flying a Basant kite; as Rustam gazed up stage at the door to Baptista's house, expecting Kiran to emerge from there, she surprised him by entering instead through the audience. She then completely ignored him, concentrating, instead, on miming flying a kite. This mimed movement shifted almost immediately into a kite-flying dance, beautiful, joyful, and also seemingly unselfconscious. When Rustam, who clearly liked what he saw, interrupted Kiran's dance, her annoyance was intense, and this interruption sparked the anger that fuelled their first confrontation. I asked the Urdu speakers sitting in front of me about the significance of the Basant kites, and they spoke enthusiastically about kite-flying in Pakistan and India. Later I found that the annual spring kite-flying festival in Lahore has been banned for the last few years, as kite-flying has been condemned as a Hindu custom by hard-line Muslim clerics. This, for me, retrospectively inflected the whole idea of Kiran as the kite-flyer with poignancy.[11]

In an interview, the production's director, Haissam Hussain, who had not directed Shakespeare previously, spoke of initially feeling intimidated by Shakespeare's language; however, as a television and film director he is used to working with mass-media communication, and he came to believe that Shakespeare's *Shrew* can reach out beyond educated elite audiences.[12] Reaching out was something this production managed to achieve wittily at the very beginning of the performance, when the dignified but genial Salman Shahid, the production's patriarch, Baptista, came on as a prologue and announced, in English, that the performance would be in Urdu so the 'English white folk' should make the most of his speech. He joked about how many languages Pakistan has and then informed the audience that the musicians were about to play the Pakistani national anthem, but there was no need to panic: this was not a Pakistani take-over. This joke, which was received warmly by the entire audience, typified the production's approach to the play: big issues were in circulation in terms of gender and international stereotyping, but the production consistently asked the audience to choose laughter. And the wittiest example of this, for me, came during the bidding war over Bina, as Ghazi/Gremio and the disguised Mir/Tranio competed in bragging of their assets. The entire audience roared with laughter as Mir triumphantly announced – in English – 'I have a British passport.' Nothing that Ghazi could offer would trump that. But the political edge to that joke – whereby current UK visa policies are making it harder for anyone from Pakistan without a British passport to travel to the UK (unless they are participating in the Cultural Olympiad) – was very real.[13]

Theatre Wallay's *Shrew* also included rumbustious slapstick, such as jokes about the flatulence of Mukkarum Kaleem's Gremio/Ghazi;[14] the production featured a gawky, cross-cast Begum/Widow played by Hamza Kamal (who also played Grumio). This Begum was extremely tall and thin, sometimes playing coyly with her shawl, but her voice was comically raucous. Such jokes can communicate across languages, across cultures and across generations. But while Theatre Wallay were demonstrating so successfully that Pakistani culture includes laughter, clowning and wit, they were also committed to working with Pakistani communities within Britain to challenge ideas about traditional gender roles. Certain practices in *The Taming of the Shrew* connect easily with some aspects of traditional Pakistani culture: arranged marriages; patriarchal rule; dowries.[15] Theatre Wallay intended to use *The Shrew* to raise questions about 'the role of educated and strong women in a patriarchal society' and 'to use the opportunity to address stereotypical views of Pakistan (as dysfunctional and consisting mainly of terrorists and other extremists) and to build charitable, educational and cultural links across several communities in the UK'.[16]

A critical figure behind the scenes of the Theatre Wallay *Shrew* was producer Susannah Harris-Wilson, an American who worked for five years teaching young Pakistani women at Kinnaird College for Girls in Lahore. In an interview on the Talking Cranes website – a website for women of South Asian heritage – Harris-Wilson states that she very particularly wanted to produce a Pakistani *Shrew* for the Globe to Globe Festival, and she sees the play as being about an intelligent, educated woman – Elizabethan or twenty-first century – struggling to find a real partner, an equal.[17] Harris-Wilson's view is that Shakespeare was consistently 'an advocate of the intelligent woman' and that, being married to a clever businesswoman, he knew the value of such a wife.[18] Harris-Wilson's optimistic reading of *The Shrew* clearly influenced the production, and she also assembled a predominantly female creative team, including music director Valerie Kaul and three translators, Aamna Kaul, Zaibun Pasha and Mariam Pasha, all three of whom are university educated women, who presumably could sympathize with Kiran as an educated woman kicking against a society that does not always value her intelligence.[19] The virtues of the translation are outside my area of expertise, but one review, in Pakistan's English-language daily newspaper, *Dawn*, states: 'While staying faithful to the original, the translators peppered the dialogue with zingy one-liners, bawdy jokes, pop culture references and sexual innuendo. The adaptation also represented characters from Pakistan's four provinces and good naturedly poked fun at ethnic archetypes.'[20] For me, the critical thing is that the translators made it very hard not to laugh at the play, even though the gender politics of the taming remain a nightmare for Western feminism.

The commitment to creating laughter was something Theatre Wallay's *Shrew* shared with the other South Asian comedies I saw in the Festival. For example, it was clear from the beginning in the Gujarati *All's Well* that the title of the play was being honoured – all *would* end well – when the cast first appeared wearing Ganesh masks; with Ganesh presiding over the unfolding events the audience could be confident that this would be no dark reworking of the play into tragedy. The Hindi *Twelfth Night* went Bollywood, cut Act 4 Scene 2, (the incarceration of Malvolio) and featured an irrepressible Sebastian who, as narrator and translator of the play, often stopped to explain to the audience that he felt sometimes Shakespeare needed a bit of a make-over. The Bangla *Tempest* ended with Caliban happily installed as the new ruler of his island. In a similar fashion, the Pakistani *Shrew* served up the play as unquestionably funny; it rendered the play's ghastly gender politics amiable; it made Katherina's critical submission speech a physicalized, funny, theatrical two-hander; it produced a great deal of laughter even in a grumpy feminist like myself.

Despite Theatre Wallay's genial interpretation of *The Shrew* – and the production was extremely skilful both in giving agency to Kiran/Katherina and reducing the misery of her taming – I am left with some difficult questions. Were the gender issues less troubling for me because the action was relocated to Lahore, that is, away from my own usual social environment, and to a country that despite having had a female prime minister in Benazir Bhutto is, in the West, stereotypically seen to be a hard place for an educated woman to flourish? Does watching *The Shrew* set in Lahore make the play too comfortable for me? In some ways Theatre Wallay's appearance at the Globe seemed very timely, as one of the main news stories in the British press at the time was feeding the worst British stereotypes about Pakistani culture: the trial of the parents of Shafilea Ahmed (1986–2003), accused of murdering their daughter because she refused an arranged marriage, can read as a brutal taming narrative. But with Western women reputedly devouring *Fifty Shades of Grey* in their millions, I wonder if the potential for abject submission in *The Shrew* has more appeal in the West than many feminists would feel comfortable acknowledging.

The Shrew is going to speak differently to women and men in different cultures, in different historical moments and at different times of their lives; at this stage in my life I have become convinced the play is a wind-up. For me, the play invites women to respond to the taming process by turning to the nearest man (Sly?) and saying 'In your dreams!' Bianca puts it more elegantly: 'Fie, what a foolish duty call you this?' (5.2.125). Surely Elizabethan women must have been capable, like their twenty-first-century sisters, of laughing at *The Shrew*'s jokes as well as spluttering with indignation over the taming of Katherina, the intelligent, feisty woman who meets her match/nemesis/Heathcliff/Mr Knightley/Baron Von Trapp in Petruchio. You don't need to have read Mary Wollstonecraft, Simone de Beauvoir or Germaine Greer in order to feel infuriated when Katherina submits to her husband in public in a speech lasting over forty lines. I'm sure Queen Elizabeth I, Bess of Hardwick, Lady Anne Clifford, Elizabeth Cary, Moll Frith, Long Meg of Westminster and Anne

Shakespeare (née Hathaway) were quite capable of responding with 'Fie, what a foolish duty call you this?' I certainly came out of Theatre Wallay's *Shrew* laughing at the foolishness of men who want tame women.

ENDNOTES

1 Elizabeth Schafer, ed., *The Taming of the Shrew*, Shakespeare in Production (Cambridge University Press, 2002).

2 The production played in Lahore before coming to the UK, where it played Oxford and then the Globe (25–6 May 2012) before moving on to Rotherham and Bradford.

3 Recorded interview with Omair Rana (Rustam/Petruchio), Globe archive. Theatre Wallay received no government support, and they had no proper rehearsal space – director Haissam Hussain speaks of rehearsing on rooftops. At the time of writing their fundraising page was still active, www.justgiving.com/UrduTaming2012, 7 November 2012.

4 While in the First Folio text of 1623 Sly disappears after the end of Act 1 Scene 1, in another early text, the quarto *The Taming of a Shrew*, Sly continues to be unimpressed by *The Shrew*; he is only interested when the clown is on stage and is so outraged when it looks likely that a character might be arrested that he attempts to intervene. But by the end of the inner play Sly accepts the story as a pedagogic demonstration on how to tame a shrewish wife; so he sets off to tame Mistress Sly. It seems likely that if Mistress Sly has a saucepan to hand, Sly is in for a rude awakening.

5 Producer Susannah Harris-Wilson in an interview on the Talking Cranes website speaks of the narrator as a 'sunderbund', a weaver of threads, who will bring the audience and performers together, as well as the threads of the story. Harris-Wilson here talks of a male figure – Abu Hassan – and his metamorphosis into the female Ravi, which is significant, given the positive way the production presented the play; see http://talkingcranes.com/arts/taming-of-the-shrew-in-urdu, 7 November 2012.

6 The musicians played harmonium, sitar, flutes and tabla. The band, the Mekaal Hasan Band, are well known in Pakistan.

7 This theatrically dull moment was accompanied by 'the off-stage recitation of the Fajr prayer', so this may have worked better for non-Anglophones. See http://dawn.com/2012/06/03/theatre-review-shakespeare-at-the-globe-in-urdu/, 7 November 2012.

8 At the performance I saw someone from the audience called out after 'Thus have I politicly . . . ', and on the matinee recording one person clapped three times before falling quiet.

9 Querying the 'sun' is a joke that goes back at least to Louisa Nisbett in 1844 and really introduces a sense of Katherina learning improvisational skills. See *Shrew* Schafer, p. 209. The Urdu translation – which has stage directions in English – specifies 'Glances at Rustam as if to confirm that it is indeed the sun'.

10 Kiran was not required to 'Kiss me, Kate' (5.1.116), presumably because it would have been culturally inappropriate.

11 The Basant kite motif also, in English, puns on kites, in the sense of 'birds of prey'; Petruchio's taming methods are based on those used by a falcon trainer (4.1.166). The company actually began by working with Shakespeare's text in English and then moved on to the Urdu translation (recorded interview with Omair Rana (Rustam/ Petruchio),

Globe archive). For a denunciation of the banning of the Basant kite festival, see http://dawn.com/2012/06/03/theatre-review-shakespeare-at-the-globe-in-urdu/, 7 November 2012.

12 Recorded interview with Haissam Hussain, Globe archive.

13 For Urdu speakers, the joke was made funnier because Gremio had first boasted of being in possession of a five-month British visa before Tranio outbid a mere visa with a full passport.

14 The translation (Globe archive) specifies three occasions when 'Ghazi breaks wind loudly'.

15 Both director Haissam Hussain and the production's Petruchio, Omair Rana, spoke of these kinds of connection in an interview, Globe archive.

16 The fundraising site also indicates how underfunded the company were, something raised in an interview by both director Haissam Hussain and actor Omair Rana. See www.justgiving.com/UrduTaming2012, 7 November 2012.

17 See http://talkingcranes.com/arts/taming-of-the-shrew-in-urdu, 7 November 2012.

18 For Anne Shakespeare (née Hathaway) as a businesswoman, see Germaine Greer, *Shakespeare's Wife* (London: Bloomsbury, 2007).

19 The original director was also a woman, Naveen Shahzad.

20 See dawn.com/2012/06/03/theatre-review-shakespeare-at-the-globe-in-urdu/, 7 November 2012.

CHAPTER THIRTY-THREE

FOREIGN SHAKESPEARE AND THE UNINFORMED THEATRE-GOER

Part II, A Turkish *Antony and Cleopatra*

Michael Dobson

There's no doubt that Zerrin Tekindor is a bewitchingly attractive actress, and a good many men in that Saturday matinee audience at the Globe – who audibly included a substantial proportion of her Turkish-speaking fans – would have been quite as unthinkingly happy to fight by sea at her request as was Haluk Bilinger's Antony. A leonine, grizzled, barrel-chested figure, this Antony was a comically susceptible lover first and a doomed world leader only second, if at all. The show opened with the Roman and the Egyptian, surrounded by Cleopatra's female, musical, belly-dancing court, exchanging what were evidently straightforward and sincere endearments (gone was the prefatory disapproving exchange between Demetrius and Philo), and this remained its keynote throughout. Cleopatra eventually applied the asp on the leather chaise longue on which the couple had been seated when Antony dismissed the messenger, and just as the venom took effect Antony, or a comfortably corporeal ghost of him, simply walked back on, reappearing from the dead in the white kaftan he had worn in the first scene. Evidently their mutual self-indulgence would continue for an afterlife even more cosily connubial than the one each separately imagines in the play (see Colour Plate 13).

Actually, to describe this *Antony and Cleopatra* as 'the Roman and the Egyptian' is slightly misleading, since no togas or eagles were on view; Mert Firat's macho and un-Machiavellian Octavius and his faction wore black, but for the most part everyone looked unspecifically Mediterranean, in costumes which could have come from one of the same trunks as those of the Armenian *King John*. With the play's central opposition thus minimized, this seemed very much an *Antony and Cleopatra* 'lite'. The evidently colloquial, prose translation had been shorn not only of passages inconvenient for a company of twelve players but also of passages which might have demanded a genuinely tragic or historical register. The soothsayer was gone; Enobarbus' Cydnus speech was gone; Octavius' account of Antony and Cleopatra mustering the kings of the earth for war was gone; the god Hercules forsaking

Antony was gone; 'I dreamed there was an Emperor Antony...' (5.2.75) was all but gone (Cleopatra's suicide followed Antony's after only a swift intervening interview with Octavius); and the queenly robes for the death scene were gone too.

What remained, as far as I could see at the time, was essentially the sitcom of the messenger scene. A cheerful, festive first half (its tone set by a strangely carefree Enobarbus) was followed by a second which never found a different gear. It's true that the company tried to make a spectacle out of Actium by having Antony and Octavius whirl wet maces towards each other (a piece of choreography confusingly reiterated for the tiny naval skirmish Antony later witnesses during the fall of Alexandria), and it is also true that the production tried to bring a note of real suffering into the humiliation of Thidias, whose agonized cries were plainly audible throughout his offstage whipping. Unfortunately, nobody on stage seemed remotely bothered by this: it plainly never crossed this Cleopatra's mind that she might be next. Tekindor's Cleopatra was touchingly and seductively over the top, but she never conveyed a sense of vulnerability, political cunning or danger, any more than did her Antony: the first time she simulated a wheezing attack and mock-fainted into the arms of her ladies (on 'Cut my lace, Charmian' (1.3.71)) it was funny, but this business was repeated throughout the play, on occasions that might have called for much less affected or insincere responses.

At the time what seemed most awkward about this *Antony and Cleopatra*, though, was the difficulty it had in getting dead characters from the stage; some were dragged off, but others, such as Enobarbus and even Antony, simply walked off when they had finished dying, looking bashful. I wondered briefly whether this was a convention the director might have imitated, at first or second hand, from Stephen Pimlott's RSC production of 1999, but I have since learned that it meant something else entirely. Here the absence of programme notes supplying more information about the background of each show in the Globe to Globe Festival seems lamentable, even for those not hoping for mug's guides by which to claim a spurious authority to write about the productions later. The glossy cast lists that supplied the only facts one could obtain on-site about these shows said nothing about their provenance, or about the restrictions imposed by the Globe on every production in the Festival. The cutting of the major soliloquies from *Antony and Cleopatra*, I have since gathered, which I took at the time as the expression of a preference for rapid narrative movement and a purposeful avoidance of intellectual and emotional engagement at any level deeper than that of soap opera, was in fact a side-effect of the Festival's insistence that no show should last longer than two and a quarter hours. (When any Shakespeare script gets cut in a hurry, it is the soliloquies, which make nothing happen, that tend to go first – the Smock Alley promptbook of *Macbeth*, prepared in Dublin during the 1670s, provides the classic example.) The embarrassed self-removing corpses, similarly, weren't a gesture towards the non-realist but merely awkward symptoms of a company more accustomed to playing in modern indoor theatres with lighting, here obliged to work in broad daylight. Everywhere else this *Antony and Cleopatra* was performed there were blackouts between scenes, during which the slain could sneak off in decent privacy.

Nor were these two shows, it transpires, exactly visiting from Armenia and Turkey respectively: they were brought into being specifically for the Festival. What I read at the time, then, as two folksy and even crude productions making themselves temporarily at home in the folksiest theatre in central London, were in fact devised with this difficult and unaccustomed space in mind, and then performed in it after being allowed only a single rehearsal on the Globe's stage. For all I know, Gasparyan and Aydoğan may both specialize the rest of the time in producing subtly nuanced versions of Shakespeare in tiny spaces lit by candles, in the manner of early Katie Mitchell. I am not sure what I think about this. On the one hand, if I were the actor-manager of a troupe famous for its three-actor, modern-dress studio adaptation of *Oedipus Rex* which got invited to stage a new *Elektra* for a worldwide Sophocles festival at Epidauros, I doubt if I would feel obliged to make my cast experiment with wearing masks and intoning hexameters for the occasion, incongruous as my production might seem in that space without them. On the other, if I were organizing a worldwide Sophocles festival at Epidauros and that was the only venue at my disposal, I'm not sure I would choose to invite any companies whose work normally depended for its effect on intimacy and modern lighting. Having belatedly realized that Gasparyan's *King John* and Aydoğan's *Antony and Cleopatra* were only produced under the anomalous circumstances of this Festival, I now have a curious impression that I haven't really seen the work of either director at all, just two very similar enforced compromises between their own artistic styles and the house style of the Globe itself. I came to these productions in ignorance, and the main thing I preserve from both is a now even deeper appreciation of that ignorance – which is salutary, no doubt, but a less satisfying result than I would normally expect from witnessing such encounters between major global theatre companies and a major global playwright.

'DIDST HEAR HER SPEAK? IS SHE SHRILL-TONGUED OR LOW?'

Conversation with Janet Suzman following a performance of *Antony and Cleopatra*, 26 May 2012

Janet Suzman

So what I thought I was seeing was Noel Coward, maybe *Private Lives*. I mean it is a perfectly legitimate, if slightly unrewarding reading – *Antony and Cleopatra* 'lite', that's all. And that is what they chose to do, and it was completely consistent. They decided to skate over the story in a sort of pretty way, in a Hollywood way, I would say because she was very glamorous and he was very Antonine. I thought there were the embryos of some really good performances there, actually. I was much taken by the young man who plays the messenger, and the actor playing Eros and Thidias. They actually squeezed feeling out of those very cut parts. I think the two protagonists rather relied on their leading lady–leading man star power back home to carry them and obviously there were many people in the audience who recognized them and loved them. And they were both very, very fetching; indeed, there is no question about that (see Colour Plate 13).

She had found the actress Cleopatra, so she kept doing her asphyxiating act, her 'I can't breathe' act, but the production missed the motivations of why she does that, what mockery she is using on Antony, which is to do with lying and play-acting. She emulates a bad actress since she is trying to point out to Antony that he is a bad actor in the matter of grief. They had clearly decided, since there is great intelligence behind it, that she was a picture-book Cleopatra, but what she didn't have was power and the fear of an autocrat. She didn't have any vulnerability at all, so she didn't allow you into her worst excesses. It was just like, 'She does that every day and so she will go on doing it.' Similarly, I think they cut short Antony's inner life, really crucially badly, and branded him a clown, a joke figure with a strange white hat. I didn't quite see what they were getting at, because it was imposed rather than enacted. I didn't feel that intense assumption of a drama which you have to feel when an actor walks into that space and then tells us a story. You didn't have any of

The quotation in the title is from *Antony and Cleopatra* 3.3.12.

the terrible turmoil, Antony makes one bad decision after another throughout the play from the moment he handles Cleopatra rather badly by not grieving for Fulvia. You know he does agree to marry Octavia, and doing the sea battle rather than the land battle. He just does everything wrong and ends up not even being able to kill himself. He botches that too. He dies of shame, his heart breaks.

There wasn't anything at stake, loss wasn't at stake, and the loss of an empire wasn't at stake and the terrible foolishness of making a wrong decision wasn't at stake. In fact no markers, which appear like huge traffic lights where you change direction, appeared to me. I just saw a very smooth road stretching to their inevitable doom because I know the play. But this is where I think we must understand that the language makes all the difference. And I wish I could understand the language but it sounded like it was prosaic all the way through. I didn't feel verse as pillars of feelings, holding up feelings, elevating them.

I found it interesting that Antony and Eros had a sort of father–son, or father–child at any rate, relationship, which was quite touching. And I quite liked the idea, too, of him being an Athenian, Eros, dressed as a cupid in white, although it was jarring. I could have wished that that had been followed through more, that we could have understood his Herculean ambitions, his Greek ambitions, but we didn't really. So I think it was a production quite full of ideas that weren't really consistently attended to.

What was lacking was danger, the danger of her taking to the monument, the danger of her lying to him. I particularly cocked an eye to see that it was Charmian that suggested that they go to the monument and suggested 'Tell him you're dead.' It's Charmian's idea, and Cleopatra is so panic-stricken that she picks up on it. But she couldn't get panic-stricken, because the scene before, which should panic-strike her, when Antony tries to tear her eyes out, wasn't there. I think all the grand moments were gone, which is why I started by saying this is the play 'lite'. It's been gutted of its grandeur.

So what was left was Bette Davis at home with her girls and a really friendly relationship with Antony, really chummy. No problems, her ruffling his hair, no Antony drunk talking to his retinue, saying 'You may never see me again' and them saying 'Buck up, stop it, stop behaving like this', and no sign of her changing the mood with 'It's my birthday' and him saying 'Right let's drink, let's drink.' All of that was gone. It was very steady, friendly daylight that infused it all. There was certainly no politics in it. I didn't see any of the now necessary, because we are all of course post-feminist, there is a necessary element to that play now which was completely missing, and that, I think, is the Turkish view that women remain completely unimportant. And the only thing she is good for is sex and nothing else. So that was a little bit old-fashioned, let me put it that way.

There was also very little sense of East and West. The fact that Turkey stands exactly at the crossroads of East and West I would have thought would have provoked a more stringent look at what joining the EU or remaining on the Asian side might mean, but that was never injected into the production. And maybe we are all addicted to seeing Shakespeare's plays as a representation of the status quo, and that there is no point in looking at *Antony and Cleopatra* unless you are looking at Washington marching with its boots into Baghdad you know, Rome and Egypt.

So I came out charmed but unenlightened. There was no doom in the play. On the stage at the Globe I think you can do big things very well. The more difficult thing is the expectations we have of serious confrontation in drama, and that is more difficult on this stage to achieve. I think this play swerves. It's like it's a big movie. It's a helicopter-shot to Athens, vroooom, a helicopter-shot to Rome, vroooom, someone's house in Rome, back to a sea battle, it's big sweeps of a camera and then it contracts in the last two acts to that little room and the monument. Antony just appeared at the end, and then his death went for nothing. She climbed onto his body and went limp for a bit, and then they said 'Empress, empress, madam, madam, empress', and then she woke up, but it had no inner life. I didn't see his suffering, his terrible shame, his utter humiliation. They had naturalized the language, which is very forgivable, but I think what it did was deflate it rather to a very ordinary size. They weren't mythical figures. They felt very suburban. I sound scabrous about this, but it's impossible to look at what you know is in a play and see it not there without having a sense of disappointment.

WEEK SIX

CHAPTER THIRTY-FIVE

HABIMA MERCHANT OF VENICE

Performances inside and outside the Globe

Suzanne Gossett

For an American Jewish academic specializing in Shakespeare, hearing that the Habima company chose *The Merchant of Venice* for its Globe to Globe performance, and that a boycott and protest were planned by pro-Palestinian activists because the company has also performed in the Settlements, created a series of conflicting feelings. The choice of play seemed at once brave, perhaps unwise and finally over-determined; the protest, especially since the Festival advertised a production of *Richard II* in Palestinian Arabic by the Ramallah-based Ashtar Theatre, similarly over-determined. One wondered what would have happened if Habima had chosen to act, for instance, *Troilus and Cressida* – would Greeks and Trojans have to be made representatives of the Middle Eastern populations? How would the sides be allotted?

One effect of the anticipated protest was that for this audience member there were, effectively, two performances, one on the stage and the other everywhere else, outside and inside the Globe, with symbolic blocking important in both cases. Outside the Globe on May 28, as we took our place in the queue to go through airport-style security, we passed first the pro-Palestinian protestors and then the Zionist defenders. The pro-Palestinians were kept further away from the entrance, but the queue led directly past the Zionists with their large 'Israel is God's country' banner: presumably this was simply a tactical judgement about the possible actions of each group, but it would have been easy to read as a political statement. Inside the theatre, even before the peaceful but conspicuous protests began – the Palestinian flags unfurled from the Globe's galleries had clearly not been found and removed by the searches to which each audience member was subjected on entrance to the theatre – I noticed a burly gentleman standing behind my section, apparently without ticket, seat or overt identification but apparently there in a security capacity and chatting familiarly with the uniformed security guard. Was he there to protect the unidentified Israeli woman and teenager seated next to me? (They said they 'knew the play', but its meaning for them, whatever that was, didn't seem to carry much weight with the protesters.) We saw more symbolic blocking by the protesters who, once their flags had been confiscated by the numerous security guards at each of the Globe's levels, stood throughout the performance with their mouths covered in adhesive tape, studiously looking everywhere but the stage. And, as it happened, returning to the Globe on 29 May for an afternoon performance of the Spanish *King Henry VIII*, with our minds fixed on the early sixteenth century, we emerged at 4pm into one of the largest collections of security personnel and sniffer dogs that I have ever seen, with significant parts of the area around the Globe shut off to us. The convention in Shakespeare's own time of closing the theatres when they violated the current political 'line' – say, after Thomas Middleton's *A Game at Chesse* – began to seem quite contemporary.

The performance on stage by the Habima company was fine: presumably they are accustomed to acting on through protests, but they also dealt very well indeed with the open spaces of the Globe arena. Certainly, they did their very best to give the anxious audience an evening of professional theatre, beginning with a lively opening dance intended, clearly, to help us focus back on the play after Globe Artistic Director Dominic Dromgoole's carefully scripted welcome and warning of possible protests. Many recent productions of *The Merchant*, both in the USA and in Britain, have of course been updated, with, for example, Shylock recast as a Wall Street trader and the stage full of cell phones and ticker tapes. Habima chose instead to keep the play in Venice and approximately in its original period, although the striking costumes were stylized in a postmodern way. The style and the political 'take' were both apparent in a brief scene staged before the play's opening line. Shylock, the small and excellent Jacob Cohen, clearly a very experienced actor, came on stage wrapped in a *tallit* or ritual shawl, only to be kicked to the ground by a group of Venetians, dressed in white and wearing traditional Venetian masks. It was a shock when, having removed his mask, Antonio was revealed as one of the bullies and delivered the first line of the play, 'In sooth, I know not why I am so sad' (1.1.1). In recent years this line has often been made the first of many suggestions that Antonio is suffering because Bassanio has taken his previously homoerotic love elsewhere, but in this production the sadness seemed one unappealing after-effect of ethnic violence.

One of the most difficult challenges for a production of *The Merchant of Venice* is managing the balance of the plots: the tendency for the conflict in Venice between Shylock and Antonio to dominate is strong, with Portia becoming of interest only in her cross-dressed role in the courtroom. Historically there have been productions that ended after Antonio is freed and Shylock defeated, simply removing the final act with its return to Belmont and the bawdy jokes about Portia and Nerissa's 'rings'.

Habima, however, did a splendid and very theatrical job of relating the situations to each other. Portia, who complains in her first scene that 'I may neither choose who I would nor refuse who I dislike; so is the will of a living daughter curbed by the will of a dead father' (1.2.19–21), was literally 'curbed', tied up in a cage of ribbon-like ropes as her suitors came and went. Strikingly, the same ropes bound Antonio, naked to the waist, in the courtroom as he awaited Shylock's knife (see Colour Plate 14), and then, after Portia's triumph at the trial, were redeployed to suspend the defeated Shylock. In this world no one is free, even those apparently rich and belonging to the dominant religion. The production also highlighted the similar ways in which money and contracts bound both Portia and Antonio: when Bassanio solved the riddle he extracted an endless roll of financial print-out from the casket – the 'full sum of' (3.2.157) Portia's wealth – which he studied with great attention, ignoring his new wife in his enthusiasm for the material advantages of the marriage. In this acquisitive context, it seemed only sensible of Jessica to hesitate before throwing her own casket, full of Shylock's stolen gold, down to Lorenzo.

The production, then, externally and internally, took its place with earlier ones that refuse to see *The Merchant of Venice*, despite the ostensibly 'happy ending', as a comedy. Even the fifth-act sections that have traditionally been staged to restore a comic or romantic tone, like the poetic exchange between Lorenzo and Jessica under the evening moonlight, where 'the floor of heaven / Is thick inlaid with patens of bright gold' (5.1.58–9), and which includes Shakespeare's famous lines about 'the sweet power of music' (5.1.79), were disturbing: Habima took seriously the implications of the pair's not-very-playful listing of faithless classical lovers and treated the scene as a serious lovers' quarrel, promising little future harmony between these two. And, as has become a familiar interpretation in recent performances and in the Al Pacino film,[1] in Belmont Jessica clearly found that even if, as she told Launcelot, she would 'end this strife, / Become a Christian and [a] loving wife' (2.3.19–20), she would nevertheless continue to be slighted and ignored.

Overall, then, a production as sensitive as this to the forms of oppression and suffering created between divided groups in a society, performed in a context of simmering protest on several sides, inevitably raised the question of how, and how much, artistic works and artistic organizations should be forced to participate in, or be judged by, cultural conflict. There are those in Israel who do not think Wagner's music should be performed there, or by an Israeli orchestra. The Globe to Globe Festival brought in troupes from other countries (e.g. Afghanistan, China) whose treatment of their minorities has also been challenged. One protestor in the audience when I attended declaimed (though, oddly, not at the appropriate moment), 'Hath not a Palestinian eyes?' Those who thought the Globe did well to have Habima participate in its festival would argue that Shakespeare's play, and the

Israeli troupe's performance, created precisely the opportunity to think through this very contemporary problem.

ENDNOTE

1 Michael Radford, William Shakespeare's *The Merchant of Venice* (2004), USA: Shylock Trading Ltd and Sony Pictures Classic.

CHAPTER THIRTY-SIX

PATRIOTISM, PRESENTISM AND THE SPANISH HENRY VIII

The tragedy of the migrant queen

Juan F. Cerdá

When Rakatá's performance of *Henry VIII* took place in late May, almost at the closing of the Globe to Globe Festival, Spain was about to win their third consecutive international football tournament and to hear from its government that the economic crisis that had started four years ago was only getting worse. I wonder if, at some point before the Madrid-based company took the stage, the organizers of the Festival asked themselves whether they would be getting the Spain that wins consecutive Euro Cups or the Spain whose possible financial rescue was on the verge of doing half the continent irremediable economic damage.[1] Rakatá's project sprang from the second scenario. Recently renamed Fundación Siglo de Oro (Golden Age Foundation) – probably seeking not only to market the project as an exclusively early modern enterprise but also to facilitate their search for financial help from public administrations – the company struggled to land the part of the budget required to accept the Globe's (only part-funded) invitation. Weeks before the performance, the same newspapers that had triumphantly announced the first Spanish expedition to the Globe echoed the company's complaints about the lack of institutional support. Thus, the prospects of Rakatá's portrayal of Henry VIII's reign, which was to defend Spanish cultural pride by 'bearing our country's flag in the London Cultural Olympiad',[2] were momentarily clouded as a consequence of the country's long economic backlash. Rakatá's protest was expressed by its 'profoundly disappointed' founder and director, Rodrigo Arribas, within the rhetorical boundaries of the two hottest topics in Spain around the late spring/early summer of 2012: football and the economy – 'it is as if the players in the national team had to pay for their boots and shirts themselves'.[3]

The company's views are symptomatic of a typically post-Francoist reliance on subsidized culture, which, as Keith Gregor notes, has been behind Shakespeare's large success in Spain in the last two to three democratic decades,[4] and which could now be in danger of collapsing. Only time will tell if the Bard will survive without institutional support in these distant and economically troubled lands, but, despite all financial adversities, the Spanish company drew unanimous rave reviews, especially after the second show. Apparently, a tweet from 'one of the Globe higher-ups' circulated after the performance noting that, almost at the end of the cycle, Rakatá's was the 'loudest and longest curtain call of a festival not short of loud and long curtain calls'.[5] Such an enthusiastic reception was largely obtained from an audience filled with Spanish speakers, institutionally led by the Spanish ambassador, who clapped profusely from his VIP box to the upper-right of the stage. The company's success was echoed back in the Spanish press – 'Golden medal in Shakespeare'[6] – and, encouraged by the performance at the Globe, the company closed the deal to bring their production to the San Javier and the Olite summer theatre festivals back in Spain, cashing in on their foreign success with perhaps more to follow next year.

This summary of the production's trajectory provides an initial perspective on the company's strategic patriotism, initially fostered by the nationalistic hype of the Spanish press but met and even surpassed by the company's adaptation of Shakespeare and Fletcher's play. As much as the Globe to Globe Festival provided a potentially multicultural scenario, the company anticipated the crowd's predominantly Spanish spectatorship and manufactured an adaptation that decidedly appealed to a nationalistic sense of 'Spanishness'. Through the gambit of restructuring the play around the exiled Catalina de Aragón and relying on the audience's identification with the Spanish queen, the production appealed to a nostalgic empathy from the Spanish community in London that has lately been enlarged through a predominantly economic diaspora provoked by dismal unemployment figures. Consequently, the production displayed a firm monoculturalism whose success had been predicted by Rakatá's earlier previews at the *Corral de comedias* in Almagro and was later confirmed by its promising future back in the Spanish theatrical circuit, in what can be seen as a natural return to the production's cultural habitat after its English venture.

Despite its extraordinary success, however, adjusting Shakespeare and Fletcher's inevitably foreign and distant playtext to a Spanish interpretation of history cannot be carried out without unearthing a number of problematic perspectives. Rakatá's intervention not only rewrites and challenges the already complex enactment of Henry VIII's reign but it relocates the play's political, religious and moral conflicts in a new light, interpellating the displaced Spanish community in present-day London in multiple and conflicting ways. In short, apart from the patriotic perspective, and as much as Rakatá cleverly rearranged the play, even the Spanish queen proves to be a difficult character to identify with from some (equally Spanish) socio-ideological positions.

HENRY VIII'S SPANISH REPAIR KIT

With the objective of producing a Spanish-friendly product, Rakatá altered the English foundations of a text that Shakespeare and Fletcher creatively produced from the historical narratives of Holinshed and Foxe, Speed, and Stow. The result of Rakatá's adaptation of the play feels as if it had been chiselled from Spanish sixteenth-century historiography like the *Ecclesiastical History* (1588) of orthodox Jesuit, Father Pedro Ribadeneyra from which Calderón de la Barca constructed *La cisma de inglaterra* (*The Schism in England*, c. 1627), the Spanish early modern theatrical version of the Henry–Katherine–Anne imbroglio. Through textual and directorial choices, the Madrid-based company reinscribed the English text into a tradition of Spanish nationalism. Shakespeare and Fletcher's contradictory playtext is a product of the anxieties that surrounded the Reformation, still in its early stages under James I's reign. In turn, Calderón's less dubitative dramatization of some of those same historical events is characterized by the fact that, as Ann L. Mackenzie notes, Calderón was writing *La cisma de Inglaterra* 'for the Spanish stage and to please devoutly Roman Catholic and anti-English theatre-goers'.[7] Rakatá was commissioned by the Globe to Globe organizers to engage with Shakespeare and Fletcher's play, yet, specializing as they do in early modern Spanish drama, they decided to put together a production that is closer in spirit to Calderón's dramatization of Henry VIII's reign.

However, as much as the complexities of the English text were not to get in the way of the company's vindication of Katherine's tragic end, and as much as the company intended to please the Spanish community in London, Rakatá was not performing for either 'devoutly Roman Catholic' or 'anti-English theatre-goers' but for Spaniards who had had to leave their home in search of a better job and for Spaniards who were about to win the Euro Cup 2012. If those spectators at the performances are to be conceptualized as a more or less homogenous 'audience', the conclusion is simple: they unproblematically loved the production.

Obviously, Katherine is in a propitious position to turn the relocated Spanish audience's sentiments of displacement, longing and vulnerability into a sympathetic sense of solidarity:

I am a most poor woman and a stranger,
Born out of your dominions, having here
No judge indifferent nor more assurance
Of equal friendship and proceeding

(2.4.13–6)

Beseech you, sir, to spare me till I may
Be by my friends in Spain advised, whose counsel
I will implore.

(2.4.52–4)

Shakespeare and Fletcher's text, together with the acting style and the company's alterations, reinforced the Spanish audience's sense of community and effectively mobilized the spectator's allegiances – as when Katherine regrets setting foot in England, 'Would I had never trod this English earth / Or felt the flatteries that grow upon it' (3.1.143–4), lines that could bear special resonance for those spectators who might be struggling in London. And even if the topicality of the queen's exiled condition only added favourably to Shakespeare and Fletcher's already kind depiction of the Spanish queen, Rakatá further tweaked the text and shaped the acting to secure a performance celebrating Katherine's martyrdom.

In their reinterpretation of *Henry VIII*, Rakatá constructed a much less likeable Henry by cutting his defence of Buckingham in Act 1 and reassigning some of Wolsey's lines to him. Also, throwing much of the textual ambiguity out of the window, they added the exchange of a love letter between Henry and Anne, in which the king promises to 'have [Anne] as his only lover, doing away with all [her] competitors',[8] a comment that undermines much of the king's credibility, especially to an audience that is well aware that he would marry a few more times after Anne. On top of this, in order to counteract the audience's potentially sympathetic reaction to Anne Bullen, the company cut the text's positive depictions of the character while Sara Moraleda played her as an overtly sexual character in contrast to Katherine's temperance. Also, Rakatá inserted a dumb-show in which Anne stole the crown from a disempowered Katherine, so by the time Anne is made queen at the beginning of Act 4, the audience's allegiance to Katherine is secured beyond what Shakespeare and Fletcher could ever have expected.

But the key directorial choice was to save the play's final words for Katherine, a character who, according to Shakespeare and Fletcher, should have made her last exit in Act 4 of a play that was written to finish with the celebration of the baby Elizabeth I's baptism. Instead, Rakatá inserted the climactic tragedy of the queen's death. Before that, Jesús Teyssiere had worked hard in delivering a rather disturbing interpretation of Cranmer, the champion of Protestantism in the English play and who in this production is constructed as a sinister fanatic, much closer to the personality of the mentally unbalanced head of an extremist sect than to the noble defender of the future creed of the British empire. Sobbing and screaming some added lines ('Although stripped of the queen's title, bury me, I beg you, as a queen and as the daughter of a king. I can't stand it any longer!'),[9] Elena González ran around the stage like a ghost, unnoticed by the rest of the characters, yet ruining for the audience the baptism of the queen who would eventually defeat the Spanish Armada (see Colour Plate 15).

CATALINA, OUR CONTEMPORARY

Not unlike Calderón, Rakatá went to great lengths to turn the English court into a celebration of Spanish dynastic pride, and the Globe to Globe Festival made it all happen at the most fitting of locations. In all its performance history, I doubt Shakespeare and Fletcher's story of Spanish Katherine has ever been delivered for an audience as ready to sympathize with the exiled queen as this one. The expectation of the audience's Spanishness felt especially powerful at those instances where Katherine was depicted as a fragile alien in a court of strangers. Then, in order to render the heroic fall of the Spanish queen effectively, the rest of the main characters were articulated through their most conflictive features and, especially, through undermining Henry's credibility. The success of the production was undeniable. The audience, the reviewers and the Spanish Ambassador all rejoiced in a feast of Spanishness that I, and perhaps others, however few, found somewhat problematic.

Even within the particularly Spanish perspective I am describing here, the production offered multiple experiences, and it was possible to take up different relationships to Rakatá's work, especially at those 'non-discursive' moments described by Terence Hawkes as when a 'play's own continuity appears to break down and it seems suddenly to leap out at us . . . to reach beyond itself and its text, to touch us directly and often wordlessly'.[10] From this presentist point of view, it is possible to complicate the way Rakatá's performance anticipated the audience response at the Globe and show how the vindication of the Spanish queen is a theatrically effective but also an ideologically problematic manoeuvre. Thus, while Rakatá worked hard to gather the audience's support for Queen Katherine, they also produced an English court that resonated with the problems of the present-day Spanish monarchy. This is less of a leap than it may at first seem. After all, Katherine is a Spanish regent, and her sobriety and temperance are familiar traits of Queen Sofía of Spain, the Greek exile in the current Spanish court. Together with this, as I was reminded by the two Spanish women sitting next to me, Fernando Gil (the actor playing Henry) briefly stepped into the spotlight less than two years ago when he played the present Prince of Asturias in the prime-time broadcast of the TV drama mini-series *Felipe y Letizia* (2010), which dramatized the engagement and early years of the prince's marriage to Letizia Ortiz.[11] The potential inter-theatricality of the actor's performance only adds to the fact that, among his Spanish subjects, the public image of King Juan Carlos I of Spain has in recent months deteriorated since an unfortunate accident at a recent safari in Botswana eventually uncovered the monarch's extramarital affair.[12] Chiefly because of the company's adaptation of the original text along with their performance style, but also reinforced by the ghostly resonances of the 'Botswana situation', I believe that no Spaniard in the audience doubted that the reasons behind Henry's abandonment of Katherine were other than his infatuation with Anne.

But, in a presentist context, Rakatá's Katherine proves problematic, as in her obstinate rejection of divorce that clashes with contemporary attitudes. In fact, the cause of divorce spearheaded the struggles of Spanish feminism in the early demo-cratic years, Congress passing the Divorce Bill in 1981. For some, this crucial step in Spanish women's emancipation was an act of restitution, as the new regulation could be understood to restore the 1932 divorce laws of the Second Republic – that is, the reform could be seen as a re-establishment of what the dictatorship had taken away. More recently (2005), the last Socialist administration updated the divorce laws and passed the Same-Sex Marriage Bill. From these perspectives, the perfor-mance of the queen's traditional sense of womanhood could be problematic for those who might be thinking that it is actually Katherine who should be asking for a divorce. Rakatá's production efficiently managed to show Wolsey's Machiavellian duplicity, Cranmer's sinister fanaticism, Anne's sexualized ambitions and Henry's intemperance, but at the same time the audience was left with a fervently religious Katherine as the only alternative.

In recent years, academic criticism has read Shakespeare and Fletcher's *Henry VIII* as a sophisticated and contradictory work that makes it virtually impossible for the reader/spectator to resolve the events portrayed on the page/stage. Perception of the play's relativism has emerged through what Ewan Fernie calls 'the dominant fashion of reading Shakespeare historically',[13] a methodology that has its origins in the Foucaultian historicized analysis of power relations and of which much of Gordon McMullan's very suggestive introduction for the Arden Shakespeare Third Series is a clear example. In short, what this tells us is that the play's unresolved nature is a consequence of Shakespeare and Fletcher's reaction to the period's equally unresolved state of affairs. As a result, Shakespeare and Fletcher's reworking of historical accounts, what McMullan refers to as the playwrights' 'filtering of events', sustains a 'sense of radical uncertainty throughout the play'[14] which can only be understood in its full complexity through its triangulation with the period's political and religious context. This is, according to such New Historicist perspectives, what ultimately explains the play and its characters' conflicts.

In turn, both inside and outside academe, the play has accumulated a cohort of detractors, like reviewer Matt Wolf, who believed that Rakatá's 'fire and pizzazz' was the right antidote to this 'potentially fusty history play'.[15] 'Now, here's a surprise', he continued, '[i]n English, *Henry VIII* gets dismissed as a Shakespearean dud (well, let's apportion the blame as well to the play's generally acknowledged co-author, John Fletcher)'; by contrast, the 'contribution from Spain [. . . and] its brio-filled, impassioned cast' has produced an interpretation of *Henry VIII* that 'pulsated with life', as opposed to the 'glum-faced decorousness and pomp that have attended most homegrown stagings'.[16] Just as in Wolf's review, the authorship question around *Henry VIII* – whether the play is not Shakespeare's work or whether it is the product of diminishing collaborative work (debates which recent criticism has largely exposed as excuses to save the sacrosanct Bard from the accusations of poor playwriting) – has often been a starting-point for negative appraisals of the play. A mixed bag of negative criticism has, among other things, pointed at the play's patchy, disjointed assemblage, and an episodic arrangement of events that fails to provide a more desirable cause–effect structure. Furthermore, the same irresolute relativism that has dominated recent scholarship can also be an obstacle to more decisive approaches to performance of the play. For example, in terms of the play's underlying ideology, McMullan documents the 'continuing role *Henry VIII* has played at times of national crisis and triumph' and the 'conservativism' exemplified in productions that helped celebrate British patriotism – such as at the end of the Pacific War or the accession of Elizabeth II. On the other hand, McMullan also illustrates a 'few "radical" productions which . . . treat the text as a piece of glorified propaganda and set out to debunk it'.[17] It seems as if, within the play's British performance history, there has been a side-taking tendency that effectively clears the text's grey areas – an approach not unlike Rakatá's in their vindication of the Spanish character in the play.

One of the ways British productions have moulded the play to fit their interests has been to end the play at different points: after Wolsey's final lines, after Katherine's death, or after Anne's coronation.[18] However, Rakatá's objectives required a deeper textual and theatrical intervention. The company's standpoint was that theirs was not so much an interpretation of Shakespeare and Fletcher's play, but a separate project altogether, as expressed by the actor playing the king when, in a newspaper interview, he differentiated between 'the original version' of *Henry VIII* and 'the one we are realising'.[19] It seems as if the company perceived that Shakespeare and Fletcher had produced a piece that needed fixing: '[it is] an extremely political play but we have been able to find the conflict's ins and outs to *make it interesting*'.[20] The Spanish company streamlined the performance by reordering, cutting, rewriting and even adding lines to transform Shakespeare and Fletcher's *Henry VIII* into a one-sided narrative that perhaps should have more accurately been entitled *The Tragedy of Catalina of Aragón*. Not only does this fit with a tradition of (heavily) rewritten Spanish performances of Shakespeare's plays that dates back to the late eighteenth century, but the title of the only other production of *Henry VIII* by a Spanish company – *Catalina de Aragón* by the theatre group La Carbonera (1965)[21] – suggests that, however tentative, Rakatá's production bespeaks a trend in the short Spanish performance history of the play. For the Spanish eye this should hardly be surprising, since Rakatá's production relocates to the Globe the version of the story that has often circulated within Spanish culture – that is, the familiar tale of the hypocritical, womanizing English ruler and the noble, self-sacrificing Spanish queen.

In any case, as subversive as this may look at the home of the English Bard, the fact is that Rakatá's undoing of the celebration of British expansionism was only replaced by a vindication of Spanish colonialism, a nostalgic narrative of the great conquering nation. Within Spanish culture, this is frequently associated with conservative ideologies that traditionally celebrate the historical highlights of the Spanish nation: the great Spanish empire, the War of Independence against France or, for radical nationalism, Franco's fascist regime. This production tried hard to take over Shakespeare and Fletcher's playtext, block its ambiguities and contradictions, and provide a one-dimensional reading of the play, yet, just as *Henry VIII* has often been read as a piece of propaganda for British identity, the Globe to Globe Festival invitation resulted in a similarly conservative version of national spirit, only this time Spanish. In the light of the production's patriotic monoculturalism, Rakatá's *Henry VIII* raises questions about the role of the Spanish contribution within the Festival and the cultural transactions enabled by it. On the Spanish side, the arrangement is at once logical and profitable: Rakatá devised a production whose patriotism works well both to wave the flag in the Shakespeare Olympics to the general acclaim of the Spanish community in London, and to go back to tour the summer festivals in Spain. This might finally improve the company's chances for future public funding, easier to request from its safely nationalistic perspective. But this only perpetuates chauvinism: conveniently, it is the national spirit of the 'other' that gets celebrated. From the perspective of Rakatá's contribution to the Festival, I find nothing especially subversive in inviting foreign cultures to do their monocultural jig at 'Shakespeare's home'. In exchange, perhaps, there is the prize of politically correct multiculturalism and the veneer of cross-cultural diversity.

ENDNOTES

1 This work is part of research project HUM-2005–02556/FILO, financed by the Ministerio de Educación and Feder.

2 Esther Alvarado, 'Larga vida al rey "Enrique VIII"', El mundo.es 20 May 2012, www.elmundo.es/elmundo/2012/05/19/cultura/1337453764.html, 29 October 2012.

3 Ibid., '[P]rofundamente decepcionado'; 'Es como si los jugadores de la selección nacional de fútbol tuvieran que pagarse ellos mismos las botas y las camisetas.'

4 See Keith Gregor, 'Spanish Shakespeare-manía: *Twelfth Night* in Madrid, 1996–7', *Shakespeare Quarterly*, 49.4 (1998): 421–2, as well as his *Shakespeare in the Spanish Theatre: 1772 to the Present* (London: Continuum, 2010).

5 Matt Wolf, 'Globe to Globe: *Henry VIII*, Shakespeare's Globe', *The Arts Desk*, 31 May 2012, www.theartsdesk.com/theatre/globe-globe-henry-viii-shakespeares-globe, 12 July 2012.

6 Esther Alvarado, 'Medalla de Oro en Shakespeare', *El mundo.es*, 31 May 2012, www.elmundo.es/elmundo/2012/05/31/cultura/1338474760.html, 29 October 2012.

7 Ann L. Mackenzie, 'Introduction', in Pedro Calderón de la Barca, *The Schism in England* (Warminster: Aris and Phillips, 1990), p. 14.

8 José Padilla, Ernesto Arias and Rafael Díez Lavín, '*Enrique VIII, Toda la verdad*, de William Shakespeare', unpublished script for Rakatá's *Henry VIII* production, p. 35. 'Os tendré como mi única enamorada, desprendiéndome de todas vuestras competidoras para serviros sólo a vos, mi Ana Bolena.'

9 Ibid., p. 52.

10 Terence Hawkes, *Shakespeare in the Present* (London: Routledge, 2002), p. 138.

11 The series depicted the private life of the Spanish Prince, Felipe de Borbón, from the breaking-off of his relationship with the Norwegian model Eva Sannum to his engagement and marriage to the journalist Letizia Ortiz, now the princess of Asturias and the future Spanish queen. Although he has acted in several films, plays and TV shows, Fernando Gil's portrayal of the Spanish prince is arguably his most memorable performance for mainstream Spanish audiences.

12 For example, the piece in *El País* entitled 'The SSWP expects an answer from the king to [public] "discontent and indignation"' (Fernando Garea and Mábel Galaz, 'El PSOE espera una respuesta del rey al "malestar e indignación"', *El País*, 18 April 2012, www.politica.elpais.com/politica/2012/04/17/actualidad/1334662276_599603.html, 29 October 2012), or another that commented on the queen's reaction to the public disclosure of the king's affair, the feature in *La Gaceta* entitled 'The Queen "greatly disappointed" for "reasons that every woman would understand"' (Ana Dávila and Segundo Sanz, 'La Reina, "enormemente enfadada" por "motivos que cualquier mujer comprende"', *La Gaceta*, 18 April 2012, www.intereconomia.com/noticias-gaceta/politica/reina-enormemente-enfadada-por-motivos-que-mujer-comprende-20120417, 29 October 2012).

13 Ewan Fernie. 'Shakespeare and the Prospect of Presentism', *Shakespeare Survey*, 58 (2005): 169.

14 Gordon McMullan, 'Introduction', William Shakespeare and John Fletcher, *Henry VIII* (London: Thomson, Arden Shakespear, 2000), p. 101.

15 Wolf, 'Globe to Globe: *Henry VIII*, Shakespeare's Globe'.

16 Ibid.

17 McMullan, 'Introduction', p. 41.

18 Ibid., pp. 30, 36, 47.

19 Amaranta Wright, 'Spain's Sweet Revenge', *Latino Life*, 28 May 2012, www.latinolife.co.uk/arts-culture/theatre/spains-sweet-revenge, 12 July 2012.

20 Miguel Ayanz, '*Enrique VIII*, una pica en Londres', *La Razón*, 20 May 2012, www.larazon.es/noticia/760-enrique-viii-una-pica-en-londres, 29 October 2012. My emphasis added.

21 Juan Carlos Mas Congost, 'Shakespeare en la cartelera teatral de Madrid y Barcelona, 1960–1992', in González Fdez. de Sevilla, ed., *Shakespeare en España: Crítica, traducciones y representaciones* (University of Alicante, 1993), p. 402.

CHAPTER THIRTY-SEVEN

TOUCH AND TABOO IN ROY-E-SABS' THE COMEDY OF ERRORS

Stephen Purcell

The climax to Afghan company Roy-e-Sabs' The Comedy of Errors gained much of its power through its physical manifestation of reunion. When Parwin Mushtahel's Zan-e Motakef (Emilia) recognized Shah Mamnoon Maqsudi's Ehsan (Egeon) as her husband, their subsequent embrace drew a spontaneous and highly emotional round of applause from the audience at Shakespeare's Globe. It was the first in a series of reunions between estranged family members – brothers, lovers, parents and children – each of which moved the audience to further applause and cheering. Here, the final hand-hold between the two Dromios (here named Bostan) was just one more in a sequence of physical embraces which had involved hugs, clasps, kisses and the cupping of faces. Roy-e-Sabs' Paris-based director, Corinne Jaber, has argued that such reunions carry a particular emotional charge for Afghan audiences, many of whom will themselves have travelled to search for lost relatives after long periods of enforced separation.[1]

The Globe audience presumably included a significant number of Afghan expatriates, since many were clearly following the Dari Persian language. This was an audience willing to express its emotional responses loudly and emphatically: from ironic wolf-whistles at Shah Mamnoon Maqsudi's drag-act Kukeb (Nell), to laughs of delight at the production's inventiveness and gasps at its plot twists. Some of the more excitable reactions came in response to the production's willingness to break Afghan cultural norms: while touching between genders is highly taboo in Afghanistan, the women in The Comedy of Errors touched the male performers frequently, and often in overtly sexual ways. Sodaba/Adriana rubbed her leg against that of Arsalan of Samarqand/Antipholus of Syracuse; Rodaba/Luciana wrestled on the floor with Arsalan of Kabul/Antipholus of Ephesus; all three women embraced their husbands in the final scene.

As I watched this joyfully life-affirming production, I dismissed my worries about the actresses' safety as stemming simply from my own naive and stereotyped

Fig. 20 Antipholus of Ephesus (Shakoor Shamshad (Arsalan of Kabul)) and Dromio of Syracuse (Shah Mohammad (Bostan of Samarqand)), *The Comedy of Errors*, Roy-e-Sabs from Kabul, Afghanistan; director Corinne Jaber.

view of Afghan culture. Afterwards, however, I began to realize that my fears were not as unfounded as I had hoped. Paul Edmondson interviewed two female Afghan audience members after the evening performance, both of whom expressed particular admiration for the actresses: one praised 'the way the women were so free, and they were able to do exactly what they wanted', while the other described herself as 'proud'. The way in which she voiced her pride, however, was couched in anxiety: 'I'm a little bit concerned about their security back in Afghanistan . . . but I'm so proud of their bravery.'[2] Indeed, the most experienced of the three actresses, Parwin Mushtahel, has warned that 'life might be difficult' for her female colleagues following the production, since many Afghans 'simply cannot accept women on the stage, not to mention women who are kissing men'.[3] Mushtahel knows this all too well: her own career in Afghan television and theatre was brutally curtailed when a campaign of physical and verbal abuse against her resulted in the murder of her husband. She fled with her children to Canada.[4]

There is, then, something of an ambiguity to the production's apparently emancipatory politics. Farzana Sayed Ahmad, who played Rodaba and the Courtesan, told *The Times of India* that the project was 'a revolution for women' and described herself as 'happy to be a part of it'.[5] Her co-star Abida Frotan (Sodaba) similarly regards her involvement in the project as 'paving the way for the next generation'.[6] But in the BBC4 documentary *Shakespeare from Kabul*, both actresses are shown struggling during rehearsals with the physical behaviour required of them by the production. The performers discuss their anxieties about touching and embracing, and Ahmad points out that while Jaber 'grew up abroad' and 'has the same freedom as the men have in Afghanistan', Afghan women face different challenges; both she and Frotan anticipate problems when they return home.[7] Jaber herself has discussed the taboo about touching strangers: 'If the women are not okay with it, I do not insist; but then there's a moment we can't do the project together. I think that's really important. I'm not here as an aid worker; I'm not here as a feminist trying to help women.'[8]

Clearly, Jaber's actresses decided to participate in her project in full knowledge of what would be asked of them, even if putting it into practice made them uncomfortable. One wonders, though, whether Jaber can disavow the political and feminist implications of her project quite so easily, especially when they could have such a substantial effect on the lives of her performers.

The Comedy of Errors was an emphatic departure from Roy-e-Sabs' previous Shakespearean work. When Jaber directed *Love's Labour's Lost* in Kabul in 2005, the female members of the cast did not touch the men until the final bows, and even that caused some controversy.[9] But whereas *Love's Labour's Lost* was performed in Afghanistan for domestic audiences, *The Comedy of Errors* was rehearsed and performed abroad.[10] *Love's Labour's Lost* had attempted, at a more optimistic moment in Afghanistan's recent history, to challenge that country's own cultural boundaries: its audiences included a large group of female students from Herat University, for example, who responded positively to the production's gentle defiance of gender taboos.[11] *The Comedy of Errors*, on the other hand, was commissioned for a British festival, and directed with totally different audiences in mind.

The production's opening scenes positioned the audience very much as Western outsiders to the Afghan world depicted. Arsalan and Bostan of Samarqand (Abdul Haq and Shah Mohammad) arrived as European-style tourists, wearing checked shirts and panama hats, and carrying cameras. The world of Kabul was as alien to them as it was to us: an early sequence of physical clowning involved them struggling to get into a *shalwar* as part of their Afghan 'disguise'. The production's scenes of physical flirtation, cross-dressing, drinking and embracing were likewise designed not for a 'home' audience of Afghans, but rather for the British, Indian, German and expatriate Afghan audiences to whom it played on its tour. It was strongly European in its style, and the influence of practitioners like Brook, Mnouchkine and Lecoq was evident.[12] Some of its cast had backgrounds in Western theatre: Abdul Haq studied theatre and puppetry in Berlin, for example, while Shakoor Shamshad (Arsalan of Kabul) is an Afghan expatriate who has lived for ten years in London. In many ways, it was a global production for a global theatre market.

The production's politics are thus highly ambiguous. Read as a challenge to Afghan cultural norms, it is very radical indeed; while Jaber has repeatedly insisted that she is 'not a feminist',[13] her project actively requires its actresses to perform actions which are, from an Afghan perspective, so radically feminist that the performers' safety may be jeopardized. The company's name, Roy-e-Sabs, translates as 'path of hope', and three different cast members have used the term 'revolution' to describe its challenges to traditional Afghan culture.[14] But *The Comedy of Errors* has also been characterized both by its cast and by its principal funder, the British Council, as an attempt to change Afghanistan's international cultural image abroad; actor Shah Mohammad (Bostan of Samarqand) has explained that a key aim is 'to show the world that Afghanistan is not what you think',[15] while Graham Sheffield, the British Council's Director of Arts, described the project as an opportunity to 'open the eyes of the British audience . . . to the rich culture of Afghanistan'.[16] It might therefore be read as an exercise in international rebranding before it is a call for domestic political change.

ENDNOTES

1 Harriet Shawcross, 'Shakespeare in Kabul', *Woman's Hour*, BBC Radio 4, 24 April 2012, www.bbc.co.uk/programmes/b01gg7cl, 17 September 2012.

2 Paul Edmondson, 'Year of Shakespeare: *The Comedy of Errors*', Audience reaction recordings, http://bloggingshakespeare.com/year-of-shakespeare-the-comedy-of-errors, 17 September 2012.

3 Amie Ferris-Rotman, 'Shakespeare Gives Hope to Afghanistan Arts Revival', Reuters, 6 June 2012, www.reuters.com/article/2012/06/06/entertainment-us-afghanistan-shakespeare-idUSBRE8550KR20120606, 17 September 2012.

4 Fuller accounts of Mushtahel's persecution can be found in Stephen Landrigan and Qais Akbar Omar, *Shakespeare in Kabul* (London: Haus Publishing, 2012), pp. 132–4, 227–9, and BBC News, 'Terrifying Plight of Afghan Actress', 25 March 2009, www.news.bbc.co.uk/1/hi/world/south_asia/7940527.stm, 17 September 2012.

5 Kim Arora, 'The Bard Speaketh Dari: Afghan Troupe Performs Shakespeare', *The Times of India*, 24 May 2012, http://timesofindia.indiatimes.com/india/The-Bard-speaketh-Dari-Afghan-troupe-performs-shakespeare/articleshow/13442664. cms, 17 September 2012.

6 Shawcross, 'Shakespeare in Kabul'.

7 Harriet Shawcross, dir., *Shakespeare from Kabul*, BBC HD, 21 July 2012 (broadcast again on BBC 4, 5 August 2012).

8 Shawcross, 'Shakespeare in Kabul'.

9 Interestingly, only two of the *Love's Labour's Lost* cast returned for *The Comedy of Errors* – Parwin Mushtahel (Zan-e Motakef/Emilia) and Shah Mohammad (Bostan of Samarqand/Dromio of Syracuse). Nabi Tanha, who was in *Love's Labour's Lost*, is listed in *The Comedy of Errors'* programme, but dropped out of the project due to 'artistic differences' with Jaber and the rest of the cast (Shawcross, *Shakespeare from Kabul*).

10 Following the bombing of the group's rehearsal space at the British Council in Kabul in August 2011, *The Comedy of Errors* was rehearsed in Bangalore. The show has toured India, Britain and Germany, but, as of February 2012, there were no concrete plans to perform it in Afghanistan itself (Harriet Shawcross and Tahir Qadiry, 'Shakespeare's Afghan Journey to the Globe', BBC News, 27 February 2012, www.bbc.co.uk/news/world-asia-17159224, 17 September 2012).

11 Landrigan and Omar, *Shakespeare in Kabul*, pp. 217–19.

12 See my own account of the performance on the 'Year of Shakespeare' website, which also considers the way in which the production positioned its audiences as 'tourists': Stephen Purcell. 'Year of Shakespeare: *The Comedy of Errors*', 31 May 2012. http://bloggingshakespeare.com/year-of-shakespeare-the-comedy-of-errors, 1 February 2013. Brook and Mnouchkine are both cited repeatedly in Landrigan and Omar, *Shakespeare in Kabul*.

13 Shawcross and Qadiry, 'Shakespeare's Afghan Journey to the Globe'.

14 Pronoti Datta, 'Even the Taliban Have Watched Our Plays', *The Times of India*, 13 May 2012, http://articles.timesofindia.indiatimes.com/2012-05-13/mumbai/31688970_1_kabul-taliban-rehearsal-space, 17 September 2012. See also Arora, 'The Bard Speaketh Dari', and Ferris-Rotman, 'Shakespeare Gives Hope'.

15 Shawcross and Qadiry, 'Shakespeare Afghan Journey to the Globe'.

16 British Council, 'Shakespeare Brings Afghan Culture to the World Stage', press release, 31 May 2012, www.britishcouncil.org/press/shakespeare-brings-afghan-culture-world-stage, 17 September 2012.

CHAPTER THIRTY-EIGHT

SHAKESPEARE AND THE EURO-CRISIS

The Bremer Shakespeare Company's *Timon aus Athen*

Jeannie Farr and Benedict Schofield

Embracing the full performative potential of Shakespeare's Globe, the Bremer Shakespeare Company's (BSC) production of *Timon aus Athen* (*Timon of Athens*) retained an essential spatial fidelity to the Globe, even as their adaptation deviated radically from Shakespeare's text. Although the production remained faithful to the emotions and moral argument of the original, the adaption shook its audience with a litany of contemporary allusions, linking the play directly to the current European financial crisis and German politics: 'Bankrupt bankers, please increase your bonuses. Politicians, give up your positions early, enjoy your severance package or pension. And if you still want to play a role, switch sides to business.'[1] Such moments demonstrate what Dennis Kennedy has called the 'direct access to the power of the plays'[2] paradigmatic of the experimental mode of 'foreign Shakespeare', and also reflect Ton Hoenselaars' argument that translation can '[make] Shakespeare into a contemporary interlocutor capable of addressing the issues that concern us today'.[3] Timon's problems with liquidity directly played on the political frisson generated by the fact that a London audience were watching Germans performing a work about a Greek financial crisis. Yet the direct concerns of that audience were also referenced, when Timon instructed the groundlings to 'burn down the Globe and replace it with a bank', since, 'after all, another bank is exactly what London needs!' Here was a typically Brechtian call to action which contributed to the sharp political tone of the production. Intriguingly, the BSC's version of *Timon* was not the only version playing in London as part of the World Shakespeare Festival to make such contemporary political allusions. The National Theatre's production similarly pursued the theme of financial crisis, albeit in the wholly updated setting of contemporary London with allusions to city sponsors, the Occupy Movement and street people. While the BSC were consistently careful to balance their political asides with a wider allegorical reading of economic shifts in power, the National's production, in comparison, rather lost this allegorical feature of Shakespeare's original, despite its far greater fidelity to the original text.

The BSC's production was broadly epic in staging, employing *gestus* and alienation, and refocusing the drama on a choice between art and commerce. Timon's invitation to the groundlings to steal his gold from the stage found a corollary in the Painter's demand that the audience engage in politics through art. No longer the hypocritical artist of the original who 'counterfeit'st most lively' (5.1.73),[4] the Painter engaged with the audience by doling out paper and pencils to the yard while proclaiming 'In this way, a crisis can also become a productive state.'[5] Apemantus also utilized epic style, taunting Timon by singing the Beatles song 'Yesterday' in English from the balcony. While singing, the actress appeared to 'corpse', i.e. lose her focus and laugh out of character on stage. It became clear that this was intentionally being used to control the audience's own laughter, alienating them both from empathy with Timon and wry laughter at the world – the true cynic's position. Perhaps these elements did feel closer to Brecht than to Shakespeare, yet Brecht himself had been fascinated with *Timon* because of its epic nature, identifying in it, like Marx before him, a critique of an economy based on the commercialization of all objects and relations.[6]

The performance began with a lengthy pre-show, which expressed the company's intense sense of ownership of the space. The edgy relationship this created with the audience sowed the emotional soil for the rest of the performance. Timon entered, moving quickly down stage and greeting the audience as they arrived, transforming the groundlings into the guests for his feast in Act 1. The remaining five performers entered either from the stage or through the yard. They interacted with the entire theatre, using wide, rhetorical gestures, winking at and joking with specific members of the audience, seemingly making no distinction between German and non-German speakers. The pre-show also gave the audience ample opportunity to register various elements of the set, including a large blue trampoline which became a central performance tool and a liminal emotional space during the rest of the production. Timon established his centrality by being the first to jump on the trampoline, setting up a convention of appeals for applause with his increasingly acrobatic leaps. Direct engagement with the audience was established, both emotionally and viscerally, allowing the multilingual groundlings to take pleasure in the non-textual, non-psychological Brechtian performance skills of the actors.

Indeed, the use of the trampoline was pivotal in allowing the audience to engage with the production regardless of their native tongue. At times, the trampoline was a clear space of performative excess: marked out as a place of friendship, fun and liberation for Timon and his guests, as well as a space in which to test physical prowess and skill. At other times, the trampoline became a site of exclusion rather than inclusion. When the military captain Alcibiades entered to be greeted by Timon, the guests drew Timon back to a collective on the trampoline, from where Alcibiades was mocked, prefiguring his later banishment. Yet in the very next scene, after hearing news of Timon's financial problems, Timon himself was hounded onto the trampoline by creditors, who disturbingly hit him with their tailcoats – emblems of their power, as well as, ironically, their indebtedness to Timon. This time, there were no appeals for audience applause. This noisy, heightened piece of stage action was followed by a quiet, intimate scene between Flaminius and Timon during which Flaminius informed Timon of the disastrous state of his affairs. Rejected by his beneficiaries, Timon invited his friends to a second dinner, at which they had to eat by crawling underneath the trampoline. Mirroring the water imagery in Shakespeare's original, Timon then brought out a hose, directed it at his friends and fired – spraying real water, much to the delight of the audience. Protected by the trampoline, the friends did not get wet, and thus the trampoline came to represent symbolically the protection of the rich life that Timon's generosity had enabled them to enjoy. The act ended with wild energy, culminating in the trampoline being overturned – the state it remained in for the rest of the show as Timon's tragedy played itself out in the second half. The shift between these scenes exemplified the skill of this company at moving from an aggressive, alienated emotional positioning to an emotionally engaged one, matching precisely what Wilhelm Hortmann has argued is the BSC's 'recipe for keeping audiences responsive and animated by constantly changing attitude, aspect and emotional temperature'.[7]

The BSC were unique among Festival participants in being the only dedicated Shakespeare company to perform in the season.[8] Well-versed in producing dialogic, non-illusionistic theatre, their version of *Timon* transferred smoothly from its original proscenium theatre to the 'more open'[9] space of the Globe. Rejecting full 'theatrical illusion' in favour of staging that was 'fairly bare ... or non-realistic'[10] also reflected many of the original practices associated with the Globe.[11] It could be argued that the BSC's unique contribution to the Festival was its ability to fuse a twenty-first-century performance aesthetic with an early modern one (see Colour Plate 16).

One of the most striking features of the production was its use of language. The production was in modern German and largely in prose (unlike Shakespeare's original, which is 75 per cent verse).[12] The adaptation by Sebastian Kautz nevertheless delighted in games with register, switching from everyday to coarse language, from the biblical to the militaristic, from the bureaucratic to the poetic. Significantly, though, much of the imagery of the original was intelligently preserved. Cannibalism, fate, the ebb and flow of nature, and above all else the relation of gold to dirt, venereal disease and corruption informed the use of language throughout.[13] Vitally for a production where many of the audience did not speak German, these images were also presented performatively, with Timon vomiting and excreting gold, and, in the final scene, Alcibiades and the Senators gulping down barbecued meat while Timon expired in the foreground as his flesh was consumed metaphorically. This ending reinforced Alcibiades' lines from Act 1, Scene 2, in which he describes his military victims as food to feast on: 'there's no meat like / 'em' (74–5). This image was not simply translated into the German, but radically expanded for a further fifteen lines (without basis in the original), as Alcibiades explained the best marinades and cooking times for human flesh: 'Quickly fry the meat with a dash of olive oil on each side for around two minutes . . . and then cook according to taste: raw, medium, well done.'[14] When Alcibiades began to barbecue at the end of the play – using a functional grill and real meat – we were thus left in no doubt that it was Timon that was now being eaten. Viscerally engaging our sense of smell, the ending offered an alienating contrast between the sensory comfort offered by the aroma of cooked meat and staging that intensified and made explicit some of the darkest imagery of cannibalism in the play.

The production held an intriguing position in the Globe to Globe Festival. The day before, Rakatá had performed *Enrique VIII* (*Henry VIII*), which directly appropriated the play for Spanish national ends by decentring Anne Bullen in favour of Katherine of Aragon. The day after, Compagnie Hypermobile performed a largely faithful version of *Beaucoup de bruit pour rien* (*Much Ado About Nothing*). *Timon* sat somewhere between the appropriation of *Enrique VIII* and the fidelity of *Beaucoup de bruit*: a radically altered, yet in so many ways thematically and linguistically faithful, and performatively revelatory, version of Shakespeare's original.

ENDNOTES

1 'Bankrotte Banker, bitte erhöht euch die Boni. Politiker, legt eure Ämter vorzeitig nieder, genießt eure Abfindung oder Pension. Und wollt Ihr weiter wirken, wechselt in die Wirtschaft': the English in the body of the essay is from Sebastian Kautz's translation of *Timon aus Athen, Spielfassung* (Performance Text dated 11 October 2011), p. 37. All German quotations are taken from this edition, referred to henceforth as *Timon Spielfassung*. The English translations are by the authors of this chapter. We would like to thank Sebastian Kautz for his permission to cite his translation.

2 See Dennis Kennedy ed., *Foreign Shakespeare: Contemporary Performance* (Cambridge University Press, 1993), p. 5.

3 Ton Hoenselaars, 'Introduction', in Ton Hoenselaars, ed., *Shakespeare and the Language of Translation* (London: Arden Shakespeare, 2004), p. 20.

4 William Shakespeare, *Timon of Athens* (London: Arden Shakespeare, 2008). All subsequent references are to this edition.

5 '[s]o kann auch eine Krise ein produktiver Zustand sein', *Timon Spielfassung*, p. 48.

6 On the importance of *Timon* for other German dramatists, see Ina Schabert, ed., *Shakespeare-Handbuch* (Stuttgart: Kröner, 2009), pp. 570–5. For a more detailed overview

of Marx's interest in *Timon*, see Armin Gerd Kukhoff, '*Timon von Athen*: Konzeption und Aufführungspraxis', *Shakespeare-Jahrbuch*, 100–1 (1965): 135–59.

7   Wilhelm Hortmann, *Shakespeare on the German Stage: The Twentieth Century* (Cambridge University Press, 1998), p. 343.

8   For a fuller discussion of the development of the BSC's theatrical engagement with Shakespeare, see Hortmann, *Shakespeare on the German Stage*, pp. 341–9. On the lengthy relationship between Shakespeare's Globe and the BSC, see www.shakespearesglobe.com/about-us/ todays-globe/international/germany, 16 July 2012.

9   A comment by Peter Lüchinger, a member of the BSC company, in an interview undertaken as part of the digital documentation of Globe to Globe. See http://globetoglobe. shakespearesglobe.com/plays/timon-athens/interview, 16 July 2012. None of the BSC actors in this production had previously performed at the Globe, despite the relationship between the two institutions.

10 See the BSC's online manifesto for Shakespeare in performance: www.shakespeare-company.com/en/, 16 July 2012.

11 On original practices see Alan C. Dessen, '"Original Practices" at the Globe: A Theatre Historian's View', in Christie Carson and Farah Karim-Coooper, eds., *Shakespeare's Globe: A Theatrical Experiment* (Cambridge University Press, 2008), pp. 45–54. On original practice in contrast to modern audience engagement, see Christie Carson, 'Democratising the Audience?', ibid., pp. 115–26.

12 For a breakdown of the linguistic medium of Shakespeare's *Timon*, see Jonathan Bate and Eric Rasmussen, eds., *The RSC Shakespeare Complete Works* (Houndmills: Macmillan, 2007), p. 1748.

13 On the significance of these images to the play, see Anthony B. Dawson and Gretchen E. Minton's introduction to their edition of William Shakespeare. *Timon of Athens* (London: Arden Shakespeare, 2008), esp. pp. 71–89.

14 'Das [Fleisch] in einem Schuss Olivenöl von beiden Seiten circa zwei Minuten scharf anbraten . . . und je nach Geschmack garen lassen: raw, medium, well done', *Timon Spielfassung*, p. 19.

CHAPTER THIRTY-NINE

RESTAGING RECEPTION

Translating the *mélange des genres* in Beaucoup de bruit pour rien

David Calder

Compagnie Hypermobile debuted *Beaucoup de bruit pour rien* at the Cartoucherie, a factory-turned-theatre outside Paris. With each production, the Cartoucherie is completely transformed: directors alter seating and build new interior structures to suit their needs. For *Beaucoup de bruit pour rien*, Hypermobile turned the Cartoucherie into a stuffy, vaguely Edwardian Italian restaurant. But when director Clément Poirée brought the production to the Globe, he had to leave the set behind. The new setting became the Globe itself.

Publicity for Hypermobile's Globe performance continued to identify the setting as an Italian restaurant, causing some critical confusion. Hannah August claimed that 'the production's design lacked coherence and the whole thing felt very much as though it had been transported from a proscenium arch theatre to the Globe stage'.[1] Chris Michael writes, 'It's apparently set in the only Italian restaurant on Earth that doesn't bother with such fripperies as food, tables or diners.'[2] Matt Wolf (understandably) did not even register a restaurant setting. He criticizes the 'cumbersome stage business involving the Globe stage being swept clean [by Borachio]';[3] however, in the production's original setting this was not metatheatrical cliché but served to establish atmosphere and clarify Borachio's position in the labour hierarchy. By contrast, Paul Edmondson characterized the lack of set as exemplary of a 'clarity' and 'straightforwardness' that kept the emphasis on the storytelling.[4] I agree that the lack of set did not spoil the performance, but I do not see the unadorned Globe stage as symbolically neutral. On the contrary, the moment the setting of the play shifted to the Globe, Poirée's stylistic choices became a commentary on the history of French Shakespeare. In what follows I analyse Hypermobile's Globe performance not only as a restaging of the Cartoucherie performance, but also as a restaging of Shakespeare's reception in France.

No French translations of Shakespeare existed prior to the mid eighteenth century. These first, partial translations attempted to bend Shakespeare's verse to adhere to the Aristotelian unities, verisimilitude and decorum. In his *Lettres philosophiques* (1734), Voltaire describes Shakespeare as possessing 'a natural genius of force and fecundity with neither the slightest spark of good taste nor the slightest knowledge of formal rules'.[5] This remained the dominant French interpretation of Shakespeare throughout the eighteenth century: a wild genius to be cautiously curtailed. For most of that century Shakespeare remained a literary figure for the French and not a theatrical one. Unlike stage performers, translators could include addenda condemning excessive sex and violence. Pierre-Antoine de la Place became the first French translator to tackle an entire Shakespeare play with *Othello* (1746). La Place situated his translation between the prevailing universalism of art and a cultural relativism tinged with French superiority.[6] The universal perfection of Art belonged to no one nation, and therefore it was acceptable to study the aesthetic achievements of foreign cultures. La Place even cited the material conditions of production as a reason to forgive Shakespeare's baser passages: Shakespeare produced plays for the mixed-class audiences of English theatres and thus had to mix high and low in his work. La Place fit *Othello* as best he could into a French neo-classical tragic structure, with a new scene for every entrance and exit, and alexandrine rhyme for the most important passages. The most sexual or violent scenes he simply summarized. La Place upheld verisimilitude and decorum, but in this he did not differ from English writers then adapting Shakespeare. France's reception was not of Elizabethan/Jacobean Shakespeare, but of an already adapted eighteenth-century version.

Jean-François Ducis became the first to stage a French version of Shakespeare with his 1765 adaptation of *Hamlet*, in which Hamlet kills Claudius off stage, Gertrude takes her own life, and Hamlet and Ophelia survive the play and presumably marry. Ducis' *Othello* (1792) deviated even more wildly from Shakespeare's text: Ducis replaced Iago with Pézare, a mere shadow of Shakespeare's complex villain, and he made Othello a white man 'of a copper complexion' so as not to offend delicate (read: female) spectators with a Moorish hero. Even these drastic changes proved insufficient. Desdemona's fate shocked audiences,[7] so Ducis cut the death mid run, sending in a helpful messenger to stay Othello's hand. In 1822, a troupe of English actors performed an untranslated *Othello* at the Théâtre Porte-Saint-Martin, with disastrous results.[8] Just five years later, another troupe of English actors – this one including William Macready and Harriet Smithson – performed *Othello* at the Odéon and Favart theatres. This production proved a critical and commercial success, playing in France from 1827 to 1828, and it marked a major turning-point for the adoption of Shakespeare by the French Romantics. Hector Berlioz attended, became infatuated with Harriet Smithson as Desdemona and went on to adapt numerous Shakespeare plays.[9] The French Romantics embraced Shakespeare as an individual artistic genius exemplary of Romantic ideals.

Alfred de Vigny translated *Othello* into French verse for a production that opened 24 October 1829 at the Comédie Française. Contrary to Vigny's subsequent accounts, his *Othello* was not a riotous attack on neo-classical sensibilities. In the nineteenth century as in the eighteenth, adaptations of Shakespeare continued to expurgate the plays' more shocking elements. Vigny's *Othello* left out nearly all of Iago's sexual puns. Berlioz's opera adaptation of *Much Ado About Nothing* eliminated the Hero–Claudio fidelity plot. Vigny purged *Othello* of its comedy, and Berlioz purged *Much Ado About Nothing* of its tragedy. Such production choices undermined the rationale behind the Romantics' adoption of Shakespeare – namely, Shakespeare's fusion of tragedy and comedy in the form of the drama.

In his preface to *Cromwell*, the manifesto of French Romanticism, Victor Hugo praises Shakespeare's synthesis of tragedy and comedy. With the advent of Christianity, Hugo argues, humankind recognizes its double nature as both spirit and flesh. In doing so, the individual turns inward on him- or herself and feels pity for all humankind. Hugo describes this modern affliction as melancholy. Paired with melancholy is the form of the drama. Via the *mélange des genres* (mixture of genres), drama represents reality's harmony of opposites. The Romantics were not attempting to overthrow art's mimetic relationship to the real; they simply argue that one cannot accurately represent reality without representing the ugly alongside the beautiful. For Hugo, 'Shakespeare is the drama, and the drama, which utters in one breath the grotesque and the sublime, the terrible and the clown, tragedy and comedy, the drama is the character proper to the third epoch of poetry.'[10] But even the Romantic Vigny censored the ribald punning that made Iago grotesque. Published texts, not embodied stagings, remained the safer spaces in which to explore Shakespeare's Romanticism.

I have focused on the reception of Shakespeare in the eighteenth and nineteenth centuries because I see in Hypermobile's *Beaucoup de bruit pour rien* a restaging of many of the same concerns, namely the mixture of tragic and comic elements – the *mélange des genres* – and the prevalence of melancholy. And I have focused up to now on *Othello* because, first, that play was easily the most famous of Shakespeare's plays during the initial hundred years of their reception in France and because, second, *Much Ado*, with its false accusations of a woman's infidelity, is *Othello*'s comic double. I turn now to those moments of Hypermobile's Globe performance intelligible within the history of French Shakespeare.

The French *mélange des genres* encompasses both genre- and gender-mixing, both of which were on display in Hypermobile's production. Beatrice began the play dressed in tweed pants, waistcoat and tie, and she regularly carried a pipe. Benedick wore a Spanish matador's jacket and an eye-searing purple kilt. Once both had privately acknowledged their love, Beatrice donned a dress and Benedick put on trousers. But the costume design undermined its own apparent restoration of

Fig. 21 Benedick (Bruno Blairet), *Much Ado About Nothing*, Compagnie Hypermobile, from Paris, France; director Clément Poirée.

gender norms. Beatrice's unstructured dress hid the figure that the tweed pants had accentuated. As for Benedick, his trousers were cut from the same loud plaid, and his transformation north of the neck – from wild hair and goatee to slick coiffure and neat moustache – made him the spitting image of Marcel Proust, arguably France's most famous closet homosexual. This distinctly French sight gag added another layer of comedy to Benedick's realization of his own desire and his reluctant 'coming out'. It also retroactively cast doubt on why, exactly, Benedick would be so invested in preserving his company of bachelors, including the oddly camp Claudio. Most importantly, it visually situated Benedick within a lineage of French melancholics plagued by inexpressible desire.

Benedick's gestural vocabulary reinforced his double nature. Even as he insulted Beatrice and the institution of marriage, he adopted an exaggerated courtship stance – weight on the left foot, right leg extended to present the calf muscle – that appears frequently in stagings of Molière or Corneille. In perfect Romantic fashion, Benedick's body and mind were at odds, which actor Bruno Blairet played to great comic effect. Beatrice experiences a similar phenomenon in a more tragic vein. When, after Claudio spurned Hero, actress Alix Poisson delivered the French equivalent of the line, 'Oh God, that I were a man! I would eat his heart / In the market-place' (4.1.294–5), she seemed to bitterly regret not her biological sex so much as her chosen costume change, as if by confessing her love for Benedick she had lost a part of herself and the power that came with it. In this production, tragedy and comedy both derived from such acts of doubling and splitting, and every comic doubling had its tragic counterpart.

This production's most hilarious piece of stage business also managed, intentionally or otherwise, to bind itself to *Much Ado*'s tragic cousin *Othello*. When Borachio explained his plan to deceive Claudio, he demonstrated how he would have sex with Marguerite by performing numerous unspeakable acts on a handkerchief. Every review of the Globe performance singled out this scene as comic genius. But the handkerchief stood in for Marguerite (who later stood in for Hero) just as the character of Marguerite/Margaret is the structural equivalent of Desdemona's handkerchief: both are objects (and this sexual economy certainly reduces Marguerite to an object) that offer supposed proof of a woman's infidelity. Claudio/Othello discovers Marguerite/handkerchief and judges Hero/Desdemona. Marguerite recognized her place in this economy as she wistfully set up the chairs for Hero's wedding. At that wedding, Claudio shamed Hero by mistaking her for Marguerite. Everyone rushed to defend or condemn Hero, leaving Marguerite alone, stage right, to ponder her worth.

If nineteenth-century English troupes brought to France a tragedy laced with ribald jokes, Hypermobile returned to England a comedy weighed down by melancholy. In his interview with the Globe, Poirée cited the play's melancholic undertones as his primary interest. Love, Poirée explains, is 'nothing',[11] a fabrication, a facilitated lie that we collectively accept as truth, not unlike the performers and spectators of theatre. In Poirée's production, the dual nature of reality is not the sublime and the grotesque, but reality itself and its image. These terms are not balanced; just as deceit produces Beatrice and Benedick's love, so illusion creates reality. A representation of reality thus becomes a representation of an image, of a mask, of nothing.

The directorial and acting choices described above were of course present at the Cartoucherie. But the change in location – heightened by the lack of additional set – made each choice an act of translation. At the Globe, Hypermobile did not perform a twenty-first-century adaptation of sixteenth-century Shakespeare, but a restaging of a history of transmission and exchange. Elements that, centuries earlier, French critics dismissed as suitable only for the English – particularly genre-mixing – were translated and re-presented to a mixed French and British audience in a distinctly French physical, visual and verbal language.

ENDNOTES

1 Hannah August, 'Globe to Globe Week 6: *Much Ado About Nothing*', *Stet: An Online Postgraduate Research Journal*, 4 June 2012, www.stetjournal.org/blogs/tag/compagnie-hypermobile/, 17 October 2012.

2 Chris Michael, '*Much Ado About Nothing* – Review', *Guardian*, 5 June 2012, www.guardian.co.uk/stage/2012/jun/05/much-ado-about-nothing-french/newsfeed=true, 17 October 2012.

3 Matt Wolf, 'Globe to Globe: *Much Ado About Nothing*, Shakespeare's Globe', *The Arts Desk*, 3 June 2012, www.theartsdesk.com/theatre/globe-globe-much-ado-about-nothing-shakespeares-globe, 17 October 2012.

4 Paul Edmondson, 'Year of Shakespeare: *Much Ado About Nothing*', 2 June 2012, http://bloggingshakespeare.com/year-of-shakespeare-much-ado-about-nothing, 17 October 2012.

5 Voltaire, 'Letter XVIII: On Tragedy', *Letters on the English, or Lettres philosophiques*, www.fordham.edu/halsall/mod/1778voltaire-lettres.asp#Letter%20XVIII, 17 October 2012.

6 See Christian Biet, '*Le Théâtre Anglois d'Antoine de la Place (1746–1749), ou la difficile émergence du théâtre de Shakespeare en France*', in P. Dorval and J.-M. Maguin, eds., *Shakespeare et la France: Actes du colloque* (Paris: Société Française Shakespeare, 2000), pp. 29–50.

7 Plenty of female characters die in French neo-classical tragedy, but these deaths always serve a 'higher' purpose (e.g. family honour).

8 Accounts differ as to why: some claim that, once again, Desdemona's death proved too much for French audiences; others point to hatred of the English left over from the 1815 defeat of Napoleon at Waterloo. Stirling Haig claims that someone in the audience cried, 'Down with Shakespeare, Wellington's aide-de-camp', though this remains unsupported (see Haig's 'Vigny and *Othello*', *Yale French Studies*, 33 (1964): 53). All agree that spectators pelted the performers with apples and eggs.

9 Berlioz composed a *King Lear* overture (1831), a *Romeo and Juliet* symphony (1839), a *Funeral March for the Last Scene of Hamlet* (1848), a song 'The Death of Ophelia' (1848), a musical drama *The Trojans* (1858) based on *Troilus and Cressida*, and the comic opera *Beatrice and Benedick* (1862) based on *Much Ado About Nothing*.

10 Victor Hugo, *Preface du Cromwell* (Oxford: Clarendon Press, 1909), pp. 19–20.

11 Clément Poirée, interview with Globe Theatre Education Department, London, May 2012, http://globetoglobe.shakespearesglobe.com/plays/much-ado-about-nothing/interview, 17 October 2012.

CHAPTER FORTY

REVIVING HAMLET? NEKROŠIUS'
LITHUANIAN 'CLASSIC'

Ann Thompson

Three days before I saw this Lithuanian production of *Hamlet* at the Globe to Globe Festival, I saw the *Comedy of Errors* from Afghanistan, which I thought was excellent, but I heard a woman in the audience say loudly to her companion, 'Of course this isn't Shakespeare: they've turned it into a farce.' Unfortunately, her words could have been applied, and more appropriately, to *Hamlet*. The publicity assured us that the director, Eimuntas Nekrošius, and the production were 'legendary' and that this *Hamlet* had toured the world to great acclaim since it was first performed in 1997, becoming 'one of the most celebrated Shakespearean productions of our age'.[1] It was, frankly, hard to see why, and I don't think it was just the cold, rainy circumstances of the Sunday evening performance.

In the world of opera we are accustomed in the UK to seeing revivals of very old productions with new casts, but not in the world of theatre. It seems, however, to have been common in the former Soviet Union and Eastern Europe to keep productions in the repertory for many years, and this is not always a bad thing. Yuri Lyubimov's *Hamlet*, for example, first performed at the Taganka Theatre in Moscow in 1971, was successfully revived at the Leicester Haymarket Theatre in 1989, and its politics still seemed relevant. Several of the productions in the Festival were 'vintage' productions of this kind, while others were newly commissioned. This gave London audiences the chance to see productions that have become 'classics' in their own countries, as well as to see how actors and directors are re-creating Shakespeare today. Experiencing the show with the diverse audiences has been one of the great pleasures of the Festival: even when the production has been less than brilliant, there has been a palpable sense of warmth and pride: 'This is our language; these are our actors; this is our Shakespeare.'

Having edited *Hamlet* for the Arden Shakespeare series (2006), I've seen a large number of productions of the play, including many in foreign languages, and I don't think I have particularly conservative or 'academic' views about it. One of my

Fig. 22 Hamlet (Andrius Mamontovas) and Margarita Žiemelytè, Algirdas Dainavičius and Vaidas Vilius as the players, *Hamlet*, Meno Fortas from Vilnius, Lithuania; director Eimuntas Nekrošius.

favourite productions in recent years was in fact the *Kupenga Kwa Hamlet*, a two-man version of the First Quarto, performed by the Zimbabwean theatre company called Two Gents (who appropriately, and delightfully, offered *Two Gentlemen of Verona* to this season). It was fresh, imaginative, funny and moving. The Lithuanian *Hamlet* had none of these qualities. It was the only production out of eight I saw in this Festival that failed to hold the attention of the audience. The actors behaved as if they were in a proscenium arch theatre and did not even try to make use of the unique relationship to the audience available at the Globe; they seemed to me hysterical and declamatory. Their production took a kaleidoscopic approach to the play: throw all the pieces up in the air and let them fall how they will. Props seemed arbitrary and self-indulgent: enormous glass goblets (admittedly quite striking), a block of ice, an outsized pipe for Ophelia to smoke. The rationale for any of this was unclear.

The general recipe seems to have been, 'Given a detail in Shakespeare's *Hamlet*, Nekrošius' *Hamlet* will duly "subvert" it.' The Nekrošius version thus becomes a travesty of its original, in the sense of 'travesty' which goes back to Scarron's *Le Vergile Travesty en vers burlesques* (1648).[2] But while the 'grotesque or debased imitation' aspect of the travesty is intended to incite laughter (as do, in our more current vocabulary, *Hamlet* parodies, of which there have been many), Nekrošius is not looking for, or even tolerating, laughter. The Great Director is too superior to his material for him to have his own work laughed at. A leading feature of the production is its immense, though strangely cheerless, self-satisfaction.

Floating around, given the use of fur, is some sort of reference to shamanism, and possibly to the early works of Joseph Beuys (who had earned their use). Less clear is where the repertoire of physical movement comes from, notably the arbitrary stamping and jumping. Movement in general is made very ugly, of course deliberately so. One notable exception to the 'Distort, distort!' aesthetic is the music, which in its sombre, mournful way would grace a better production. Needless to say, *Hamlet* as a mourning play is antithetical to Nekrošius' vision. Indeed, the villain of the play turns out to be Hamlet's father, who hurtles around throughout the action and ends it with a great, very theatrical, howl of anguish: it is *he* who has destroyed his son. Unfortunately, you can't pull a Big Heartrending Howl out of a hat if you've systematically drained the play of emotion earlier.

John Morrison, in his splendid and brief blog entry on the production, puts it in the context of Eastern European theatre pre-1989.

I was watching a theatrical fossil. Productions that stay in the repertoire for decades are an East European specialty; when I lived in Moscow the theatres were full of them. They're a leftover from Soviet days, when it was such an enormous struggle to get anything past the censors that it was always easier to keep reviving existing works rather than to try anything new.[3]

He concludes his assessment, in my view correctly, 'Too old and long in the tooth, this pretentious show has lost any vestige of freshness. The actors' eyes are completely dead and at no point do they even attempt to open a channel to the audience.' Morrison left after twenty-five minutes; I dutifully held on to the end. As Morrison says, it is a shame that the wonderful Globe international season ended with so dire an offering, but, 'Ah well, you can't win them all.'

To be fair, I should report that the production was received rapturously by the audience. Presumably Nekrošius has succeeded in imposing himself as, to borrow the Japanese term, a Living National Treasure.

ENDNOTES

1 'Hamlet: Meno Fortas', Shakespeare's Globe London (2012), http://globetoglobe. shakespearesglobe.com/plays/hamlet/english-45, 26 October 2012.

2 'travesty, adj. and n.', OED Online, September 2012, Oxford University Press, www.oed.com/ view/Entry/205300/isAdvanced=true&result=1&rskey=yXApFi&, 10 October 2012.

3 John Morrison, 'Globe To Globe: Hamlet (Meno Fortas)', 2 June 2012, www.blackpig. typepad.com/john_morrison/2012/06/index.html, 10 October 2012.

AFTERWORDS

'FROM THENCE TO ENGLAND'

Henry V at Shakespeare's Globe

Abigail Rokison

As the play with which to open the Globe season in the summer of the Queen's Jubilee and the London Olympic Games, *Henry V*, generally perceived as Shakespeare's most nationalistic play, might seem an ideal choice. As Alice Jones wrote in the *Independent*, 'it's not hard to see why the play, centred on the English triumph over the French at Agincourt, with its patriotism, "band of brothers" underdog spirit and even a romance with a beautiful Princess Catherine has captured the imagination in 2012',[1] a year which also saw prominent productions of the play on BBC television (directed by Thea Sharrock) and on stage by Edward Hall's all-male company, Propeller. As the play with which to close the Globe to Globe Festival – a celebration of Shakespeare performed by different cultures and in different languages – the choice seemed slightly more suspect. The play presents its non-English characters as culturally and linguistically inferior, and Dominic Dromgoole's production did little to play down this mockery, with an idiotic, if charming, Fluellen and an incomprehensible Scottish Captain Jamy, while the English pronunciation of Alice in particular was hyperbolically absurd, clearly designed to elicit laughter from the audience.

So why did Dromgoole choose this play at this particular time? The answer to the question is by no means straightforward, and, indeed, neither was Dromgoole's take on the play, which swung between the poles of nationalism and scepticism.

On the one hand the production's exaggerated ridiculing of the non-English characters, and its cutting of the final chorus to finish the play on a note of triumph rather than impending doom, removing references to Henry's 'small' reign and England's subsequent descent into civil war, seemed to play up the play's potential patriotism. On the other hand, the production showed an acute awareness of the ambiguity inherent in the chorus' invocation of Henry's heroic actions – its status as what Gwilym Jones terms 'an unreliable narrator' conveniently missing out

1 *Henry VI* 4.1.1936.

elements which 'puncture Henry's chivalric narrative'[2] – and a somewhat sceptical approach to a reading of the play as 'a blunt straightforward Englishman's paean to English glory',[3] particularly evident in the nuanced, sensitive performance of Jamie Parker as Henry. In spite of the apparent surge of nationalistic feeling which surrounded the summer of 2012, the production reflected the fact that it was, and perhaps still is, difficult to be unreservedly proud, male and English.

In many of these respects Edward Hall's Propeller production might be seen to contrast with Dromgoole's Globe offering. As an all-male company comprised mostly of young men, Propeller's members seem to revel in a certain laddish-ness, their productions unabashedly testosterone-fuelled and boisterous. Unlike Parker's Henry, Dugald Bruce-Lockhart, in the title role, displayed little sense of vulnerability or uncertainty in his quest against the French, clearly at home on the field of battle and leading his soldiers with confidence. While Dromgoole's depiction of the eve of Agincourt undermined the chorus' assertions about Henry '[w]alking from watch to watch from tent to tent' (4.0.30) and greeting his men, the king conspicuous in his absence from the scene, Bruce-Lockhart's Henry was seen bounding from one group of soldiers to the next, vigorously shaking hands and slapping backs.

By contrast, although Hall's production may have been less sceptical than Drom-goole's about Henry's status as an heroic leader, its attitude to the final victory was far more ambiguous. Far from removing the final chorus speech to finish the play on Henry's triumph, Hall used its sentiments as the basis of the framing device of his production – a chorus of soldiers now under the reign of Henry VI (albeit in modern-day fatigues) telling the story of the glory of a previous era which was all too transient – a feeling of pride and victory which soon descended into civil war. As Sarah Hemming notes, with the 'group of squaddies' presenting the play – assuming roles as they assumed pieces of costume – the focus was firmly on 'the importance of the common soldier', with the play's staging reinforcing 'the endur-ing concerns of Shakespeare's play'.[4]

With even Bruce-Lockhart's Henry initially part of this 'band of brothers' before donning the crown, Propeller's production had (as does most of their work) a true sense of ensemble playing. As Rachel Halliburton comments, often Henry V 'has helped to confirm the status of the title performer, but here the emphasis is on blokeish collaboration', perhaps appropriate in a political climate in which 'people are more likely to sympathise with soldiers than their leaders'.[5] Although less obvi-ously an ensemble piece than Propeller's, Dromgoole's production showed a similar lack of concern with star casting, Parker being relatively young and inexperienced to take on the play's title role. In this respect, in particular, Dromgoole's production was notably different from the last production of the play at Shakespeare's Globe – Richard Olivier's production with Mark Rylance as Henry V – which opened the

Fig. 23 Princess Katherine (Olivia Ross) and Henry V (Jamie Parker), *Henry V*, Shakespeare's Globe from London, England; director Dominic Dromgoole.

theatre's first season in 1997. This choice of opening play may have been largely motivated by theories that *Henry V* was the first of Shakespeare's plays to have been performed at the original Globe Theatre in 1599;[6] however, its story of a charismatic ruler leading his people to victory might also have seemed an appropriate one for Rylance to begin his own reign with.

Indeed, one might assert that in each of these three productions – Olivier's, Hall's and Dromgoole's – we glimpsed not only the spirit of the times but of the company itself, actor-led, ensemble-led and director-led. While Rylance's casting was reminiscent of that of Laurence Olivier and Kenneth Branagh, both of whom chose the play for their first ventures as leading actors in their own films, Propeller seemed more concerned with the story of Henry as a shared legend, and Dromgoole with the overall shape of the Globe's repertoire. Jamie Parker's performance was highly accomplished, but the production as a whole was less about the leading actor than about exploring the continuity and discontinuity between the character of Hal as played by Parker in Dromgoole's 2010 production of 1 and 2 *Henry IV*, and that of King Henry in *Henry V*. It also fit neatly into the Globe's ongoing repertoire, which was to see productions of all three parts of *Henry VI* in 2013.

Dromgoole's production, was, of course, most notably distinguished from those of Hall and Olivier in its casting of women in the female roles (and, in the case of Olivia Ross as the Boy, in a male role). Unlike in Hall's and Olivier's productions, where the chorus' lines were divided among the cast of male actors, in

Dromgoole's production the role of the chorus was also, unusually, taken by a woman – Brid Brennan – who, rather than declaiming the lines, as is so often the case in productions of the play, evoked place and time with intimate clarity. Having a woman in this authoritative role again helped to temper the sense of machismo in the play, particularly when, for example, the chorus commented ironically, 'Now all the youth of England are on fire' (2.0.1), while Nym made crude hand gestures in the direction of Pistol and Mistress Quickly.

Although the reviews of the production noted, for the most part, Dromgoole's ambiguous stance on the play's patriotism, almost all focused on the perceived appropriateness of 'Shakespeare's most stirring history play',[7] a 'celebration of our country, our way of life and our willingness to defend it',[8] to the English 'summer of national celebration'.[9] Tim Walker commented on the timing 'to perfection' of the production at a point in England's history at which there was a 'renewed sense of nationhood that the Diamond Jubilee celebrations engendered',[10] and Paul Taylor described it as 'stirringly inaugurat[ing] the Globe's own season ... in a year when, with the Jubilee and the Olympics, there's a perceived duty to fly the flag (even ironically) for England'.[11] However ironic elements of the flag-flying in England for the Jubilee and Olympics may have been, there can be no doubting the pervading sense of nationalistic fervour and its influence on the moods of audiences and reviewers, many of whom, in spite of Parker's portrait of the king as a rather tentative leader of men, seemed moved to follow him into his dubious quest for victory over the French – 'you see how a call to arms can work like a charm';[12] 'I swear that if this Henry had strode off the stage and out of the theatre at the end, everyone would have followed him';[13] 'you feel the entire theatre would rise up to march behind him'.[14] As if anticipating such an audience response, Dromgoole's production had Parker turn to the groundlings to complete his rallying cry to war – 'Cry God for Harry. . . . ' Invariably they did – though with a characteristically English dose of embarrassment.[15]

ENDNOTES

1 Alice Jones, 'We Happy Two: Jamie Parker and Tom Hiddleston Tackle Shakespeare's Henry V', *Independent*, 19 July 2012, www.independent.co.uk/arts-entertainment/theatre-dance/features/we-happy-two-jamie-parker-and-tom-hiddleston-tackle-shakespeares-henry-v-7956970.html, 10 February 2013.

2 Gwilym Jones, 'Piece out His – or Her – Imperfections', *Around the Globe*, 51 (summer 2012): 12.

3 Gary Taylor, ed., *Henry V* (Oxford University Press, 1998), p. 1.

4 Sarah Hemming, '*Henry V/The Winter's Tale*, Hampstead Theatre, London', *The Financial Times*, 9 Jul, 2012, www.ft.com/cms/s/2/8a4dea0e-c9af-11e1-a5e2-00144feabdc0.html#axzz2KaEomsff, 10 February 2013.

5 Rachel Halliburton, 'Henry V', *Time Out*, 10 July 2012, www.timeout.com/london/theatre/henry-v-4.

6 Andrew Gurr states that *Henry V* 'has a good claim to be the first play definitely written for the Globe': see Andrew Gurr, ed., *Henry V* (Cambridge University Press, 1992), p. 6.

7 Dominic Cavendish, '*Henry V*, Shakespeare's Globe – Review', *Telegraph*, 14 June 2012, www.telegraph.co.uk/culture/theatre/theatre-reviews/9329868/Henry-V-Shakespeares-Globe-review.html, 10 February 2013.

8 Tim Walker, '*Henry V* at Shakespeare's Globe – *Seven Magazine* Review', *Sunday Telegraph*, 20 June 2012, www.telegraph.co.uk/culture/theatre/theatre-reviews/9344141/Henry-V-at-Shakespeares-Globe-Seven-magazine-review.html, 10 February 2013.

9 Fiona Mountford, '*Henry V*, Globe – Review', *Evening Standard*, 14 June 2012, www.standard.co.uk/arts/theatre/henry-v-globe–review-7850779.html, 10 February 2013.

10 Walker, '*Henry V* at Shakespeare's Globe'.

11 Paul Taylor, '*Henry V*, Shakespeare's Globe, London', *Independent*, 15 June 2012, www.independent.co.uk/arts-entertainment/theatre-dance/reviews/henry-v-shakespeares-globe-london-7854958.html, 10 February 2013.

12 Cavendish, '*Henry V*, Shakespeare's Globe'.

13 Lyn Gardner, '*Henry V* – Review', *Guardian*, 14 June 2012 www.guardian.co.uk/stage/2012/jun/14/henry-v-review, 10 February 2013.

14 Taylor, '*Henry V*, Shakespeare's Globe, London'.

15 Zoe Craig reports that on the first night, 'When our lovely leader cries "God for Harry, England, and Saint George!" some audience members around us, straining forward on the very edges of their seats, even joined in. Then looked nervously at their neighbours – we were s'posed to shout back, weren't we?' See Zoe Craig, 'Theatre Review: *Henry V* at Shakespeare's Globe', *Londonist*, 14 June 2012, http://londonist.com/2012/06/theatre-review-henry-v-at-shakespeares-globe.php, 10 February 2013.

DECENTRING SHAKESPEARE

A hope for future connections

Bridget Escolme

The production at the Globe to Globe Festival that delighted me most was Arpana Theatre's revision of *All's Well That Ends Well*. Peter Kirwan, reviewing it in Chapter 30 of this volume, rightly suggests that it solved the 'problem' that this play remains for many scholars and newspaper critics. It produced *All's Well* as a comedy, and the audience was clearly expected wholeheartedly to invest in its closure. This *All's Well* offered a resolution of recognition and realization – not in the literal sense of disguises uncovered or twins reunited – but in the emotional homecoming of Bharatram/Bertram to Heli/Helena once he has learned that the values of dedication, resourcefulness and familiar friendship ultimately outweigh that of social status, economic gain and novelty. I was particularly interested in how the Bhangwadi form of popular theatre – one that emerged from the entertainment needs of daily wage labourers in late nineteenth-century Mumbai and which was still being performed there in the 1970s – had been used to open up the source text to its mixed Gujarati- and English-speaking audiences at the Globe. It is a form that uses dance, song and direct-address storytelling to engage its audiences, to invite them into the play of recognition upon which the denouement turns. The form assumes that the audience share the hopes and fears of the figures on stage, particularly Heli, who gets some of the best songs; as we (and a 'we' is, I think, generated by this production) accept each song and dance turn for the glorious entertainment that it is, as we meet each of Heli's hopeful or desperate gazes out into the yard, the closure that we know is coming becomes entirely unproblematic. We want this girl to get what she wants. We know Bharahtram is right to decide that he wants her after all. Bhangwadi seemed, then, like a perfect form through which to revise a Shakespearean comedy.

Having seen the production I had many questions about this apparently rich and engaging form. Were its narratives varied or formulaic? Was it celebratory, pacifying entertainment for those Mumbai daily wage labourers, or could it be used to subvert or satirize? Were its heroines resourceful like Heli/Helena; did they push at the limits of gendered convention? But it is relatively difficult to find anything out about Bhangwadi theatre. Today's familiar quick-search internet and journal database resources uncover passing comments on the form and the now-demolished Bhangwadi theatre building, but little by way of detailed history or cultural analysis. A British Library search comes up with 'Did you mean "Bhangra"?' Of course there are other resources; director of *All's Well* Sunil Shanbag, who performed himself in a Bhangwadi piece during the 1970s, is proving an invaluable and generous human resource as I try to find out more. But I am disconcerted by the form's invisibility in places where an audience member who had seen *All's Well* at the Festival, and was intrigued to find more, might go to look. Of course, it goes without saying that there is plenty about Shakespeare in these places. On the first page of Google entries for 'Bhangwadi' and 'theatre' there are three mentions of him: because of Arpana's production. The British used him as a colonial tool, and now he colonizes the internet. My hope is that the Globe to Globe Festival could paradoxically be the beginning of a decentring of Shakespeare in global knowledge production. What questions might this Festival continue to provoke that aren't about Shakespeare? And how might theatres and universities start to explore and answer them?

ICONOGRAPHIES OF PASTNESS

How do theatrical cultures reproduce – or indeed produce – the past on stage? What are the theatrical sign systems that indicate 'pastness' in different cultural traditions? What versions of the past are produced in the theatre, and what ideological and emotional relationships are audiences being invited to have with them? I found myself fascinated by my own lack of knowledge, not only everywhere I listened at the Festival (I saw many productions in languages of which I could not recognize a sound) but everywhere I looked. I did not know, for example, whether a native speaker of Mandarin, watching the National Theatre of China's *Richard III*, would have regarded the highly stylized performance adopted by Lady Anne, as Richard interrupts the mourning of her father-in-law, as a living tradition, still recognizable as mourning to a modern Chinese theatre-goer, or whether Anne's performance would have been considered distant and archaic. And what do I mean by a 'living tradition'? The phrase suggests a nostalgic valuing of the past-in-the-present which I certainly think permeates British culture; I have far less knowledge about the ideological work that the past does in Chinese art and history, or in the art produced within a political system that has so carefully policed the stories of its own cultural origins. I could only guess at the origins of the strong sense of community produced by the National Theatre Belgrade, as the actors pushed the curved brass structures of their 1 *Henry VI* about the Globe stage to make barricades and castles, and hiding and meeting places. I read the relative silence of the mainly Serbian audience at what I found to be an absolutely hilarious rendition of Mortimer's succession speech (2.5.61–92), mimed by the two figures that mainly played messengers and working people, in the light of Serbia's recent history. I stifled my laughter in the face of what I assumed to be the sensitivities of a people who knew only too well how a civil war begins. But this was not, unlike Ashtar's Palestinian *Richard II*, a modern-dress version of a history play. Costumes were a version of medieval, and I know little of how a Serbian might describe the wars of his or her country's distant centuries: within an iconography of past glories or shames that can be connected to present questions about Serb nationalism? Or as something quite distinct from the recent conflict? Are there any Serbian dramas about medieval or early modern wars? The Globe to Globe Festival has provoked some questions its audiences might not otherwise have thought to ask about history and its uses.

BEYOND REALISM

What kind of staging and acting conventions produce emotion and affect in the theatre? British theatre, in much of its Shakespeare production, tends to answer: realism. To feel in the theatre is to feel empathy with a plausibly rounded, psychologically drawn 'character'. It is not that the traditions of realist drama do not produce some brilliant theatre in this country. But they render a play like *All's Well* a 'problem' because they struggle to make Helena's love for Bertram plausible and struggle even more with Bertram's conversion to Helena. The Arpana production shifted between theatrical traditions, as Bharatram played the realist role of a young Indian man seeking his fortune in colonial India and Heli played the less 'realistic' one of a young Indian woman leaving the safety of her home to roam the country to cure patriarchs and stage-manage bed tricks. The National Theatre recently acknowledged the folkloric nature of Helena's narrative in *All's Well* with the scenography of fairy tale (Helena went off on her travels in a red riding hood and performed the bed trick as Dick Whittington's cat). But the attractive fairy-tale motifs seemed to me to undermine the emotional stakes of the play, whilst a Bhangwadi Helena can perform empathetic emotion through song, dance and direct address. Grupo Galpão's Brazilian Portuguese *Romeo and Juliet* produced idealized lovers teetering prettily on stilts, their fragile and literally precarious performances always foregrounding their fate. Even the, to me, wearying jokes about the Nurse's sagging fabric breasts and the helplessly staring wooden women, like the figureheads of ships, with whom Mercutio and company dance at the Capulets' party, posed interesting questions about what meanings may be generated if we stage the gender constructions of the past without attention to modern political sensibilities. What does loving a woman mean in a world where men figure women as Mercutio does? The huge variety of non-realist form offered by the Globe to Globe productions, so highly appropriate to this consciously theatrical, presentational space, allowed politics and emotion, and the politics of emotion, onto the stage in ways that are rarely seen in Shakespeare production here, despite assumptions that his are the most politically astute and emotionally heightened plays in our theatre history.

NOT SHAKESPEARE?

Shakespeare's use in the ex-Eastern bloc as an allegorical means of critiquing power and political corruption is well documented. Much was made in the press of the fact that the Belarus Free Theatre were not permitted to perform their *King Lear* at home and had to rehearse in secret. Vakhtangov Theatre's Russian *Measure for Measure* had the Duke doubling as Angelo, with the Duke figure performing the same relentless and violent sexual pursuit of a frail Isabella as Angelo; and Teatr im. Kochanowskiego's Polish *Macbeth* portrayed all men in power, including the source's good King Duncan, as grotesque drunks, and staged a rape of Lady Macduff. These productions gave rise, among my own peer group, to accusations that they unquestioningly staged women as both victims and objects of consumption. I sympathized with those views. But the productions were daring in the clarity of their use of 400-year-old plays to make explicit critiques of current power and patriarchy – as was the Palestinian *Richard II*, where Richard's favourites were not fashionable young men but ageing politicos – clearly the favourites of failed regime after failed regime. We are certainly used to seeing our early modern dramas in our own contemporary clothing here. But how daring are our allegories? How genuinely disturbing are the moments of political violence we stage? Perhaps if Russia, Poland and Palestine are so well able to explore their own cultural and political moments through 400-year-old English drama, we should be looking to sources and theatrical forms outside our own theatre history to produce the history plays of today, as well as at the ways in which a Shakespeare beyond English might re-teach us Shakespeare.

I hope that the relationships forged between Shakespeare's Globe and the companies who performed in this Festival continue to develop. I would like to think that larger and larger audiences might be given the opportunity to see some of the work documented and explored in this volume – and wonder about where it came from. In the summer of 2012 I was provoked to ask again and again: what theatrical and cultural histories generated this work? Does it produce the past in similar or analogous ways to the way the British Shakespeare industry does? Or is the past quite a different country to each theatrical culture? How do other theatres use their own past to critique their present? I would like to think that these questions might become so interesting that they could be in danger of decentring Shakespeare and rendering more precarious our certainties about his significance. I would like to think that more and more theatre-goers would look to find out about theatrical cultures that are new to them and, in their frustration at finding nothing but Shakespeare, demand more information, ask new questions and make new relationships. This is a responsibility not only for theatres but for universities and the current 'impact' agenda for research in the humanities. I hope that as a result of the Globe to Globe Festival we will eventually be seeing not only more *haka* and *waiata* Shakespeare, more postmodern Polish Shakespeare, more Bhangwadi Shakespeare – but more *haka* and *waiata*, more postmodern Polish, more Bhangwadi theatre.

INDEX